Emile Durkh

MODERNITY AND SOCIETY

General Editor: *Ira J. Cohen*

Modernity and Society is a series of readers edited by the most eminent scholars working in social theory today. The series makes a distinctive and important contribution to the field of sociology by offering one-volume overviews that explore the founding visions of modernity originating in the classic texts. In addition, the volumes look at how ideas have been reconstructed and carried in new directions by social theorists throughout the twentieth century. Each reader builds a bridge from classical selections to modern texts to make sense of the fundamental social forces and historical dynamics of the twentieth century and beyond.

Emile Durkheim

SOCIOLOGIST OF MODERNITY

Edited by
Mustafa Emirbayer

Series Editor
Ira J. Cohen

Blackwell
Publishing

Editorial material and organization © 2003 by Blackwell Publishing Ltd

BLACKWELL PUBLISHING
350 Main Street, Malden, MA 02148-5020, USA
9600 Garsington Road, Oxford OX4 2DQ, UK
550 Swanston Street, Carlton, Victoria 3053, Australia

The right of Mustafa Emirbayer to be identified as the Author of the Editorial
Material in this Work has been asserted in accordance with the UK Copyright,
Designs, and Patents Act 1988.

First published 2003 by Blackwell Publishing Ltd

2   2006

Library of Congress Cataloging-in-Publication Data has been applied for.

ISBN-13: 978-0-631-21990-3 (hardback)
ISBN-10: 0-631-21990-0 (hardback)
ISBN-13: 978-0-631-21991-0 (paperback)
ISBN-10: 0-631-21991-9 (paperback)

A catalogue record for this title is available from the British Library.

Set in 10/12pt Book Antiqua
by Graphicraft Ltd, Hong Kong

For further information on
Blackwell Publishing, visit our website:
www.blackwellpublishing.com

Contents

General Editor's Foreword

Mustafa Emirbayer's volume on Durkheim and modernity is the latest volume to appear in the *Modernity and Society* series. I had yet to meet Mustafa when I began to cast my net for an accomplished theorist to compose the Durkheim volume, but I knew the project would require a very special scholar. Now, with the results in hand, it is clear that Mustafa met the needs for this volume with unusual wisdom and great skill, talents I have come to know he brings to all of his endeavors. Lest these seem idle words, let me summarize the theoretical frame of mind this project required and how Mustafa met these requirements so well.

When I began planning the *Modernity and Society* series I envisioned that each volume would provide a broad and sturdy bridge that would link the most central and enduring insights of one of the great classical thinkers to the issues of foremost concern to contemporary theorists. Like many others, I knew that over the course of the twentieth century both historical events and empirical evidence have made it impossible to accept without qualification many of the major tenets of any of the classical theorists. After all, over the past four generations the human race at large and intellectuals of all persuasions have been stunned by two world wars, great capitalist contractions and expansions, sweeping technological revolutions, surging social movements, and the surprising reinvigoration of religious faith and zeal in the face of the relentless secularization of many institutional orders. But just as I knew that the classical social thinkers failed to anticipate many of the most dramatic and consequential developments of the twentieth century, I also knew that the depth and scope of their ideas still provide irreplaceable resources that all of us need in order to develop theories that comprehend the twenty-first century conditions of modernity. The editors of the volumes in the *Modernity and Society* series would need to have a fine sense of intellectual balance to accentuate the living heritage of the classics while letting their missteps and misstatements slip into the background.

What makes the central perceptions of theorists such as Emile Durkheim, Karl Marx, and Max Weber irreplaceable after so many unanticipated historical twists and turns? The classical era in social theory, which began in the second quarter of the nineteenth century and concluded at the end of World War I, coincided with the Industrial Revolution, the permanent institutionalization of capitalism, and the transition from tradition-bound practices and solidarities to liberal rights and moralities based on the autonomy of the individual. Interacting with and against one another, these forces dissolved all but the most peripheral remnants of feudal and aristocratic life in Western Europe, and set in motion the development of new societies in North America and Australia. Today, new conjunctions and tension between these forces influence historical developments around the globe. But the classical social theorists came on the scene when this new era in human civilization was new and raw. In these early years of modernity, they accepted the challenge to identify and define the unprecedented forces that made the crust of society heave and quake beneath their feet.

The classical theorists could not know what was to come, and they committed blunder after blunder when it comes to their philosophies of history. But they possessed two significant advantages over their successors. First, the raw forces of capitalism, the Industrial Revolution, and movements to empower civil society were easier to discern when modernity was new. In many ways these forces continue to operate in the same basic ways today, although each has grown more complex, and they all perpetually interact in historically tangled ways. Second, it makes a significant difference that the classical theorists wrote at an intellectual moment nourished by deeper philosophical roots than our own. By the turn of the nineteenth century, metaphysics and theology had lost their persuasive powers. Their successors, the theories we describe as classical today, appealed to evidence and reason rather than mysteries and faith to persuade readers of the plausibility of their views. But the classical theorists still retained the historical scale and moral depth and passionate spirit of the general philosophers of the past. Evidence and events may have taught contemporary theorists to be even more cautious of speculation than their classical forebears. And yet, if the social sciences are to be anything more than a dry historical record, they need the depth and vision that only classical theory can supply.

Emile Durkheim's writings epitomize the scale, depth, and spirit of classical theory. A true successor to philosophers such as Rousseau and Kant, Durkheim understood that at the core of the most profound speculative ideas of the past lie kernels of empirical insight from which a sociology suited to modernity could be nurtured and grown. A true believer in Enlightenment ideals and moral solidarity, Durkheim recognized that modernity would challenge society at large to reconcile cold facts and heart-felt moral values. And yet, as a practicing social researcher, Durkheim insisted that all his lofty beliefs would need to be conceptualized, specified, and empirically pinned down.

But now back to my search for an editor for the Durkheim volume. Making Durkheim relevant to contemporary theorists would not be easy. Precisely because Durkheim kept one foot in his philosophical heritage as he stepped forward to advance empirically relevant insights into modernity, many critics have found his work sociologically naïve. It was Mustafa Emirbayer's sparkling defense of Durkheim in the face of a most erudite and astute critic that convinced me of his surpassing qualifications to produce this volume.

The critic was Charles Tilly, who included in his collection *As Sociology Meets History* (1981) a polemic provocatively entitled "Useless Durkheim." Tilly's claim, in brief, was that Durkheim's ideas, especially his cultural lines of thought, and all else that was beholden to his philosophical heritage did not hold up when put to the test against the historical record. In an essay in *Sociological Theory*, 14 (3) (1996), Mustafa published a subtle, wise, and generous rejoinder to Tilly entitled "Useful Durkheim." He drew on the latest historical sociological scholarship and the strongest and most empirically relevant contemporary theoretical models to demonstrate that Durkheim's classical writings not only endure, but provide irreplaceable cornerstones for the development of contemporary accounts of modernity at large and consequential historical situations. When I finished my first reading of "Useful Durkheim," I knew that he was just the scholar I was looking for to edit this book.

Mustafa advances his belief in the continuing significance of Durkheim's thought in both his extensive introductory essay and the careful selections in the present volume. Mustafa distinguishes himself from more parochial social theorists by his willingness to acknowledge the weaknesses and oversights in Durkheim's intellectual development. Critics who write on a smaller scale often contend that once you have shown that a given theorist contradicts one idea expressed in one work by a second idea expressed in another place, then you are free to dismiss that theorist out of hand. Mustafa more generously acknowledges that Durkheim occasionally contradicted himself, and often lost sight of his profound early arguments as his career moved on. Yet Emirbayer asks us to consider Durkheim's best insights on their own, leaving his inconsistencies and shifts in emphasis out of account. Taking another tack, he is well aware that, like all thinkers, Durkheim shaped his theoretical writings to draw upon the intellectual resources of his time and respond to the social and political debates of his local context. To be familiar with Durkheim's intellectual biography is to discover a true child of the Third Republic in France. Yet, here again, while Mustafa acknowledges the contextuality of Durkheim's ideas, he asks us to look past that context. He clearly understands that only historians of ideas are duty-bound to keep a theorist's best insights rooted in their local contexts. If we need Durkheim's ideas, we can extract them with fully acknowledged qualifications and redeploy or refashion them to suit our purposes today.

All of this comes through in the way Emirbayer has organized the writings of Durkheim and his successors in this volume. Selection by selection, Mustafa brings us the best of Durkheim. His ten thematic sections are grouped into four broad topics: Durkheim's operating principles (his Sociological Methodology), the fundamentals of Durkheim's thought (A Topography of Modernity), state, economy, and civil society (The Institutional Order Of Modern Societies) and moral individualism (Morality and Modernity). Each of the ten chapters also includes excerpts from contemporary theorists who do not so much *tell* us that Durkheim is still important as *show* us that Durkheim's insights are alive and well. Beyond all else, these contemporary insights show us that Durkheim is still capable of provoking contemporary theorists to craft some of the most original and empirically incisive ideas of our time. From Pierre Bourdieu and Claude Lévi-Strauss, to Erving Goffman and Basil Bernstein, to bell hooks and Viviana Zelizer, to Robert Bellah and James Scott, Emirbayer leaves no doubt that Durkheim matters here and now.

For those who are new to Mustafa Emirbayer, I should add that he is much more than an exponent of Durkheim's work. He is, in fact, one of the most broad-ranging theorists in the current generation. Many readers know Mustafa as the author or coauthor of a series of articles in the *American Journal of Sociology* (1994, 1997, 1998), in which he establishes new foundations for social theory based on the primacy of social relationships. He has also written or coauthored essays on the political sociology of modern educational reform and the concepts and methods for studying publics in history and historical sociology. But it is not just the sum of Mustafa's scholarship, but the quality, that sets him apart. All in all, Mustafa's full range of scholarship has had a substantial influence among social theorists and beyond.

On a warm summer afternoon over a fine lunch in a restaurant in Greenwich Village, Mustafa agreed to produce the Durkheim volume in the *Modernity and Society* series. This was just days before he assumed a faculty position at the University of Wisconsin–Madison. The work he has done on this project is important to this series. But it is more important to social theory. For students and scholars in the twenty-first century, Durkheim comes alive in these pages with insight and inspiration that will sustain theories of modernity for generations yet to come.

Ira J. Cohen

Acknowledgments

The author and publishers gratefully acknowledge the following for permission to reproduce copyright material:

Alexander, Jeffrey C., "Culture and Political Crisis: 'Watergate' and Durkheimian Sociology," *Durkheimian Sociology, Cultural Studies*, 1988 © Cambridge University Press.

Bellah, Robert, *Beyond Belief: Essays on Religion in a Post-Traditional World*. Copyright © 1991 The University of California Press. Used by permission of The Regents of the University of California.

Berger, Peter L., and Richard John Neuhaus, *To Empower People: From State to Civil Society* (American Enterprise Institute for Public Policy Research, Washington DC, 1977).

Bernstein, Basil, *Class, Codes and Control*, vol. 3, *Towards a Theory of Educational Transmissions*, 2nd edn. (Routledge, London, 1975).

Bloch, Marc, *The Royal Touch: Sacred Monarchy and the Scrofula in England and France*, trans. J. E. Anderson (Routledge and Kegan Paul, London, 1973).

Bourdieu, Pierre, *Distinction: A Social Critique of the Judgment of Taste*, trans. Richard Nice (Harvard University Press, Cambridge, MA, 1984).

Collins, Randall, "Stratification, emotional energy and transient emotions," from *Research Agendas in the Sociology of Emotions*, ed. Theodore D. Kemper (SUNY Press, 1990).

Douglas, Mary, *Purity and Danger: An Analysis of the Concepts of Pollution and Taboo* (Ark, London, 1984).

Durkheim, Emile, *The Division of Labor in Society*. Reprinted with the permission of The Free Press, an imprint of Simon & Schuster Adult Publishing Group, from *The Division of Labor in Society* by Emile Durkheim, translated by W. D. Halls. Introduction by Lewis and Coser. Introduction, copyright © 1984 by Lewis A. Coser. Translation, copyright © by Higher & Further Education Division, Macmillan Publishers Ltd.

Durkheim, Emile, *Education and Sociology*. Reprinted with the permission of The Free Press, an imprint of Simon & Schuster Adult Publishing Group, from *Education and Sociology*, translated with an introduction by Sherwood D. Fox. Copyright © 1956, copyright renewed 1984 by The Free Press.

Durkheim, Emile, *The Elementary Forms of Religious Life*. Reprinted with the permission of The Free Press, an imprint of Simon & Schuster Adult Publishing Group, from *The Elementary Forms of Religious Life* by Emile Durkheim, translated with an introduction by Karen E. Fields. Translation and introduction, copyright © 1995 by Karen E. Fields.

Durkheim, Emile, *Emile Durkheim: Essays on Morals and Education*, trans. H. L. Sutcliffe, ed. W. S. F. Pickering (Routledge and Kegan Paul, London, 1979).

Durkheim, Emile, *Emile Durkheim: On Institutional Analysis*, trans. and ed. Mark Traugott (The University of Chicago Press, Chicago, 1978).

Durkheim, Emile, *Emile Durkheim: On Morality and Society*, trans. Charles Blend, ed. Robert N. Bellah (The University of Chicago Press, 1973).

Durkheim, Emile, *The Evolution of Educational Thought: Lectures on the Formation and Development of Secondary Education in France*, trans. Peter Collins (Routledge, London, 1992 and Presses Universitaires, Paris).

Durkheim, Emile, *Moral Education*. Reprinted with the permission of The Free Press, an imprint of Simon & Schuster Trade Publishing Group, from *Moral Education: A Study in the Theory and Application of the Sociology of Education* by Emile Durkheim, translated by Everett K. Wilson and Hermann Schnurer. Copyright © 1961, 1973 by The Free Press.

Durkheim, Emile, and Marcel Mauss, *Primitive Classification*, trans. Rodney Needham (The University of Chicago Press and Routledge and Kegan Paul, 1963).

Durkheim, Emile, *Professional Ethics and Civic Morals*, trans. Cornelia Brookfield (Routledge, London, 1992 and Presses Universitaires, Paris).

Durkheim, Emile, *The Rules of Sociological Method*. Reprinted with the permission of The Free Press, an imprint of Simon & Schuster Trade Publishing Group, from *The Rules of Sociological Method and Selected Texts on Sociology and its Method*, by Emile Durkheim, translated by W. D. Halls. Edited with an introduction by Steven Lukes. Introduction and selection copyright © 1982 by Steven Lukes. Translation copyright © 1983 by Macmillan Press Ltd.

Durkheim, Emile, *Socialism and Saint-Simon* (Antioch Press, Yellow Springs, OH, 1958).

Durkheim, Emile, *Sociology and Philosophy*, trans. D. F. Pocock (The Free Press, 1974, copyright Routledge and Kegan Paul Limited, London).

Durkheim, Emile, *Suicide: A Study in Sociology*. Reprinted with the permission of The Free Press, an imprint of Simon & Schuster Adult Publishing Group, from *Suicide: A Study in Sociology* by Emile Durkheim, translated by John A. Spaulding and George Simpson. Edited by George Simpson. Copyright © 1951, copyright renewed 1979 by The Free Press.

Erikson, Kai, *Wayward Puritans: A Study in the Sociology of Deviance* (Macmillan, New York, 1966).

Etzioni, Amitai, *The Moral Dimension: Toward a New Economics.* Reprinted with the permission of The Free Press, an imprint of Simon & Schuster Trade Publishing Group, from *The Moral Dimension: Toward a New Economics* by Amitai Etzioni. Copyright © 1988 by Amitai Etzioni.

Foucault, Michel, *Discipline and Punish: The Birth of the Prison*, trans. Alan Sheridan (Vintage, New York, 1979. Copyright Les Éditions du Seuil, Paris).

Goffman, Erving, *Interaction Ritual: Essays on Face-to-Face Behavior* (Pantheon, New York, 1967).

Gramsci, Antonio, *Selections from the Prison Notebooks*, trans. Quintin Hoare and Geoffrey Nowell Smith (International Publishers, New York, 1971).

hooks, bell, *Teaching to Transgress: Education as the Practice of Freedom.* Copyright © 1994. From *Teaching to Transgress* by bell hooks. Reproduced by permission of Routledge, Inc., part of the Taylor & Francis Group.

Lévi-Strauss, Claude, *The Savage Mind* (The University of Chicago Press and Weidenfeld and Nicolson, 1966).

Parsons, Talcott, *Social Structure and Personality.* Reprinted with the permission of The Free Press, an imprint of Simon & Schuster Adult Publishing Group, from *Social Structure and Personality* by Talcott Parsons. Copyright © 1964 by The Free Press. Copyright renewed 1992 by Charles D. Parsons and Susan P. Cramer.

Scott, James C., *The Moral Economy of the Peasant: Rebellion and Subsistence in Southeast Asia* (Yale University Press, 1976).

Sewell, William H., "Historical Events as Transformations of Structures: Inventing Revolution at the Bastille," *Theory and Society* 25 (1996), pp. 864–71. With kind permission of Kluwer Academic Publishers.

Turner, Victor, *The Ritual Process: Structure and Anti-Structure* (Cornell University Press, Ithaca, 1969, copyright Adline de Gruyter).

Zelizer, Viviana, *Pricing the Priceless Child: The Changing Social Value of Children* (Princeton University Press, Princeton 1994, copyright Basic Books Inc.).

The publishers apologize for any errors or omissions in the above list and would be grateful to be notified of any corrections that should be incorporated in the next edition or reprint of this book.

Emile Durkheim: Sociologist of Modernity

Mustafa Emirbayer

Often described as "the father of sociology," Emile Durkheim ranks among the most important and influential figures in modern social thought. If anything, his work has gained in stature in recent years, with the enhanced interest among sociologists in cultural analysis, the sociology of the emotions, and the study of civil society. Durkheimian perspectives have emerged regarding a wide range of other topics as well, from social structure to individual and collective agency, from the state and political public sphere to economic life, and from sociological methodology to moral critique. The significance of Durkheim's contributions to the sociology of modernity has possibly never been as fully appreciated across the scholarly world as it is today.

This volume attempts to capture the enduring value and import of Durkheimian sociology, focusing upon the diverse points of view – methodological, theoretical, substantive, and even normative – from which it approaches the analysis of modern social life. It includes extracts from Durkheim's best-known writings (e.g., on the division of labor in modern society, on suicide and the maladies of modern moral culture, and on ritual and symbolic classification in religious life), as well as selections from less widely read texts that similarly address central themes in the sociology of modernity. Together, these various selections give us the compelling image of a "useful Durkheim," one who continues to provide important and penetrating insights into the sociology of the modern world. This volume includes not only these many selections, brought together within a conceptual framework that allows one to see both the expansiveness and the unity (or coherence) of Durkheim's vision, but also a wide range of selections by more recent thinkers who were themselves deeply influenced by Durkheimian social thought. It illuminates conceptual linkages among his various writings and continuities between those writings and later traditions in social and historical analysis. Through such juxtapositions, it seeks to establish the living vitality of the Durkheimian sociology of modernity, as well as to project this sociology forward into new horizons of inquiry. By providing this bridge between the past and the future, it aims to further the analysis of modern social life itself.

The volume is divided into four major sections. The first is a methodological prelude that treats of Durkheim's insights into sociological explanation. It alerts the reader to methodological themes and concerns that inform many of the more substantive selections that follow. The second section then turns to the topics of social structure, culture, and collective emotions, as well as individual and collective agency. It shows how modern social life, as Durkheim conceived of it, is structured in terms of relatively enduring matrices of social relations, cultural symbols and practices, and shared sentiments, as well as how these are both reproduced and sometimes transformed through ritualized social action. The third section maps these theoretical insights onto a range of substantive inquiries into the major institutional sectors or complexes of modern society. It presents Durkheim's most significant insights into modern administrative-bureaucratic states, industrial-capitalist economies, and the voluntary associations, organizations, and institutions of civil society, including occupational groups, the family, and educational institutions. Finally, a normative coda brings the reader back to Durkheim's fundamental concerns with individual autonomy and self-determination. Here we see him confronting head-on the normative problems facing modernity and proposing ways to address them. Having started out with explanatory issues, the reader thus returns ultimately to the reconstructive aspirations always so close to the heart of Durkheimian sociology.

One theme that all sections of the volume develop is the Durkheimian concern with individualism in modern societies. His writings all take on the task of thinking through the significance for modern social life of the moral integration and regulation of the individual and of the deleterious impact, in particular, of modern tendencies towards egoism and anomie. An ongoing concern with individualism thus becomes one of the central threads tying together the various discrete sections of this volume. It was, to be sure, among the major concerns of Durkheim's entire sociology of modernity.

In this introductory essay, I shall review the key themes and insights of Durkheim's work, following closely the organizational format that I have chosen for the core chapters of the volume. After a brief biographical sketch, I shall turn to Durkheim's writings on social structure, culture, and collective psychology, as well as on individual and collective agency, and show how they inform his analyses of the major institutional sectors of modern society: the state, economy, and civil society. Along the way, I shall also respond to alternative critical interpretations of Durkheim that fail to do justice to the full complexity of his theoretical vision. Finally, I shall offer some closing thoughts regarding alternative possible ways of presenting Durkheim's sociological ideas.

Biographical Sketch

During the middle decades of the twentieth century, the canonical interpretation of Durkheim's work held that it was primarily concerned with "the problem of social order," the Hobbesian question as to how society is possible given the mutual incompatibility of individual ends, goals, and desires (see especially Parsons, 1937). Durkheim's writings, in other words, were seen as a massive and lifelong response to the challenges of utilitarian social thought, an attempt to elaborate in the face of those challenges a general theory of social cohesion. Such an interpretation was fundamentally wrong-headed.

> Durkheim's overriding concern with the sources and forms of solidarity did not stem from an intellectual polemic against British utilitarianism and a subsequent attempt at theorizing societal integration *in abstracto;* it found its roots in the concrete experience of the crisis of traditional European societies in the face of rationalism, individualism, and capitalist industralization. His lifework was a sustained and remarkably coherent effort to diagnose this crisis, uncover its origins, and formulate the means to overcome it. (Wacquant, 1993, p. 1)

Durkheim was very much a man of his times. To begin to understand his sociology, then, one has to turn back to the specific historical circumstances within which he lived and worked.

Durkheim was born in Epinal, France, a town in the eastern province of Lorraine, on April 5, 1858. He was descended from a long line of rabbis, which included his father, and thus came from a relatively elite (albeit not an especially wealthy) family, one that held an esteemed place in the rather insular Ashkenazi community of that region of France. (Sephardic Jews, by contrast, settled largely in the southwestern part of the country, in such locales as Bayonne and Bordeaux, where Durkheim himself would later teach, and were assimilated to a much greater degree into contemporary French culture (Coser, 1971, pp. 161–3).) Although Durkheim originally aspired to become a rabbi, as an adolescent he moved decisively away from Judaism – indeed, from all forms of religious engagement – and became a resolute agnostic. "His intense involvement with secular French society and with the *nation francaise* allowed him to cut his umbilical ties to the religious community he was so deeply involved in during his early formative years. French republican and secular society became for him a passionate object of love, replacing his attachment to the religious community of his native home" (Coser, 1971,

p. 162). Durkheim's early family upbringing nevertheless continued to make itself felt in a number of ways: through his intense and lifelong respect for learning, through his extraordinary seriousness and dedication to work, and through his austere and earnest moralism.

While still in Epinal, Durkheim experienced three interrelated events of the greatest historical significance for France: its defeat in 1870–1 at the hands of Prussia and its German allies; the Paris Commune of 1871, an urban insurrection that culminated in a fratricidal bloodletting, reignit-ing long-standing tensions (extending back to the Great Revolution of 1789) between the forces of tradition and order and those of revolutionary change; and the establishment, finally, of a moderate new political regime in France, the Third Republic. These events were still fresh in collective memory when Durkheim concluded his studies at Epinal and moved to Paris, where he enrolled in the prestigious École Normale Supérieure, a training ground for the French intellectual elite, in 1879. There he studied social and political philosophy, as well as history, and developed a political perspective aligned "strongly with republicanism and progress-ive social reform, in the face of the reactionary sentiments of the mon-archists and the Catholic right" (Giddens, 1978, p. 17). It was during this period, in fact, that Durkheim first emerged as an ardent defender of the liberal ideals of the Third Republic. "Efforts to create a new repub-lican France were in the air he breathed and continually affected him" (Bellah, 1973, p. xiii). . . . "To the extent that the Third Republic stood for an appropriation of the ideals of the French Revolution and their stable institutionalization in a social order, to be in favor of the Third Republic meant that one was necessarily a democrat, a political liberal, and prob-ably if not a socialist at least concerned with major reforms of the social and economic order, all of which Durkheim was" (Bellah, 1973, p. xvi). By no means was the Third Republic a very secure regime, however. The young Durkheim was acutely aware of its endemic internal tensions, which manifested themselves in a series of political crises. Much of his work was shaped by these tensions and by a concern to reconcile them at both prac-tical and theoretical levels.

Durkheim graduated from the École in 1882, determined to engage in the scientific study of society and indeed to construct a sociology that would address and contribute to resolving the moral and political problems of his times. For several years he taught in provincial *Lycées* in the vicinity of Paris, while also taking a leave of absence to spend one academic year in Germany (mostly in Berlin and Leipzig), on a fellowship to study methods of instruction and the state of the social sciences in that country. The two reports on what he encountered there, published soon after his return from Germany, enabled him to gain his first academic appointment, at the University of Bordeaux, in 1887. (It was during this same year that he married Louise Dreyfus, with whom he would have two children, Marie and André.) Durkheim would spend the next 15 years at Bordeaux, surely the most productive and fruitful phase of his intellectual career. He would work out during this period his most distinctive diagnoses of, and prescriptions for, the maladies of his age. Already this was foreshadowed in his Inaugural Lecture at Bordeaux, in which he characterized the problems of his day, to which even the most basic political divisions could be traced, as ultimately *moral* problems, as having to do with a loosening of social bonds and a breakdown of moral solidarity, which sociology could help to restore:

> [T]he collective spirit has been weakened in us. Each of us has so overwhelming a sense of self that he no longer perceives the limits which hem him in on all sides. . . . We must react with all our energy against this dispersive tendency. . . . I believe that sociology, more than any other science, is in a position to [do this]. It is sociology which will make the individual understand what society is, how it completes him, and how little he really is when reduced to his own forces alone. (Durkheim, 1978b [1888], p. 69).

At Bordeaux, Durkheim was charged with teaching courses in the areas of pedagogy as well as sociology. Included under the former rubric were courses on the theory, history, and practice of education, while the latter category included lecture series on topics such as social solidarity, the family, religion, law, morality, the history of socialism, and the history of sociological doctrines (Lukes, 1973, pp. 617–20). In addition to his prodigious efforts in teaching, Durkheim also founded a major scholarly journal, *L'Année Sociologique*, a collaborative enterprise to which he recruited an extraordinarily talented group of young scholars and protegés to serve as co-editors and through which he disseminated his emerging ideas regarding the nature and mission of sociology. Most importantly, he published during this period two of his most important works, both of them masterpieces: *The Division of Labor in Society* (1893), based upon his doctoral dissertation; and *Suicide* (1897).

In *The Division of Labor*, Durkheim argued that a major historical shift was under way from a "mechanical" type of solidarity based upon resemblances to an "organic" type based upon differences and the division of labor. This entailed a shift from a segmental type of social structure marked by little interdependence to a more organized type marked by high degrees of differentiation and coordination of functions; at the cultural level, correspondingly, this meant an evolution from a collective conscience (or consciousness) marked by generalized conformity and absolute collective authority to a normative order marked by a high esteem for the dignity and moral autonomy of the individual (for a useful summary, see Lukes, 1973, p. 158). In Durkheim's view, the current state of society was a transitional one in which the development of this latter form of collective consciousness remained incomplete, even as the old moral framework of the past was now obsolete. Hence the moral crises of his times, which he analyzed as abnormal or pathological forms of the division of labor: most significantly, an "anomic" form resulting from insufficient moral regulation of social relations and a "forced" variant resulting from external inequalities in the conditions of struggle.

In *Suicide*, Durkheim explored these moral problems in even greater depth, arguing that suicide "as it exists today is precisely one of the forms through which the collective affection from which we suffer is transmitted," that " from our study [should thus emerge] suggestions concerning the causes of the general contemporary maladjustment being undergone by European societies" (Durkheim, 1951 [1897], p. 37, and p. 32 below). Durkheim found that two types of suicide occurred with abnormal frequency in today's societies: an "egoistic" and an "anomic" type. These were caused, respectively, by a pathological detachment from, and a lack of regulation by, normative structures. The crises of modern society, then, could ultimately be traced back to the breakdown of social bonds and of moral community, the failure of a new normative order to replace the older one that had irretrievably passed away.

While at Bordeaux, Durkheim sought to specify institutional and normative remedies for the moral problems which he was diagnosing. In his famous "Preface to the Second Edition" of *The Division of Labor* (published in his final year at Bordeaux, but featuring ideas long in the making), he proposed the formation of occupational groups as a functional substitute for the normative structures that were fast disappearing, one that would be more institutionally appropriate to the changing conditions of modern social life. Occupational groups, in his view, "would develop rules and regulations governing all aspects of the life of the occupation including working conditions, wages, and hours. . . . This vigorous group life would provide the moral forces that would prevent the development of egoistic and anomic tendencies and would provide an environment of justice and equity so necessary if a highly differentiated society is to function without pathology" (Bellah, 1973, p. xxxi). At the level of cultural ideals, moreover, Durkheim ardently defended, and sought to further, the progress of moral individualism. In the late 1890s, he involved himself in the so-called Dreyfus Affair, a controversy that rocked the Third Republic by raising in acute form all the enduring issues of Right versus Left, of "spiritual heirs of the *ancien régime* [versus] inheritors of the tradition of the French Revolution," refracted also through an intense debate over anti-Semitism (Coser, 1971, p. 159). Durkheim argued strenuously against the forces of conservatism and tradition, reaffirming the principles of moral autonomy, liberalism, and of respect for the right of the individual, and distinguishing these carefully from utilitarian individualism and the "egoistic cult of the self." "Not only is individualism not anarchical," he asserted, "but it henceforth is the only system of beliefs which can ensure the moral unity of the country" (Durkheim, 1973 [1898], p. 50, and p. 276 below). Durkheim's interventions in the Dreyfus Affair marked one of the high points in his career as a thinker oriented toward practical social reform.

In 1902, Durkheim left Bordeaux for the Sorbonne in Paris, where he would continue to teach until his death in 1917. While at the Sorbonne, Durkheim offered a range of new courses on pedagogy and educational history, as well on the sociologies of religion and morality and the philosophy of pragmatism. His work on *L'Année* continued. And his growing fame as a scholar, combined with his new institutional location at the center of French academic life, greatly enhanced his stature as a public figure. He became an advisor to key political figures in the Third Republic and a consultant to many governmental agencies, such as the Ministry of Education, and came to exert a considerable influence over the educational policies of the Third Republic. "The convergence between his sociology and the official ideology of republicanism was so great that some contemporary critics spoke caustically of the pervasive hold of 'State Durkheimianism' in the educational system" (Giddens, 1978, pp. 23–4).

Moreover, it was during this Sorbonne period that Durkheim published his third masterpiece of sociology, *The Elementary Forms of Religious Life* (1912). In this work, he demonstrated that "there is something eternal in religion that is destined to outlive the succession of particular symbols in which religious thought has clothed itself." This eternal element was the need in all societies "at regular intervals to maintain and strengthen the collective feelings and ideas that provide its coherence and its distinct individuality. This moral remaking can be achieved," he wrote, "only through [collective experiences] in which the individuals, pressing close to one another, reaffirm in common their common sentiments" (Durkheim, 1995 [1912], p. 429, and p. 118 below). While not applying this insight directly or systematically to modern societies, Durkheim elaborated here a theory of ritual process – and of moral communion and regeneration – that was meant to be valid for all types of society, "primitive" or modern. As for the other key component of religion – beliefs and symbols – Durkheim acknowledged that modern science was gradually replacing these with its own accounts and theories based upon reason. However, he added that even "the essential notions of scientific logic are [themselves] of religious origin. . . . [S]cientific thought is only a more perfected form of religious thought" (Durkheim, 1995 [1912], p. 431, and p. 120 below). Moreover, he put forward a theory of the organization of classification systems in terms of the religious polarity of "sacred and profane" that was meant to apply to a wide range of modern discourses and belief systems. In sum, Durkheim's contribution in *The Elementary Forms* was to elaborate a thoroughly "religious" model of modern society, one that encompassed both the practical and the intellectual domains.

Durkheim also reaffirmed his idea of the "cult of the individual" as the true and rightful religion of modern life, and presented sociology as the discipline that would argue the importance of this cult and propose institutional reforms to make it into an empirical and concrete reality.

With the onset of World War I, Durkheim shifted his energies to the war effort, not out of jingoism or war hysteria, but rather, out of a concern for what he described as the "moral sustenance of the country" (quoted in Lukes, 1973, p. 553). He wrote pamphlets attacking pan-Germanism (his only ventures into political journalism since the Dreyfus Affair), organized a committee on the publication of studies and documents relating to the war, and served on a dozen or more other committees, all the while continuing to teach and to do scholarly work. The war took a heavy toll upon him. It left him exhausted and depleted. It also claimed the lives of many of his most talented young students and collaborators from the group around *L'Année*. And in late 1915, it brought about the death of his only son, himself a talented young scholar who had emerged as one of the leading lights of the *L'Année* circle. It was a blow from which Durkheim was never to recover. Overworked and emotionally devastated, his health deteriorated, and finally, on November 15, 1917, he died of a stroke at the age of 59. Durkheim had been part of an illustrious generation of sociological thinkers, one that also included Georg Simmel and Max Weber. All three had been born within a few years of each other, and all three would pass away nearly contemporaneously – during or in the immediate aftermath of World War I.

What are we to make of Durkheimian sociology? My claim is that it can usefully be approached from two different theoretical vantage-points. (Much of what follows draws upon Emirbayer, 1996b.) One concerns his insights into the problematic of structure and agency – that is, the ways in which social action is constrained and enabled by social, cultural, and collective-emotional structures, while simultaneously reproducing and potentially transforming these in turn. The other concerns his insights into the major institutions and institutional sectors of modern society: the state, the economy, and civil society. In what follows, I shall take up each of these vantage-points in turn and show how, from both perspectives, Durkheim sought to shed better light upon the possibilities and challenges facing modern society.

A Topography of Modernity

First let us consider the problematic of structure and agency. All empirical instances of social action can be said to be shaped and channeled, on the one hand, by social structure, culture, and collective emotions. We can say that these three structural contexts of action intersect and overlap with one another and yet are mutually autonomous, that they designate relatively enduring patterns of relationships that each operates according to its own independent logic. We can say, moreover, that this complex multidimensional topography is ongoingly shaped and reshaped by social action itself, as individual and collective actors agentically engage with – and sometimes seek to transform – the very structural contexts that constrain and enable them. Durkheim had many insights in respect to each of these areas of inquiry. In each domain, however, profound misreadings of his work persist, which we shall now have to deal with in turn.

Social structure

One important line of criticism of Durkheim portrays him as an idealist who consistently neglected the material and demographic infrastructure of modern society. Based upon a selective emphasis upon *The Elementary Forms*, this interpretive line sees him as concerned primarily with the normative order, as disinterested in the internal organization and history of social-structural formations (Coser, 1964; Aron, 1970; Birnbaum, 1976; Bottomore, 1981; see also Sorel, 1895). This criticism is often quite accurate and telling, especially when directed against Durkheim's later writings. It is certainly true, for example, that Durkheim devoted less attention in his later years to the kinds of factors he discussed in *The Division of Labor*, where he argued that functional differentiation, specialization, and the evolution of the division of labor (brought about by increases in "material and moral density") had destroyed traditional forms of moral integration and produced a new type of (organic) solidarity, one marked by interdependence and a greater scope for individual initiative. The heavy culturalism of his later writings does seem to leave such developments mostly out of consideration.

On the other hand, even in this later, more "idealist" phase of production, Durkheim continued to be interested in the impact of morphological structures and processes upon institutional change. In his lecture course on *The Evolution of Educational Thought* (1904–5), for example, he wove morphological transformations deeply into his causal explanations, locating the wellspring of Humanist educational ideals in the emergent domain of "polite society," a "leisured class" that owed its existence to a complex configuration of social-structural causes: the establishment of order and security by means of better government and more efficient administration, the growth of population and the proliferation of urban centers, the spread of communications, and the stimulation of economic activity and the expansion of markets through the discovery and exploitation of new routes of trade. Durkheim suggested that the increasing social mobility and social wealth that accompanied these changes greatly narrowed the gulf between the various levels of society and fostered among the middle strata a new desire to emulate the ways of life of the aristocracy. The breakup of Christendom into a multiplicity of national units, each with "its own special mode of thought and feeling," further enhanced these aspirations and resulted in a "movement towards individualism and differentiation" that ultimately found expression in new Humanist doctrines of pedagogy. Durkheim combined such morphological considerations with rigorous cultural analysis to produce a rich causal narrative of institutional change in French civil society during the Renaissance period. (For a detailed discussion of this work, see Emirbayer, 1996a.)

On a general analytical level as well, Durkheim continued to lay stress upon the element of social morphology. In a programmatic essay on "Sociology and the Social Sciences," for example, he carved out a special place for scientific inquiry that "has as its object the external and material form of society" (Durkheim, 1978f [1909], p. 79). Under this rubric fell empirical researches on social differentiation, changing class structure, political centralization, and demographic tendencies of various kinds. Elsewhere, in a brief prefatory note on social morphology in L'Année, he suggested that social infrastructures vary, "depending on whether the population is more or less sizable, more of less dense; depending on whether it is concentrated in cities or dispersed in the countryside; depending on the way in which the cities and the houses are constructed; depending on whether the space occupied by the society is more or less extensive; depending on the borders which define its limits, the avenues of communication which traverse it." Social morphology as a science then aimed to investigate "how the [changing] constitution of this substratum directly or indirectly affects all social phenomena" (Durkheim, 1978d [1897–8], p. 88, and p. 77 below).

The significance of Durkheim's later empirical and theoretical writings lies in the fact that they show us, on the one hand, how morphological structures and processes, the social substratum of modern life, are implicated in the genesis and functioning of social institutions, and, on the other hand, how they interact historically with other kinds of structures and processes. Social structure denotes but one dimension of what is in fact a complex, multifaceted reality; social and morphological configurations help to channel the empirical social action that unfolds within concrete empirical settings, but they do so only partially and in complex interaction with cultural and collective-emotional structures. Thus, for Durkheim, modern social structures are marked by a high degree of differentiation and scope for individual autonomy and initiative. However, these features of contemporary social relations, while deeply influencing the makeup of social institutions, are by no means fully determinative of them; one must also inquire into the symbolic and affectual dimensions of those institutions, in order to know how much room is truly opened up in them for individual freedom. Durkheim always took social-structural considerations extremely seriously, but he also took special pains always to delimit their explanatory scope and power.

Culture

A second common misreading of Durkheim, the very opposite of the misreading mentioned above, is based in large part upon his first major work, *The Division of Labor*. It holds that even in his later writings, those most often seen as contributing to a new perspective upon the cultural context of action, Durkheim never quite abandoned his earlier commitment to a "base/superstructure" mode of analysis, that he remained a "materialist" in some form or other throughout his career. This interpretation, shared by a wide range of commentators, insists that although Durkheim decisively rejected economic materialism in the Marxian mode, he continued to espouse a sort of "generic materialism" that related collective representations (or cultural formations) back to broader patterns in social organization, to the so-called material substratum (Benoit-Smullyan, 1948; Giddens, 1977; Traugott, 1978). This argument comes easiest, of course, with respect to *The Division of Labor*; yet its proponents apply it even to the later writings of Durkheim's "religious" period, and thereby connect Durkheim as a whole back to the Marxian tradition. In one interpreter's words: "[O]n this basic point the convergence [between Durkheim and Marx is] . . . a natural and necessary consequence of their assumptions concerning the systemic character of society and the need for a group unit of analysis" (Traugott, 1978, p. 260, n. 60).

The portrayal of Durkheim as a "generic materialist" has considerable merits, to be sure: most prominent among them, the insight that Durkheim never forgot to acknowledge the social situatedness of symbolic formations, even as he insisted upon their relative autonomy. "He [was] always careful to insist that such propositions [as 'society is the ideal'] must be interpreted to mean that ideals are *creations* of human society, not 'given' forces which determine social conduct" (Giddens, 1977, p. 290). Yet this reading also carries with it an important weakness: it loses sight of the truly radical nature of Durkheim's later turn toward cultural analysis, his new-found understanding (especially in *The Elementary Forms*) of the internal complexity and causal significance of cultural structures.

The other "founding fathers" of sociology never did develop such a far-reaching program for cultural analysis. Despite the fact that later theorists in the Marxian tradition made many positive contributions to cultural studies, one can discern in Marx's writings themselves only the vaguest lineaments of a sociological theory of modern culture (Althusser, 1971; Williams, 1977; Thompson, 1979; Hall, 1986). While Weber's "verstehen" sociology did much to advance the cause of hermeneutic analysis, Weber's own boldly stated theses of the "loss of meaning" and the spread of "mechanized petrification" in the contemporary world made it difficult to elaborate a Weberian theory of cultural modernity (Habermas, 1984, pp. 243–54; Alexander, 1989a, p. 189; see also Walzer, 1965). And finally, while certain of Tocqueville's writings (e.g., in vol. 2 of *Democracy in America*) did include rich insights into the "manners and mores" of modern societies marked by an equality of conditions, Tocqueville never himself articulated a systematic program for cultural analysis (Bellah, 1975). The later Durkheim, by contrast, did provide us with a useful set of tools for the investigation of symbolic structures and processes in the modern world. His "religious" sociology opened up new possibilities for analyzing the cultural context of action. It was in his later period that he arrived, after all, at his crucial insights into the enduring significance, even in the modern world, of "sacred' ideals, images, and symbols, and into the importance in cultural life of the opposition of "sacred" and "profane" (for a review, see Alexander, 1988).

Durkheim suggested in *The Elementary Forms* that religious beliefs and, by extension, other cultural formations are organized according to a binary logic, that they embody *symbolic polarities* that divide social and metaphysical reality into such antithetical categories as the rational and the irrational, the intelligible and the mysterious, the sacred and the profane. Within the fundamental "genus" of the sacred, moreover, he postulated additional subdivisions: between, for instance, the pure and the impure, the divine and the diabolical, and the guardians of order and the dispensers of chaos. Symbolic formations, in short, exhibited for him a complex internal structure and organization. Durkheim maintained that in the modern world, it is the ideal of moral autonomy to which the quality of sacredness most powerfully attaches itself. It is the rights and freedoms of the individual that come to be exalted over all other principles. Durkheim showed how, no less than the internal logics of social-structural or collective-emotional formations, these cultural logics of moral individualism can constrain and enable action in all the institutional sectors of modern society. Sometimes they can even stand at variance with dominant social-structural and collective-emotional configurations and demand the latter's reorganization in their own image. Categories of purity and pollution, Durkheim maintained, can provide directions and legitimations for actions that seek to reshape given structures and to establish a new order: once such schemas and representation "are constituted, they are, by that very fact, realities *sui generis*, autonomous and capable of being causes in turn, capable of producing new phenomena. . . . [O]nce they exist, they become, in turn, creative sources of action, they have an effectiveness all their own, and they react on the very causes on which they depend" (Durkheim, 1978d [1897], p. 130).

Collective emotions

The third of the criticisms of Durkheim currently prevalent in the secondary literature suggests that he misconstrued the role of collective-emotional factors in the historical process. One variant of this view, quite similar to that discussed immediately above, holds that as a "generic materialist,"Durkheim simply undervalued the independent role of collective-emotional engagements in social life. Another (somewhat different) view holds that Durkheim actually *misrepresented* the historical role of collective emotions, particularly in his analysis of extra-institutional processes. This latter perspective depicts Durkheim as anticipating the collective behavior tradition in social movement theory, an approach to collective action that stresses its irrationality, volatility, and emergence from situations of "social strain." (For a review and extensive bibliography, see Marx and Wood, 1975.) In "Useless Durkheim," Charles Tilly elaborates a particularly powerful version of this critique. He extracts three specific hypotheses about collective action from Durkheim's writings, in particular from *Suicide* and *The Division of Labor*: (1) that levels of social conflict increase as traditional controls upon individuals and groups weaken; (2) that periods or areas of rapid social change exhibit greater levels of social conflict and protest; and (3) that levels of all forms of disorder, ranging from individual suicide to collective protest, all rise or fall together. Scanning data on collective action in Europe over the past several hundred years, he voices "profound skepticism" in regard to each of these three hypotheses (Tilly, 1981, p. 107).

Tilly quite rightly underscores the inadequacies of arguments that take as their fundamental point of departure such notions as "anomie," social strain, and sociopathology. He correctly points out that Durkheim himself often had recourse to such notions – as in (once again) *The Evolution of Educational Thought*, where he depicted the pedagogical reforms of the Jesuits as "retrograde" developments, "conservative and even reactionary," whose real aim was to contain an advancing tide of secular Humanism that could scarcely be reversed. Even so, Tilly also fails to acknowledge that there are other, more positive aspects to the Durkheimian legacy. These include, preeminently, Durkheim's idea of *social solidarity* as "the universal concomitant of group action." As another commentator puts it, for Durkheim, "solidarity constitutes the defining characteristic of group life. It is, by extension, the *sine qua non* of collective action." Far from stressing emotional disintegration, "Durkheim typically characterizes the variations in solidarity associated with social movements as *intensifications* of . . . integrative bonds" (Traugott, 1984, p. 325). Indeed, even in explaining school reform in France, he portrayed the Jesuits as a group bound tightly together by dense matrices of emotional ties, hardly suffering at all from affective disorientation or other irrational disturbances. In pursuit of their goals, he saw the Jesuits as engaged in action that was both instrumentally rational *and* expressive in nature. Durkheim was in this sense just as much a precursor of theories deeply at odds with the older orthodoxies – theories that deny a deep division between rationality and emotion, for example – as he was of the collective behavior line (Calhoun, 1991, 1993, 1994; Morris and Mueller, 1992; Larana, Johnston, and Gusfield, 1994).

These theoretical insights extend as well into the study of more established and institutionalized settings. Here, too, Durkheim suggested that among the most important channeling influences upon action are collective-emotional formations. In *The Elementary Forms*, he argued that enhanced levels of the physical density of interaction, together with the increasing ecological boundedness of a given group, raise its focus of attention and the intensity of common emotions. The collective emotions generated in such moments of collective effervescence crystallize into transpersonal patterns both of cultural or symbolic identification and of emotional commitment. The former "are items on which a group has focused attention during [a ritual]. Such symbols come to represent membership in the group.... Durkheim called them 'sacred objects'" (Collins, 1993, p. 212). The latter entail varying patterns of emotional coordination – structured webs of emotional commitments – that exhibit their own distinctive properties as constraining and enabling forces. For Durkheim, the most important collective emotions in modern society had to do, not surprisingly by now, with the value and dignity of the individual personality. It was the morally autonomous individual who enjoyed in contemporary societies the most exalted emotional status and who served as the object and focus of the most powerful emotional attachments, commitments, and investments.

Durkheim, then, showed that the emotional dimension of social life is *transpersonal*, that emotions have a *relational* grounding. He also demonstrated that interpersonal interactions (within and without institutions) themselves have an emotional foundation. Such ideas could be – and have been – applied in a number of substantive areas of inquiry. Collective action, for example, is now often seen as unfolding within several different structural contexts at once – the social-structural, the cultural, *and* the collective-emotional. Although most studies today tend to focus upon the first two of these contexts, some recent writings incorporate explicitly collective-emotional concepts into their frameworks of analysis and stress the passional as well as cultural and morphological underpinnings of solidarity (see, for example, Goodwin, Jasper, and Polletta, 2001). Nationalism, too (to take another example), is seen to emerge within multiple structural environments. For some analysts today, it consists just as much in ritual processes that enhance group solidarity and emotional energy – across the imagined community of the nation – as it does in the pursuit of certain material interests or symbolic aims (see, for example, Scheff, 1994). Finally, democratic structures and processes are seen as requiring not only particular morphological configurations and cultural ideals in order to flourish, but also patterns of emotional commitments truly conducive to a broad and inclusive citizenship (for references, see Emirbayer and Sheller, 1999). For such work, the nature and limitations of the democracy that emerges in a given historical setting are often greatly influenced by the transpersonal patterns of love and aggression that bind groups and institutions together within that setting and split them apart from others; in a phrase, they are deeply determined by matters of "emotional economy."

Individual and collective agency

A final, long-standing line of interpretation of Durkheim views him as a theorist of "social equilibrium" and of structural functionalism – with few if any real affinities with historical research. Based upon Durkheim's study of rituals and ceremonials in *The Elementary Forms*, this interpretation portrays him as interested primarily in the "disciplinary, cohesive, vitalizing, and euphoric social forces" serving "to remake individuals and groups morally" (Alpert, 1965, p. 141). Durkheim then becomes an "anthropologists' sociologist," far more concerned with the regenerative functions of rituals in "static and 'unhistorical' societies" than with historical change in the contemporary world (Bottomore, 1981, p. 907). Even when he analyzes social development, Durkheim is taken to task for treating it, as one of his critics charges, "as a gradual process of social differentiation that necessarily produces . . . social solidarity" rather than genuine innovation (Bottomore, 1981, p. 912).

Of course, those who hold to such a view capture an undeniable aspect of Durkheim's thought. There are indeed powerful traces of static reproductionism scattered throughout his writings. But these same critics also neglect the crucial fact that Durkheim often saw rituals and ceremonials – and, more broadly, moments of collective effervescence – as potentially creative and dynamic moments. It was precisely in such moments, he felt, that one finds the wellsprings of human agency, of the capacity not only to reproduce, but also (under certain conditions) to creatively reconfigure and transform the relational structures within which action unfolds. "Under the influence of some great collective shock in certain historical periods," in his words, "social interactions become much more frequent and active. Individuals seek out one another and come together more. The result is the general effervescence that is characteristic of revolutionary or creative epochs. . . . People live differently and more intensely than in normal times" (Durkheim, 1995 [1912], pp. 212–13, and p. 141 below). In *The Elementary Forms*, Durkheim also provided an account of *individual* leadership and agency. "Sometimes," he wrote, the individual "feels possessed by a moral force greater than he, of which he is only the interpreter. This is the hallmark of what has often been called the demon of oratorical inspiration. This extraordinary surplus of forces is quite real and comes to him from the very group he is addressing. . . . It is then no longer a mere individual who speaks but a group incarnated and personified" (Durkheim, 1995 [1912], p. 212, and p. 141 below).

Examples of creative effervescence of individual and group action abound in Durkheim's later writings. In the history of French secondary education, for example, these include "the crisis of Christendom" in the twelfth and thirteenth centuries, which gave rise to Scholasticism; the periods of the Renaissance and the Reformation; the Revolutionary epoch; and the ongoing institutional crises of the eighteenth and nineteenth centuries. In the political sphere, Durkheim included as well the Crusades and "the many savage or sublime moments in the French Revolution." Durkheim noted that during the French Revolution, "We [saw] the most mediocre or harmless bourgeois transformed by the general exaltation into a hero or an executioner. And the mental processes [were] so clearly the same as those at the root of religion that the individuals themselves conceived the pressure they yielded to in explicitly religious terms" (Durkheim 1995 [1912], p. 213, and p. 141 below). During such junctures, moreover, the complex symbolic forms operative in civil society, as well as long-standing configurations of social structure and collective emotions, became focal points for conflict. Historical actors such as the Humanists, the Jesuits, and French revolutionaries strove to advance their own ends by wresting control over the very organization of culture, social structure, and emotional investments. In Durkheim's view, the apparent unity of prevailing structures in these environments masked intense processes of contestation among multiple social groups. The dynamics of power once gave rise to these structures, and the realities of social conflict persisted in them still. "Functionalist" or not, Durkheim was hardly blind to the struggles that shape – and transform – social life.

The Institutional Order of Modern Societies

Having considered Durkheim's work in terms of the problematic of structure and agency, we now turn to his various institutional analyses. Each of these encompasses all the different analytical elements discussed above; for Durkheim, any institution or institutional complex can be said simultaneously to encompass social relations, cultural structures, and collective emotions, and to be ongoingly reproduced and transformed through individual and collective agency. It is useful, then, to see the topographical schema that was elaborated in earlier sections as relevant to each of the institutional sectors that Durkheim examined. I shall now discuss in turn his analyses of the modern state, economy, and civil society. (For a general assessment of Durkheim's institutional theorizing, see Poggi, 1971.)

The modern state and the political public sphere

Interpreters of Durkheim are often more guilty of an error of omission when it comes to his political sociology than of one of commission, for it is not uncommon to find his theory of the state almost completely neglected, or else relegated to a peripheral place, in discussions of his overall body of work. This is due in large part to an accident of publication history: his major analysis of the modern state, in a lecture course on *Professional Ethics and Civic Morals* (1898–1900), did not actually appear in print until 1950, leaving readers after his death with only a few disjointed texts from which to piece together a coherent framework. Unsurprisingly, interpretive schemas were developed in which Durkheim's political sociology was decidedly marginalized, schemas that would endure for decades thereafter and deeply shape the later reception of his work. (The most influential of these, surely, was Parsons, 1937.) One other error (of commission) might be cited here as well: to the extent that his political sociology was taken seriously, it was typically presented as the work of an ideological conservative (Coser, 1964; Nisbet, 1974). This latter interpretation was most often grounded in his analyses of moral solidarity in *The Division of Labor*. It was not entirely without basis, for Durkheim was, in fact, very concerned with many of the same themes as was political conservatism: for example, the importance of tradition, community, and moral authority in modern life.

As a number of scholars have come to appreciate in recent years, however, Durkheim not only elaborated a highly original political sociology and state theory, he also elaborated a thoroughgoing criticism of political conservatism (Giddens, 1971; Cladis, 1992; Cotterrell, 1999). While, on the one hand, he acknowledged that the scope and functions of the state expand concomitantly with the division of labor, such that one cannot (unlike classical liberals and socialists) properly speak of a minimalist state destined to fold into society and disappear, he did argue, on the other hand, against traditionalists and conservatives (among whom he included idealists in the Hegelian tradition) who envision an all-powerful and autocratic state that looms over and dominates society. The modern state is a strong state, he contended, with significant positive functions; but it must also be a moral actor that respects and implements the rights and dignity of the individual. In the modern age, it is the "cult of the indi-

vidual" that this state must seek above all else to promote within civil
society: "the main function of the State is to liberate the individual personalities," its distinctive purpose is to embody and promote the fundamental principles of moral individualism (Durkheim, 1992 [1898–1900],
p. 62, and p. 181 below). As one commentator expresses it, " it is the state
which, in the modern type of society, is the institution which is concerned
with the implementation and the furtherance of individual rights"....
(Giddens, 1971, p. 496). "The specific role of the [modern] state is not
to subordinate the individual to itself, but in fact to provide for his self-
realization" (Giddens, 1971, p. 502). Here we see a direct connection between
Durkheimian state theory and the political practice in which he engaged
as a defender and moral conscience of the Third Republic.

   In his political sociology, Durkheim also set forth a distinctive conception of democracy. The state could become autocratic and dominate the
individual, he argued, if not counterbalanced by a set of intermediary societal institutions, or secondary groupings, interposed between the individual
and the state. (Conversely, those mediating institutions could themselves
become hostile to the cause of individual freedom if not counterbalanced
by a powerful state.) Democracy required a proper juxtaposition of – and
productive tension between – such agencies. Historically, among the
most significant of the former had been the family, suggested Durkheim,
but under conditions of modern society, it was gradually being supplanted
by occupational groups or professional associations (of the sort discussed
above). It was in these institutions – and in their communicative interplay with the modern state – that he invested his hopes for a future democracy. Durkheim distinguished between the administrative and coercive
apparatus of government and "the state" proper; while the principal function of the former was "to act" and "to achieve," it fell upon the latter to
"elevate" the ideals and beliefs of the pre-reflective masses. "The state is
a special organ," Durkheim wrote, "whose responsibility it is to work out
certain representations which hold good for the collectivity. These representations are distinguished from [others] by their higher degree of consciousness and reflection" (Durkheim 1992 [1898–1900], p. 50, and p. 177
below). Durkheim saw occupational groups as constituting an important
medium between the pre-reflective representations of the collectivity and
the far higher levels of state consciousness. Occupational groups, with their
internal mechanisms of deliberation, obviated the need for a direct
democracy (which Durkheim saw as a vehicle for societal traditionalism)
by channeling, filtering, and focusing public opinion.

   In these discussions of political sociology, Durkheim brought to bear
all the key analytical concepts of his topography of modern society. The rise
of the modern state could be analyzed, in his view, in terms of the growth
of the division of labor and of an organized type of social structure. The
state itself could be seen as embodying the cultural ideals of moral

individualism. Moreover, it could be understood as the focal point and repository of collective sentiments and emotions, again centering on the autonomous individual. And it could be seen as an institution continually produced and reproduced through agentic processes of deliberation and communicative interaction. The concepts of his theoretical schema of structure and agency thus folded usefully into his analyses of the modern state and the political public sphere.

The modern economy

An important variant of two of the misreadings of Durkheim mentioned above – that he was a theorist not of historical change but of social cohesion and stasis, and that he was an idealist – holds that he neglected to analyze the dynamics of class conflict or, more generally, of economic inequality. This misreading, which focuses primarily upon *The Elementary Forms*, stresses that Durkheim had little of value to say about the modern industrial-capitalist economy (for a more sophisticated version of this critique, see Poggi, 1971). As with the other accounts that I have covered, there is an element of truth to this. As compared to Marx or even Weber, Durkheim had only a relatively underdeveloped theory of economic structures and processes. Moreover, purely economic changes and remedies were ultimately less vital to him than was the task of moral reconstruction.

Nevertheless, it cannot be said that Durkheim failed to grasp the significance of class conflict or that he gave short shrift to the other problems of industrialism in his times. He was both a moralist *and* a probing analyst (and severe critic) of contemporary economic life. He was acutely aware of the economic disturbances that were rocking European societies to their very foundations, disturbances that he called abnormal forms – anomic and forced – of the division of labor. These included recurrent industrial crises, a widespread alienation from work, unbridled economic egoism, a lack of equal opportunity, and deep-seated hostilities between labor and capital. Durkheim's assessments of these problems were multidimensional, taking into account simultaneously their morphological, symbolic, and affectual aspects. Ultimately, however, he always came back to the same conclusion: namely, that these maladies were all symptoms – not causes – of a fundamental moral breakdown. These pathologies could all be traced back to the transitional nature of contemporary societies themselves, still only part way between the moral framework of traditionalism and the fully developed normative structures of modernity. The solution was not to be found, then, within the economic order alone. Certainly it was not to include socialist revolution or the abolition of private property. Durkheim wrote sympathetically about socialism, and he was generally positive toward certain socialist tendencies within the Third Republic. But these tended to be largely of an evolutionary variety, and far removed from the class-based socialism promoted by Marx, which he found far too one-sidedly economistic.

For Durkheim, the only true solution to the economic problems and challenges of his day was the reconstitution of moral authority. This meant, ultimately, the development of a new set of moral rules to govern economic transactions, a new kind of normative order within which economic activities could unfold. It meant, in a word, a new moralization of economic bonds themselves. The renovated normative order that Durkheim envisioned would involve regulations of individual desires and appetites – the very dignity and happiness of the individual were impossible without them – but only within an economic framework that could be broadly agreed upon as just and fair. Once again, his proposal for a new set of occupational groups and professional associations was relevant here, as a way of instituting a moral community that would properly regulate and integrate the individual economic actor. Durkheim's "constantly echoed assertion that 'the social problem' (i.e., then problem of class conflict) cannot be solved through purely economic measures [thus] has to be read against his equally emphatic stress upon the basic changes in the economic order which have to be made to complete the institutionalization of moral individualism" (Giddens, 1971, p. 505).

Civil society

It has been suggested that at least since the 1960s, historical sociology has been oriented primarily around two "master concepts": the modern state and the industrial-capitalist economy. "In the case of Western countries over the last few hundred years," as one writer has put it, "the program [of the new historical sociology] begins by recognizing that the development of capitalism and the formation of powerful, connected national states dominated all other social processes and shaped all social structures. . . . It goes on by following the creation and destruction of different sorts of structures by capitalism and statemaking, then tracing the relationship of other processes . . . to capitalism and statemaking" (Tilly, 1984, pp. 14–15). Such an assessment is accurate enough, to be sure; classes and class conflict have indeed been the guiding concerns behind much (Marxist) scholarship during this period (Moore, 1966; Anderson, 1974a, 1974b). And states as autonomous organizations with their own distinctive interests and goals (the Weberian perspective) – and the complex interactions of states with economic actors and class structures (Tocqueville's contribution) – have also been key concerns for the new "state-centered" historical sociology (Skocpol, 1979, 1985; Evans, Rueschemeyer, and Skocpol, 1985).

However, while extremely useful for exploring certain kinds of substantive problems, both class-oriented and state-centered strategies of analysis have left undertheorized a potentially important distinction between *economic* class structures, on the one hand, and *associational* relations of civil life, on the other (Emirbayer and Sheller, 1999). Both have remained content to take the basic dichotomy of "state versus society" as their theoretical point of departure, without disaggregating the concept of "society" itself into its distinct analytical components.

It is precisely at this theoretical juncture, "in between" the modern state and the industrial-capitalist economy (the two "master concepts" of the above quotation), that one begins to discern a new relevance for Durkheimian concerns. For of all the classical sociological theorists, it was surely Durkheim himself (along with Tocqueville) who provided for us the most perceptive analyses of the structures and practices of civil society. It is the intermediate domains of social life – the domestic and associational institutions of society – that Durkheim analyzed most acutely. More insightfully even than Marx and Weber, he explored the internal logic of these structures and practices and assessed their contributions to social integration, willed community, and individual autonomy; in so doing, he provided a useful corrective to those who would devote themselves primarily to the study of state formation and/or industrial-capitalist development. In addition, Durkheim examined the institutions of civil society (as he did the state and economy as well) from multiple points of view. He devoted attention to their social-structural bases, their cultural aspects, and even their collective-emotional organization. This lent to his studies a special analytical depth and substantive rigor.

Most significant among Durkheim's studies of civil society were his inquiries into the evolution of three distinct types of institutional structure – the three domains of societal interaction that Hegel before him had termed the key moments of "ethical life" (Hegel, 1967 [1821]). The first of these was the modern family. Durkheim followed historically the formation of the modern family unit across a series of discrete stages: the diffuse clan, the differentiated family of maternal or paternal lineage, the joint family of agnates, the patriarchal family, the paternal-maternal family, and, finally, the modern family itself. Today, he argued (in language reminiscent of Hegel), family life has come to consist in "two different associations, [one that] unites two members of the same generation [and another that] unites one generation to the next" (quoted in Wallwork, 1972, p. 96). More than ever before, such patterns of relationships "allow . . . the personalities of the family members to come forth more and more. . . . Each individual increasingly [now] assume[s] his own character, his personal manner of thinking and feeling" (Durkheim, 1978a [1891–2], pp. 233–4, p. 227 below). Even in the modern age, moreover, the conjugal-nuclear family also remains a focal point for group norms and emotional attachments – and a key matrix for individual moral development. In addition, the marital bond itself becomes stronger and comes to serve a moral function, enhancing "moral health and happiness" and providing "a respected form of regulation which creates social bonds among individuals" (Durkheim, 1978c [1906], p. 248). Durkheim investigated the various historical forces that threaten family solidarity in the present day, including a wide range of economic, legal, and spiritual transformations.

Durkheim also inquired into the moral and historical significance of modern corporations and professional bodies. He examined the manner in which occupational groups evolved over time, beginning with the Roman collegia and then moving on to the medieval guilds that arose in the eleventh and twelfth centuries. Today, he argued (as we have seen), a new system of professional bodies is needed to remedy the lack of moral authority in economic life, to provide a new focal point for moral community and group attachments, and to mediate the "individualistic particularism" of economic interests within the public sphere.

Finally, Durkheim saw modern education as serving an important mediating function. Its role was to connect "two kinds of moralities, the affective morality of family life and the more rigorous, impersonal faith that controls civic [sic] society"and the state (Alexander, 1982, pp. 279–80). In *The Evolution of Educational Thought*, he examined the unfolding of this moral and educational process across more than eleven centuries of cultural and institutional development, following the evolution of French secondary education from its origins in the early Church up through the time of the "educational crisis" of the late nineteenth century. Although its title suggests a study in the history of educational ideals alone, this work actually blended together the analysis of abstract pedagogical doctrines and the study of structural and organizational forces. In highlighting the causal significance of ritual processes and of the sacred in this complex story, it involved the most extensive application of Durkheim's later religious sociology to a particular substantive problem. In numerous other writings as well, Durkheim addressed the topic of education, often with more theoretical concerns. He explored the curricular and pedagogical means by which education instills a sense of discipline and group attachment in young children, as well as a capacity for moral autonomy and individualism. Schoolteachers, he observed, are like secular priests of contemporary societies, helping to produce and reproduce a new kind of moral community for the modern age. It is worth noting here that both of Durkheim's major academic appointments – in Bordeaux and at the Sorbonne – were originally in the field of education, so important was this area of inquiry for his overall project of developing an institutional analysis of the key sectors of modern society.

Alternative Ways of Approaching Durkheim

In this introduction, I have highlighted Durkheim's major contributions along a number of different analytical lines, clustering around the problematic of structure and agency and the institutional analysis of modern society. I have surveyed his multidimensional topography of the social, cultural, and collective-emotional structures that help to shape modern social life and the individual and collective agency that reproduces and transforms those structures. In addition, I have featured his schema of the key institutions and institutional complexes (state, economy, and civil society) that are located within that topography. By way of conclusion, let me step back and assess the strengths and limitations of this particular approach. The organizational format that I have chosen for this volume is but one of several alternative ways of presenting Durkheim's work. It is important that readers be aware of its major disadvantages as well as advantages.

Surely the most obvious weakness of the format that I have chosen is that it approaches Durkheim in terms of analytical distinctions that are in part not of his own making. Nowhere does Durkheim put forward, for example (at least in so many words), the tripartite distinction upon which I have relied, of social structure, culture, and collective emotions, although the first two of those concepts are surely present throughout his lifework, and the third is clearly implicit. Nor does he operate (again, in so many words) with the specific idea of civil society that I have counterposed in this volume to state and economy. I have used these terms not only because I believe they help to capture the key themes and ideas in Durkheim's *oeuvre*, but also because they help to link his insights to present-day concerns (for a better sense of how I define and use these concepts, see Emirbayer and Sheller, 1999). But the strategy of presenting Durkheim in ways that resonate with contemporary debates brings in its train the difficulty that concepts must be invoked that do not have exact correlates in his own analytical vocabulary.

A second significant shortcoming of the framework that I have chosen is that it shifts the reader's attention away from the crucial question of how the very categories and research agendas that Durkheim put forward were themselves shaped by his location within a certain landscape of intellectual production, by his implication in such tendencies and currents as Eurocentrism, and by his own race-, gender-, and sexuality-based privileges. Durkheim was certainly influenced by the Eurocentrism of his day, as well as by hegemonic ways of thinking about race, gender, and sexuality. These (largely unspoken and untheorized) commitments deeply structured his analyses of the nature of modern European societies and their contrast with contemporary non-European as well as "primitive" social orders; they also manifested themselves in his prescriptions for social reform. One cannot fully understand Durkheim (or any other classical figure, for that matter) without systematically considering the relation of his work to such projects of racial, patriarchal, heterosexual, and civilizational domination (see, for example, Lehmann, 1994; Connell, 1997; Seidman, 1998). It is difficult fully to do justice to such issues, however, within the organizational format that I have chosen. One compensating feature, at least, is that the textual material for such an approach is largely present in the selections that I have included. When making those selections, I was determined not to relegate passages on "primitive" societies, for example – or any number of other revealing passages – to a textually segregated chapter or two at the conclusion of the volume. Instead, I included those passages in many different places throughout the text, so as to illustrate just how pervasive such ways of thinking are in Durkheim's overall body of work.

A third and related disadvantage of the format that I have selected is that it fails to underscore the intrinsic ambiguities, inconsistencies, and contradictions in Durkheim's thinking. It tends to render the tensions within his work less than fully visible, highlighting instead the ways in which that lifework can be said to cohere or to represent a seamless whole. Many commentators have noted the deep ambivalences in Durkheim's writings, whether on a theoretical level (e.g., the issue of idealism versus materialism), on a methodological plane (e.g., positivism versus interpretivism), or on the level of his normative and political commitments (e.g., conservatism versus liberalism) (for an exhaustive review of these debates, see Alexander, 1982). These and other such ambivalences cannot be as fully or deeply explored within the present framework as might be desirable. The gain of presenting Durkheim's ideas as a systematic whole is at least partially offset by the cost of slightly flattening them out or ridding them of some of their most interesting, and perhaps telling, wrinkles.

Finally, an important shortcoming of this framework is that it treats Durkheim's lifework as if it were an integral entity outside time, a body of work that never changed in its emphases or its theoretical logic. The consensus among Durkheim scholars has long been, by contrast, that his thinking did undergo major transitions, although the number, timing, and nature of those transitions have always been a source of debate. (One commentator, for example, places the crucial dividing line at 1895, when Durkheim began fully to appreciate the significance of religion in social life and thence shifted to a more culturalist perspective. This commentator writes: "The vast implications of Durkheim's religious revelation have never been fully appreciated. It is scarcely realized that after 1896 he systematically revised every piece of his sociological writings, and every one of his sets of lectures as well, to make them reflect his new understanding" (Alexander, 1989b, p. 143).) The present volume's design cannot by its very nature convey such shifts in theorization, although it does have the partial virtue, at least, of highlighting the continuities in Durkheim's thought that nonetheless spanned the various phases of his development. An alternative approach to Durkheim that works its way text by text, period by period, along his entire theoretical trajectory would more easily have shown how Durkheim went about continually elaborating and sometimes revising his ideas, although (once again) this would have made it correspondingly more difficult to isolate specific themes or to dramatize basic continuities over time.

On the other hand, hopefully the most important advantage of the organizational format of this volume is that it successfully captures the full array of theoretical approaches that Durkheim brought to bear upon modern society. It allows us to see, first, the different analytical vantage-points (of structure and agency) from which he approached modernity – and then the ways in which these perspectives came together in his various institutional analyses. A focus upon his key theoretical contributions, in sum, is precisely what the present volume is best designed to facilitate. Durkheim had much to say, for example, on theoretical issues pertaining to cultural analysis, or with respect to educational institutions, the family, and occupational groups. But without dissecting his overall contributions into distinct topical clusters, it would have been difficult to grasp the full nature and significance of his insights in either area of study. One related advantage here is that the carving out of such themes and concerns permits a more direct linkage to recent work in corresponding areas of inquiry, such as contemporary cultural sociology or the emerging field of civil society studies. Two additional chapters in the volume – the opening and closing chapters – allow us similarly to highlight the methodological and normative themes that Durkheim also wove into the complex fabric that constitutes his assessment of modern social life.

Durkheim's work is certainly inexhaustible, and it will reward careful study from any number of different theoretical vantage-points. Even as modern societies themselves continue to evolve, perhaps in directions that Durkheim may not have anticipated, his sociology will remain a crucial source of ideas to help us chart their development and will shed important light upon their dynamics, emergent problems, and future possibilities.

Acknowledgments

I would like to thank Shamus Khan for his invaluable assistance in the preparation of this volume; Chad Goldberg and Elliot Weininger for helpful suggestions along the way; and Ira Cohen for his inspiring enthusiasm and support since the very beginning of this project.

References

Alexander, Jeffrey C. 1982: *Theoretical Logic in Sociology*, vol. 2. Berkeley: University of California Press.

—— (ed.) 1988: *Durkheimian Sociology: Cultural Studies*. Cambridge: Cambridge University Press.

——. 1989a: "The Dialectic of Individuation and Domination: Weber's Rationalization Theory and Beyond." In *Max Weber, Rationality, and Modernity*, ed. Sam Whimsler and Scott Lash, London: Allen and Unwin, pp. 185–206.

——. 1989b: "Rethinking Durkheim's Intellectual Development." In *Structure and Meaning*, New York: Columbia University Press, pp. 123–55.

Alpert, Harry. 1965: "Durkheim's Functional Theory of Ritual." In *Emile Durkheim*, ed. Robert A. Nisbet, Englewood Cliffs, NJ: Prentice-Hall, pp. 137–41.

Althusser, Louis. 1971: "Ideology and Ideological State Apparatuses." In *Lenin and Philosophy and other Essays*, trans. Ben Brewster, New York: Monthly Review, pp. 127–86.

Anderson, Perry. 1974a: *Lineages of the Absolutist State*. London: New Left Books.

——. 1974b: *Passages from Antiquity to Feudalism*. London: New Left Books.

Aron, Raymond. 1970: *Main Currents in Sociological Thought*, trans. Richard Howard and Helen Weaver. New York: Anchor Books.

Bellah, Robert A. 1973: "Introduction." In *Emile Durkheim: On Morality and Society*, ed. Robert A. Bellah, Chicago and London: University of Chicago Press, pp. ix–lv.

——. 1975: *The Broken Covenant*. New York: Seabury.

Benoit-Smullyan, Emile. 1948: "The Sociologism of Emile Durkheim and his School." In *An Introduction to the History of Sociology*, ed. H. E. Barnes, Chicago: University of Chicago Press, pp. 499–537.

Birnbaum, Pierre. 1976: "La Conception durkheimienne de l'état." *Revue française de sociologie* 17: 247–58.

Bottomore, Tom. 1981: "A Marxist Consideration of Durkheim." *Social Forces* 59: 902–17.

Calhoun, Craig. 1991: "The Problem of Identity in Collective Action." In *Macro-Micro Linkages in Sociology*, ed. Joan Huber, Newbury Park, CA: Sage Publications, pp. 51–75.

——. 1993: "'New Social Movements' of the Early Nineteenth Century." *Social Science History* 17: 385–428.

——. 1994: *Neither Gods nor Emperors*. Berkeley: University of California Press.

Cladis, Mark S. 1992: *A Communitarian Defense of Liberalism*. Stanford, CA: Stanford University Press.

Collins, Randall. 1993: "Emotional Energy as the Common Denominator of Rational Action." *Rationality and Society* 5: 203–30.

Connell, R. W. 1997: "Why is Classical Theory Classical?" *American Journal of Sociology* 102: 1511–57.

Coser, Lewis A. 1964: "Durkheim's Conservatism and its Implications for his Sociological Theory." In *Essays on Sociology and Philosophy by Emile Durkheim et al.*, ed. Kurt Wolff, New York: Harper, pp. 211–32.

——. 1971. *Masters of Sociological Thought*, 2nd edn. San Diego, CA: Harcourt Brace Jovanovich.

Cotterrell, Roger. 1999: *Emile Durkheim: Law in a Moral Domain*. Stanford, CA: Stanford University Press.

Durkheim, Emile. 1951 [1897]: *Suicide: A Study in Sociology*, trans. John A. Spaulding and George Simpson. New York: Free Press.

——. 1973 [1898]: "Individualism and the Intellectuals." In *Emile Durkheim: On Morality and Society*, trans. Charles Blend, ed. Robert N. Bellah, Chicago and London: University of Chicago Press, pp. 43–57.

——. 1978a [1891–2]: "The Conjugal Family." In *Emile Durkheim: On Institutional Analysis*, ed. and trans. Mark Traugott, Chicago and London: University of Chicago Press, pp. 229–39.

——. 1978b [1888]: "Course in Sociology: Opening Lecture." In *Emile Durkheim: On Institutional Analysis*, ed. and trans. Mark Traugott, Chicago and London: University of Chicago Press, pp. 43–70.

——. 1978c [1906]: "Divorce by Mutual Consent." In *Emile Durkheim: On Institutional Analysis*, ed. and trans. Mark Traugott, Chicago and London: University of Chicago Press, pp. 240–52.

——. 1978d [1897–8]: "Note on Social Morphology." In *Emile Durkheim: On Institutional Analysis*, ed. and trans. Mark Traugott, Chicago and London: University of Chicago Press, pp. 88–90.

——. 1978e [1897]: "Review of Antonio Labriola, *Essais sur la conception materialiste de l'histoire*." In *Emile Durkheim: On Institutional Analysis*, ed. and trans. Mark Traugott, Chicago and London: University of Chicago Press, pp. 123–30.

——. 1978f [1909]: "Sociology and the Social Sciences." In *Emile Durkheim: On Institutional Analysis*, ed. and trans. Mark Traugott, Chicago and London: University of Chicago Press, pp. 71–87.

——. 1992 [1898–1900]: *Professional Ethics and Civic Morals*, trans. Cornelia Brookfield. London: Routledge.

——. 1995 [1912]: *The Elementary Forms of Religious Life*, trans. Karen E. Fields. New York: Free Press.

Emirbayer, Mustafa. 1996a: "Durkheim's Contribution to the Sociological Analysis of History." *Sociological Forum* 11: 263–84.

——. 1996b: "Useful Durkheim." *Sociological Theory* 14: 109–30.

Emirbayer, Mustafa, and Mimi Sheller. 1999: "Publics in History." *Theory and Society* 28: 145–97.

Evans, Peter B., Dietrich Rueschemeyer, and Theda Skocpol (eds) 1985: *Bringing the State Back In*. New York: Cambridge University Press.

Giddens, Anthony. 1971: "Durkheim's Political Sociology." *Sociological Review* 19: 477–519.

——. 1977: "The 'Individual' in the Writings of Emile Durkheim." In *Studies in Social and Political Theory*, New York: Basic Books, pp. 273–96.

——. 1978: *Emile Durkheim*. Harmondsworth: Penguin.

Goodwin, Jeff, James M. Jasper, and Francesca Polletta (eds) 2001: *Passionate Politics*. Chicago and London: University of Chicago Press.

Habermas, Jürgen. 1984: *The Theory of Communicative Action*, vol 1, trans. Thomas McCarthy. Boston: Beacon Press.

Hall, Stuart. 1986: "Cultural Studies: Two Paradigms." In *Media, Culture, and Society: A Critical Reader*, ed. Richard Collins et al. Beverly Hills, CA: Sage Publications, pp. 9–32.

Hegel, G. W. F. 1967 [1821]: *Hegel's Philosophy of Right*, trans. T. M. Knox. Oxford: Oxford University Press.

Larana, Enrique, Hank Johnston, and Joseph R. Gusfield (eds) 1994: *New Social Movements*. Philadelphia: Temple University Press.

Lehmann, Jennifer M. 1994: *Durkheim and Women*. Lincoln, NE, and London: University of Nebraska Press.

Lukes, Steven. 1973: *Emile Durkheim: His Life and Work. A Historical and Critical Study*. Stanford, CA: Stanford University Press.

Marx, Gary, and James Wood. 1975: "Strands of Theory and Research in Collective Behavior." *Annual Review of Sociology* 1: 368–428.

Moore, Barrington, Jr. 1966: *Social Origins of Dictatorship and Democracy*. Boston: Beacon Press.

Morris, Aldon D., and Carol McClurg Mueller (eds) 1992: *Frontiers in Social Movement Theory*. New Haven and London: Yale University Press.

Nisbet, Robert A. 1974: *The Sociology of Emile Durkheim*. New York: Oxford University Press.

Parsons, Talcott. 1937: *The Structure of Social Action*, 2 vols. New York: Free Press.

Poggi, Gianfranco. 1971: "The Place of Religion in Durkheim's Theory of Institutions." *European Journal of Sociology* 12: 229–60.

Scheff, Thomas J. 1994: *Bloody Revenge*. Boulder, CO: Westview Press.

Seidman, Steven. 1998: *Contested Knowledge*, 2nd edn. Malden, MA: Blackwell.

Skocpol, Theda. 1978: *States and Social Revolutions*. New York: Cambridge University Press.

——. 1985: "Bringing the State Back In." In *Bringing the State Back In*, ed. Peter B. Evans, Dietrich Rueschemeyer, and Theda Skocpol, New York: Cambridge University Press, pp. 3–37.

Sorel, Georges. 1895: "Les Theories de M. Durkheim." *Le Devenir* 1: 1–25, 148–80.

Thompson, E. P. 1979: *The Poverty of Theory and Other Essays*. London: Merlin.

Tilly, Charles. 1981: "Useless Durkheim." In *As Sociology Meets History*, New York: Academic Press, pp. 95–108.

——. 1984: *Big Structures, Large Processes, Huge Comparisons*. New York: Russell Sage Foundation.

Traugott, Mark. 1978: "Introduction." In *Emile Durkheim: On Institutional Analysis*, ed. and trans. Mark Traugott, Chicago and London: University of Chicago Press, pp. 1–39, 253–60.

——. 1984: "Durkheim and Social Movements." *Archives Européennes de Sociologie* 25: 319–26.

Wacquant, Loic J. D. 1993: "Solidarity, Morality and Sociology." *Journal of the Society for Social Research* 1: 1–8.

Wallwork, Ernest. 1972: *Durkheim: Morality and Milieu*. Cambridge, MA: Harvard University Press.

Walzer, Michael. 1965: *The Revolution of the Saints*. Cambridge, MA: Harvard University Press.

Williams, Raymond. 1977: *Marxism and Literature*. Oxford and New York: Oxford University Press.

part 1

Sociological Methodology

chapter 1

An Agenda for Sociology

Introduction

The extracts from *Suicide* that follow serve as a useful introduction to Durkheim's methodological agenda. They make the case that even the most seemingly private of acts – suicide – is a subject matter best treated not by individual psychology, but rather by a sociology concerned with the objectivistic study of social facts. Durkheim classifies and explains the different social types of suicide by the different social causes or "suicidogenic currents" that generate them; he contends that these currents, at least within certain limits, are phenomena of a "normal sociology"; and argues that in contemporary societies those limits have been exceeded, and that "the rising tide of suicide originates in a pathological state just now accompanying the march of civilization" (p. 48). Such conclusions lead to practical suggestions for social reform (see ch. 8). While these excerpts might easily be read alone, they are perhaps most profitably studied in tandem with another of Durkheim's major works – *The Rules of Sociological Method* – selections from which appear in the Appendix. (As Durkheim himself notes, *Suicide* treats in "concrete and specific form . . . the chief methodological problems" discussed "in greater detail" in that other work (p. 32).) *Suicide*, however, is not merely a work of applied sociological methodology. It is also a major theoretical study that introduces Durkheim's key categories of social integration and social regulation and, more specifically, his concepts of egoism, altruism, anomie, and fatalism. It also stands as one of his most important substantive contributions to the sociology of modernity, for while it is outwardly concerned with variations in suicide rates, at a much deeper level it investigates "the causes of the general contemporary maladjustment being undergone by European societies" (p. 32). The concluding selection from Pierre Bourdieu's *Distinction* similarly spans methodological, theoretical, and substantive levels of analysis. It takes the most seemingly private of faculties – taste – and shows how its variations can also be explained sociologically; it also provides new theoretical perspectives upon class formation and opens up important new vistas upon the structuring and dynamics of modern societies.

From *Suicide*

Emile Durkheim, *Suicide: A Study in Sociology*, trans. John A. Spaulding and George Simpson (New York: Free Press, 1951), pp. 36–9, 46–51, 145–60, 198–215, 217–28, 241–76, 323–5, 361–87.

Suicide has been chosen as [our] subject, among the various subjects that we have had occasion to study in our teaching career, because few are more accurately to be defined and because it seemed to us particularly timely; its limits have even required study in a preliminary work. On the other hand, by such concentration, real laws are discoverable which demonstrate the possibility of sociology better than any dialectical argument. The ones we hope to have demonstrated will appear. . . .

Moreover, by thus restricting the research, one is by no means deprived of broad views and general insights. On the contrary, we think we have established a certain number of propositions concerning marriage, widowhood, family life, religious society, etc., which, if we are not mistaken, are more instructive than the common theories of moralists as to the nature of these conditions or institutions. There will even emerge from our study some suggestions concerning the causes of the general contemporary maladjustment being undergone by European societies and concerning remedies which may relieve it. . . .

Finally, in the course of this work, but in a concrete and specific form, will appear the chief methodological problems elsewhere stated and examined by us in greater detail. [*Les règles de la Méthode sociologique*, Paris, F. Alcan, 1895. (Translated into English as *The Rules of Sociological Method*, and published by the Free Press, Glencoe, Illinois, 1950.)] Indeed, among these questions there is one to which the following work makes a contribution too important for us to fail to call it immediately to the attention of the reader.

Sociological method as we practice it rests wholly on the basic principle that social facts must be studied as things, that is, as realities external to the individual. There is no principle for which we have received more criticism; but none is more fundamental. Indubitably for sociology to be possible, it must above all have an object all its own. It must take cognizance of a reality which is not in the domain of other sciences. But if no reality exists outside of individual consciousness, it wholly lacks any material of its own. In that case, the only possible subject of observation is the mental states of the individual, since nothing else exists. That, however, is the field of psychology.... On the pretext of giving the science a more solid foundation by establishing it upon the psychological constitution of the individual, it is thus robbed of the only object proper to it. *It is not realized that there can be no sociology unless societies exist, and that societies cannot exist if there are only individuals.* Moreover, this view is not the least of the causes which maintain the taste for vague generalities in sociology. How can it be important to define the concrete forms of social life, if they are thought to have only a borrowed existence?

But it seems hardly possible to us that there will not emerge, on the contrary, from every page of this book, so to speak, the impression that the individual is dominated by a moral reality greater than himself: namely, collective reality.... Thus it will appear more clearly why sociology can and must be objective, since it deals with realities as definite and substantial as those of the psychologist or the biologist....

... Since suicide is an individual action affecting the individual only, it must seemingly depend exclusively on individual factors, thus belonging to psychology alone. Is not the suicide's resolve usually explained by his temperament, character, antecedents and private history?

The degree and conditions under which suicides may be legitimately studied in this way need not now be considered, but that they may be viewed in an entirely different light is certain. If, instead of seeing in them only separate occurrences, unrelated and to be separately studied, the suicides committed in a given society during a given period of time are taken as a whole, it appears that this total is not simply a sum of independent units, a collective total, but is itself a new fact *sui generis*, with its own unity, individuality and consequently its own nature – a nature, furthermore, dominantly social. Indeed, provided too long a period is not considered, the statistics for one and the same society are almost invariable, ...

If a longer period of time is considered, more serious changes are observed. Then, however, they become chronic; they only prove that the structural characteristics of society have simultaneously suffered profound changes. It is interesting to note that they do not take place with the extreme slowness that quite a large number of observers has attributed to them, but are both abrupt and progressive. After a series of years, during which these figures have varied within very narrow limits, a rise suddenly appears which, after repeated vacillation, is confirmed, grows and is at last fixed. This is because every breach of social equilibrium, though sudden in its appearance, takes time to produce all its consequences. Thus, the evolution of suicide is composed of undulating movements, distinct and successive, which occur spasmodically, develop for a time, and then stop only to begin again. . . .

At each moment of its history, therefore, each society has a definite aptitude for suicide. The relative intensity of this aptitude is measured by taking the proportion between the total number of voluntary deaths and the population of every age and sex. We will call this numerical datum *the rate of mortality through suicide, characteristic of the society under consideration.* It is generally calculated in proportion to a million or a hundred thousand inhabitants.

Not only is this rate constant for long periods, but its invariability is even greater than that of leading demographic data. General mortality, especially, varies much more often from year to year and the variations it undergoes are far greater. . . .

. . . The average rate of mortality, furthermore, achieves this regularity only by being general and impersonal, and can afford only a very imperfect description of a given society. It is in fact substantially the same for all peoples of approximately the same degree of civilization; at least, the differences are very slight. . . . On the contrary, the suicide-rate, while showing only slight annual changes, varies according to society by doubling, tripling, quadrupling, and even more. . . . Accordingly, to a much higher degree than the death-rate, it is peculiar to each social group where it can be considered as a characteristic index. It is even so closely related to what is most deeply constitutional in each national temperament that the order in which the different societies appear in this respect remains almost exactly the same at very different periods. . . .

The suicide-rate is therefore a factual order, unified and definite, as is shown by both its permanence and its variability. For this permanence would be inexplicable if it were not the result of a group of distinct characteristics, solidary one with another, and simultaneously effective in spite of different attendant circumstances; and this variability proves the concrete and individual quality of these same characteristics, since they vary with the individual character of society itself. In short, these statistical data express the suicidal tendency with which each society is collectively afflicted. . . .

. . .[I]t would seem to be best to inquire first whether the tendency [to suicide] is single and indestructible or whether it does not rather consist of several different tendencies, which may be isolated by analysis and which should be separately studied. If so, we should proceed as follows. As the tendency, single or not, is observable only in its individual manifestations, we should have to begin with the latter. . . .

Unfortunately, no classification of the suicides of sane persons can be made in terms of their morphological types or characteristics, from almost complete lack of the necessary data. . . .

But our aim may be achieved by another method. Let us reverse the order of study. Only in so far as the effective causes differ can there be different types of suicide. For each to have its own nature, it must also have special conditions of existence. The same antecedent or group of antecedents cannot sometimes produce one result and sometimes another, for, if so, the difference of the second from the first would itself be without cause, which would contradict the principle of causality. Every proved specific difference between causes therefore implies a similar difference between effects. Consequently, we shall be able to determine the social types of suicide by classifying them not directly by their preliminarily described characteristics, but by the causes which produce them. Without asking why they differ from one another, we will first seek the social conditions responsible for them; then group these conditions in a number of separate classes by their resemblances and differences, and we shall be sure that a specific type of suicide will correspond to each of these classes. In a word, instead of being morphological, our classification will from the start be aetiological. Nor is this a sign of inferiority, for the nature of a phenomenon is much more profoundly got at by knowing its cause than by knowing its characteristics only, even the essential ones. . . .

First let us see how the different religious confessions affect suicide.

If one casts a glance at the map of European suicide, it is at once clear that in purely Catholic countries like Spain, Portugal, Italy, suicide is very little developed, while it is at its maximum in Protestant countries, in Prussia, Saxony, Denmark. . . .

Nevertheless, this first comparison is still too summary. In spite of undeniable similarities, the social environments of the inhabitants of these different countries are not identical. The civilizations of Spain and Portugal are far below that of Germany and this inferiority may conceivably be the reason for the lesser development of suicide which we have just mentioned. If one wishes to avoid this source of error and determine more definitely the influence of Catholicism and Protestantism on the suicidal tendency, the two religions must be compared in the heart of a single society. . . .

. . . [E]verywhere without exception, Protestants show far more suicides than the followers of other confessions. . . .

The aptitude of Jews for suicide is always less than that of Protestants; in a very general way it is also, though to a lesser degree, lower than that of Catholics. . . . [T]heir religion has the fewest suicides of all.

These facts established, what is their explanation?

The only essential difference between Catholicism and Protestantism is that the second permits free inquiry to a far greater degree than the first. Of course, Catholicism by the very fact that it is an idealistic religion concedes a far greater place to thought and reflection than Greco-Latin polytheism or Hebrew monotheism. It is not restricted to mechanical ceremonies but seeks the control of the conscience. So it appeals to conscience, and even when demanding blind submission of reason, does so by employing the language of reason. None the less, the Catholic accepts his faith ready made, without scrutiny. He may not even submit it to historical examination since the original texts that serve as its basis are proscribed. A whole hierarchical system of authority is devised, with marvelous ingenuity, to render tradition invariable. All *variation* is abhorrent to Catholic thought. The Protestant is far more the author of his faith. The Bible is put in his hands and no interpretation is imposed upon him. The very structure of the reformed cult stresses this state of religious individualism. . . .

. . . So if Protestantism concedes a greater freedom to individual thought than Catholicism, it is because it has fewer common beliefs and practices. Now, a religious society cannot exist without a collective *credo* and the more extensive the *credo* the more unified and strong is the society. For it does not unite men by an exchange and reciprocity of services, a temporal bond of union which permits and even presupposes differences, but which a religious society cannot form. It socializes men only by attaching them completely to an identical body of doctrine and socializes them in proportion as this body of doctrine is extensive and firm. The more numerous the manners of action and thought of a religious character are, which are accordingly removed from free inquiry, the more the idea of God presents itself in all details of existence, and makes individual wills converge to one identical goal. Inversely, the greater concessions a confessional group makes to individual judgment, the less it dominates lives, the less its cohesion and vitality. We thus reach the conclusion that the superiority of Protestantism with respect to suicide results from its being a less strongly integrated church than the Catholic church.

This also explains the situation of Judaism. Indeed, the reproach to which the Jews have for so long been exposed by Christianity has created feelings of unusual solidarity among them. Their need of resisting a general hostility, the very impossibility of free communication with the rest of the population, has forced them to strict union among themselves. Consequently, each community became a small, compact and coherent society with a strong feeling of self-consciousness and unity. Everyone thought and lived alike; individual divergences were made almost impossible by the community of existence and the close and constant surveillance of all over each. The Jewish church has thus been more strongly united than any other, from its dependence on itself because of being the object of intolerance. By analogy with what has just been observed apropos of Protestantism, the same cause must therefore be assumed for the slight tendency of the Jews to suicide in spite of all sorts of circumstances which might on the contrary incline them to it. Doubtless they owe this immunity in a sense to the hostility surrounding them. But if this is its influence, it is not because it imposes a higher morality but because it obliges them to live in greater union. They are immune to this degree because their religious society is of such solidarity. . . .

. . . [M]arriage has . . . a preservative effect of its own against suicide. But it is very limited and also benefits one sex only. . . . [T]he family is the essential factor in the immunity of married persons, that is, the family as the whole group of parents and children. Of course, since husband and wife are members, they too share in producing this result, however not as husband or wife but as father or mother, as functionaries of the family association. If the disappearance of one increases the chances that the other may commit suicide, it is not because the bonds uniting them personally are broken, but because a family disaster occurs, the shock of which the survivor undergoes. Reserving the special effect of marriage for later study, we shall say that domestic society, like religious society is a powerful counteragent against suicide.

This immunity even increases with the density of the family, that is with the increase in the number of its elements. . . .

. . . Why does family density have this effect upon suicide? . . . It is . . . because the functioning of the family varies with its greater or less density, that the number of its component elements affects the suicidal tendency.

That is, the density of a group cannot sink without its vitality diminishing. Where collective sentiments are strong, it is because the force with which they affect each individual conscience is echoed in all the others, and reciprocally. The intensity they attain therefore depends on the number of consciences which react to them in common. For the same reason, the larger a crowd, the more capable of violence the passions vented by it. Consequently, in a family of small numbers, common sentiments and memories cannot be very intense; for there are not enough consciences in which they can be represented and reenforced by sharing them. No such powerful traditions can be formed there as unite the members of a single group, even surviving it and attaching successive generations to one another. Small families are also inevitably short-lived; and without duration no society can be stable. Not only are collective states weak in such a group, but they cannot be numerous. . . .

But for a group to be said to have less common life than another means that it is less powerfully integrated; for the state of integration of a social aggregate can only reflect the intensity of the collective life circulating in it. It is more unified and powerful the more active and constant is the intercourse among its members. Our previous conclusion may thus be completed to read: just as the family is a powerful safeguard against suicide, so the more strongly it is constituted the greater its protection.

If statistics had not developed so late, it would be easy to show by the same method that this law applies to political societies. History indeed teaches us that suicide, generally rare in young societies in process of evolution and concentration, increases as they disintegrate. . . .

Great political upheavals are sometimes said to increase the number of suicides. But Morselli has conclusively shown that facts contradict this view. All the revolutions which have occurred in France during this century reduced the number of suicides at the moment of their occurrence. . . .

Mild as they are, mere election crises sometimes have the same result. . . . Great national wars have the same effect as political disturbances. . . .

These facts are therefore susceptible of only one interpretation; namely, that great social disturbances and great popular wars rouse collective sentiments, stimulate partisan spirit and patriotism, political and national faith, alike, and concentrating activity toward a single end, at least temporarily cause a stronger integration of society. The salutary influence which we have just shown to exist is due not to the crisis but to the struggles it occasions. As they force men to close ranks and confront the common danger, the individual thinks less of himself and more of the common cause. Besides, it is comprehensible that this integration may not be purely momentary but may sometimes outlive its immediate causes, especially when it is intense.

We have thus successively set up the three following propositions:

Suicide varies inversely with the degree of integration of religious society.
Suicide varies inversely with the degree of integration of domestic society.
Suicide varies inversely with the degree of integration of political society.

This grouping shows that whereas these different societies have a moderating influence upon suicide, this is due not to special characteristics of each but to a characteristic common to all. . . . The cause can only be found in a single quality possessed by all these social groups, though perhaps to varying degrees. The only quality satisfying this condition is that they are all strongly integrated social groups. So we reach the general conclusion: suicide varies inversely with the degree of integration of the social groups of which the individual forms a part.

But society cannot disintegrate without the individual simultaneously detaching himself from social life, without his own goals becoming preponderant over those of the community, in a word without his personality tending to surmount the collective personality. The more weakened the groups to which he belongs, the less he depends on them, the more he consequently depends only on himself and recognizes no other rules of conduct than what are founded on his private interests. If we agree to call this state egoism, in which the individual ego asserts itself to excess in the face of the social ego and at its expense, we may call egoistic the special type of suicide springing from excessive individualism. . . .

. . . What is there then in individualism that explains this result?

If, . . . as has often been said, man is double, that is because social man superimposes himself upon physical man. Social man necessarily presupposes a society which he expresses and serves. If this dissolves, if we no longer feel it in existence and action about and above us, whatever is social in us is deprived of all objective foundation. All that remains is an artificial combination of illusory images, a phantasmagoria vanishing at the least reflection; that is, nothing which can be a goal for our action. Yet this social man is the essence of civilized man; he is the masterpiece of existence. Thus we are bereft of reasons for existence; for the only life to which we could cling no longer corresponds to anything actual; the only existence still based upon reality no longer meets our needs. Because we have been initiated into a higher existence, the one which satisfies an animal or a child can satisfy us no more and the other itself fades and leaves us helpless. So there is nothing more for our efforts to lay hold of, and we feel them lose themselves in emptiness. . . .

But this is not all. This detachment occurs not only in single individuals. One of the constitutive elements of every national temperament consists of a certain way of estimating the value of existence. There is a collective as well as an individual humor inclining peoples to sadness or cheerfulness, making them see things in bright or sombre lights. . . . For individuals share too deeply in the life of society for it to be diseased without their suffering infection. What it suffers they necessarily suffer. Because it is the whole, its ills are communicated to its parts. Hence it cannot disintegrate without awareness that the regular conditions of general existence are equally disturbed. Because society is the end on which our better selves depend, it cannot feel us escaping it without a simultaneous realization that our activity is purposeless. . . . As these currents are collective, they have, by virtue of their origin, an authority which they impose upon the individual and they drive him more vigorously on the way to which he is already inclined by the state of moral distress directly aroused in him by the disintegration of society. Thus, at the very moment that, with excessive zeal, he frees himself from the social environment, he still submits to its influence. However individualized a man may be, there is always something collective remaining – the very depression and melancholy resulting from this same exaggerated individualism. He effects communion through sadness when he no longer has anything else with which to achieve it.

Hence this type of suicide well deserves the name we have given it. Egoism is not merely a contributing factor in it; it is its generating cause. In this case the bond attaching man to life relaxes because that attaching him to society is itself slack. The incidents of private life which seem the direct inspiration of suicide and are considered its determining causes are in reality only incidental causes. The individual yields to the slightest shock of circumstance because the state of society has made him a ready prey to suicide. . . .

. . . If, as we have just seen, excessive individuation leads to suicide, insufficient individuation has the same effects. When man has become detached from society, he encounters less resistance to suicide in himself, and he does so likewise when social integration is too strong.

It has sometimes been said that suicide was unknown among lower societies. Thus expressed, the assertion is inexact. To be sure, egoistic suicide, constituted as has just been shown, seems not to be frequent there. But another form exists among them in an endemic state. . . .

Suicide, . . . is surely very common among primitive peoples. But it displays peculiar characteristics. All the facts . . . fall into one of the following three categories:

1   Suicides of men on the threshold of old age or stricken with sickness.
2   Suicides of women on their husbands' death.
3   Suicides of followers or servants on the death of their chiefs.

Now, when a person kills himself, in all these cases, it is not because he assumes the right to do so but, on the contrary, *because it is his duty*. If he fails in this obligation, he is dishonored and also punished, usually, by religious sanctions. . . . The weight of society is thus brought to bear on him to lead him to destroy himself. To be sure, society intervenes in egoistic suicide, as well; but its intervention differs in the two cases. In one case, it speaks the sentence of death; in the other it forbids the choice of death. In the case of egoistic suicide it suggests or counsels at most; in the other case it compels and is the author of conditions and circumstances making this obligation coercive.

This sacrifice then is imposed by society for social ends. . . .

This description sufficiently defines the cause of these suicides. For society to be able thus to compel some of its members to kill themselves, the individual personality can have little value. For as soon as the latter begins to form, the right to existence is the first conceded it; or is at least suspended only in such unusual circumstances as war. But there can be only one cause for this feeble individuation itself. For the individual to occupy so little place in collective life he must be almost completely absorbed in the group and the latter accordingly, very highly integrated. . . .

We thus confront a type of suicide differing by incisive qualities from the preceding one. Whereas the latter is due to excessive individuation, the former is caused by too rudimentary individuation. One occurs because society allows the individual to escape it, being insufficiently aggregated in some parts or even in the whole; the other, because society holds him in too strict tutelage. Having given the name of *egoism* to the state of the ego living its own life and obeying itself alone, that of *altruism* adequately expresses the opposite state, where the ego is not its own property, where it is blended with something not itself, where the goal of conduct is exterior to itself, that is, in one of the groups in which it participates. So we call the suicide caused by intense altruism *altruistic suicide.* . . .

. . . One is related to the crude morality which disregards everything relating solely to the individual; the other is closely associated with the refined ethics which sets human personality on so high a pedestal that it can no longer be subordinated to anything. Between the two there is, therefore, all the difference between primitive peoples and the most civilized nations.

However, if lower societies are the theatre par excellence of altruistic suicide, it is also found in more recent civilizations. Under this head may notably be classified the death of some of the Christian martyrs. . . .

In our contemporary societies, as individual personality becomes increasingly free from the collective personality, such suicides could not be widespread. Some may doubtless be said to have yielded to altruistic motives, such as soldiers who preferred death to the humiliation of defeat, like Commandant Beaurepaire and Admiral Villeneuve, or unhappy persons who kill themselves to prevent disgrace befalling their family. For when such persons renounce life, it is for something they love better than themselves. But they are isolated and exceptional cases. Yet even today there exists among us a special environment where altruistic suicide is chronic: namely, the army.

It is a general fact in all European countries that the suicidal aptitude of soldiers is much higher than that of the civilian population of the same age. The difference varies between 25 and 900 per cent. . . .

But society is not only something attracting the sentiments and activities of individuals with unequal force. It is also a power controlling them. There is a relation between the way this regulative action is performed and the social suicide-rate. . . .

No living being can be happy or even exist unless his needs are sufficiently proportioned to his means. . . .

In the animal, at least in a normal condition, this equilibrium is established with automatic spontaneity because the animal depends on purely material conditions. . . .

This is not the case with man, because most of his needs are not dependent on his body or not to the same degree. . . . Such appetites, however, admittedly sooner or later reach a limit which they cannot pass. But how determine the quantity of well-being, comfort or luxury legitimately to be craved by a human being? Nothing appears in man's organic nor in his psychological constitution which sets a limit to such tendencies. . . .

But if nothing external can restrain this capacity, it can only be a source of torment to itself. Unlimited desires are insatiable by definition and insatiability is rightly considered a sign of morbidity. Being unlimited, they constantly and infinitely surpass the means at their command; they cannot be quenched. Inextinguishable thirst is constantly renewed torture. . . . To pursue a goal which is by definition unattainable is to condemn oneself to a state of perpetual unhappiness. . . .

To achieve any other result, the passions first must be limited. Only then can they be harmonized with the faculties and satisfied. But since the individual has no way of limiting them, this must be done by some force exterior to him. A regulative force must play the same role for moral needs which the organism plays for physical needs. This means that the force can only be moral. . . . Either directly and as a whole, or through the agency of one of its organs, society alone can play this moderating role; for it is the only moral power superior to the individual, the authority of which he accepts. It alone has the power necessary to stipulate law and to set the point beyond which the passions must not go. Finally, it alone can estimate the reward to be prospectively offered to every class of human functionary, in the name of the common interest. . . .

But when society is disturbed by some painful crisis or by beneficent but abrupt transitions, it is momentarily incapable of exercising this influence; thence come the sudden rises in the curve of suicides which we have pointed out above.

In the case of economic disasters, indeed, something like a declassification occurs which suddenly casts certain individuals into a lower state than their previous one. Then they must reduce their requirements, restrain their needs, learn greater self-control. All the advantages of social influence are lost so far as they are concerned; their moral education has to be recommenced. But society cannot adjust them instantaneously to this new life and teach them to practice the increased self-repression to which they are unaccustomed. So they are not adjusted to the condition forced on them, and its very prospect is intolerable; hence the suffering which detaches them from a reduced existence even before they have made trial of it.

It is the same if the source of the crisis is an abrupt growth of power and wealth. . . . The scale is upset; but a new scale cannot be immediately improvised. Time is required for the public conscience to reclassify men and things. So long as the social forces thus freed have not regained equilibrium, their respective values are unknown and so all regulation is lacking for a time. The limits are unknown between the possible and the impossible, what is just and what is unjust, legitimate claims and hopes and those which are immoderate. Consequently, there is no restraint upon aspirations. . . .

This explanation is confirmed by the remarkable immunity of poor countries. Poverty protects against suicide because it is a restraint in itself. . . .

If anomy never appeared except, as in the above instances, in intermittent spurts and acute crisis, it might cause the social suicide-rate to vary from time to time, but it would not be a regular, constant factor. In one sphere of social life, however – the sphere of trade and industry – it is actually in a chronic state.

For a whole century, economic progress has mainly consisted in freeing industrial relations from all regulation. Until very recently, it was the function of a whole system of moral forces to exert this discipline. . . .

Actually, religion has lost most of its power. And government, instead of regulating economic life, has become its tool and servant. The most opposite schools, orthodox economists and extreme socialists, unite to reduce government to the role of a more or less passive intermediary among the various social functions. . . . [I]ndustry, instead of being still regarded as a means to an end transcending itself, has become the supreme end of individuals and societies alike. Thereupon the appetites thus excited have become freed of any limiting authority. By sanctifying them, so to speak, this apotheosis of well-being has placed them above all human law. Their restraint seems like a sort of sacrilege. For this reason, even the purely utilitarian regulation of them exercised by the industrial world itself through the medium of occupational groups has been unable to persist. Ultimately, this liberation of desires has been made worse by the very development of industry and the almost infinite extension of the market. . . .

We may even wonder if this moral state is not principally what makes economic catastrophes of our day so fertile in suicides. In societies where a man is subjected to a healthy discipline, he submits more readily to the blows of chance. The necessary effort for sustaining a little more discomfort costs him relatively little, since he is used to discomfort and constraint. But when every constraint is hateful in itself, how can closer constraint not seem intolerable? There is no tendency to resignation in the feverish impatience of men's lives. When there is no other aim but to outstrip constantly the point arrived at, how painful to be thrown back! ...

Industrial and commercial functions are really among the occupations which furnish the greatest number of suicides. ...

Anomy, therefore, is a regular and specific factor in suicide in our modern societies; one of the springs from which the annual contingent feeds. So we have here a new type to distinguish from the others. It differs from them in its dependence, not on the way in which individuals are attached to society, but on how it regulates them. Egoistic suicide results from man's no longer finding a basis for existence in life; altruistic suicide, because this basis for existence appears to man situated beyond life itself. The third sort of suicide, the existence of which has just been shown, results from man's activity's lacking regulation and his consequent sufferings. By virtue of its origin we shall assign this last variety the name of *anomic suicide*.

Certainly, this and egoistic suicide have kindred ties. Both spring from society's insufficient presence in individuals. But the sphere of its absence is not the same in both cases. In egoistic suicide it is deficient in truly collective activity, thus depriving the latter of object and meaning. In anomic suicide, society's influence is lacking in the basically individual passions, thus leaving them without a check-rein. In spite of their relationship, therefore, the two types are independent of each other. We may offer society everything social in us, and still be unable to control our desires; one may live in an anomic state without being egoistic, and vice versa. These two sorts of suicide therefore do not draw their chief recruits from the same social environments; one has its principal field among intellectual careers, the world of thought – the other, the industrial or commercial world. ...

... [T]here is a type of suicide the opposite of anomic suicide, just as egoistic and altruistic suicides are opposites. It is the suicide deriving from excessive regulation, that of persons with futures pitilessly blocked and passions violently choked by oppressive discipline. It is the suicide of very young husbands, of the married woman who is childless. So, for completeness' sake, we should set up a fourth suicidal type. But it has so little contemporary importance and examples are so hard to find aside from the cases just mentioned that it seems useless to dwell upon it. However it might be said to have historical interest. Do not the suicides of slaves, said to be frequent under certain conditions, ... belong to this type, or all suicides attributable to excessive physical or moral despotism? To bring out the ineluctable and inflexible nature of a rule against which there is no appeal, and in contrast with the expression "anomy" which has just been used, we might call it *fatalistic suicide*.

The role of individual factors in the origin of suicide can now be more precisely put. If, in a given moral environment, for example, in the same religious faith or in the same body of troops or in the same occupation, certain individuals are affected and certain others not, this is undoubtedly, in great part, because the former's mental constitution, as elaborated by nature and events, offers less resistance to the suicidogenetic current. But though these conditions may share in determining the particular persons in whom this current becomes embodied, neither the special qualities nor the intensity of the current depend on these conditions. A given number of suicides is not found annually in a social group just because it contains a given number of neuropathic persons. Neuropathic conditions only cause the suicides to succumb with greater readiness to the current. Whence comes the great difference between the clinician's point of view and the sociologist's. The former confronts exclusively particular cases, isolated from one another. He establishes, very often, that the victim was either nervous or an alcoholic, and explains the act by one or the other of these psychopathic states. In a sense he is right; for if this person rather than his neighbors committed suicide, it is frequently for this reason. But in a general sense this motive does not cause people to kill themselves, *nor, especially, cause a definite number to kill themselves in each society in a definite period of time.* The productive cause of the phenomenon naturally escapes the observer of individuals only; for it lies outside individuals. To discover it, one must raise his point of view above individual suicides and perceive what gives them unity. . . .

. . . Should the present state of suicide among civilized peoples be considered as normal or abnormal? According to the solution one adopts, he will consider reforms necessary and possible with a view to restraining it, or, on the contrary, will agree, not without censure, to accept it as it is.

Some are perhaps astonished that this question could be raised.

It is true, we usually regard everything immoral as abnormal. Therefore, if suicide offends the public conscience, as has been established, it seems impossible not to see in it a phenomenon of social pathology. But we have shown elsewhere [see *Règles de la Méthode sociologique,* ch. III] that even the preeminent form of immorality, crime itself, need not necessarily be classed among morbid manifestations. . . .

Now there is no society known where a more or less developed criminality is not found under different forms. No people exists whose morality is not daily infringed upon. We must therefore call crime necessary and declare that it cannot be non-existent, that the fundamental conditions of social organization, as they are understood, logically imply it. Consequently it is normal. . . . And we have actually shown how crime may be of service. But it serves only when reproved and repressed. The mere fact of cataloguing it among the phenomena of normal sociology has been wrongly thought to imply its absolution. If it is normal that there should be crimes, it is normal that they should be punished. Punishment and crime are two terms of an inseparable pair. One is as indispensable as the other. Every abnormal relaxation of the system of repression results in stimulating criminality and giving it an abnormal intensity.

Let us apply these ideas to suicide.

We have not sufficient data, it is true, to be sure that there is no society where suicide is not found. . . . At any rate, it is certain that suicidogenetic currents of different intensity, depending on the historical period, have always existed among the peoples of Europe; statistics prove it ever since the last century, and juridical monuments prove it for earlier periods. Suicide is therefore an element of their normal constitution, and even, probably, of any social constitution.

It is also possible to see their mutual connection.

This is especially true of altruistic suicide with respect to lower societies. Precisely because the strict subordination of the individual to the group is the principle on which they rest, altruistic suicide is there, so to speak, an indispensable procedure of their collective discipline. If men, there, did not set a low value on life, they would not be what they should be; and from the moment they value it so lightly, everything inevitably becomes a pretext for them to abandon it. So there is a close connection between the practice of this sort of suicide and the moral organization of this sort of society. It is the same today in those special settings where abnegation and impersonality are essential. Even now, military esprit can only be strong if the individual is self-detached, and such detachment necessarily throws the door open to suicide.

For opposite reasons, in societies and environments where the dignity of the person is the supreme end of conduct, where man is a God to mankind, the individual is readily inclined to consider the man in himself as a God and to regard himself as the object of his own cult. When morality consists primarily in giving one a very high idea of one's self, certain combinations of circumstances readily suffice to make man unable to perceive anything above himself. Individualism is of course not necessarily egoism, but it comes close to it; the one cannot be stimulated without the other being enlarged. Thus, egoistic suicide arises. Finally, among peoples where progress is and should be rapid, rules restraining individuals must be sufficiently pliable and malleable; if they preserved all the rigidity they possess in primitive societies, evolution thus impeded could not take place promptly enough. But then inevitably, under weaker restraint, desires and ambitions overflow impetuously at certain points. As soon as men are inoculated with the precept that their duty is to progress, it is harder to make them accept resignation; so the number of the malcontent and disquieted is bound to increase. The entire morality of progress and perfection is thus inseparable from a certain amount of anomy. Hence, a definite moral constitution corresponds to each type of suicide and is interconnected with it. One cannot exist without the other, for suicide is only the form inevitably assumed by each moral constitution under certain conditions, particular, to be sure, but inescapably arising.

We shall be answered that these varied currents cause suicide only if exaggerated; and asked whether they might not have everywhere a single, moderate intensity? This is wishing for the conditions of life to be everywhere the same, which is neither possible nor desirable. There are special environments in every society which are reached by collective states only through the latter being modified; according to circumstances, they are strengthened or weakened. For a current to have a certain strength in most of the country, it therefore has to exceed or fail to reach this strength at certain points.

But not only are these excesses in one or the other direction necessary; they have their uses. For if the most general state is also the one best adapted to the most general circumstances of social life, it cannot be so related with unusual circumstances; yet society must be capable of being adapted to both. A man in whom the taste for activity never surpassed the average could not maintain himself in situations requiring an unusual effort. Likewise, a society in which intellectual individualism could not be exaggerated would be unable to shake off the yoke of tradition and renew its faiths, even when this became necessary. Inversely, where this same spiritual state could not on occasion be reduced enough to allow the opposite current to develop, what would happen in time of war, when passive obedience is the highest duty? But, for these forms of activity to be produced when they are needed, society must not have totally forgotten them. Thus, it is indispensable that they have a place in the common existence; there must be circles where an unrelenting spirit of criticism and free examination is maintained, others, like the army, where the old religion of authority is preserved almost intact. . . .

The different currents of collective sadness which derive from these three moral states have their own reasons for existence so long as they are not excessive. Indeed, it is wrong to believe that unmixed joy is the normal state of sensibility. Man could not live if he were entirely impervious to sadness. Many sorrows can be endured only be being embraced, and the pleasure taken in them naturally has a somewhat melancholy character. So, melancholy is morbid only when it occupies too much place in life; but it is equally morbid for it to be wholly excluded from life. . . . This certainly does not mean that the current of pessimism is eventually to submerge the other, but it proves that it does not lose ground and that it does not seem destined to disappear. Now, for it to exist and maintain itself, there must be a special organ in society to serve as its substratum. There must be groups of individuals who more especially represent this aspect of the collective mood. But the part of the population which plays this role is necessarily that where ideas of suicide easily take root.

But it does not follow from the fact that a suicidogenetic current of a certain strength must be considered as a phenomenon of normal sociology, that every current of the same sort is necessarily of the same character. If the spirit of renunciation, the love of progress, the taste for individuation have their place in every kind of society, and cannot exist without becoming generators of suicide at certain points, it is further necessary for them to have this property only in a certain measure, varying with various peoples. It is only justified if it does not pass certain limits. Likewise, the collective penchant for sadness is only wholesome as long as it is not preponderant. So the above remarks have not settled the question whether the present status of suicide among civilized nations is or is not normal. We need further to consider whether its tremendous aggravation during the past century is not pathological in origin. . . .

. . . [T]his aggravation springs not from the intrinsic nature of progress but from the special conditions under which it occurs in our day, and nothing assures us that these conditions are normal. For we must not be dazzled by the brilliant development of sciences, the arts and industry of which we are the witnesses; this development is altogether certainly taking place in the midst of a morbid effervescence, the grievous repercussions of which each one of us feels. It is then very possible and even probable that the rising tide of suicide originates in a pathological state just now accompanying the march of civilization without being its necessary condition.

The rapidity of the growth of suicides really permits no other hypothesis. Actually, in less than fifty years, they have tripled, quadrupled, and even quintupled, depending on the country. On the other hand, we know their connection with the most ineradicable element in the constitution of societies, since they express the mood of societies, and since the mood of peoples, like that of individuals, reflects the state of the most fundamental part of the organism. Our social organization, then, must have changed profoundly in the course of this century, to have been able to cause such a growth in the suicide-rate. So grave and rapid an alteration as this must be morbid; for a society cannot change its structure so suddenly. Only by a succession of slow, almost imperceptible modifications does it achieve different characteristics. The possible changes, even then, are limited. Once a social type is fixed it is no longer infinitely plastic; a limit is soon reached which cannot be passed. Thus the changes presupposed by the statistics of contemporary suicides cannot be normal. . . .

In resume, just as suicide does not proceed from man's difficulties in maintaining his existence, so the means of arresting its progress is not to make the struggle less difficult and life easier. If more suicides occur today than formerly, this is not because, to maintain ourselves, we have to make more painful efforts, nor that our legitimate needs are less satisfied, but because we no longer know the limits of legitimate needs nor perceive the direction of our efforts. Competition is of course becoming keener every day, because the greater ease of communication sets a constantly increasing number of competitors at loggerheads. On the other hand, a more perfected division of labor and its accompanying more complex cooperation, by multiplying and infinitely varying the occupations by which men can make themselves useful to other men, multiplies the means of existence and places them within reach of a greater variety of persons. The most inferior aptitudes may find a place here. At the same time, the more intense production resulting from this subtler cooperation, by increasing humanity's total resources, assures each worker an ampler pay and so achieves a balance between the greater wear on vital strength and its recuperation. Indeed, it is certain that average comfort has increased on all levels of the social hierarchy, although perhaps not always in equal proportions. The maladjustment from which we suffer does not exist because the objective causes of suffering have increased in number or intensity; it bears witness not to greater economic poverty, but to an alarming poverty of morality. . . .

From *Distinction: A Social Critique of the Judgment of Taste*
Pierre Bourdieu

Pierre Bourdieu, *Distinction: A Social Critique of the Judgment of Taste*, trans. Richard Nice (Cambridge, MA: Harvard University Press, 1984), pp. 50–8.

Neutralization and the universe of possibles   Unlike non-specific perception, the specifically aesthetic perception of a work of art (in which there are of course degrees of accomplishment) is armed with a pertinence principle which is socially constituted and acquired. This principle of selection enables it to pick out and retain, from among the elements offered to the eye (e.g., leaves or clouds considered merely as indices or signals invested with a denotative function – "It's a poplar", "There's going to be a storm"), all the stylistic traits – and only those – which, when relocated in the universe of stylistic possibilities, distinguish a particular manner of treating the elements selected, whether clouds or leaves, that is, a style as a mode of representation expressing the mode of perception and thought that is proper to a period, a class or class fraction, a group of artists or a particular artist. No stylistic characterization of a work of art is possible without presupposing at least implicit reference to the compossible alternatives, whether simultaneous – to distinguish it from its contemporaries – or successive – to contrast it with earlier or later works by the same or a different artist. . . .

The aesthetic disposition, understood as the aptitude for perceiving and deciphering specifically stylistic characteristics, is thus inseparable from specifically artistic competence. The latter may be acquired by explicit learning or simply by regular contact with works of art, especially those assembled in museums and galleries, where the diversity of their original functions is neutralized by their being displayed in a place consecrated to art, so that they invite pure interest in form. This practical mastery enables its possessor to situate each element of a universe of artistic representations in a class defined in relation to the class composed of all the artistic representations consciously or unconsciously excluded. . . .

In short, a grasp of the resemblances presupposes implicit or explicit reference to the differences, and vice versa. Attribution is always implicitly based on reference to "typical works", consciously or unconsciously selected because they present to a particularly high degree the qualities more or less explicitly recognized as pertinent in a given system of classification. Everything suggests that, even among specialists, the criteria of pertinence which define the stylistic properties of "typical works" generally remain implicit and that the aesthetic taxonomies implicitly mobilized to distinguish, classify and order works of art never have the rigour which aesthetic theories sometimes try to lend them. . . .

But the celebrant's or devotee's intention is not that or understanding, and, in the ordinary routine of the cult of the work of art, the play of academic or urbane references has no other function than to bring the work into an interminable circuit of inter-legitimation, . . .

Analogy, functioning as a circular mode of thought, makes it possible to tour the whole area of art and luxury *without ever leaving it.* . . .

Distance from necessity   To explain the correlation between educational capital and the propensity or at least the aspiration to appreciate a work "independently of its content", as the culturally most ambitious respondents put it, and more generally the propensity to make the "gratuitous" and "disinterested" investments demanded by legitimate works, it is not sufficient to point to the fact that schooling provides the linguistic tools and the references which enable aesthetic experience to be expressed and to be constituted by being expressed. What is in fact affirmed in this relationship is the dependence of the aesthetic disposition on the past and present material conditions of existence which are the precondition of both its constitution and its application and also of the accumulation of a cultural capital (whether or not educationally sanctioned) which can only be acquired by means of a sort of withdrawal from economic necessity. The aesthetic disposition which tends to bracket off the nature and function of the object represented and to exclude any "naive" reaction – horror at the horrible, desire for the desirable, pious reverence for the sacred – along with all purely ethical responses, in order to concentrate solely upon the mode of representation, the style, perceived and appreciated by comparison with other styles, is one dimension of a total relation to the world and to others, a life-style, in which the effects of particular conditions of existence are expressed in a "misrecognizable" form. These conditions of existence, which are the precondition for all learning of legitimate culture, whether implicit and diffuse, as domestic cultural training generally is, or explicit and specific, as in scholastic training, are characterized by the suspension and removal of economic necessity and by objective and subjective distance from practical urgencies, which is the basis of objective and subjective distance from groups subjected to those determinisms.

To be able to play the games of culture with the playful seriousness which Plato demanded, a seriousness without the "spirit of seriousness", one has to belong to the ranks of those who have been able, not necessarily to make their whole existence a sort of children's game, as artists do, but at least to maintain for a long time, sometimes a whole lifetime, a child's relation to the world. (All children start life as baby bourgeois, in a relation of magical power over others and, through them, over the world, but they grow out of it sooner or later.) This is clearly seen when, by an accident of social genetics, into the well-policed world of intellectual games there comes one of those people (one thinks of Rousseau or Chernyshevsky) who bring inappropriate stakes and interests into the games of culture; who get so involved in the game that they abandon the margin of neutralizing distance that the *illusio* (belief in the game) demands; who treat intellectual struggles, the object of so many pathetic manifestos, as a simple question of right and wrong, life and death. This is why the logic of the game has already assigned them rôles – eccentric or boor – which they will *play* despite themselves in the eyes of those who know how to stay within the bounds of the intellectual illusion and who cannot see them any other way.

The aesthetic disposition, a generalized capacity to neutralize ordinary urgencies and to bracket off practical ends, a durable inclination and aptitude for practice without a practical function, can only be constituted within an experience of the world freed from urgency and through the practice of activities which are an end in themselves, such as scholastic exercises or the contemplation of works of art. In other words, it presupposes the distance from the world . . . which is the basis of the bourgeois experience of the world. Contrary to what certain mechanistic theories would suggest, even in its most specifically artistic dimension the pedagogic action of the family and the school operates at least as much through the economic and social conditions which are the precondition of its operation as through the contents which it inculcates. . . .

Economic power is first and foremost a power to keep economic necessity at arm's length. This is why it universally asserts itself by the destruction of riches, conspicuous consumption, squandering, and every form of *gratuitous* luxury. . . .

Material or symbolic consumption of works of art constitutes one of the supreme manifestations of *ease*, in the sense both of objective leisure and subjective facility. The detachment of the pure gaze cannot be separated from a general disposition towards the "gratuitous" and the "disinterested", the paradoxical product of a negative economic conditioning which, through facility and freedom, engenders distance vis-à-vis necessity. At the same time, the aesthetic disposition is defined, objectively and subjectively, in relation to other dispositions. Objective distance from necessity and from those trapped within it combines with a conscious distance which doubles freedom by exhibiting it. As the objective distance from necessity grows, life-style increasingly becomes the product of what Weber calls a "stylization of life", a systematic commitment which orients and organizes the most diverse practices – the choice of a vintage or a cheese or the decoration of a holiday home in the country. This affirmation of power over a dominated necessity always implies a claim to a legitimate superiority over those who, because they cannot assert the same contempt for contingencies in gratuitous luxury and conspicuous consumption, remain dominated by ordinary interests and urgencies. The tastes of freedom can only assert themselves as such in relation to the tastes of necessity, which are thereby brought to the level of the aesthetic and so defined as vulgar. This claim to aristocracy is less likely to be contested than any other, because the relation of the "pure", "disinterested" disposition to the conditions which make it possible, i.e., the material conditions of existence which are rarest because most freed from economic necessity, has every chance of passing unnoticed. The most "classifying" privilege thus has the privilege of appearing to be the most natural one.

The aesthetic sense as the sense of distinction Thus, the aesthetic disposition is one dimension of a distant, self-assured relation to the world and to others which presupposes objective assurance and distance. It is one manifestation of the system of dispositions produced by the social conditionings associated with a particular class of conditions of existence when they take the paradoxical form of the greatest freedom conceivable, at a given moment, with respect to the constraints of economic necessity. But it is also a distinctive expression of a privileged position in social space whose distinctive value is objectively established in its relationship to expressions generated from different conditions. Like every sort of taste, it unites and separates. Being the product of the conditionings associated with a particular class of conditions of existence, it unites all those who are the product of similar conditions while distinguishing them from all others. And it distinguishes in an essential way, since taste is the basis of all that one has – people and things – and all that one is for others, whereby one classifies oneself and is classified by others.

Tastes (i.e., manifested preferences) are the practical affirmation of an inevitable difference. It is no accident that, when they have to be justified, they are asserted purely negatively, by the refusal of other tastes. In matters of taste, more than anywhere else, all determination is negation; and tastes are perhaps first and foremost distastes, disgust provoked by horror or visceral intolerance ("sick-making") of the tastes of others. . . . Aversion to different life-styles is perhaps one of the strongest barriers between the classes; class endogamy is evidence of this. . . . At stake in every struggle over art there is also the imposition of an art of

living, that is, the transmutation of an arbitrary way of living into the legitimate way of life which casts every other way of living into arbitrariness. . . .

Objectively and subjectively aesthetic stances adopted in matters like
cosmetics, clothing or home decoration are opportunities to experience
or assert one's position in social space, as a rank to be upheld or a distance to be kept. It goes without saying that the social classes are not equally
inclined and prepared to enter this game of refusal and counter-refusal;
and that the strategies aimed at transforming the basic dispositions of
a life-style into a system of aesthetic principles, objective differences
into elective distinctions, passive options (constituted externally by the
logic of the distinctive relationships) into conscious, elective choices are
in fact reserved for members of the dominant class, indeed the very top
bourgeoisie, and for artists, who as the inventors and professionals of the
"stylization of life" are alone able to make their art of living one of the
fine arts. By contrast, the entry of the petite bourgeoisie into the game of
distinction is marked, inter alia, by the anxiety of exposing oneself to
classification by offering to the taste of others such infallible indices of
personal taste as clothes or furniture, even a simple pair of armchairs, as
in one of Nathalie Sarraute's novels. As for the working classes, perhaps
their sole function in the system of aesthetic positions is to serve as a foil,
a negative reference point, in relation to which all aesthetics define themselves, by successive negations. Ignoring or ignorant of manner and
style, the "aesthetic" (in itself) of the working classes and culturally most
deprived fractions of the middle classes defines as "nice", "pretty",
"lovely" (rather than "beautiful") things that are already defined as such
in the "aesthetic" of calendars and postcards: a sunset, a little girl playing with a cat, a folk dance, an old master, a first communion, a children's
procession. The striving towards distinction comes in with petit-bourgeois
aestheticism, which delights in all the cheap substitutes for chic objects
and practices – driftwood and painted pebbles, cane and raffia, "art" handi-
crafts and art photography. . . .

part 2

A Topography of Modernity

chapter 2

Social Structure and Collective Consciousness

Introduction

This chapter and the two that follow are all concerned with the different structural contexts – namely, social structure (or, in Durkheim's term, "social morphology"), culture, and collective emotions – which constrain and enable social interaction. The present chapter draws primarily upon *The Division of Labor in Society*. It introduces Durkheim's famous distinction between two major forms of social solidarity, which he terms "mechanical" and "organic," and shows how each corresponds in his view to a different species of law (the latter thereby playing a key methodological role as empirical indicator). We see how Durkheim conceives of these solidaristic forms as involving not only very different types of cultural structure (or what he terms "collective consciousness"), but also very different patterns of collective emotions. Most importantly, we see how he traces these two configurations of culture and collective emotion back to the social-structural (or morphological) bases to which they correspond: segmentary organization and the division of labor, respectively. And we are presented with the causal argument whereby he explains the rise to predominance of the latter type, which for him is emblematic of modern society. A brief "Note on Social Morphology" then underscores this pre-eminence of social-structural considerations in Durkheim's account of the nature and genesis of modern societies. A concluding selection by Basil Bernstein illustrates these points by reference to the different forms of social organization, common beliefs, and shared sentiments that mark different patterns of schooling within two distinct periods in British educational history.

From *The Division of Labor in Society*

Emile Durkheim, *The Division of Labor in Society*, trans. W. D. Halls (New York: Free Press, 1984), pp. 24–9, 30–61, 68–83, 126–39, 179, 200–12.

. . . [S]ocial solidarity is a wholly moral phenomenon which by itself is not amenable to exact observation and especially not to measurement. . . . we must therefore substitute for this internal datum, which escapes us, an external one which symbolises it, and then study the former through the latter.

That visible symbol is the law. Indeed where social solidarity exists, in spite of its non-material nature, it does not remain in a state of pure potentiality, but shows its presence through perceptible effects. . . . In fact, social life, wherever it becomes lasting, inevitably tends to assume a definite form and become organised. Law is nothing more than this very organisation in its most stable and precise form. Life in general within a society cannot enlarge in scope without legal activity simultaneously increasing in proportion. Thus we may be sure to find reflected in the law all the essential varieties of social solidarity. . . .

Thus our method is clearly traced out for us. Since law reproduces the main forms of social solidarity, we have only to classify the different types of law in order to be able to investigate which types of social solidarity correspond to them. It is already likely that one species of law exists which symbolises the special solidarity engendered by the division of labour. Once we have made this investigation, in order to judge what part the division of labour plays it will be enough to compare the number of legal rules which give it expression with the total volume of law. . . .

In order to proceed methodically, we have to discover some characteristic which, whilst essential to juridical phenomena, is capable of varying as they vary. Now, every legal precept may be defined as a rule of behaviour to which sanctions apply. Moreover, it is clear that the sanctions change according to the degree of seriousness attached to the precepts, the place they occupy in the public consciousness, and the role they play in society. Thus it is appropriate to classify legal rules according to the different sanctions that are attached to them.

These are of two kinds. The first consist essentially in some injury, or at least some disadvantage imposed upon the perpetrator of a crime. Their purpose is to do harm to him through his fortune, his honour, his life, his liberty, or to deprive him of some object whose possession he enjoys. These are said to be repressive sanctions, such as those laid down in the penal code. It is true that those that appertain to purely moral rules are of the same character. Yet such sanctions are administered in a diffuse way by everybody without distinction, whilst those of the penal code are applied only through the mediation of a definite body – they are organised. As for the other kind of sanctions, they do not necessarily imply any suffering on the part of the perpetrator, but merely consist in *restoring the previous state of affairs*, re-establishing relationships that have been disturbed from their normal form. This is done either by forcibly redressing the action impugned, restoring it to the type from which it has deviated, or by annulling it, that is depriving it of all social value. Thus legal rules must be divided into two main species, according to whether they relate to repressive, organised sanctions, or to ones that are purely restitutory. The first group covers all penal law; the second, civil law, commercial law, procedural law, administrative and constitutional law, when any penal rules which may be attached to them have been removed.

Let us now investigate what kind of social solidarity corresponds to each of these species.

The bond of social solidarity to which repressive law corresponds is one the breaking of which constitutes the crime. We use the term "crime" to designate any act which, regardless of degree, provokes against the perpetrator the characteristic reaction known as punishment. To investigate the nature of this bond is therefore to ask what is the cause of the punishment or, more precisely, what in essence the crime consists of.

Assuredly crimes of different species exist. But it is no less certain that all these species of crime have something in common. This is proved by the reaction that they provoke from society: the fact that punishment, except for differences in degree, always and everywhere exists. The oneness of the effect reveals the oneness of the cause. . . .

. . . Indeed, the only feature common to all crimes is that, saving some apparent exceptions to be examined later, they comprise acts universally condemned by the members of each society. Nowadays the question is raised as to whether such condemnation is rational and whether it would not be wiser to look upon crime as a mere sickness or error. But we need not launch into such discussions, for we are seeking to determine what is or has been, not what should be. The real nature of the fact we have just established cannot be disputed, viz., that crime disturbs those feelings that in any one type of society are to be found in every healthy consciousness. . . .

Yet crime has not been defined when we have stated that it consists of an injury done to the collective sentiments, since some of these may be wounded without any crime having been committed.... Thus the collective sentiments to which a crime corresponds must be distinguished from other sentiments by some striking characteristic: they must be of a certain average intensity. Not only are they written upon the consciousness of everyone, but they are deeply written. They are in no way mere halting, superficial caprices of the will, but emotions and dispositions strongly rooted within us....

We are now in a position to conclude. The totality of beliefs and sentiments common to the average members of a society forms a determinate system with a life of its own. It can be termed the collective or common consciousness. Undoubtedly the substratum of this consciousness does not consist of a single organ. By definition it is diffused over society as a whole, but nonetheless possesses specific characteristics that make it a distinctive reality. In fact it is independent of the particular conditions in which individuals find themselves. Individuals pass on, but it abides. It is the same in north and south, in large towns and in small, and in different professions. Likewise it does not change with every generation but, on the contrary, links successive generations to one another. Thus it is something totally different from the consciousnesses of individuals, although it is only realised in individuals. It is the psychological type of society, one which has its properties, conditions for existence and mode of development, just as individual types do, but in a different fashion. For this reason it has the right to be designated by a special term....

Thus, summing up the above analysis, we may state that an act is criminal when it offends the strong, well-defined states of the collective consciousness.

This proposition, taken literally, is scarcely disputed, although usually we give it a meaning very different from the one it should have. It is taken as if it expressed, not the essential characteristics of the crime, but one of its repercussions. We well know that crime offends very general sentiments, but ones that are strongly held. But it is believed that their generality and strength spring from the criminal nature of the act, which consequently still remains wholly to be defined. It is not disputed that any criminal act excites universal disapproval, but it is taken for granted that this results from its criminal nature. Yet one is then hard put to it to state what is the nature of this criminality. Is it in a particularly serious form of immorality? I would concur, but this is to answer a question by posing another, by substituting one term for another. For what *is* immorality is precisely what we want to know – and particularly that special form of immorality which society represses by an organised system of punishments, and which constitutes criminality. Clearly it can only derive from one or several characteristics common to all varieties of crime. Now the only characteristic to satisfy that condition refers to the opposition that exists between crime of any kind and certain collective sentiments. It is thus this opposition which, far from deriving from the crime, constitutes the crime. In other words, we should not say that an act offends the common consciousness because it is criminal, but that it is criminal because it offends that consciousness. We do not condemn it because it is a crime, but it is a crime because we condemn it. . . .

. . . What characterises a crime is that it determines the punishment. Thus if our own definition of crime is exact it must account for all the characteristics of the punishment. . . .

. . . we must establish what those characteristics are.

In the first place, punishment constitutes an emotional reaction. This characteristic is all the more apparent the less cultured societies are. Indeed primitive peoples punish for the sake of punishing, causing the guilty person to suffer solely for the sake of suffering and without expecting any advantage for themselves from the suffering they inflict upon him. . . .

It would indeed be mistaken to believe that vengeance is mere wanton cruelty. It may very possibly constitute by itself an automatic, purposeless reaction, an emotional and senseless impulse, and an unreasoned compulsion to destroy. But in fact what it tends to destroy was a threat to us. Therefore in reality it constitutes a veritable act of defence, albeit instinctive and unreflecting. We wreak vengeance only upon what has done us harm, and what has done us harm is always dangerous. The instinct for revenge is, after all, merely a heightened instinct of self-preservation in the face of danger. . . . Thus between the punishment of today and yesterday there is no great gulf, and consequently it had no need to change to accommodate itself to the role that it plays in our civilised societies. The whole difference lies in the fact that punishment now produces its effects with a greater awareness of what it is about. . . .

Thus punishment constitutes essentially a reaction of passionate feeling, graduated in intensity, which society exerts . . . over those of its members who have violated certain rules of conduct.

Now the definition of crime we have given quite easily accounts for all these characteristics of punishment.

Why this resistance is organised remains to be expounded.

This trait can be explained if we note that an organised repression is not in opposition to a diffuse repression, but is distinguished from it by a mere difference in degree: the reaction is more united. The greater intensity of the sentiments, and their more definite nature, which punishment proper avenges, easily account for this more complete state of unity. If the feeling that has been denied is weak, or is only weakly offended, it can only provoke a weak concentration of those consciousnesses that have been outraged. However, quite the contrary occurs if the state of feeling is strongly offended and if the offence is grave: the entire group attacked closes ranks in the face of danger and, in a manner of speaking, clings closer together. One is no longer content to exchange impressions when the occasion presents itself, nor draw closer together when the chance occurs or when meeting is convenient. On the contrary, the anxiety that has spread from one person to another impels forcibly together all those who resemble one another, causing them to assemble in one place. This physical concentration of the whole group, bringing the interpenetration of minds ever closer, also facilitates every concerted action. Emotional reactions enacted within each individual consciousness are thus afforded the most favourable conditions in which to coalesce together. Yet if they were too diverse in quantity or quality a complete fusion would not be possible between those elements which were partially heterogeneous and irreducible. But we know that the sentiments that determine these reactions are very definite and in consequence very uniform. Thus, partaking of the same uniformity, as a result they merge very naturally with one another, blending into a single amalgam, which serves as a surrogate for each one, a surrogate that is utilised, not by each individual in isolation, but by the body social constituted in this way. . . .

We can therefore see what kind of solidarity the penal law symbolises. In fact we all know that a social cohesion exists whose cause can be traced to a certain conformity of each individual consciousness to a common type, which is none other than the psychological type of society. Indeed under these conditions all members of the group are not only individually attracted to one another because they resemble one another, but they are also linked to what is the condition for the existence of this collective type, that is, to the society that they form by coming together. Not only do fellow-citizens like one another, seeking one another out in preference to foreigners, but they love their country. They wish for it what they would wish for themselves, they care that it should be lasting and prosperous, because without it a whole area of their psychological life would fail to function smoothly. Conversely, society insists upon its citizens displaying all these basic resemblances because it is a condition for its own cohesion. Two consciousnesses exist within us: the one comprises only states that are personal to each one of us, characteristic of us as individuals, whilst the other comprises states that are common to the whole of society. The former represents only our individual personality, which it constitutes; the latter represents the collective type and consequently the society without which it would not exist. When it is an element of the latter determining our behaviour, we do not act with an eye to our own personal interest, but are pursuing collective ends. Now, although distinct, these two consciousnesses are linked to each other, since in the end they constitute only one entity, for both have one and the same organic basis. Thus they are solidly joined together. This gives rise to a solidarity *sui generis* which, deriving from resemblances, binds the individual directly to society. . . .

It is this solidarity that repressive law expresses, at least in regard to what is vital to it. Indeed the acts which such law forbids and stigmatises as crimes are of two kinds: either they manifest directly a too violent dissimilarity between the one who commits them and the collective type; or they offend the organ of the common consciousness. In both cases the force shocked by the crime and that rejects it is thus the same. It is a result of the most vital social similarities, and its effect is to maintain the social cohesion that arises from these similarities. It is that force which the penal law guards against being weakened in any way. At the same time it does this by insisting upon a minimum number of similarities from each one of us, without which the individual would be a threat to the unity of the body social, and by enforcing respect for the symbol which expresses and epitomises these resemblances, whilst simultaneously guaranteeing them. . . .

The very nature of the restitutory sanction is sufficient to show that the social solidarity to which that law corresponds is of a completely different kind.

The distinguishing mark of this sanction is that it is not expiatory, but comes down to a mere *restoration of the "status quo ante"*. Suffering in proportion to the offence is not inflicted upon the one who has broken the law or failed to acknowledge it; he is merely condemned to submit to it. If certain acts have already been performed, the judge restores them to what they should be. He pronounces what the law is, but does not talk of punishment. Damages awarded have no penal character: they are simply a means of putting back the clock so as to restore the past, so far as possible, to its normal state. . . .

. . . [T]he relationships that are regulated by co-operative law, with its restitutory sanctions, and the solidarity these relationships express, result from the social division of labour. Moreover, it is explicable that, in general, co-operative relationships do not carry with them any other form of sanctions. Indeed, special tasks, by their very nature, are exempt from the effects of the collective consciousness. This is because if something is to be the object of shared sentiments, the first condition is that it should be shared, that is, present in every consciousness, and that each individual may be able to conceive of it from a single, identical viewpoint. Doubtless, so long as functions are of a certain general nature, everyone can have some feeling for them. Yet the more specific they become the more also the number is restricted of those who are aware of each and every function. Consequently the more they overflow beyond the common consciousness. The rules that determine them cannot therefore possess that superior force and transcendent authority which, when it suffers harm, exacts expiation. It is indeed also from public opinion that their authority springs, just as do penal rules, but from an opinion that is specific to certain sectors of society.

Moreover, even in those special circles where the rules are applied, and where consequently they are evoked in the minds of people, they do not reflect any very acute feelings, nor even in most cases any kind of emotional state. For, since they determine the manner in which the different functions should work together in the various combinations of circumstances that may arise, the objects to which they relate are not ever-present in the consciousness. We are not always having to administer a guardianship or a trusteeship, nor having to exercise our rights as creditor or buyer, etc. Above all, we do not have to exercise them in particular conditions. But the states of consciousness are strong only in so far as they are permanent. The infringement of these rules does not therefore touch to the quick the common spirit of society, nor, at least usually, that of these special groups. Consequently the infringement cannot provoke more than a very moderate reaction. All that we require is for the functions to work together in a regular fashion. Thus if this regularity is disturbed, we are satisfied if it is re-established. This is most certainly not to say that the development of the division of labour cannot have repercussions in the penal law. There are, as we already know, administrative and governmental functions where certain relationships are regulated by repressive law, because of the special character marking the organ of the common consciousness and everything appertaining to it. In yet other cases, the bonds of solidarity linking certain social functions may be such that once they are broken repercussions occur that are sufficiently general to provoke a reaction of punishment. But for reasons we have already stated, these consequences are exceptional.

In the end this law plays a part analogous in society to that of the nervous system in the organism. That system, in effect, has the task of regulating the various bodily functions in such a way that they work harmoniously together. Thus it expresses in a very natural way the degree of concentration that the organism has reached as a result of the physiological division of labour. Therefore we can at the different levels of the animal scale ascertain the measure of that concentration according to the development of the nervous system. Likewise this means that we can ascertain the measure of concentration that a society has reached through the social division of labour, according to the development of co-operative law with its restitutory sanctions. One can foresee that such a criterion will be of great utility to us. . . .

... [I]t is a law of history that mechanical solidarity, which at first is isolated, or almost so, should progressively lose ground, and organic solidarity gradually become preponderant. But when the way in which men are solidly linked to one another is modified, it is inevitable that the structure of societies should change. The shape of a body must needs be transformed, when the molecular affinities within are no longer the same. Consequently, if the foregoing proposition is accurate, there must be two social types, corresponding to these two kinds of solidarity.

If, by a process of thought, we attempt to constitute the ideal type of a society whose cohesion would result exclusively from resemblances, we would have to conceive of it as consisting of an absolutely homogeneous mass whose parts would not be distinguishable from one another and consequently not be arranged in any order in relation to one another. In short, the mass would be devoid of any definite form or articulation. This would be the real social protoplasm, the germ from which all social types would have emerged. The aggregate we have characterised in this way we propose to call a *horde.*

It is true that we have not yet observed, with complete authentication, societies that correspond in every respect to this description. Yet what gives us the right to postulate their existence is the fact that lower societies, those that in consequence are the most akin to this primordial stage, are formed by a mere replication of aggregates of this kind. We find an almost wholly pure model of this social organisation among the Indians of North America. For example, each Iroquois tribe is made up of a number of incomplete societies (the most extensive includes eight of them) which present all the features we have just pointed out. ...

We shall give the term "clan" to a horde that has ceased to be independent and has become an element in a more extensive group, and that of *segmentary societies based upon clans* to those peoples that have been constituted from an association of clans. We term such societies "segmentary" to denote that they are formed from the replication of aggregates that are like one another, analogous to the rings of annelida worms. We also term this elementary aggregate a clan because this word aptly expresses its mixed nature, relating both to the family and to the body politic. It is a family in the sense that all the members who go to make it up consider themselves kin to one another, and indeed it is true that for the most part they share a blood relationship. The affinities produced by sharing a blood kinship are mainly what keeps them united. What is more, they sustain mutual relationships that might be termed domestic, since these are to be found elsewhere in societies whose family character is undisputed: I mean collective revenge, collective responsibility and, as soon as individual property makes an appearance, mutual heredity. Yet on the other hand it is not a family in the true sense of the word, for in order to form part of it, there is no need to have a clear-cut blood relationship

with the other clan members. It is enough to exhibit some external criterion, which usually consists in bearing the same name. Although this
sign is esteemed to denote a common origin, such an official status really
constitutes very ineffective proof, one that is very easy to copy. Thus the
clan comprises a large number of strangers, which allows it to attain a
size that the family proper never reaches: very often it numbers several
thousand people. Moreover, it is the basic political unit; the clan chiefs
are the sole authorities in society.

Thus this organisation might also be termed politico-familial. . . .

Yet, whatever term we assign to it, this organisation, just like that of
the horde, whose extension it merely is, plainly does not possess any other
solidarity save that which derives from similarities. This is because the
society is made up of similar segments and these in turn comprise only
homogeneous elements. Doubtless each clan has its own peculiar features
and is consequently distinct from the others. But their solidarity is the
weaker the more heterogeneous they are, and vice versa. For a segmentary organisation to be possible, the segments must both resemble one
another (or else they would not be united) and yet be different from
one another. Otherwise they would become so lost in one another as to
vanish. Depending upon the society, these two opposing necessities are
met in different proportions, but the social type remains the same.

This time we have emerged from the sphere of prehistory and conjec-
ture. Not only is this social type far from hypothetical: it is almost the
most widespread of all among lower societies. And we know that these
are the most numerous. . . .

The arrangement of clans within society and thus the overall shape of
the latter can, it is true, vary. Sometimes they are simply juxtaposed so
as to form a kind of linear series: this is the case for many Indian tribes
in North America. In other instances – and this is the distinguishing mark
of a higher organisation – each one is embedded within a larger group
which, having been formed by the coming together of several clans, has
its own life and special name. Each one of these groups in turn may be
embedded with several other groups in an even more extensive aggregate, and it is from the successive series formed by the embedding process that results the unity of the whole society. . . .

These societies are the home *par excellence* of mechanical solidarity, so
much so that it is from this form of solidarity that they derive their main
physiological characteristics.

We know that in them religion pervades the whole of social life. This
is because social life is made up almost entirely of common beliefs and
practices that draw from their unanimous acceptance a very special kind
of intensity. Using the analysis of classical texts alone to go back to an
era exactly similar to the one we are discussing, Fustel de Coulanges discovered that the primitive organisation of societies was of the family type

and that, moreover, the constitution of the primitive family was based upon religion. Only he mistook cause for effect. After having postulated the religious idea, without tracing its derivation from anything, he deduced from it the social arrangements which he noted, whilst, on the contrary, it is these arrangements that explain the power and nature of the religious idea. Since all such social masses were formed from homogeneous elements, that is to say, since the collective type is very highly developed in them whereas individual types are rudimentary, it was inevitable that the entire psychological life of society should assume a religious character.

From this also springs the notion of communism, which has often been noted among these peoples. In fact, communism is the necessary product of the special cohesion that swallows up the individual within the group, the part into the whole. In the end property is merely the extension of the idea of the person to things. Thus where the collective personality is the sole existing one, property itself is inevitably collective. It can only become individual when the individual, freeing himself from the mass of the people, has also become a personal, distinctive being, not only as an organism, but as a factor in social life.

This type can even be modified without the nature of social solidarity suddenly changing on this account. Indeed not all primitive peoples display that lack of centralisation we have just observed. On the contrary, some of them are subject to an absolute power. The division of labour has therefore appeared in them. However, the link which in this case binds the individual to the chief is identical to that which joins things to persons. The relationships of the barbaric despot to his subjects, like those of the master to his slaves or the father of the Roman family to his descendants, are indistinguishable from those of the owner to the object he possesses. There is nothing about them which corresponds to that reciprocity which brings about the division of labour. It has been rightly stated that they are unilateral. Thus the solidarity they express remains mechanical. The difference lies entirely in the fact that it links the individual no longer directly to the group, but to the one who is its image. But the unity of the whole rules out as before any individuality in the parts. . . .

Thus there is a social structure of a determinate nature to which mechanical solidarity corresponds. What characterises it is that it comprises a system of homogeneous segments similar to one another.

But the structure of societies where organic solidarity is preponderant is entirely different.

These are constituted, not by the replication of similar homogeneous elements, but by a system of different organs, each one of which has a special role and which themselves are formed from differentiated parts.

The elements in society are not of the same nature, nor are they arranged in the same manner. They are neither placed together end-on, as are the rings of an annelida worm, nor embedded in one another, but co-ordinated and subordinated to one another around the same central organ, which exerts over the rest of the organism a moderating effect. This organ itself is no longer of the same character as outlined above, for, if the others depend upon it, in turn it depends upon them. Undoubtedly it still enjoys a special place and, one may say, a privileged one. But this is due to the nature of the role that it fulfils and not to some cause external to its functions or to some force imparted to it from outside. Thus it has nothing more than what is temporal and human about it; between the other organs and itself there is no longer any difference save in degree. Thus, with an animal, the priority of the nervous system over the other systems comes down to the right, if it may be so expressed, of receiving a choicer form of sustenance and of taking its share first. But it has need of the other organs, just as they have need of it.

This social type relies upon principles so utterly different from the preceding type that it can only develop to the extent that the latter has vanished. Indeed individuals are distributed within it in groups that are no longer formed in terms of any ancestral relationship, but according to the special nature of the social activity to which they devote themselves. Their natural and necessary environment is no longer that in which they were born, but that of their profession. It is no longer blood relationship, whether real or fictitious, that determines the place of each one, but the functions he fulfils Undoubtedly, when this new organisation begins to appear, it attempts to use the existing one and to assimilate it to itself. The way in which functions are distributed is therefore modelled as closely as possible upon the way in which society is already divided up. The segments, or at least groups of segments linked by particular affinities, become organs. Thus the clans which as an entity constitute the tribe of the Levites, appropriate for themselves the priestly functions among the Jewish people. Generally it may be said that classes and castes have probably no other origin or nature: they spring from the mixing of the professional organisation, which is just emerging, with a pre-existent family organisation. But this mixed arrangement cannot last for long because, between the two elements that it takes upon itself to reconcile, there is an hostility that must in the end break out. Only a very rudimentary division of labour can fit into these rigid, well-defined moulds, which were not fashioned for it. The division of labour can only increase in so far as it frees itself from the frame that hedges it in. Once it has gone beyond a certain stage of development no longer is there any connection between the fixed number of segments and the ever-increasing number of functions that become specialised, nor between the hereditarily determined properties of the former and the new aptitudes that the latter demand. Thus the social substance must enter into entirely new combinations in order to be organised on completely different foundations. Now the old structure, so long as it subsists, is hostile to this. This is why it must disappear.

The history of these two types indeed shows that the one has only made progress in the proportion to which the other has regressed. . . .

But it is far from true that the organised type subsists alone, in its pristine state, once the clan has disappeared. The organisation based upon clans is in fact only one species of a more extensive *genus*, the segmentary organisation. The distribution of society into similar compartments corresponds to needs that persist even in new societies where social life is established, needs that nevertheless produce their effects in another form. The mass of the population is no longer divided up according to blood relationships, whether real or fictitious, but according to land divisions. The segments are no longer family aggregates but territorial constituencies.

Moreover, it was through a slow process of evolution that the passage from one state to another took place when the memory of the common origin had faded. When the domestic relationships that sprang from it, but as we have seen often outlive it, have themselves vanished, the clan has no longer any consciousness of itself save as a group of individuals who occupy the same parcel of territory. It becomes the village proper. Thus all those peoples who have passed beyond the stage of the clan are made up from territorial districts (the mark, the commune, etc.) which, just as the Roman *gens* had become implicated in the *curia*, are inserted in other districts of the same kind, but larger in size, termed in one place *hundred*, elsewhere *Kreis* or *arrondisssement*, which in turn are often swallowed up in other entities, even more extensive (county, province, *département*) which unite to form a society. This process of insertion can moreover be more or less an hermetical sealing-off. Likewise the links that join together the most general kind of districts can either be very close, as with the centralised countries of present-day Europe, or more relaxed, as in simple confederations. But the principle behind the structure remains the same, and this is why mechanical solidarity persists even in the highest societies.

Nevertheless, in the same way as mechanical solidarity is no longer preponderant, the arrangement in the form of segments is no longer, as previously, the sole anatomical structure or even the essential structure of society. Firstly, the territorial divisions have necessarily something artificial about them. The ties that arise from living together have not their source so deeply in men's hearts as those arising from blood-relationship. Thus they have a much weaker power of resistance. When one is born into a clan, one cannot change anything more, so to speak, than one's relatives. The same reasons do not prevent one's changing one's town or province. Doubtless, geographical distribution corresponds roughly to a certain moral distribution of the population. For example, each province, each territorial division, has its own special morality and customs, a life peculiarly its own. Thus it exerts over individuals imbued with its spirit an attraction that tends to keep them on the spot and, moreover, to repel others. But within a single country such differences cannot be very numerous or clear-cut. The segments are therefore more open to one another. Indeed, from the Middle Ages onwards "after the formation of towns, foreign artisans travelled as freely and as far and wide as did goods". Segmentary organisation had lost its contours.

It is increasingly losing them as societies develop. It is indeed a general law that the partial aggregates that make up a more extensive aggregate see their individuality as growing less and less distinctive. At the same time as the family organisation, local religions have disappeared for ever, yet local customs continue to exist. Gradually these merge into one another and unify, at the same time as dialects and patois dissolve into a single national language and regional administration loses its autonomy. In this fact a simple consequence of the law of imitation has been discerned. However, it seems as if it is rather a levelling-out analogous to that which occurs between two liquids which intermingle together. The partitions that separate the various cells of social life, being less thick, are breached more often. Their permeability increases the more they are penetrated. Consequently they lose their consistency and gradually collapse, and to the same extent environments become mingled together. Now local diversity can only be maintained in so far as a diversity of environments subsists. Territorial divisions are therefore less and less based upon the nature of things, and consequently lose their significance. One might almost say that a people is the more advanced the more superficial its character.

On the other hand, as segmentary organisation vanishes organisation by professions covers it ever more completely with its network. It is true that at the beginning it establishes itself only within the boundaries of the more simple segments, without extending beyond. Every town, with its immediate neighbourhood, forms a group within which work is divided up, but that strives to be self-sufficient. . . .

. . . Doubtless to a certain extent this professional organisation attempts to adapt itself to the one that existed before it, as it had originally done for the organisation of the family. This is what emerges from the very description given above. Moreover, it is a very general fact that new institutions are shaped initially in the mould of previous institutions. The territorial regions therefore tend to be specialised in relation to their complexion, organs and different mechanisms, just as was the clan in former times. But just like the latter, they are really incapable of maintaining this role. In fact a town always includes either different organs or parts of organs. Conversely there are hardly any organs that are wholly included within the limits of a particular district, whatever its size. Almost always the district extends beyond them. Likewise, although fairly frequently those organs which are most closely linked to one another tend to draw together, yet in general their physical proximity reflects only very imperfectly the degree of closeness of their relationships. Some are very distant, although depending directly upon one another. Others are physically very close, although their relationships are indirect and distant. The way in which men are grouped together as a result of the division of labour is thus very different from the way the spatial distribution of the population occurs. The professional environment no more coincides with the territorial environment than it does with the family environment. It is a new framework that is substituted for the others. Thus the substitution is only possible to the extent that the others have vanished.

If therefore this social type is nowhere to be observed in a state of absolute purity, likewise nowhere is organic solidarity to be met with in isolation. But at least it frees itself increasingly from any amalgam, just as it becomes increasingly preponderant. Such predominance is all the more rapid and complete because at the very moment when its structure becomes more prominent, the other becomes more indistinct. The segment formed by the clan, so well-defined, is replaced by the territorial district. At least originally, the latter corresponded, although in somewhat vague and approximate fashion, to the real and moral division of the population. But it gradually loses this character, to become no more than an arbitrary combination, one that is a mere convention. As these barriers are lowered, they are covered over by systems of organs which are more and more developed. If therefore social evolution remains subject to the effect of the same determining causes – and we shall see later that this is the sole feasible hypothesis – we may predict that this dual movement will continue in the same direction, and the day will come when the whole of our social and political organisation will have an exclusively, or almost exclusively, professional basis.

Moreover, the studies that follow will establish that this professional organisation is not even today all that it is destined to become; that abnormal causes have prevented it from reaching the stage of development that our present social state requires. From this we may judge the importance that it is destined to assume in the future.

What are the causes of the division of labour?

Undoubtedly there can be no question of finding one single formula to account for all the possible forms of the division of labour. Such a formula does not exist. Each particular case depends upon special causes that can only be determined by a special investigation. The problem that we are posing is less wide. If we leave out of account the various forms that the division of labour assumes according to the conditions of time and space, the general fact remains that the division develops regularly as history proceeds. This fact certainly depends on causes that are likewise constant, causes that we shall investigate. . . .

. . . [I]t is in certain variations of the social environment that we must seek the cause that explains the progress of the division of labour. . . .

In fact we have seen that the organised structure, and consequently the division of labour, develops regularly as the segmentary structure vanishes. It is therefore this disappearance that is the cause of this development. . . .

But the disappearance of this type can only bring about this result for the following reason. It is because there occurs a drawing together of individuals who were separated from one another, or at least they draw more closely together than they had been. Hence movements take place between the parts of the social mass which up to then had no reciprocal effect upon one another. . . . Social life, instead of concentrating itself in innumerable small foci that are distinct but alike, becomes general. Social relationships – more exactly we should say intra-social relationships – consequently become more numerous, since they push out beyond their original boundaries on all sides. Thus the division of labour progresses the more individuals there are who are sufficiently in contact with one another to be able mutually to act and react upon one another. If we agree to call dynamic or moral density this drawing together and the active exchanges that result from it, we can say that the progress of the division of labour is in direct proportion to the moral or dynamic density of society.

But this act of drawing together morally can only bear fruit if the real distance between individuals has itself diminished, in whatever manner. Moral density cannot therefore increase without physical density increasing at the same time, and the latter can serve to measure the extent of the former. Moreover, it is useless to investigate which of the two has influenced the other; it suffices to realise that they are inseparable.

The progressive increase in density of societies in the course of their historical development occurs in three main ways:

(1) Whilst lower societies spread themselves over areas that are relatively vast in comparison with the number of individuals that constitute them, amongst more advanced peoples the population is continually becoming more concentrated. . . .

The changes wrought successively in the industrial life of nations demonstrate how general this transformation is. The activity of nomadic tribes, whether hunters or shepherds, entails in fact the absence of any kind of concentration and dispersion over as wide an area as possible. Agriculture, because it is of necessity a settled existence, already presumes a certain drawing together of the social tissues, but one still very incomplete, since between each family tracts of land are interposed. In the city, although the condensation process was greater, yet houses did not adjoin one another, for joined building was not known in Roman law. This was invented on our own soil and demonstrates that the social ties have become tighter. Moreover, from their origins European societies have seen their density increase continuously in spite of a few cases of temporary regression.

(2) The formation and development of towns are a further symptom, even more characteristic, of the same phenomenon. The increase in average density can be due solely to the physical increase in the birth rate and can consequently be reconciled with a very weak concentration of people, and the very marked maintenance of the segmentary type of society. But towns always result from the need that drives individuals to keep constantly in the closest possible contact with one another. They are like so many points where the social mass is contracting more strongly than elsewhere. They cannot therefore multiply and spread out unless the moral density increases. Moreover, we shall see that towns recruit their numbers through migration to them, which is only possible to the extent that the fusion of social segments is far advanced. . . .

(3) Finally, there is the number and speed of the means of communication and transmission. By abolishing or lessening the vacuums separating social segments, these means increase the density of society. Moreover, there is no need to demonstrate that they are the more numerous and perfect the higher the type of society. . . .

But this factor is not the only one.

If the concentration of society produces this result, it is because it multiplies intra-social relationships. But these will be even more numerous if the total number of members in a society also becomes larger. If it includes more individuals, as well as their being in closer contact, the effect will necessarily be reinforced. Social volume has therefore the same influence over the division of labour as density.

In fact, societies are generally more voluminous the more advanced they are and consequently labour is more divided up in them. . . .

. . . An increase in social volume . . . does not always speed up the progress of the division of labour, but only when the mass condenses at the same time and to the same degree. Consequently it is, one may say, only an additional factor. Yet, when joined to the first factor, it extends the effects by an action peculiarly its own, and thus requires to be distinguished from it.

We can therefore formulate the following proposition:

> *The division of labour varies in direct proportion to the volume and density of societies and if it progresses in a continuous manner over the course of social development it is because societies become regularly more dense and generally more voluminous.*

At all times, it is true, it has been clearly understood that there was a relationship between these two orders of facts. This is because, for functions to specialise even more, there must be additional co-operating elements, which must be grouped close enough together to be able to co-operate. Yet in societies in this condition we usually see hardly more than the means by which the division of labour is developed, and not the cause of this development. The cause is made to depend upon individual aspirations towards wellbeing and happiness, which can be the better satisfied when societies are more extensive and more condensed. The law we have just established is completely different. We state, not that the growth and condensation of societies *permit* a greater division of labour, but that they *necessitate* it. It is not the instrument whereby that division is brought about; but it is its determining cause.

Yet how can we represent to ourselves the way in which this dual cause produces its effect?

If labour becomes increasingly divided as societies become more voluminous and concentrated, it is not because the external circumstances are more varied, it is because the struggle for existence becomes more strenuous.

Darwin very aptly remarked that two organisms vie with each other more keenly the more alike they are. Having the same needs and pursuing the same purposes, they are everywhere to be found in a state of rivalry. So long as they possess more resources than each needs, they can still live cheek by jowl. But if each happens to increase in number in such proportions that all appetites can no longer be sufficiently assuaged, war breaks out and it is the more violent the more striking the shortfall, that is, the numbers vying with one another are greater. The situation is totally different if the individuals coexisting together are of different species or varieties. As they do not feed in the same way or lead the same kind of life, they do not impede one another. What causes some to flourish lacks value for others. The occasions for conflict are therefore less, as are the occasions of meeting, and this is all the more the case when these species or varieties are more distant from one another. . . .

Men are subject to the same law. In the same town different occupations can coexist without being forced into a position where they harm one another, for they are pursuing different objectives. The soldier seeks military glory, the priest moral authority, the statesman power, the industrialist wealth, the scientist professional fame. Each one of them can therefore reach his goal without preventing others from reaching theirs. This is the case even when the functions are less remote from one another. The medical eye specialist does not compete with the one who cares for the mentally ill, the shoemaker does not compete with the hatter, the mason with the cabinet-maker, the physician with the chemist, etc. As they perform different services they can perform them in harmony.

However, the closer the functions are to one another, the more points of contact there are between them, and, as a result, the more they tend to conflict. As in this case they satisfy similar needs by different means, it is inevitable that they should seek, more or less, to encroach upon others. The magistrate is never in competition with the industrialist. But the brewer and the winegrower, the draper and the maker of silks, the poet and the musician often attempt mutually to supplant each other. As for those that discharge exactly the same function, they cannot prosper save to the detriment of their fellows. If therefore one represents these different functions in the form of a cluster of branches springing from a common root, the struggle is least between the extreme points, whilst it increases steadily as it approaches the centre. This is the case not only within each town but over society as a whole. Similar occupations located at different sites over an area enter into fiercer rivalry the more alike they are, provided that difficulties of communications and transport do not constrain their sphere of action.

This having been said, it is easy to understand that any concentration in the social mass, particularly if accompanied by a growth in population, necessarily determines the progress of the division of labour.

In fact, let us imagine an industrial centre that supplies a certain area of the country with a special product. The development that it is capable of reaching is restricted in two ways: firstly by the extent of the needs that have to be satisfied, or the so-called size of the market, and secondly, by the capacity of the means of production at its command. Normally it does not produce more than is necessary, even less does it produce more than it can. But if it is impossible for it to exceed these limits, as set out, it strives to reach them, for it is in the nature of a force to deploy all its energy so long as nothing brings it to a halt. Once it has arrived at this point, it has adapted to the conditions of its existence; it finds itself in a position of equilibrium that cannot change if nothing changes.

But there may be some region, until then independent of the centre, that becomes linked to it by a means of communication which partly does away with distance. At a single stroke one of the barriers that prevented its upward ascent is broken down or at least is lowered. The market becomes more extensive, there are now more needs to be satisfied. Undoubtedly if all the individual undertakings that it includes had already reached their possible peak of production, as they could not expand further, things would stay as they were. However, such a situation is wholly an ideal one. In reality there is always a certain number of undertakings that have not reached their limit and which, so to speak, consequently have sufficient speed in reserve to go further. As an empty space has opened up for them, their needs must seek to spread over it and fill it. If they meet with similar undertakings that are capable of resisting them, these latter contain them, they impose mutual limits upon one another, and consequently their mutual relationships remain unchanged. To be sure, there are more competitors, but as they share a larger market, the share of each one on the two sides remains the same. Yet if there are some that manifest some kind of inferiority, they will have to yield ground that they occupied up to then, where they can no longer sustain themselves in the new conditions in which the struggle is fought out. They then have no longer any option but either to disappear or to transform themselves, and this transformation must necessarily result in a fresh specialisation. For if instead of creating at once yet another speciality, the weakest preferred to adopt a different kind of business, but which existed already, they would have to enter into competition with those who had been engaged in it up to then. The struggle would therefore no longer be over, but simply change its location, producing its consequences in a different place. Finally, somewhere there would certainly have to be either an elimination or a fresh differentiation. It would be pointless to add that if a society in fact comprises more members, and at the same time they have drawn closer to one another, the struggle is even fiercer and the specialisation that emerges from it more rapid and more complete.

In other works, to the extent that the social constitution is a segmentary one, each segment has its own organs that are, so to speak, protected and kept at a distance from similar organs by the partitions separating the different segments. But, as these partitions disappear, it is inevitable that organs similar to one another come into contact, embark upon a struggle and try to substitute themselves for one another. However, in whatever way this substitution occurs, some advance along the road to specialisation cannot fail to be the outcome. For on the one hand, the segmentary organ that triumphs, if we may speak in those terms, cannot be sufficient to undertake the larger task that now falls to it in the future save by a greater division of labour. On the other hand, the vanquished can only continue to exist by concentrating upon one part only of the total function that they fulfilled up to that time. The small employer becomes a foreman, the small shopkeeper an employee, etc. This share can moreover be of greater or lesser size depending on whether their inferiority is more or less glaring. It can even happen that the original function simply becomes split into two parts of equal importance. Instead of entering into competition, or remaining so, two similar undertakings find their equilibrium again by sharing their common task: instead of one becoming subordinate to the other, they co-ordinate their activities. But in every case new specialities appear.

Although the above examples are especially taken from economic life, this explanation is applicable to all social functions without distinction. Work, whether scientific, artistic, or otherwise, does not divide up in any other way or for any other reasons. It is still because of these same causes that, as we have seen, the central regulatory mechanism absorbs to itself the local regulatory organs, reducing them to the role of specialised auxiliary ones. . . .

"Note on Social Morphology"

Emile Durkheim: On Institutional Analysis, ed. and trans. Mark Traugott (Chicago and London: University of Chicago Press, 1978), pp. 88–90.

Before analyzing the works which we have assembled under this rubric, we must first indicate the meaning of the term.

Social life rests upon a substratum which is determinate both in its extent and in its form. It is composed of the mass of individuals who comprise the society, the manner in which they are disposed upon the earth, and the nature and configuration of objects of all sorts which affect collective relations. Depending on whether the population is more or less sizable, more or less dense; depending on whether it is concentrated in cities or dispersed in the countryside; depending on the way in which the cities and the houses are constructed; depending on whether the space occupied by the society is more or less extensive; depending on the borders which define its limits, the avenues of communication which traverse it, and so forth, this social substratum will differ. From another point of view, the constitution of this substratum directly or indirectly affects all social phenomena, just as all psychic phenomena are placed in mediate or immediate relationship with the brain. Thus, we have a whole collection of problems which are of obvious interest to sociology and which, because they all refer to a single and identical object, must come within the jurisdiction of a single science. It is this science which we propose to call *social morphology*.

The works which deal with these questions now have their origin in different disciplines. It is geography which studies the territorial forms of nations. It is history which retraces the evolution of rural or urban groups. It is demography which covers all that concerns the distribution of population. We believe there is an advantage to be gained by drawing these fragmentary sciences out of their isolation and placing them in contact by assembling them under a single rubric. They will thus achieve an awareness of their unity. The reader will learn below of how a school of geography is now attempting an analogous synthesis under the name of *political geography*. But we fear that this expression may create certain confusions. In effect, this new field will study, not the forms of the earth, but the forms which affect societies as they establish themselves on the earth, which is quite a different matter. There is no doubt that watercourses, mountains, and the like enter as elements in the constitution of the social substratum; but they are neither the only nor the most essential elements. Now the word *geography* almost fatally leads to according them an importance which they do not have, and we shall have occasion to see that this is so. The number of individuals, the way in which they are grouped, and the form of their habitations in no way constitute geographic facts. Why then should we retain a term which has been so changed from its ordinary meaning? For these reasons, a new rubric seems necessary. The one we propose has the advantage of placing in sharp relief the unity of the object upon which all this research bears, namely the tangible, material forms of societies or, in other words, the nature of their substratum.

Moreover, social morphology does not consist in a simple science of observation which describes these forms without accounting for them. It can and must be explanatory. It must investigate the conditions which cause variations in the political territory of different peoples, the nature and aspect of their borders, and the unequal density of the population. It must ask how urban agglomerations are born, what the laws of their evolution are, how they are recruited, what their role might be, and so forth. It does not, therefore, merely consider the social substratum already established in order to present a descriptive analysis; it observes it in the process of creation in order to see how it is constituted. This is not a purely static science; rather, it quite naturally includes the movements from which result the conditions which it studies. In addition, it, like all the other branches of sociology, finds indispensable auxiliaries in history and comparative ethnography.

From "Open Schools – Open Society?"
Basil Bernstein

Basil Bernstein, *Class, Codes and Control*, vol. 3: *Towards a Theory of Educational Transmissions*, 2nd edn (London: Routledge and Kegan Paul, 1975), pp. 67–73.

. . . The approach to current changes in the structure of the contemporary school system, which I attempt in this article, was initially set out by Durkheim over seventy years ago in his book, *The Division of Labour*. I shall interpret the changes in terms of a shift of emphasis in the principles of social integration – from "mechanical" to "organic" solidarity. Such changes in social integration within schools are linked to fundamental changes in the character of the British educational system: a change from education in depth to education in breadth. I shall raise throughout this article the question of the relationship between the belief and moral order of the school, its social organization and its forms of social integration. . . .

Consider, first, the forms of social control. In secondary schools there has been a move away from the transmission of common values through a ritual order and control based upon position or status, to more personalized forms of control where teachers and taught confront each other as individuals. The forms of social control appeal less to shared values, group loyalties and involvements; they are based rather upon the recognition of differences between individuals. And with this there has been a weakening of the symbolic significance and ritualization of punishment.

Look now at the division of labour of the school staff. Irrespective of the pupil/teacher ratios, the staff is now much larger. The division of labour is more complex from the point of view of the range of subjects taught. Within the main subjects, the hierarchy of responsibility has become more differentiated. The teacher's role itself has fragmented to form a series of specialized roles (vocational, counselling, housemaster, social worker and so on). Still within the broad category of the division of labour consider – very briefly, for the moment – the organization of pupils. The pupils' position in the new schools in "principle" is less likely to be fixed in terms of sex, age or IQ, for ideally their position, within limits, is achieved in terms of their individual qualities.

Thus we find (a) a movement towards a more complex division of labour among the staff and a greater differentiation of the teacher's role; and (b) at the same time, the pupils' relationships with other pupils in principle arise from their expression of their educational differences. This is good evidence of a shift towards organic solidarity.

Let us turn, next, to shifts in emphasis in the curriculum, pedagogy, the organization of teaching groups and teaching and pupil roles. Here we are at the heart of the instrumental order of the school: the transmission of skills and sensitivities.

Take the organization of teaching groups first. Here we can begin to see a shift from a situation where the teaching group is a fixed structural unit of the school's organization (the form or class), to secondary schools where the teaching group is a flexible or variable unit of the social organization. . . .

Now for the changes in pedagogy. There is a shift – from a pedagogy which, for the majority of secondary school pupils, was concerned with the learning of standard operations tied to specific contexts – to a pedagogy which emphasizes the exploration of principles. From schools which emphasized the teacher as a solution-giver to schools which emphasize the teacher as a problem-poser or creator. Such a change in pedagogy (itself perhaps a response to changed concepts of skill in industry) alters the authority relationships between teacher and taught, and possibly changes the nature of the authority inherent in the subject. The pedagogy now emphasizes the *means* whereby knowledge is created and principles established, in a context of self-discovery by the pupils. The act of learning itself celebrates choice.

But what about the curriculum? I mean by curriculum the principles governing the selection of, and relation between, subjects. We are witnessing a shift in emphasis away from schools where the subject is a clear-cut definable unit of the curriculum, to schools where the unit of the curriculum is not so much a subject as an *idea* – say, topic-centred inter-disciplinary enquiry. Such a shift is already under way at the university level. . . .

In the older schools, integration between subjects, when it existed, was determined by the public examination system, and this is one of the brakes on the shift I am describing. In the new schools, integration at the level of idea involves a new principle of social integration of staff: that of organic solidarity. This shift in the basis of the curriculum from subject to idea may point towards a fundamental change in the character of British education: a change from education in depth to education in breadth.

As a corollary of this, we are moving from secondary schools where the teaching roles were insulated from each other, where the teacher had an assigned area of authority and autonomy, to secondary schools where the teaching role is less autonomous and where it is a shared or co-operative role. There has been a shift from a teaching role which is, so to speak, "given" (in the sense that one steps into assigned duties), to a role which has to be *achieved* in relation with other teachers. It is a role which is no longer made but *has to be made*. The teacher is no longer isolated from other teachers, as where the principle of integration is the relation of his subject to a public examination. The teacher is now in a complementary relation with other teachers at the level of his day-by-day teaching.

Under these conditions of co-operative, shared teaching roles, the loss of a teacher can be most damaging to the staff because of the inter-dependence of roles. Here we can begin to see the essence of organic solidarity as it affects the crucial role of teacher. The act of teaching itself expresses the organic articulation between subjects, teachers and taught. The form of social integration, in the central area of the school's function, is organic rather than mechanical.

How is the role of pupil affected? I said that, under mechanical solid-arity, social roles were likely to be fixed and ascribed, aspirations would be limited, and individuals would relate to each other through common beliefs and shared sentiments. These beliefs and sentiments would regu-late the details of social action. In the older secondary schools, individual choice was severely curtailed, aspirations were controlled through careful streaming, and streaming itself produced homogeneous groups accord-ing to an imputed similarity in ability. The learning process emphasized the teacher as solution-giver rather than problem-poser. The role of pupil was circumscribed and well defined.

Now there has been a move towards giving the pupil greater choice. Aspirations are likely to be raised in the new schools, partly because of changes in their social organization. The learning process creates greater autonomy for the pupil. The teaching group may be either a hetero-geneous unit (unstreamed class) or a series of different homogeneous units (sets) or even both. The pupil's role is less clearly defined. Of equal significance, his role conception evolves out of a series of diverse con-texts and relationships. The enacting of the role of pupil reveals less his similarity to others, but rather his difference from other.

I suggested earlier that, where the form of social integration was mechanical, the community would tend to become sealed off, self-enclosed, and its boundary relationship would be sharply defined. Inside and outside would be clearly differentiated. These notions can apply to changes both within the school and to its relation to the outside.

Schools' boundary relations, both within and without, are now more open. This can be seen at many levels. First of all, the very architecture of the new schools points up their openness compared with the old schools. The inside of the institution has become visible. Of more significance, the boundary relation between the home and school has changed, and parents (their beliefs and socializing styles) are incorporated within the school in way unheard of in the older schools. The range and number of non-school adults who visit the school and talk to the pupils have increased. The barrier between the informal teenage subcultures and the culture of the school has weakened: often the non-school age group subculture becomes a content of a syllabus. The outside penetrates the new schools in other fundamental ways. The careful editing, specially for schools, of books, papers, films, is being replaced by a diverse representation of the outside both within the library and through films shown to the pupils.

Within the school, as we have seen, the insulation between forms and between teaching roles has weakened, and authority relationships are less formal. The diminishing of a one-to-one relation between a given activity, a given space and a given time – i.e. flexibility – must reduce the symbolic significance of particular spaces and particular times. The controls over flow in the new schools carry a different symbolic significance from the controls over flow in the old schools. . . .

chapter 3

Culture and Symbolic Classification

Introduction

In this chapter, we see Durkheim once again developing arguments that encompass social structure and culture, as well as collective emotions, although this time I have chosen selections that highlight his contributions to cultural sociology. The chapter draws heavily upon *The Elementary Forms of Religious Life*. It begins with the methodological considerations that go into Durkheim's choice of "the simplest and most primitive religion[s]" (p. 85) as privileged sites for the analysis of religious phenomena in general. It then follows his reasoning past alternative conceptualizations of religion until it arrives at Durkheim's own comprehensive definition. Important to that definition is the distinction between religious beliefs and practices. The present chapter focuses primarily upon religious beliefs, while the subsequent chapter focuses more upon religious practices. Durkheim contends that all religious beliefs consist in a "division of the world into two domains, one containing all that is sacred and the other all that is profane" (p. 87). He shows how the sacred itself represents a transfigura-tion of the anonymous, impersonal, and awe-inspiring emotional force of society *vis-à-vis* the individual. In a brief excerpt from *Primitive Classifica-tion* (co-authored with anthropologist Marcel Mauss, who was his nephew), Durkheim further explores how systems of symbolic classification – down to the most basic categories of knowledge themselves – have a social origin and are produced through social interaction. And in an excerpt from "Individual and Collective Representations," he discusses how such cultural formations, once produced, gain a certain autonomy relative to the social substratum, the social structure, out of which they emerged. The selections that follow – by Marc Bloch, Claude Lévi-Strauss, Mary Douglas, Kai Erikson, and Michel Foucault – further develop Durkheim's ideas regard-ing symbolic classification and symbolic boundaries. Together, they indicate one major line of inquiry that leads straight from Durkheim's religious soci-ology into contemporary studies in cultural analysis, studies that shed light upon the cultural sociology of traditional and modern societies alike.

From *The Elementary Forms of Religious Life*

Emile Durkheim, *The Elementary Forms of Religious Life*, trans. Karen E. Fields (New York: Free Press, 1995), pp. 1–7, 21–44, 190–2.

I propose in this book to study the simplest and most primitive religion that is known at present, to discover its principles and attempt an explanation of it. A religious system is said to be the most primitive that is available for observation when it meets the two following conditions: First, it must be found in societies the simplicity of whose organization is nowhere exceeded; second, it must be explainable without the introduction of any element from a predecessor religion. . . .

. . . This choice is solely for reasons of method. . . .

. . . Since all religions may be compared, all being species within the same genus, some elements are of necessity common to them all. . . . At the foundation of all systems of belief and all cults, there must necessarily be a certain number of fundamental representations and modes of ritual conduct that, despite the diversity of forms that the one and the other may have taken on, have the same objective meaning everywhere and everywhere fulfill the same functions. It is these enduring elements that constitute what is eternal and human in religion. They are the whole objective content of the idea that is expressed when *religion* in general is spoken of.

How, then, can those elements be uncovered?

Surely it is not by observing the complex religions that have arisen in the course of history. Each of those religions is formed from such a variety of elements that it is very hard to distinguish what is secondary to them from what is primary, and what is essential from what is accessory. . . .

The case is altogether different in the lower societies. The lesser development of individuality, the smaller scale of the group, and the homogeneity of external circumstances all contribute to reducing the differences and variations to a minimum. . . . Inessential, secondary, and luxurious developments have not yet come to hide what is primary. Everything is boiled down to what is absolutely indispensable, to that without which there would be no religion. But the indispensable is also the fundamental, in other words, that which it is above all important for us to know.

Thus, primitive civilizations are prime cases because they are simple cases. . . .

But primitive religions do not merely allow us to isolate the constituent elements of religion; their great advantage is also that they aid in its explanation. Because the facts are simpler, the relations between them are more apparent. The reasons men invoke to explain their actions to themselves have not yet been refined and revamped by sophisticated thought: They are closer and more akin to the motives that caused those actions. . . . The remainder of this work will be an illustration and a test of this methodological point. We will see how, in the primitive religions, the religious phenomenon still carries the visible imprint of its origins. It would have been much more difficult for us to infer those origins by considering more developed religions alone. . . .

In order to identify the simplest and most primitive religion that observation can make known to us, we must first define what is properly understood as a religion. If we do not, we run the risk of either calling a system of ideas and practices religion that are in no way religious, or of passing by religious phenomena without detecting their true nature. . . .

One notion that is generally taken to be characteristic of all that is religious is the notion of the supernatural. By that is meant any order of things that goes beyond our understanding; the supernatural is the world of mystery, the unknowable, or the incomprehensible. Religion would then be a kind of speculation upon all that escapes science, and clear thinking generally. . . .

Certainly the role played by the feeling of mystery has not been unimportant in certain religions, including Christianity. Even so, the importance of this role has shown marked variation at different moments of Christian history. . . .

What is certain, in any case, is that this idea appears very late in the history of religions. It is totally alien not only to the peoples called primitive but also to those who have not attained a certain level of intellectual culture. . . .

Furthermore, as we will see in the course of this work, the idea of natural forces is very likely derived from that of religious forces. . . .

Besides, the idea of the supernatural, as we understand it, is recent. It presupposes an idea that is its negation, and that is in no way primitive. To be able to call certain facts supernatural, one must already have an awareness that there is a *natural order of things*, in other words, that the phenomena of the universe are internally linked according to necessary

relationships called laws. Once this principle is established, anything that
departs from those laws necessarily appears as beyond nature and, thus,
beyond reason: For what is in this sense natural is also rational, those
relations expressing only the manner in which things are logically connected. Now, the idea of universal determinism is of recent origin; even
the greatest thinkers of classical antiquity did not achieve full awareness of it. That idea is territory won by the empirical sciences; it is the
postulate on which they rest and which their advancement has proved.
So long as this postulate was lacking or not well established, there was
nothing about the most extraordinary events that did not appear perfectly
conceivable. So long as what is immovable and inflexible about the order
of things was unknown, and so long as it was seen as the work of contingent wills, it was of course thought natural that these wills or others
could modify the order of things arbitrarily. For this reason, the miraculous interventions that the ancients ascribed to their gods were not in their
eyes miracles, in the modern sense of the word. To them, these interventions
were beautiful, rare, or terrible spectacles, and objects of surprise and
wonder (θαύματα, *mirabilia, miracula*); but they were not regarded as
glimpses into a mysterious world where reason could not penetrate. . . .

Another idea by which many have tried to define religion is that of
divinity. . . .
    But however obvious this definition may seem, given habits of mind
that we owe to our own religious upbringing, there are many facts to which
it is not applicable but that nevertheless belong to the domain of religion.
    In the first place, there are great religions from which the idea of gods
and spirits is absent, or plays only a secondary and inconspicuous role.
This is the case in Buddhism. . . .
    But many rites that are wholly independent of any idea of gods or spir-
itual beings are found even in deistic religions. . . .
    Thus there are rites without gods, and indeed rites from which gods
derive. Not all religious virtues emanate from divine personalities, and
there are cult ties other than those that unite man with a deity. Thus, religion is broader than the idea of gods or spirits and so cannot be defined
exclusively in those terms.

With these definitions set aside, let us now see how we can approach the
problem.
    First, let us note that, in all these formulas, scholars have been trying
to express the nature of religion as a whole. Although religion is a whole
composed of parts – a more or less complex system of myths, dogmas,
rites, and ceremonies – they operate as if it formed a kind of indivisible
entity. Since a whole can be defined only in relationship to the parts that
comprise it, a better method is to try to characterize the elementary

phenomena from which any religion results, and then characterize the system produced by their union. . . .

Religious phenomena fall into two basic categories: beliefs and rites. The first are states of opinion and consist of representations; the second are particular modes of action. Between these two categories of phenomena lies all that separates thinking from doing.

The rites can be distinguished from other human practices – for example, moral practices – only by the special nature of their object. Like a rite, a moral rule prescribes ways of behaving to us, but those ways of behaving address objects of a different kind. It is the object of the rite that must be characterized, in order to characterize the rite itself. The special nature of that object is expressed in the belief. Therefore, only after having defined the belief can we define the rite.

Whether simple or complex, all known religious beliefs display a common feature: They presuppose a classification of the real or ideal things that men conceive of into two classes – two opposite genera – that are widely designated by two distinct terms, which the words *profane* and *sacred* translate fairly well. The division of the world into two domains, one containing all that is sacred and the other all that is profane – such is the distinctive trait of religious thought. Beliefs, myths, dogmas, and legends are either representations or systems of representations that express the nature of sacred things, the virtues and powers attributed to them, their history, and their relationships with one another as well as with profane things. Sacred things are not simply those personal beings that are called gods or spirits. A rock, a tree, a spring, a pebble, a piece of wood, a house, in a word anything, can be sacred. A rite can have sacredness; indeed there is no rite that does not have it to some degree. There are words, phrases, and formulas that can be said only by consecrated personages; there are gestures and movements that cannot be executed by just anyone. . . .

But I have confined myself thus far to enumerating various sacred things as examples: I must now indicate the general characteristics by which they are distinguished from profane things.

One might be tempted to define sacred things by the rank that is ordinarily assigned to them in the hierarchy of beings. They tend to be regarded as superior in dignity and power to profane things, and particularly to man, in no way sacred when he is only a man. Indeed, he is portrayed as occupying a rank inferior to and dependent upon them. While that portrayal is certainly not without truth, nothing about it is truly characteristic of the sacred. Subordination of one thing to another is not enough to make one sacred and the other not. Slaves are subordinate to their masters, subjects to their king, soldiers to their leaders, lower classes to ruling classes, the miser to his gold, and the power seeker to the power holders. If a man is sometimes said to have the religion of beings or things in which he recognizes an eminent value and a kind of superiority to him, it is obvious that, in all such cases, the word is taken in a metaphorical sense, and there is nothing in those relations that is religious in a strict sense.

On the other hand, we should bear in mind that there are things with which man feels relatively at ease, even though they are sacred to the highest degree. An amulet has sacredness, and yet there is nothing extraordinary about the respect it inspires. Even face to face with his gods, man is not always in such a marked state of inferiority, for he very often uses physical coercion on them to get what he wants. He beats the fetish when he is displeased, only to be reconciled with it if, in the end, it becomes more amenable to the wishes of its worshipper. To get rain, stones are thrown into the spring or the sacred lake where the god of the rain is presumed to reside; it is believed that he is forced by this means to come out and show himself. Furthermore, while it is true that man is a dependent of his gods, this dependence is mutual. The gods also need man; without offerings and sacrifices, they would die. I will have occasion to show that this dependence of gods on their faithful is found even in the most idealistic religions.

However, if the criterion of a purely hierarchical distinction is at once too general and too imprecise, nothing but their heterogeneity is left to define the relation between the sacred and the profane. But what makes this heterogeneity sufficient to characterize that classification of things and to distinguish it from any other is that it has a very particular feature: *It is absolute.* In the history of human thought, there is no other example of two categories of things as profoundly differentiated or as radically opposed to one another. . . .

This is not to say that a being can never pass from one of these worlds to the other. But when this passage occurs, the manner in which it occurs demonstrates the fundamental duality of the two realms, for it implies a true metamorphosis. Rites of initiation, which are practiced by a great many peoples, demonstrate this especially well. Initiation is a long series of rites to introduce the young man into religious life. For the first time, he comes out of the purely profane world, where he has passed his childhood, and enters into the circle of sacred things. This change of status is conceived not as a mere development of preexisting seeds but as a transformation *totius substantiae.* At that moment, the young man is said to die, and the existence of the particular person he was, to cease – instantaneously to be replaced by another. He is born again in a new form. Appropriate ceremonies are held to bring about the death and the rebirth, which are taken not merely in a symbolic sense but literally. Is this not proof that there is a rupture between the profane being that he was and the religious being that he becomes?

Indeed, this heterogeneity is such that it degenerates into real antagonism. The two worlds are conceived of not only as separate but also as hostile and jealous rivals. Since the condition of belonging fully to one is fully to have left the other, man is exhorted to retire completely from the profane in order to live an exclusively religious life. From thence comes monasticism, which artificially organizes a milieu that is apart from, outside of, and closed to the natural milieu where ordinary men live a secular life, and that tends almost to be its antagonist. From thence as well comes mystic asceticism, which seeks to uproot all that may remain of man's attachment to the world. Finally, from thence come all forms of religious suicide, the crowning logical step of this asceticism, since the only means of escaping profane life fully and finally is escaping life altogether.

The opposition of these two genera is expressed outwardly by a visible sign that permits ready recognition of this very special classification, wherever it exists. The mind experiences deep repugnance about mingling, even simple contact, between the corresponding things, because the notion of the sacred is always and everywhere separate from the notion of the profane in man's mind, and because we imagine a kind of logical void between them. The state of dissociation in which the ideas are found in consciousness is too strongly contradicted by such mingling, or even by their being too close to one another. The sacred thing is, par excellence, that which the profane must not and cannot touch with impunity. . . .

Now we have a first criterion of religious beliefs. No doubt, within these two fundamental genera, there are secondary species that are themselves more or less incompatible with each other. But characteristically, the religious phenomenon is such that it always assumes a bipartite division of the universe, known and knowable, into two genera that include all that exists but radically exclude one another. Sacred things are things protected and isolated by prohibitions; profane things are those things to which the prohibitions are applied and that must keep at a distance from what is sacred. Religious beliefs are those representations that express the nature of sacred things and the relations they have with other sacred things or with profane things. Finally, rites are rules of conduct that prescribe how man must conduct himself with sacred things.

When a certain number of sacred things have relations of coordination and subordination with one another, so as to form a system that has a certain coherence and does not belong to any other system of the same sort, then the beliefs and rites, taken together, constitute a religion. . . .

Even so, this definition is not yet complete, for it fits equally well two orders of things that must be distinguished even though they are akin: magic and religion.

Magic, too, is made up of beliefs and rites. . . .

Must we therefore say that magic cannot be rigorously differentiated from religion – that magic is full of religion and religion full of magic and, consequently, that it is impossible to separate them and define the one without the other? . . .

Here is how a line of demarcation can be drawn between these two domains.

Religious beliefs proper are always shared by a definite group that professes them and that practices the corresponding rites. Not only are they individually accepted by all members of that group, but they also belong to the group and unify it. The individuals who comprise the group feel joined to one another by the fact of common faith. A society whose members are united because they imagine the sacred world and its relations with the profane world in the same way, and because they translate this common representation into identical practices, is what is called a Church. In history we do not find religion without Church. . . .

. . . A Church is not simply a priestly brotherhood; it is a moral community made up of all the faithful, both laity and priests. Magic ordinarily has no community of this sort. . . .

We arrive thus at the following definition: *A religion is a unified system of beliefs and practices relative to sacred things, that is to say, things set apart and forbidden – beliefs and practices which unite into one single moral community called a Church, all those who adhere to them.* The second element thus holds a place in my definition that is no less essential than the first: In showing that the idea of religion is inseparable from the idea of a Church, it conveys the notion that religion must be an eminently collective thing.

We have seen that [Australian] totemism places figurative representations of the totem in the first rank of the things it considers sacred; then come the animals or plants whose name the clan bears, and finally the members of the clan. Since all these things are sacred in the same right, albeit unequally so, their religiousness cannot arise from any of the particular traits that distinguish them from one another. . . . Obviously the similar feelings that these dissimilar kinds of things evoke in the consciousness of the faithful, and that constitute their sacredness, can derive only from a principle that is shared by all alike – totemic emblems, people of the clan, and individuals of the totemic species. This is the common principle to which the cult is in reality addressed. In other words, totemism is not the religion of certain animals, certain men, or certain images; it is the religion of a kind of anonymous and impersonal force that is identifiable in each of these beings but identical to none of them. None possesses it entirely, and all participate in it. Such is its independence from the particular subjects in which it is incarnated that it both precedes and outlives them. The individuals die; the generations pass on and are replaced by others; but this force remains always present, alive, and the same. It animates the generations of today as it animated those of yesterday and will animate those of tomorrow. Taking the word "god" in a very broad sense, one could say that it is the god that each totemic cult worships. But it is an impersonal god, without name, without history, immanent in the world, diffused in a numberless multitude of things. . . .

But the Australian does not conceive of this impersonal force abstractly. Influences that we will have to seek out led him to conceive of it in the form of an animal or plant, that is, in the form of a material thing. Here, in reality, is what the totem amounts to: It is the tangible form in which that intangible substance is represented in the imagination; diffused through all sorts of disparate beings, that energy alone is the real object of the cult. We are now in a better position to comprehend what the native means when he affirms, for example, that the people of the Crow phratry are crows. He does not exactly mean that they are crows in the everyday empirical sense of the word, but that the same principle is found in all of them. That principle constitutes what they all most fundamentally are, is shared between people and animals of the same name, and is conceptualized as having the outward form of the crow. In this way the universe, as totemism conceives it, is pervaded and enlivened by a number of forces that the imagination represents in forms that, with only a few exceptions, are borrowed from either the animal or the plant kingdom. There are as many of these forces as there are clans in the tribe, and each of them pervades certain categories of things of which it is, the essence and the life-principle.

When I speak of these principles as forces, I do not use the word in a metaphorical sense; they behave like real forces. In a sense, they are even physical forces that bring about physical effects mechanically. . . .

And in addition to their physical nature, they have a moral nature. . . . All the beings that participate in the same totemic principle consider themselves, by that very fact, to be morally bound to one another; they have definite obligations of assistance, vengeance, and so on, toward each other, and it is these that constitute kinship. Thus, the totemic principle is at once a physical force and a moral power, and we will see that it is easily transformed into divinity proper. . . .

From *Primitive Classification* (with Mauss)

Emile Durkheim and Marcel Mauss, *Primitive Classification*, trans. Rodney Needham (Chicago: University of Chicago Press, 1963), pp. 10–13, 82–4.

The most simple systems of classification known are those found among the tribes of Australia.

The most widespread form of social organization among these societies is well known. Each tribe is divided into two large fundamental sections which we shall call moieties. Each moiety, in turn, comprises a certain number of clans, i.e. groups of individuals with the same totem. In principle, the totems of one moiety are not found in the other. In addition to this division into clans, each moiety is divided into two classes which we shall call "marriage classes". We give them this name because their purpose, above all, is to regulate marriage: a particular class of one moiety may marry only with a particular class of the other moiety. . . .

All the members of the tribe are classed in this way in definite categories which are enclosed one in the other. *Now the classification of things reproduces this classification of men.*

Cameron has already observed that among the Ta-ta-thi "everything in the universe is divided among the different members of the tribe". "Some", he says, "claim the trees, others the plains, others the sky, stars, wind, rain, and so forth." Unfortunately, this information lacks precision. We are not told to which groups of individuals the different groups of things are related in this way. But we have facts from another source which are extremely significant.

The tribes of the Bellinger River are each divided into two moieties; and, according to Palmer, this division applies equally to nature. "All nature is divided into class names and said to be male and female. The sun and moon and stars are said to be men and women, and to belong to classes just as the blacks themselves." This tribe is fairly close to another tribe, that of Port Mackay in Queensland, in which we find the same system of classification. According to the answers made by Bridgeman to the questionnaires of Curr, Smyth, and Lorimer Fison, this tribe, like its neighbours, is divided into two moieties, one called Youngaroo, the other Wutaroo. As a matter of fact, there are marriage classes as well; but these do not appear to have affected cosmological notions. On the contrary, the division into moieties is considered "as a universal law of nature". "All things, animate and inanimate," says Curr after Bridgeman, "are divided by these tribes into two classes, named *Youngaroo* and *Wootaroo*." The same observer reports (according to Smyth) that "they divide everything into moieties. They tell you that alligators are Youngaroo and kangaroos are Wootaroo – the sun is Youngaroo and the moon is Wootaroo; and so on with the constellations, with the trees, and with the plants." And Fison relates that: "Everything in nature, according to them, is divided between the two classes. The wind belongs to one, and the rain to the other. . . . If a star is pointed out they will tell you to which division [moiety] it belongs."

Such a classification is of extreme simplicity, since it is simply bipartite. Everything is distributed in the two categories corresponding to the two moieties. The system becomes more complex when it is no longer only the division into moieties which is the framework for the division of things, but also the division into four marriage classes. This is the case among the Wakelbura of north-central Queensland. . . .

. . . Far from it being the case, as Frazer seems to think, that the social relations of men are based on logical relations between things, in reality it is the former which have provided the prototype for the latter. According to him, men were divided into clans by a pre-existing classification of things; but, quite on the contrary, they classified things because they were divided by clans.

We have seen, indeed, how these classifications were modelled on the closest and most fundamental form of social organization. This, however, is not going far enough. Society was not simply a model which classificatory thought followed; it was its own divisions which served as divisions for the system of classification. The first logical categories were social categories; the first classes of things were classes of men, into which these things were integrated. It was because men were grouped, and thought of themselves in the form of groups, that in their ideas they grouped other things, and in the beginning the two modes of grouping were merged to the point of being indistinct. Moieties were the first genera; clans, the first species. Things were thought to be integral parts of society, and it was their place in society which determined their place in nature. . . .

Not only the external form of classes, but also the relations uniting them to each other, are of social origin. It is because human groups fit one into another – the sub-clan into the clan, the clan into the moiety, the moiety into the tribe – that groups of things are ordered in the same way. Their regular diminution in span, from genus to species, species to variety, and so on, comes from the equally diminishing extent presented by social groups as one leaves the largest and oldest and approaches the more recent and the more derivative. And if the totality of things is conceived as a single system, this is because society itself is seen in the same way. It is a whole, or rather it is *the* unique whole to which everything is related. Thus logical hierarchy is only another aspect of social hierarchy, and the unity of knowledge is nothing else than the very unity of the collectivity, extended to the universe.

Furthermore, the ties which unite things of the same group or different groups to each other are themselves conceived as social ties. We recalled in the beginning that the expressions by which we refer to these relations still have a moral significance; but whereas for us they are hardly more than metaphors, originally they meant what they said. Things of the same class were really considered as relatives of the individuals of the same social group, and consequently of each other. They are of "the same flesh", the same family. Logical relations are thus, in a sense, domestic relations. Sometimes, too, as we have seen, they are comparable at all points with those which exist between a master and an object possessed, between a chief and his subjects. We may even wonder whether the idea of the pre-eminence of genus over species, which is so strange from a positivistic point of view, may not be seen here in its rudimentary form. Just as, for the realist, the general idea dominates the individual, so the clan totem dominates those of the sub-clans and, still more, the personal totems of individuals; and wherever the moiety has retained its original stability it has a sort of primacy over the divisions of which it is composed and the particular things which are included in them. Though he may be essentially Wartwut and partially Moiwiluk, the Wotjobaluk . . . is above all a Krokitch or a Gamutch. Among the Zuñi, the animals symbolizing the six main clans are set in sovereign charge over their respective sub-clans and over creatures of all kinds which are grouped with them. . . .

From "Individual and Collective Representations"

Emile Durkheim, *Sociology and Philosophy*, trans. D. F. Pocock (New York: Free Press, 1974), pp. 23–6.

If representations, once they exist, continue to exist in *themselves* without their existence being perpetually dependent upon the disposition of the neural centres, if they have the power to react directly upon each other and to combine according to their own laws, they are then realities which, while maintaining an intimate relation with their substratum, are to a certain extent independent of it. Certainly their autonomy can only be a relative one; there is no realm of nature that is not bound to others. Nothing could be more absurd than to elevate psychic life into a sort of absolute, derived from nothing and unattached to the rest of the universe. It is obvious that the condition of the brain affects all the intellectual phenomena and is the immediate cause of some of them (pure sensation). But, on the other hand, it follows from what has been said earlier that representational life is not inherent in the intrinsic nature of nervous matter, since in part it exists by its own force and has its own particular manner of being. A representation is not simply an aspect of the condition of a neural element at the particular moment that it takes place, since it persists after that condition has passed, and since the relations of the representations are different in nature from those of the underlying neural elements. It is something quite new which certain characteristics of the cells certainly help to produce but do not suffice to constitute, since it survives them and manifests different properties. To say that the mental condition does not derive directly from the cell is to say that it is not included in it, that it forms itself in part outside it and is to that extent exterior to it. If it was directly derived it would be within it, since its reality would derive from no other source.

When we said elsewhere that social facts are in a sense independent of individuals and exterior to individual minds, we only affirmed of the social world what we have just established for the psychic world. Society has for its substratum the mass of associated individuals. The system which they form by uniting together, and which varies according to their geographical disposition and the nature and number of their channels of communication, is the base from which social life is raised. The representations which form the network of social life arise from the relations between the individuals thus combined or the secondary groups that are between the individuals and the total society. If there is nothing extraordinary in the fact that individual representations, produced by the action and reaction between neural elements, are not inherent in these elements, there is nothing surprising in the fact that collective representations, produced by the action and reaction between individual minds that form the society, do not derive directly from the latter and consequently surpass them. The conception of the relationship which unites the social substratum and the social life is at every point analogous to that which undeniably exists between the physiological substratum and the psychic life of individuals, if, that is, one is not going to deny the existence of psychology in the proper sense of the word. The same consequences should then follow on both sides. The independence, the relative externality of social facts in relation to individuals, is even more immediately apparent than is that of mental facts in relation to the cerebral cells, for the former, or at least the most important of them, bear the clear marks of their origin. While one might perhaps contest the statement that all social facts without exception impose themselves from without upon the individual, the doubt does not seem possible as regards religious beliefs and practices, the rules of morality and the innumerable precepts of law – that is to say, all the most characteristic manifestations of collective life. All are expressly obligatory, and this obligation is the proof that these ways of acting and thinking are not the work of the individual but come from a moral power above him, that which the mystic calls God or which can be more scientifically conceived. The same law is found at work in the two fields.

Furthermore, it can be explained in the same way in the two cases. If one can say that, to a certain extent, collective representations are exterior to individual minds, it means that they do not derive from them as such but from the association of minds, which is a very different thing. No doubt in the making of the whole each contributes his part, but private sentiments do not become social except by combination under the action of the *sui generis* forces developed in association. In such a combination, with the mutual alterations involved, *they become something else.* A chemical synthesis results which concentrates and unifies the synthesised elements and by that transforms them. Since this synthesis is the work of the whole, its sphere is the whole. The resultant surpasses the individual as the whole the part. It is *in* the whole as it is *by* the whole. In this sense it is exterior to the individuals. No doubt each individual contains a part, but the whole is found in no one. . . .

From *The Royal Touch: Sacred Monarchy and Scrofula in England and France*
Marc Bloch

Marc Bloch, *The Royal Touch: Sacred Monarchy and Scrofula in England and France*, trans. J. E. Anderson (London: Routledge and Kegan Paul, 1973), pp. 41–3.

The men of the Middle Ages – or the vast majority of them at all events – were accustomed to picture the things of religion in an extremely rational and down-to-earth fashion. And it is difficult to see how this could have been otherwise. The miraculous world to which the Christian rites gave access did not appear to them to be separated from the world they lived in by an impassable abyss, for the two worlds interpenetrated one another. How could it be possible for actions affecting the life beyond not to have an effect also on this life here below? Of course, the idea of this kind of intervention did not shock anyone, since no one had any accurate conception of natural laws. Sacred actions, objects or individuals were thus thought of not only as reservoirs of powers available beyond this present life, but also as sources of energy capable of exerting an immediate influence on this earth too. Moreover, they pictured this energy in such concrete terms that they sometimes even represented it as possessing a certain weight. Gregory of Tours tells us that a piece of material placed upon the altar of a great saint – such as St Peter or St Martin – would become heavier than before, provided always that the saint was willing to display his power.

The priest, thought to be possessed of sacred powers, was considered by many as a kind of magician, and as such was sometimes venerated and sometimes hated. In certain places, people would cross themselves as he passed by, since meeting him was considered a bad omen. In eleventh-century Denmark, the priests were held responsible for disturbances in the weather and for infections in the same way as witches, and they were sometimes persecuted as the agents of such evils, and with such bitterness that Gregory VII had to make a protest. Besides, there is no need for us to look so far north; for there is no doubt at all that the following instructive anecdote belongs to thirteenth-century France. Jacques de Vitry, the popular writer who relates it, says that he had it "on very reliable authority". An epidemic broke out in a certain village, and to put an end to it, the villagers could think of nothing better than to sacrifice their *curé*. One day, when he was wearing his robes and conducting a funeral, they threw him headlong into the grave alongside the corpse. And similar insensate practices – though in rather milder forms – still survive today.

Thus the power commonly ascribed by public opinion to a sacred person could sometimes take on formidable or adverse shapes; but, more often than not, it was of course regarded as beneficent. Now is there any greater and more perceptible benefit than health? It was an easy step to attribute healing power to everything that in some measure formed part of the consecration rite. The Host, the communion wine, the baptismal water, the ablution water in which the officiant had dipped his hands after touching the sacred elements, the very fingers of the priest – all these were regarded as so many remedies. And even today, in certain provinces, the dust from a church and the moss growing on its walls are held to partake of the same properties. This kind of idea sometimes led uneducated minds into strange aberrations. Gregory of Tours tells the story of some barbarian chieftains who, suffering pains in their feet, bathed them in a paten which was used to hold the sacred host. The clergy naturally condemned such excesses; but they allowed the continuance of those practices which they did not consider harmful to the due dignity of worship. Moreover, popular beliefs were largely out of their control. Among all the sacramentals, the holy oils, being the normal vehicle of consecrations, seemed to be particularly rich in supernatural virtues. The parties to a trial by ordeal would swallow some in order to ensure a favourable result for themselves. Above all, the holy oils were held to be marvellously effective against all bodily ills, and it proved necessary to safeguard the vessels containing them against the indiscreet attentions of the faithful. In truth, in those days the word "consecrated" implied the possession of power to heal.

Let us remember, then, what kings were at this period. Almost everyone believed, in the words of Peter of Blois, in their "holiness". But this notion went even further. Whence came this "holiness"? Largely, no doubt, in the eyes of the people, from this family predestination in which the masses, holding on to ancient ideas, had certainly not lost faith; but also since Carolingian times, more specifically and from a more Christian sentiment, from the religious rite of unction – in other words, from the consecrated oil which likewise seemed the most effective remedy for so many illnesses. Thus kings were doubly marked out for the role of beneficent wonder-workers – first by their sacred character *per se*, and then more particularly by the most apparent and venerable of its origins, through which this sacred character was held to act. Sooner or later, it would seem, they were bound to figure as healers.

Yet they did not become healers straight away, that is, not immediately after the introduction of anointing for kings in the States of Western Europe, nor in all countries. So the general considerations just put forward are not enough to explain the appearance of the royal touch in France and in England; they can do no more than show how men's minds were prepared to conceive or to admit such a practice. In order to account for its birth at a specific date and in a particular environment, we shall have to appeal to facts of a different and more fortuitous order, since they imply to a higher degree the interplay of individual wills.

From *The Savage Mind*
Claude Lévi-Strauss

Claude Lévi-Strauss, *The Savage Mind* (Chicago: University of Chicago Press, 1966), pp. 217–19.

... [A]ll classification proceeds by pairs of contrasts: classification only ceases when it is no longer possible to establish oppositions. Strictly speaking, therefore, the system knows no checks. Its internal dynamism is progressively weakened as it proceeds along its axis in either direction. And when the system comes to a halt, this is not because of any unforeseen obstacles presented by empirical properties of beings or things nor through any jamming of its mechanism but because it has completed its course and wholly fulfilled its function.

When the classificatory intention ascends, as it were, towards the greatest generality and most extreme abstraction, no diversity prevents it from applying a scheme through the operation of which reality undergoes a series of progressive purifications, whose final term will be provided, as intended, in the form of a simple binary opposition (high and low, right and left, peace and war, etc.), and beyond which it is, for intrinsic reasons, useless as well as impossible to go. The same operation can be repeated on other planes: on that of the internal organization of the social group, which the so-called totemic classifications allow to grow to the dimensions of an international society by application of a similar scheme of organization to an ever-greater number of groups; or again on the spatio-temporal plane, thanks to a mythical geography which, as an Aranda myth ... shows, permits the organization of an inexhaustible variety of landscapes by successive reductions which once again terminate in a binary opposition (in this case between directions and elements, since the contrast here is between land and water).

At the lower end there is no external limit to the system either, since it succeeds in treating the qualitative diversity of natural species as the symbolic material of an order, and its progress towards the concrete, particular and individual is not even arrested by the obstacle of personal appellations: even proper names can serve as terms for a classification.

What is in question is thus a total system, which ethnologists in vain tried to pull to pieces in order to fashion them into distinct institutions, of which totemism continues to be the most famous example. But in this way one is led only into paradoxes bordering on the absurd. Thus, Elkin, . . . in an otherwise admirable work of synthesis, taking totemism as the point of departure for his analysis of the religious thought and organization of Australian natives, when confronted by its theoretical wealth, evades the difficulty by introducing a special heading, "classificatory totemism". He thus treats classification as a special form of totemism when in fact . . . it is totemism or so-called totemism, which constitutes not even a mode of classification, but an aspect or moment of it. Comte knew nothing of totemism (and it was no doubt this which saved him from being deceived by a phantom), and though he lacked the evidence which would have confirmed his thesis, yet he had roughly gauged the importance in the history of thought of a classificatory system, whose organization and tenor he understood better than ethnologists of the present day:

> Never since that epoch have human conceptions been able to recover to a degree at all comparable, that great unity of method and homogeneity of doctrine which constitutes the fully normal state of our intelligence, and which it had then acquired spontaneously . . . (Comte, 53e leçon, p. 58).

No doubt Comte assigns this "savage mind" to a period of history – to the ages of fetishism and polytheism – while in this book it is neither the mind of savages nor that of primitive or archaic humanity, but rather mind in its untamed state as distinct from mind cultivated or domesticated for the purpose of yielding a return. This latter has appeared at certain points of the globe and at certain moments in history, and it is natural that Comte, lacking ethnographic data (and that ethnographic sense which can be acquired only by the collection and handling of data of this type) should have apprehended the former in its retrospective form, as a mode of mental activity anterior in time to the latter. We are better able to understand today that it is possible for the two to co-exist and interpenetrate in the same way that (in theory at least) it is possible for natural species, of which some are in their savage state and others transformed by agriculture and domestication, to co-exist and cross, although – from the very fact of their development and the general conditions it requires – the existence of the latter threatens the former with extinction. But, whether one deplores or rejoices in the fact, there are still zones in which savage thought, like savage species, is relatively protected. This is the case of art, to which our civilization accords the status of a national park, with all the advantages and inconveniences attending so artificial a formula; and it is particularly the case of so many as yet "uncleared" sectors of social life, where, through indifference or inability, and most often without our knowing why, primitive thought continues to flourish. . . .

From *Purity and Danger: An Analysis of the Concepts of Pollution and Taboo*
Mary Douglas

Mary Douglas, *Purity and Danger: An Analysis of the Concepts of Pollution and Taboo* (London: Ark, 1984), pp. 2–4, 35–6, 94–6.

. . . [D]irt is essentially disorder. There is no such thing as absolute dirt: it exists in the eye of the beholder. If we shun dirt, it is not because of craven fear, still less dread or holy terror. Nor do our ideas about disease account for the range of our behaviour in cleaning or avoiding dirt. Dirt offends against order. Eliminating it is not a negative movement, but a positive effort to organise the environment. . . .

In this book I have tried to show that rituals of purity and impurity create unity in experience. So far from being aberrations from the central project of religion, they are positive contributions to atonement. By their means, symbolic patterns are worked out and publicly displayed. Within these patterns disparate elements are related and disparate experience is given meaning. . . .

. . . I admit to having made society sound more systematic than it really is. But just such an expressive over-systematising is necessary for interpreting the beliefs in question. For I believe that ideas about separating, purifying, demarcating and punishing transgressions have as their main function to impose system on an inherently untidy experience. It is only by exaggerating the difference between within and without, above and below, male and female, with and against, that a semblance of order is created. In this sense I am not afraid of the charge of having made the social structure seem over-rigid. . . .

If we can abstract pathogenicity and hygiene from our notion of dirt, we are left with the old definition of dirt as matter out of place. This is a very suggestive approach. It implies two conditions: a set of ordered relations and a contravention of that order. Dirt then, is never a unique, isolated event. Where there is dirt there is system. Dirt is the by-product of a systematic ordering and classification of matter, in so far as ordering involves rejecting inappropriate elements. This idea of dirt takes us straight into the field of symbolism and promises a link-up with more obviously symbolic systems of purity.

We can recognise in our own notions of dirt that we are using a kind of omnibus compendium which includes all the rejected elements of ordered systems. It is a relative idea. Shoes are not dirty in themselves, but it is dirty to place them on the dining-table; food is not dirty in itself, but it is dirty to leave cooking utensils in the bedroom, or food bespattered on clothing; similarly, bathroom equipment in the drawing room; clothing lying on chairs; out-door things in-doors; upstairs things downstairs; under-clothing appearing where over-clothing should be, and so on. In short, our pollution behaviour is the reaction which condemns any object or idea likely to confuse or contradict cherished classifications. . . .

Granted that disorder spoils pattern; it also provides the materials of pattern. Order implies restriction; from all possible materials, a limited selection has been made and from all possible relations a limited set has been used. So disorder by implication is unlimited, no pattern has been realised in it, but its potential for patterning is indefinite. This is why, though we seek to create order, we do not simply condemn disorder. We recognise that it is destructive to existing patterns; also that it has potentiality. It symbolises both danger and power. . . .

. . . Danger lies in transitional states, simply because transition is neither one state nor the next, it is undefinable. The person who must pass from one to another is himself in danger and emanates danger to others. The danger is controlled by ritual which precisely separates him from his old status, segregates him for a time and then publicly declares his entry to his new status. Not only is transition itself dangerous, but also the rituals of segregation are the most dangerous phase of the rites. . . .

From *Wayward Puritans: A Study in the Sociology of Deviance*
Kai Erikson

Kai Erikson, *Wayward Puritans: A Study in the Sociology on Deviance* (New York: Macmillan, 1966), pp. 5–11.

One of the earliest problems the sociologist encounters in his search for a meaningful approach to deviant behavior is that the subject itself does not seem to have any natural boundaries. Like people in any field, sociologists find it convenient to assume that the deviant person is somehow "different" from those of his fellows who manage to conform, but years of research into the problem have not yielded any important evidence as to what, if anything, this difference might be. Investigators have studied the character of the deviant's background, the content of his dreams, the shape of his skull, the substance of his thoughts – yet none of this information has enabled us to draw a clear line between the kind of person who commits deviant acts and the kind of person who does not. Nor can we gain a better perspective on the matter by shifting our attention away from the individual deviant and looking instead at the behavior he enacts. Definitions of deviance vary widely as we range over the various classes found in a single society or across the various cultures into which mankind is divided, and it soon becomes apparant that there are no objective properties which all deviant acts can be said to share in common – even within the confines of a given group. Behavior which qualifies one man for prison may qualify another for sainthood, since the quality of the act itself depends so much on the circumstances under which it was performed and the temper of the audience which witnessed it.

This being the case, many sociologists employ a far simpler tactic in their approach to the problem – namely, to let each social group in question provide its own definitions of deviant behavior. In this study, as in others dealing with the same general subject, the term "deviance" refers to conduct which the people of a group consider so dangerous or embarrassing or irritating that they bring special sanctions to bear against the persons who exhibit it. Deviance is not a property *inherent in* any particular kind of behavior; it is a property *conferred upon* that behavior by the people who come into direct or indirect contact with it. The only way an observer can tell whether or not a given style of behavior is deviant, then, is to learn something about the standards of the audience which responds to it. . . .

Once the problem is phrased in this manner we can ask: how does a community decide which . . . behavioral details are important enough to merit special attention? And why, having made this decision, does it build institutions like prisons and asylums to detain the persons who perform them? The conventional answer to that question, of course, is that a society creates the machinery of control in order to protect itself against the "harmful" effects of deviation, in much the same way that an organism mobilizes its resources to combat an invasion of germs. Yet this simple view of the matter is apt to pose many more problems than it actually settles. As both Emile Durkheim and George Herbert Mead pointed out long ago, it is by no means evident that all acts considered deviant in society are in fact (or even in principle) harmful to group life. . . . Perhaps these activities *are* dangerous, but to accept this conclusion without a thoughtful review of the situation is apt to blind us to the important fact that people in every corner of the world manage to survive handsomely while engaged in practices which their neighbors regard as extremely abhorrent. In the absence of any surer footing, then, it is quite reasonable for sociologists to return to the most innocent and yet the most basic question which can be asked about deviation: why does a community assign one form of behavior rather than another to the deviant class?

The following paragraphs will suggest one possible answer to that question. . . .

. . . [C]ommunities are boundary maintaining: each has a specific territory in the world as a whole, not only in the sense that it occupies a defined region of geographical space but also in the sense that it takes over a particular niche in what might be called cultural space and develops its own "ethos" or "way" within that compass. . . .

Now people who live together in communities cannot relate to one another in any coherent way or even acquire a sense of their own stature as group members unless they learn something about the boundaries of the territory they occupy in social space, if only because they need to sense what lies beyond the margins of the group before they can appreciate the special quality of the experience which takes place within it. Yet how do people learn about the boundaries of their community? And how do they convey this information to the generations which replace them?

To begin with, the only material found in a society for marking boundaries is the behavior of its members – or rather, the networks of interaction which link these members together in regular social relations. And the interactions which do the most effective job of locating and publicizing the group's outer edges would seem to be those which take place between deviant persons on the one side and official agents of the community on the other. The deviant is a person whose activities have moved outside the margins of the group, and when the community calls him to account for that vagrancy it is making a statement about the nature and placement of its boundaries. It is declaring how much variability and diversity can be tolerated within the group before it begins to lose its distinctive shape, its unique identity. . . . [O]n the whole, members of a community inform one another about the placement of their boundaries by participating in the confrontations which occur when persons who venture out to the edges of the group are met by policing agents whose special business it is to guard the cultural integrity of the community. Whether these confrontations take the form of criminal trials, excommunication hearings, courts-martial, or even psychiatric case conferences, they act as boundary-maintaining devices in the sense that they demonstrate to whatever audience is concerned where the line is drawn between behavior that belongs in the special universe of the group and behavior that does not. . . .

From *Discipline and Punish: The Birth of the Prison*
Michel Foucault

Michel Foucault, *Discipline and Punish: The Birth of the Prison*, trans. Alan Sheridan (New York: Vintage, 1979), pp. 227–8, 271–7.

. . . Is it surprising that the cellular prison, with its regular chronologies, forced labour, its authorities of surveillance and registration, its experts in normality, who continue and multiply the functions of the judge, should have become the modern instrument of penality? Is it surprising that prisons resemble factories, schools, barracks, hospitals, which all resemble prisons?

. . . If the prison-institution has survived for so long, with such immobility, if the principle of penal detention has never seriously been questioned, it is no doubt because this carceral system was deeply rooted and carried out certain very precise functions. . . . But what role was it supposed to play?

. . . [T]he prison, apparently "failing", does not miss its target; on the contrary, it reaches it, in so far as it gives rise to one particular form of illegality in the midst of others, which it is able to isolate, to place in full light and to organize as a relatively enclosed, but penetrable, milieu. It helps to establish an open illegality, irreducible at a certain level and secretly useful, at once refractory and docile; it isolates, outlines, brings out a form of illegality that seems to sum up symbolically all the others, but which makes it possible to leave in the shade those that one wishes to – or must – tolerate. . . .

For the observation that prison fails to eliminate crime, one should perhaps substitute the hypothesis that prison has succeeded extremely well in producing delinquency, a specific type, a politically or economically less dangerous – and, on occasion, usable – form of illegality; in producing delinquents, in an apparently marginal, but in fact centrally supervised milieu; in producing the delinquent as a pathologized subject. The success of the prison, in the struggles around the law and illegalities, has been to specify a "delinquency". We have seen how the carceral system substituted the "delinquent" for the offender, and also superimposed upon juridical practice a whole horizon of possible knowledge. Now this process that constitutes delinquency as an object of knowledge is one with the political operation that dissociates illegalities and isolates delinquency from them. The prison is the hinge of these two mechanisms; it enables them to reinforce one another perpetually, to objectify the delinquency behind the offence, to solidify delinquency in the movement of illegalities. So successful has the prison been that, after a century and a half of "failures", the prison still exists, producing the same results, and there is the greatest reluctance to dispense with it.

chapter 4

Collective Emotions and Ritual Process

Introduction

The focus shifts in this chapter from religious beliefs and systems of symbolic classification – the subject matter of the preceding chapter – to religious practices and the ritual process. And although both social structure and culture continue to figure importantly here, these extracts (again, mostly from *The Elementary Forms of Religious Life*) underscore the usefulness of Durkheim's ritual theory for the development of an emotional sociology, one that pays close attention to the role of collective emotions in the structuring of social interaction. The chapter begins with Durkheim's famous description of collective effervescence in Australian ceremonials and with the contrast that he draws between these ceremonials and more mundane periods marked by the "utter colorlessness" of utilitarian pursuits. It shows how these successive phases of social activity are related in turn to totemism and to the sacred/profane distinction, themes from Durkheim's cultural analysis in chapter 3. It also explores what is "eternal" or "enduring" in religious life, concluding that while religion's cognitive functions are increasingly being supplanted by modern science, religion as a system of practices – "in a word, the cult" – will always "outlive the succession of particular symbols in which religious thought has clothed itself" (p. 118). A final, brief selection by Durkheim, an excerpt from "A Discussion on Sex Education," illustrates his ideas about the ritual process and the sacred by means of an unusual example: the meaning of the sexual act itself and of sexual intimacy. In all these extracts, Durkheim directs attention to the collective emotions that are generated in and through religious communion and the ritual process and demonstrates how they constrain and enable social interaction. Such themes are further developed in the excerpts by Victor Turner, Erving Goffman, and Randall Collins that follow, all of which extend Durkheimian insights from the study of religious life *per se* to more secular and everyday interactions. Finally, William Sewell, Jr., provides examples from the French Revolution to dramatize the applicability of these same insights to interactions of a different order: to striking and extraordinary historical events upon the world stage.

From *The Elementary Forms of Religious Life*

Emile Durkheim, *The Elementary Forms of Religious Life*, trans. Karen E. Fields (New York: Free Press, 1995), pp. 216–32, 429–33.

Life in Australian societies alternates between two different phases. In one phase, the population is scattered in small groups that attend to their occupations independently. Each family lives to itself, hunting, fishing – in short, striving by all possible means to get the food it requires. In the other phase, by contrast, the population comes together, concentrating itself at specified places for a period that varies from several days to several months. This concentration takes place when a clan or a portion of the tribe is summoned to come together and on that occasion either conducts a religious ceremony or holds what in the usual ethnographic terminology is called a *corroboree*.

These two phases stand in the sharpest possible contrast. The first phase, in which economic activity predominates, is generally of rather low intensity. Gathering seeds or plants necessary for food, hunting, and fishing are not occupations that can stir truly strong passions. The dispersed state in which the society finds itself makes life monotonous, slack, and humdrum. Everything changes when a corroboree takes place. Since the emotional and passionate faculties of the primitive are not fully subordinated to his reason and will, he easily loses his self-control. An event of any importance immediately puts him outside himself. Does he receive happy news? There are transports of enthusiasm. If the opposite happens, he is seen running hither and you like a madman, giving way to all sorts of chaotic movements: shouting, screaming, gathering dust and throwing it in all directions, biting himself, brandishing his weapons furiously, and so on. The very act of congregating is an exceptionally powerful stimulant. Once the individuals are gathered together, a sort of electricity is generated from their closeness and quickly launches them to an extraordinary height of exaltation. Every emotion expressed resonates without interference in consciousnesses that are wide open to external impressions, each one echoing the others. The initial impulse is thereby amplified each time it is echoed, like an avalanche that grows as it goes along. And since passions so heated and so free from all control cannot help but spill over, from every side there are nothing but wild movements, shouts, downright howls, and deafening noises of all kinds that further intensify the state they are expressing. Probably because a collective emotion cannot be expressed collectively without some order that permits harmony and unison of movement, these gestures and cries tend to fall into rhythm and regularity, and from there into songs and dances. But in taking on a more regular form, they lose none of their natural fury. A regulated commotion is still a commotion. The human voice is inadequate to the task and is given artificial reinforcement: Boomerangs are knocked against one another; bull roarers are whirled. The original function of these instruments, used widely in the religious ceremonies of Australia, probably was to give more satisfying expression to the excitement felt. And by expressing this excitement, they also reinforce it. The effervescence often becomes so intense that it leads to outlandish behavior; the passions unleashed are so torrential that nothing can hold them. People are so far outside the ordinary conditions of life, and so conscious of the fact, that they feel a certain need to set themselves above and beyond ordinary morality. The sexes come together in violation of the rules governing sexual relations. Men exchange wives. Indeed, sometimes incestuous unions, in normal times judged loathsome and harshly condemned, are contracted in the open and with impunity. If it is added that the ceremonies are generally held at night, in the midst of shadows pierced here and there by firelight, we can easily imagine the effect that scenes like these are bound to have on the minds of all those who take part. They bring about such an intense hyperexcitement of physical and mental life as a whole that they cannot be borne for very long. The celebrant who takes the leading role eventually falls exhausted to the ground.

To illustrate and flesh out this unavoidably sketchy tableau, here is an account of scenes taken from Spencer and Gillen.

One of the most important religious celebrations among the Warramunga concerns the snake Wollunqua. It is a series of rites that unfold over several days. What I will describe takes place on the fourth day.

According to the protocol in use among the Warramunga, representatives of the two phratries take part, some as celebrants and others as organizers and participants. Although only the people of the Uluuru phratry are authorized to conduct the ceremony, the members of the Kingilli phratry must decorate the participants, prepare the site and the instruments, and serve as the audience. In this capacity, they are responsible for mounding damp sand ahead of time, on which they use red down to make a drawing that represents the snake Wollunqua. The ceremony proper, which Spencer and Gillen attended, did not begin until nightfall. Around ten or eleven o'clock, Uluuru and Kingilli arrived on the scene, sat on the mound, and began to sing. All were in a state of obvious excitement (*"every one was evidently very excited"*). A short time later in the evening, the Uluuru brought their wives and handed them over to the Kingilli, who had sexual relations with them. The recently initiated young men were brought in, and the ceremony was explained to them, after which there was uninterrupted singing until three in the morning. Then came a scene of truly wild frenzy (*"a scene of the wildest excitement"*). With fires flickering on all sides, bringing out starkly the whiteness of the gum trees against the surrounding night, the Uluuru knelt in single file beside the mound, then moved around it, rising in unison with both hands on their thighs, kneeling again a little farther along, and so on. At the same time, they moved their bodies left and then right, at each movement letting out an echoing scream – actually a howl – at the top of their voices, *Yrrsh! Yrrsh! Yrrsh!* Meanwhile the Kingilli, in a high state of excitement, sounded their boomerangs, their chief appearing to be even more excited than his companions. When the procession of the Uluuru had circled the mound twice, they rose from their kneeling position, seated themselves, and took to singing again. From time to time, the singing would flag and almost die, then break out suddenly again. At the first sign of day, everyone jumped to their feet; the fires that had gone out were relit; urged on by the Kingilli, the Uluuru furiously attacked the mound with boomerangs, lances, and sticks, and in a few minutes it was in pieces. The fires died and there was profound silence.

The same observers were present at a yet wilder scene among the Warramunga during the fire rituals. All sorts of processions, dances, and songs had been underway by torchlight since nightfall, and the general effervescence was increasingly intense. At a certain moment, twelve of those present each took in hand a large lighted torch; and, holding his own torch like a bayonette, one of them charged a group of natives. The blows were parried with staves and lances. A general melée followed. Men jumped, kicked, reared, and let out wild screams. The torches blazed and crackled as they hit heads and bodies, showering sparks in all directions. "The smoke, the flaming torches, the rain of sparks, the mass of men dancing and screaming – all that," say Spencer and Gillen, "created a scene whose wildness cannot be conveyed in words."

It is not difficult to imagine that a man in such a state of exaltation should no longer know himself. Feeling possessed and led on by some sort of external power that makes him think and act differently than he normally does, he naturally feels he is no longer himself. It seems to him that he has become a new being. The decorations with which he is decked out, and the masklike decorations that cover his face, represent this inward transformation even more than they help bring it about. And because his companions feel transformed in the same way at the same moment, and express this feeling by their shouts, movements, and bearing, it is as if he was in reality transported into a special world entirely different from

the one in which he ordinarily lives, a special world inhabited by exceptionally intense forces that invade and transform him. Especially when
repeated for weeks, day after day, how would experiences like these
not leave him with the conviction that two heterogeneous and incom-
mensurable worlds exist in fact? In one world he languidly carries on his
daily life; the other is one that he cannot enter without abruptly entering
into relations with extraordinary powers that excite him to the point
of frenzy. The first is the profane world and the second, the world of
sacred things.

It is in these effervescent social milieux, and indeed from that very effervescence, that the religious idea seems to have been born. That such is
indeed the origin tends to be confirmed by the fact that what is properly
called religious activity in Australia is almost entirely contained within
the periods when these gatherings are held. To be sure, there is no people
among whom the great cult ceremonies are not more or less periodical,
but in the more advanced societies, there is virtually no day on which some
prayer or offering is not offered to the gods or on which some ritual
obligation is not fulfilled. In Australia, by contrast, the time apart from the
feasts of the clan and the tribe is taken up almost entirely with secular
and profane activities. Granted, even during the periods of secular activity,
there are prohibitions that must be and are observed. Freely killing or
eating the totemic animal is never permitted, at least where the prohibition has kept its original strictness, but hardly any positive rite or ceremony of any importance is conducted. The positive rites and ceremonies
take place only among assembled groups. Thus, the pious life of the
Australian moves between successive phases – one of utter colorlessness,
one of hyperexcitement – and social life oscillates to the same rhythm.
This brings out the link between the two phases. Among the peoples called
civilized, on the other hand, the relative continuity between them partially masks their interrelations. Indeed, we may well ask whether this
starkness of contrast may have been necessary to release the experience
of the sacred in its first form. By compressing itself almost entirely into
circumscribed periods, collective life could attain its maximum intensity
and power, thereby giving man a more vivid sense of the twofold existence he leads and the twofold nature in which he participates.

But this explanation is still incomplete. I have shown how the clan
awakens in its members the idea of external forces that dominate and exalt
it by the way in which it acts upon its members. But I still must ask how
it happens that those forces were conceived of in the form of the totem,
that is, in the form of an animal or plant.

The reason is that some animal or plant has given its name to the clan
and serves as the clan's emblem. It is, in fact, a well-known law that the
feelings a thing arouses in us are spontaneously transmitted to the symbol
that represents it. Black is for us a sign of mourning; therefore it evokes

sad thoughts and impressions. This transfer of feelings takes place because the idea of the thing and the idea of its symbol are closely connected in our minds. As a result, the feelings evoked by one spread contagiously to the other. This contagion, which occurs in all cases to some extent, is much more complete and more pronounced whenever the symbol is something simple, well defined, and easily imagined. But the thing itself is difficult for the mind to comprehend – given its dimensions, the number of its parts, and the complexity of their organization. We cannot detect the source of the strong feelings we have in an abstract entity that we can imagine only with difficulty and in a jumbled way. We can comprehend those feelings only in connection with a concrete object whose reality we feel intensely. Thus if the thing itself does not meet this requirement, it cannot serve as a mooring for the impressions felt, even for those impressions it has itself aroused. The symbol thus takes the place of the thing, and the emotions aroused are transferred to the symbol. It is the symbol that is loved, feared, and respected. It is to the symbol that one is grateful. And it is to the symbol that one sacrifices oneself. The soldier who dies for his flag dies for his country, but the idea of the flag is actually in the foreground of his consciousness. Indeed, the flag sometimes causes action directly. Although the country will not be lost if a solitary flag remains in the hands of the enemy or won if it is regained, the soldier is killed retaking it. He forgets that the flag is only a symbol that has no value in itself but only brings to mind the reality it represents. The flag itself is treated as if it was that reality.

The totem is the flag of the clan, so it is natural that the impressions the clan arouses in individual consciousness – impressions of dependence and of heightened energy – should become more closely attached to the idea of the totem than to that of the clan. The clan is too complex a reality for such unformed minds to be able to bring its concrete unity into clear focus. Besides, the primitive does not see that these impressions come to him from the group. He does not even see that the coming together of a certain number of men participating in the same life releases new energies that transform each one of them. All he feels is that he is lifted above himself and that he is participating in a life different from the one he lives ordinarily. He must still connect those experiences to some external object in a causal relation. Now what does he see around him? What is available to his senses, and what attracts his attention, is the multitude of totemic images surrounding him. He sees the waninga and the nurtunja, symbols of the sacred being. He sees the bull roarers and the churingas, on which combinations of lines that have the same meaning are usually engraved. The decorations on various parts of his body are so many totemic marks. Repeated everywhere and in every form, how could that image not fail to stand out in the mind with exceptionally sharp relief? Thus placed at center stage, it becomes representative. To that image

the felt emotions attach themselves, for it is the only concrete object to
which they can attach themselves.

The image goes on calling forth and recalling those emotions even after
the assembly is over. Engraved on the cult implements, on the sides of
rocks, on shields, and so forth, it lives beyond the gathering. By means
of it, the emotions felt are kept perpetually alive and fresh. It is as though
the image provoked them directly. Imputing the emotions to the image
is all the more natural because, being common to the group, they can only
be related to a thing that is equally common to all. Only the totemic emblem
meets this condition. By definition, it is common to all. During the ceremony, all eyes are upon it. Although the generations change, the image
remains the same. It is the abiding element of social life. So the mysterious forces with which men feel in touch seem to emanate from it, and
thus we understand how men were led to conceive them in the form of
the animate or inanimate being that gives the clan its name.

Having laid this foundation, we are in a position to grasp the essence
of totemic beliefs. Because religious force is none other than the collective and anonymous force of the clan and because that force can only be
conceived of in the form of the totem, the totemic emblem is, so to speak,
the visible body of the god. From the totem, therefore, the beneficial or
fearsome actions that the cult is intended to provoke or prevent will seem
to emanate. So it is to the totem that the rites are specifically addressed.
This is why the totem stands foremost in the ranks of sacred things.

Like any other society, the clan can only live in and by means of the
individual consciousnesses of which it is made. Thus, insofar as religious
force is conceived of as embodied in the totemic emblem, it seems to be
external to individuals and endowed with a kind of transcendence; and
yet, from another standpoint, and like the clan it symbolizes, it can be
made real only within and by them. So in this sense, it is immanent in
individual members and they of necessity imagine it to be. They feel within
themselves the active presence of the religious force, because it is this force
that lifts them up to a higher life. This is how man came to believe that
he had within him a principle comparable to the one residing in the totem,
and thus how he came to impute sacredness to himself – albeit a sacredness less pronounced than that of the emblem. This happens because the
emblem is the preeminent source of religious life. Man participates in it
only indirectly, and he is aware of that; he realizes that the force carrying him into the realm of sacred things is not inherent in himself but comes
to him from outside.

For another reason, the animals or plants of the totemic species had to
have the same quality to an even greater degree. For if the totemic principle is none other than the clan, it is the clan thought of in the physical
form depicted by the emblem. Now, this is also the form of the real beings
whose name the clan bears. Because of this resemblance, they could not

fail to arouse feelings similar to those aroused by the emblem itself. Because this emblem is the object of religious respect, they too should inspire respect of the same kind and appear as sacred. Given forms so perfectly identical, the faithful were bound to impute forces of the same kind to both. This is why it is forbidden to kill or eat the totemic animal and why the flesh is deemed to have positive virtues that the rites put to use. The animal looks like the emblem of the clan – like its own image, in other words. And since it looks more like the emblem than the man does, its place in the hierarchy of sacred things is superior to man's. Clearly there is a close kinship between these two beings; both share the same essence, and both incarnate something of the totemic principle. But because the principle itself is conceived of in animal form, the animal seems to incarnate it more conspicuously than the man does. This is why, if the man respects the animal and treats it as a brother, he gives it at least the respect due an older brother.

But although the totemic principle has its chief residence in a specific animal or plant species, it cannot possibly remain localized there. Sacredness is highly contagious, and it spreads from the totemic being to everything that directly or remotely has to do with it. The religious feelings inspired by the animal passed into the substances it ate, thereby making or remaking its flesh and blood; those feelings passed into the things that resemble it and into the various creatures with which it is in constant contact. Thus, little by little, subtotems attached themselves to totems, and the cosmological systems expressed by the primitive classifications came into being. In the end, the whole world was divided up among the totemic principles of the same tribe.

We now understand the source of the ambiguity that religious forces display when they appear in history – how they come to be natural as well as human and material as well as moral. They are moral powers, since they are made entirely from the impressions that moral collectivity as a moral being makes on other moral beings, the individuals. Such moral powers do not express the manner in which natural things affect our senses but the manner in which the collective consciousness affects individual consciousnesses. Their authority is but one aspect of the moral influence that society exerts on its members. From another standpoint, they are bound to be regarded as closely akin to material things because they are conceived of in tangible forms. Thus they bestride the two worlds. They reside in men but are at the same time the life-principles of things. It is they that enliven and discipline consciences; it is also they that make the plants grow and the animals multiply. Because of its double nature, religion was able to be the womb in which the principal seeds of human civilization have developed. Because religion has borne reality as a whole within itself, the material world as well as the moral world, the forces that move both bodies and minds have been conceived of in religious form. Thus it is that the most disparate techniques and practices – those that ensure the continuity of moral life (law, morals, fine arts) and those that are useful to material life (natural sciences, industrial techniques) – sprang from religion, directly or indirectly. . . .

. . . [W]e can say that the faithful are not mistaken when they believe in the existence of a moral power to which they are subject and from which they receive what is best in themselves. That power exists, and it is society. When the Australian is carried above himself, feeling inside a life overflowing with an intensity that surprises him, he is not the dupe of an illusion. That exaltation is real and really is the product of forces outside of and superior to the individual. Of course, he is mistaken to believe that a power in the form of an animal or plant has brought about this increase in vital energy. But his mistake lies in taking literally the symbol that represents this being in the mind, or the outward appearance in which the imagination has dressed it up, not in the fact of its very existence. Behind these forms, be they cruder or more refined, there is a concrete and living reality.

In this way, religion acquires a sense and a reasonableness that the most militant rationalist cannot fail to recognize. The main object of religion is not to give man a representation of the natural universe, for if that had been its essential task, how it could have held on would be incomprehensible. In this respect, it is barely more than a fabric of errors. But religion is first and foremost a system of ideas by means of which individuals imagine the society of which they are members and the obscure yet intimate relations they have with it. Such is its paramount role. And although this representation is symbolic and metaphorical, it is not unfaithful. It fully translates the essence of the relations to be accounted for. It is true with a truth that is eternal that there exists outside us something greater than we and with which we commune.

That is why we can be certain that acts of worship, whatever they may be, are something other than paralyzed force, gesture without motion. By the very act of serving the manifest purpose of strengthening the ties between the faithful and their god – the god being only a figurative representation of the society – they at the same time strengthen the ties between the individual and the society of which he is a member. . . .

. . . even though purely ideal, the powers . . . conferred on [an] object behave as if they were real. They determine man's conduct with the same necessity as physical forces. The Arunta who has properly rubbed himself with his churinga feels stronger; he is stronger. If he has eaten the flesh of an animal that is prohibited, even through it is perfectly wholesome, he will feel ill from it and may die. The soldier who falls defending his flag certainly does not believe he has sacrificed himself to a piece of cloth. Such things happen because social thought, with its imperative authority, has a power that individual thought cannot possibly have. By acting on our minds, it can make us see things in the light that suits it; according to circumstances, it adds to or takes away from the real. Hence, there is a realm of nature in which the formula of idealism is almost literally applicable; that is the social realm. There, far more than anywhere else, the idea creates the reality. Even in this case, idealism is probably not true without qualification. We can never escape the duality of our nature and wholly emancipate ourselves from physical necessities. As I will show, to express our own ideas even to ourselves, we need to attach those ideas to material things that symbolize them. But, here, the role of matter is at a minimum. The object that serves as a prop for the idea does not amount to much as compared to the ideal superstructure under which it disappears, and, furthermore, it has nothing to do with that superstructure. From all that has been said, we see what the pseudo-delirium met with at the basis of so many collective representations consists of: It is only a form of this fundamental idealism. So it is not properly called a delusion. The ideas thus objectified are well founded – not, to be sure, in the nature of the tangible things onto which they are grafted but in the nature of society.

We can understand now how it happens that the totemic principle and, more generally, how any religious force comes to be external to the things in which it resides: because the idea of it is not at all constructed from the impressions the thing makes directly on our senses and minds. Religious force is none other than the feeling that the collectivity inspires in its members, but projected outside the minds that experience them, and objectified. To become objectified, it fixes on a thing that thereby becomes sacred; any object can play this role. In principle, none is by nature predestined to it, to the exclusion of others, any more than others are necessarily precluded from it. Where religious force becomes objectified depends entirely upon what circumstances cause the feeling that generates religious ideas to settle here or there, in one place rather than another. The sacredness exhibited by the thing is not implicated in the intrinsic properties of the thing: *It is added to them.* The world of the religious is not a special aspect of empirical nature: *It is superimposed upon nature.*

Finally, this idea of the religious enables us to explain an important principle found at the root of many myths: When a sacred being is subdivided, it remains wholly equal to itself in each of its parts. In other words, from the standpoint of religious thought, the part equals the whole; the part has the same powers and the same efficacy. A fragment of a relic has the same virtues as the whole relic. The smallest drop of blood contains the same active principle as all the blood. As we will see, the soul can be broken up into almost as many parts as there are organs or tissues in the body; each of these partial souls is equivalent to the entire soul. This conception would be inexplicable if sacredness depended on the constitutive properties of the thing serving as its substrate, for sacredness would have to change with that thing, increasing and decreasing with it. But if the virtues the thing is deemed to have are not intrinsic to it, if they come to it from certain feelings that it calls to mind and symbolizes (even though such feelings originate outside it), it can play an evocative role whether it is whole or not, since in that role it does not need specific dimensions. Since the part evokes the whole, it also evokes the same feelings as the whole. A mere scrap of the flag represents the country as much as the flag itself; moreover, it is sacred in the same right and to the same degree.

That an emblem can be useful as a rallying point for any sort of group requires no argument. By expressing the social unit tangibly, it makes the unit itself more tangible to all. And for that reason, the use of emblematic symbols must have spread quickly, as soon as the idea was born. Furthermore, this idea must have arisen spontaneously from the conditions of life in common, for the emblem is not only a convenient method of clarifying the awareness the society has of itself: It serves to create – and is a constitutive element of – that awareness.

By themselves, individual consciousnesses are actually closed to one another, and they can communicate only by means of signs in which their inner states come to express themselves. For the communication that is opening up between them to end in a communion – that is, in a fusion of all the individual feelings into a common one – the signs that express those feelings must come together in one single resultant. The appearance of this resultant notifies individuals that they are in unison and brings home to them their moral unity. It is by shouting the same cry, saying the same words, and performing the same action in regard to the same object that they arrive at and experience agreement. Granted, individual representations also bring about repercussions in the body that are not unimportant; still, these effects can be treated as analytically distinct from physical repercussions that come with or after them but that are not their basis. . . .

Thus there is something eternal in religion that is destined to outlive the succession of particular symbols in which religious thought has clothed itself. There can be no society that does not experience the need at regular intervals to maintain and strengthen the collective feelings and ideas that provide its coherence and its distinct individuality. This moral remaking can be achieved only through meetings, assemblies, and congregations in which the individuals, pressing close to one another, reaffirm in common their common sentiments. Such is the origin of ceremonies that, by their object, by their results, and by the techniques used, are not different in kind from ceremonies that are specifically religious.

What basic difference is there between Christians' celebrating the principal dates of Christ's life, Jews' celebrating the exodus from Egypt or the promulgation of the Decalogue, and a citizens' meeting commemorating the advent of a new moral charter or some other great event of national life?

If today we have some difficulty imagining what the feasts and ceremonies of the future will be, it is because we are going through a period of transition and moral mediocrity. The great things of the past that excited our fathers no longer arouse the same zeal among us, either because they have passed so completely into common custom that we lose awareness of them or because they no longer suit our aspirations. Meanwhile, no replacement for them has yet been created. We are no longer electrified by those principles in whose name Christianity exhorted the masters to treat their slaves humanely; and besides, Christianity's idea of human equality and fraternity seems to us today to leave too much room for unjust inequalities. Its pity for the downcast seems to us too platonic. We would like one that is more vigorous but do not yet see clearly what it should be or how it might be realized in fact.

In short, the former gods are growing old or dying, and others have not been born. This is what voided Comte's attempt to organize a religion using old historical memories, artificially revived. It is life itself, and not a dead past, that can produce a living cult. But that state of uncertainty and confused anxiety cannot last forever. A day will come when our societies once again will know hours of creative effervescence during which new ideals will again spring forth and new formulas emerge to guide humanity for a time. And when those hour have been lived through, men will spontaneously feel the need to relive them in thought from time to time – that is, to preserve their memory by means of celebrations that regularly recreate their fruits. We have already seen how the [French] Revolution instituted a whole cycle of celebrations in order to keep the principles that inspired it eternally young. If that institution quickly perished, it is because the revolutionary faith lasted only briefly, and because disappointments and discouragements quickly replaced the first moment of enthusiasm. But although that work miscarried, it helps us to imagine what might have come to be under other conditions; and everything leads us to believe that the work will sooner or later be taken up again. There are no immortal gospels, and there is no reason to believe that humanity is incapable of conceiving new ones in the future. As to knowing what the symbols will be in which the new faith will come to express itself, whether they will resemble those of the past, whether they will better suit the reality to be expressed – that is a question that exceeds human faculties of prediction and that, moreover, is beside the point.

But feasts and rites – in a word, the cult – are not the whole of religion. Religion is not only a system of practices but also a system of ideas whose object is to express the world; even the humblest have their own cosmologies, as we have seen. No matter how these two elements of religious life may be related, they are nonetheless quite different. One is turned toward action, which it elicits and regulates; the other toward thought, which it enriches and organizes. Since they do not rest on the same conditions, then, there is reason to ask whether the ideas correspond to needs as universal and as permanent as the practices do.

When we impute specific traits to religious thought and believe its function is to express, by its own methods, a whole aspect of the real that eludes both ordinary knowledge and science, we naturally refuse to grant that the speculative role of religion could ever be overthrown. But it does not seem to me that analysis of the facts has demonstrated this specificity of religion. The religion we have just studied is one of those in which the symbols used are the most unsettling to reason. Everything about it seems full of mystery. At first glance, those beings that simultaneously participate in the most disparate kingdoms, multiply without ceasing to be one, and break up without diminishing, seem to belong to an entirely different world from the one in which we live. Some have even gone so far as to say that the thought that built it was totally ignorant of the laws of logic. Never, perhaps, has the contrast between reason and faith been so pronounced. If ever there was a moment in history when the difference between them must have stood out plainly, then that truly was the moment.

But I have noted, contrary to such appearances, that the realities to which religious speculation was applied then are the same ones that would later serve as objects of scientists' reflection. Those realities are nature, man, and society. The mystery that appears to surround them is entirely superficial and fades upon closer scrutiny. To have them appear as they are, it is enough to pull aside the veil with which the mythological imagination covered them. Religion strives to translate those realities into an intelligible language that does not differ in nature from that used by science. Both attempt to connect things to one another, establish internal relations between those things, classify them, and systematize them. We have even seen that the essential notions of scientific logic are of religious origin. Of course, science reworks those notions in order to use them. It distills out all sorts of extraneous elements and generally brings to all its efforts a critical spirit that is unknown in religion; it surrounds itself with precautions to "avoid haste and bias" and to keep passions, prejudices, and all subjective influences at bay. But these improvements in method are not enough to differentiate science from religion. In this regard, both pursue the same goal; scientific thought is only a more perfected form of religious thought. Hence it seems natural that religion should lose ground as science becomes better at performing its task.

There is no doubt, in fact, that this regression has taken place over the course of history. Although the offspring of religion, science tends to replace religion in everything that involves the cognitive and intellectual functions.

Christianity has by now definitively sanctioned that replacement, in the realm of physical phenomena. Regarding matter as a profane thing par excellence, Christianity has easily abandoned knowledge to a discipline that is alien to it, *tradidit mundum hominum disputationi*. So it is that the sciences of nature have, with relative ease, succeeded in establishing their authority and in having that authority acknowledged. But Christianity could not let the world of souls out of its grip as easily, for it is above all over souls that the god of the Christians wishes to rule. This is why the idea of subjecting psychic life to science long amounted to a kind of profanation; even today, that idea is still repugnant to many. Today, experimental and comparative psychology has been created and must be reckoned with. But the world of religious and moral life still remains forbidden. The great majority of men continue to believe that there is an order of things that the intellect can enter only by very special routes. Hence the strong resistance one encounters whenever one attempts to treat religious and moral phenomena scientifically. Yet these efforts persist despite opposition, and that very persistence makes it foreseeable that this last barrier will give way in the end, and that science will establish itself as mistress, even in this preserve.

This is what the conflict of science and religion is about. People often have a mistaken idea of it. Science is said to deny religion in principle, But religion exists; it is a system of given facts; in short, it is a reality. How could science deny a reality? Furthermore, insofar as religion is action and insofar as it is a means of making men live, science cannot possibly take its place. Although science expresses life, it does not create life, and science can very well seek to explain faith but by that very fact presupposes faith. Hence there is conflict on only a limited point. Of the two functions originally performed by religion, there is one, only one, that tends more and more to escape it, and that is the speculative function. What science disputes in religion is not its right to exist but its right to dogmatize about the nature of things, its pretensions to special expertise for explaining man and the world. In fact, religion does not know itself. It knows neither what it is made of nor what needs it responds to. Far from being able to tell science what to do, religion is itself an object for science! And on the other hand, since apart from a reality that eludes scientific reflection, religious speculation has no special object of its own, that religion obviously cannot play the same role in the future as it did in the past.

However, religion seems destined to transform itself rather than disappear.

I have said that there is something eternal in religion: the cult and the faith. But men can neither conduct ceremonies for which they can see no rationale, nor accept a faith that they in no way understand. To spread or simply maintain religion, one must justify it, which is to say one must devise a theory of it. A theory of this sort must assuredly rest on the various sciences, as soon as they come into existence: social sciences first, since religious faith has its origins in society; psychology next, since society is a synthesis of human consciousnesses; sciences of nature finally, since man and society are linked to the universe and can be abstracted from it only artificially. But as important as these borrowings from the established sciences may be, they are in no way sufficient; faith is above all a spur to action, whereas science, no matter how advanced, always remains at a distance from action. Science is fragmentary and incomplete; it advances but slowly and is never finished; but life – that cannot wait. Theories whose calling is to make people live and make them act, must therefore rush ahead of science and complete it prematurely. They are possible only if the demands of practicality and vital necessities, such as we feel without distinctly conceiving them, push thought beyond what science permits us to affirm. In this way, even the most rational and secularized religions cannot and can never do without a particular kind of speculation which, although having the same objects as science itself, still cannot be properly scientific. The obscure intuitions of sense and sensibility often take the place of logical reasons.

Thus, from one point of view, this speculation resembles the speculation we encounter in the religions of the past, while from another, it differs from them. While exercising the right to go beyond science, it must begin by knowing and drawing inspiration from science. As soon as the authority of science is established, science must be reckoned with; under pressure of need, one can go beyond science, but it is from science that one must start out. One can affirm nothing that science denies, deny nothing that science affirms, and establish nothing that does not directly or indirectly rest on principles taken from science. From then on, faith no longer holds the same sway as in the past over the system of representations that can continue to be called religious. There rises a power before religion that, even though religion's offspring, from then on applies its own critique and its own testing to religion. And everything points to the prospect that this testing will become ever more extensive and effective, without any possibility of assigning a limit to its future influence.

From "A Discussion on Sex Education"

Emile Durkheim: Essays on Morals and Education, trans. H. L. Sutcliffe, ed. W. S. F. Pickering (London: Routledge and Kegan Paul, 1979), pp. 142–7.

. . . When it is said that there is something mysterious about the sexual act, what is meant is that it cannot be grouped together with the acts of day-to-day life, that it is exceptional, that it is disconcerting and disturbing in some ways and that it awakens contradictory feelings in us. What this means is that it shocks, repels and offends us and at the same time attracts us. Now it can scarcely be that this sentiment is the product of a pure illusion. If there is such a thing as modesty, the sexual act is the immodest act *par excellence*. It negates and offends against modesty and since modesty is a virtue, the sexual act is immoral by reason of this alone. But on the other hand, there is no act which creates such strong bonds between human beings. It has an associative, and consequently moral power without compare. Is it surprising that, faced with such a complex and ambiguous relationship, moral *conscience* remains hesitant, perplexed, confused and divided against itself? It cannot advocate such an act, nor condemn it, nor can it praise, stigmatize or above all declare it unimportant. . . .

Even Kant felt that there was something about sexual relations which offended against the moral sentiment. This, he says, is because in sexual relations one individual serves as an instrument of pleasure to another, which is contrary to the dignity of the human being. But I believe the reason for the moral anxiety this act causes us is deeper and more general. The sentiment that lies at the root of our morality is the respect that man generates in his fellows. As a consequence of such respect, we keep our distance from our fellows and they keep their distance from us; we flee intimacy and do not permit it; we conceal our body as well as our inner life from prying eyes; we hide and isolate ourselves from others, and this isolation is at once the token and the consequence of the sacred character which has been vested in us. If we touch a sacred object without observing the respectful precautions laid down by ritual, we profane it and commit sacrilege. It is also a kind of desecration to fail to respect the boundaries separating men, to overstep these limits, and to intrude without due cause on other people. This is what engenders the sentiment and the duty of modesty, whether physical or moral. So there is no need to show that in the sexual act this profanation reaches an exceptionally high level, since each of the two personalities in contact is engulfed by the other. On no occasion is the abandoning of that reserve – which is merely another aspect of our dignity – so complete. This is what comprises the seed of basic immorality which is contained within this curiously complex act.

But at the same time it also contains within it the wherewithal to eradicate and redeem its constitutional immorality. For in fact this desecration also produces a communion, and a communion of the most intimate kind possible between two conscious beings. Through this communion, the two persons united become one; the limits which originally circumscribed each of them are first displaced and later transferred. A new personality is born, enveloping and embracing the other two. Should this fusion become critical and the new unity thus constituted become lasting, then from that moment onwards the desecration ceases to exist, since there are no longer two distinct, separate people, but one. Yet this result is achieved only on such terms. On the other hand, should the two individuals separate again after having become one, should each reclaim his independence after first giving himself to the other, then the desecration remains complete and irredeemable. . . .

From *The Ritual Process: Structure and Anti-Structure*
Victor Turner

Victor Turner, *The Ritual Process: Structure and Anti-Structure* (Ithaca, NY: Cornell University Press, 1969), pp. 95–129.

The attributes of liminality or of liminal *personae* ("threshold people") are necessarily ambiguous, since this condition and these persons elude or slip through the network of classifications that normally locate states and positions in cultural space. Liminal entities are neither here nor there; they are betwixt and between the positions assigned and arrayed by law, custom, convention, and ceremonial. As such, their ambiguous and indeterminate attributes are expressed by a rich variety of symbols in the many societies that ritualize social and cultural transitions. Thus, liminality is frequently likened to death, to being in the womb, to invisibility, to darkness, to bisexuality, to the wilderness, and to an eclipse of the sun or moon. . . .

What is interesting about liminal phenomena for our present purposes is the blend they offer of lowliness and sacredness, of homogeneity and comradeship. We are presented, in such rites, with a "moment in and out of time," and in and out of secular social structure, which reveals, however fleetingly, some recognition (in symbol if not always in language) of a generalized social bond that has ceased to be and has simultaneously yet to be fragmented into a multiplicity of structural ties. These are the ties organized in terms either of caste, class, or rank hierarchies or of segmentary oppositions in the stateless societies beloved of political anthropologists. It is as though there are here two major "models" for human interrelatedness, juxtaposed and alternating. The first is of society as a structured, differentiated, and often hierarchical system of politico-legal-economic positions with many types of evaluation, separating men in terms of "more" or "less." The second, which emerges recognizably in the liminal period, is of society as an unstructured or rudimentarily structured and relatively undifferentiated *comitatus*, community, or even communion of equal individuals who submit together to the general authority of the ritual elders. . . .

. . . I infer that, for individuals and groups, social life is a type of dialectical process that involves successive experience of high and low, communitas and structure, homogeneity and differentiation, equality and inequality. The passage from lower to higher status is through a limbo of statuslessness. . . . In other words, each individual's life experience contains alternating exposure to structure and communitas, and to states and transitions. . . .

Communitas breaks in through the interstices of structure, in liminality; at the edges of structure, in marginality; and from beneath structure, in inferiority. It is almost everywhere held to be sacred or "holy," possibly because it transgresses or dissolves the norms that govern structured and institutionalized relationships and is accompanied by experiences of unprecedented potency. . . .

There is a dialectic here, for the immediacy of communitas gives way to the mediacy of structure, while, in *rites de passage*, men are released from structure into communitas only to return to structure revitalized by their experience of communitas. What is certain is that no society can function adequately without this dialectic. Exaggeration of structure may well lead to pathological manifestations of communitas outside or against "the law." Exaggeration of communitas, in certain religious or political movements of the leveling type, may be speedily followed by despotism, overbureaucratization, or other modes of structural rigidification. . . . The history of any great society provides evidence at the political level for this oscillation. . . .

From "The Nature of Deference and Demeanor" Erving Goffman

Erving Goffman, *Interaction Ritual: Essays on Face-to-Face Behavior* (New York: Pantheon, 1967), pp. 53–6.

Students of society have distinguished in several ways among types of rules, as for example, between formal and informal rules; for this paper, however, the important distinction is that between substance and ceremony. A substantive rule is one which guides conduct in regard to matters felt to have significance in their own right, apart from what the infraction or maintenance of the rule expresses about the selves of the persons involved. Thus, when an individual refrains from stealing from others, he upholds a substantive rule which primarily serves to protect the property of these others and only incidentally functions to protect the image they have of themselves as persons with proprietary rights. The expressive implications of substantive rules are officially considered to be secondary; this appearance must be maintained, even though in some special situations everyone may sense that the participants were primarily concerned with expression.

A ceremonial rule is one which guides conduct in matters felt to have secondary or even no significance in their own right, having their primary importance – officially anyway – as a conventionalized means of communication by which the individual expresses his character or conveys his appreciation of the other participants in the situation. This usage departs from the everyday one, where "ceremony" tends to imply a highly specified, extended sequence of symbolic action performed by august actors on solemn occasions when religious sentiments are likely to be invoked. In my attempt to stress what is common to such practices as tipping one's hat and coronations, I will perforce ignore the differences among them to an extent that many anthropologists might perhaps consider impracticable.

In all societies, rules of conduct tend to be organized into codes which guarantee that everyone acts appropriately and receives his due. In our society the code which governs substantive rules and substantive expressions comprises our law, morality, and ethics, while the code which governs ceremonial rules and ceremonial expressions is incorporated in what we call etiquette. All of our institutions have both kinds of codes, but in this paper attention will be restricted to the ceremonial one.

The acts or events, that is, the sign-vehicles or tokens which carry ceremonial messages, are remarkably various in character. They may be linguistic, as when an individual makes a statement of praise of depreciation regarding self or other, and does so in a particular language and intonation; gestural, as when the physical bearing of an individual conveys insolence or obsequiousness; spatial, as when an individual precedes another through the door, or sits on his right instead of his left; task-embedded, as when an individual accepts a task graciously and performs it in the presence of others with aplomb and dexterity; part of the communication structure, as when an individual speaks more frequently than the others, or receives more attentiveness than they do. The important point is that ceremonial activity, like substantive activity, is an analytical element referring to a component or function of action, not to concrete empirical action itself. While some activity that has a ceremonial component does not seem to have an appreciable substantive one, we find that all activity that is primarily substantive in significance will nevertheless carry some ceremonial meaning, provided that its performance is perceived in some way by others. The manner in which the activity is performed, or the momentary interruptions that are allowed so as to exchange minor niceties, will infuse the instrumentally-oriented situation with ceremonial significance.

All of the tokens employed by a given social group for ceremonial purposes may be referred to as its ceremonial idiom. We usually distinguish societies according to the amount of ceremonial that is injected into a given period and kind of interaction, or according to the expansiveness of the forms and the minuteness of their specification; it might be better to distinguish societies according to whether required ceremony is performed as an unpleasant duty or, spontaneously, as an unfelt or pleasant one. . . .

From "On Face-Work"
Erving Goffman

Erving Goffman, *Interaction Ritual: Essays on Face-to-Face Behavior* (New York: Pantheon, 1967), pp. 29–31.

Since each participant in an undertaking is concerned, albeit for differing reasons, with saving his own face and the face of the others, then tacit cooperation will naturally arise so that the participants together can attain their shared but differently motivated objectives.

One common type of tacit cooperation in face-saving is the tact exerted in regard to face-work itself. The person not only defends his own face and protects the face of the others, but also acts so as to make it possible and even easy for the others to employ face-work for themselves and him. He helps them to help themselves and him. Social etiquette, for example, warns men against asking for New Year's Eve dates too early in the season, lest the girl find it difficult to provide a gentle excuse for refusing. . . .

Tact in regard to face-work often relies for its operation on a tacit agreement to do business through the language of hint – the language of innuendo, ambiguities, well-placed pauses, carefully worded jokes, and so on. . . .

Another form of tacit cooperation, and one that seems to be much used in many societies, is reciprocal self-denial. Often the person does not have a clear idea of what would be a just or acceptable apportionment of judgments during the occasion, and so he voluntarily deprives or depreciates himself while indulging and complimenting the others, in both cases carrying the judgments safely past what is likely to be just. The favorable judgments about himself he allows to come from the others; the unfavorable judgments of himself are his own contributions. . . .

A person's performance of face-work, extended by his tacit agreement to help others perform theirs, represents his willingness to abide by the ground rules of social interaction. Here is the hallmark of his socialization as an interactant. If he and the others were not socialized in this way, interaction in most societies and most situations would be a much more hazardous thing for feelings and faces. The person would find it impractical to be oriented to symbolically conveyed appraisals of social worth, or to be possessed of feelings – that is, it would be impractical for him to be a ritually delicate object. And as I shall suggest, if the person were not a ritually delicate object, occasions of talk could not be organized in the way they usually are. It is no wonder that trouble is caused by a person who cannot be relied upon to play the face-saving game.

From "Stratification, Emotional Energy, and the Transient Emotions" Randall Collins

Randall Collins, *Research Agendas in the Sociology of Emotions*, ed. Theodore D. Kemper (Albany, NY: State University of New York Press, 1990), pp. 27–34.

Emotion potentially occupies a crucial position in general sociological theory. As we attempt to be more precise and more empirical about sociological concepts, we find that many of the most important rest to a considerable extent upon emotional processes.

Durkheim raised the fundamental question of sociology: What holds society together? His answer is the mechanisms that produce moral solidarity; and these mechanisms, I suggest, do so by producing emotions. Parsonian sociology, which took the most reified, agentless side of Durkheim, put the argument in equivalent terms: Society is held together by values. But values, to the extent that they exist – and leaving open the issue of how far they are shared, and under what conditions – are cognitions infused with emotion. On the conflict side of sociological theory, Weber's central concepts also imply emotion: (a) the legitimacy that underlies stable power, (b) the status group ranking by which stratification

permeates everyday life, and (c) the religious world views that motivated some crucial periods of economic action. When we attempt to
translate any of these concepts into observables, it is apparent that we
are dealing with particular kinds of emotions. Marx and Engels are
perhaps farthest away from theorizing about emotional processes; in
their models, everything is structural (even alienation, which for Marx is
an ontological relationship, not a psychological one). But it is apparent
that in Marxian analyses of class mobilization and class conflict, emotion
must play a part – whether it is the mutual distrust within fragmented
classes that keeps them apart . . . or the solidarity that dominant classes
have and that oppressed classes acquire only in revolutionary situations. In
these respects, Marx and Engels' conflict theory comes close to a dynamic
and non-reified version of Durkheim's themes.

These are some reasons why the sociology of emotions should be
brought into the central questions of sociology. What holds a society
together – the "glue" of solidarity – and what mobilizes conflict – the energy
of mobilized groups – are emotions; so is what operates to uphold
stratification – hierarchical feelings, whether dominant, subservient, or
resentful. If we can explain the conditions that cause people to feel these
kinds of emotions, we will have a major part of a core sociological theory. There is of course a structural part of such a theory, and a cognitive
part, but the emotional part gives us something essential for a realistic
theory on its dynamics. . . .

. . . Goffman, like everyone else, speaks of emotion only in passing.
He focuses on the structure of micro-interaction, on its constraints and
levels, on the interplay between its subjective and objective components.
The crucial thing to see is that Goffman is applying Durkheimian theory
to micro-situations: he is concerned with how ritual solidarity is generated in the little transient groups of everyday life, at the level of the
encounter. These "natural rituals" (as I would call them) are equivalent
to the formal rituals Durkheim analyzed – religious ceremonies in abori-
gine tribes, patriotic rituals in the modern state – which produce sacred
objects and moral constraints. Goffman broadened Durkheim in a way
that shows how social order is produced on the micro-level: that is to say,
all over the map, in transient situations and local groups, which may well
be class-stratified or otherwise divided against each other, instead of in
the reified Durkheimian way (which Parsons followed) in which it seems
to be "Society" as a whole that is being integrated.

Goffmanian analysis of Interaction Ritual, then, is the analysis of a
wide-ranging and flexible mechanism, which produces pockets of moral
solidarity, but *variously* and *discontinuously* throughout society. It helps
us to connect upwards to the macro-structure, especially via stratification.
And it connects downward to the micro-details of human experience
and action, because rituals are made with emotional ingredients, and

they produce other sorts of emotions (especially moral solidarity, but also sometimes aggressive emotions) as outcomes. I will make considerable use of the Durkheimian/Goffmanian model of rituals in my stratification theory of emotions. . . .

The basic model of ritual interaction (IR) that I derive from Durkheim has the following elements:

1   A group of minimum size two assembled face-to-face. The sheer physical presence of human animals in the same place is a precondition for the emotional and cognitive processes that follow.
2   Focus of attention upon the same object or activity, and mutual awareness of each other's attention. Collective formalities, such as a church service or political protocol, are important only because they are one easy way to focus common attention. But any circumstances in everyday life that focus attention in this way . . . have the effect of producing a ritual situation. The crucial feature is that individuals become caught up in a group activity, in which they are mutually aware of what each other is doing. This makes the group itself the focus of attention, as a transindividual reality, influencing members from outside while permeating their consciousness from within.
3   Members share a common mood. It is inessential what emotion is present at the outset. The feelings may be anger, friendliness, enthusiasm, fear, sorrow, or many others. This model posits an emotional contagion among the persons present, for they are focussing attention on the same thing and are aware of each other's focus; they become caught up in each other's emotions. As a result, the emotional mood becomes stronger and more dominant; competing feelings are driven out by the main group feeling. On the ultra-micro level, this seems to happen by the process of rhythmic entrainment physiologically. . . . That is to say, activities and emotions have their own micro-rhythm, a pace in which they take place. As the focus of interaction becomes progressively more attuned, the participants anticipate each other's rhythms, and thus become caught up "in the swing of things". . . . Participants feel sadder in the course of a successful funeral, more humorous as part of a responsive audience at a comedy show, more convivial during the build-up of a party, more engrossed in a conversation as its rhythms become established.
4   The outcome of a successful build-up of emotional coordination within an interaction ritual is to produce feelings of solidarity. The emotions that are ingredients of the ritual (in no. 3 above) are transient; the outcome however is a long-term emotion, the feelings of attachment to the group that was assembled at that time. Thus, in the funeral ritual the short-term emotion was sadness, but the main

"ritual work" of the funeral was producing (or restoring) group solidarity. The emotional ingredients of a party may be friendliness or humor; the long-term result is the feeling of status group membership.

I refer to these long-term outcomes as "emotional energy" (EE). . . . This is a rather undifferentiated term, that includes various components. The most important component, I suggest, is very energy-like. It is a continuum, ranging from a high end of confidence, enthusiasm, good self-feelings; down through a middle range of lesser states, and to a low end of depression, lack of initiative, and negative self-feelings. Emotional energy is like the psychological concept of "drive" . . . but it has a specifically social orientation. High emotional energy is a feeling of confidence and enthusiasm for social interaction. It is the personal side of having a great deal of Durkheimian ritual solidarity with a group. One gets pumped up with emotional strength from participating in the group's interaction. This makes one not only an enthusiastic supporter of the group, but also a leading figure within it. One feels good with the group, and is able to be an energy-leader, a person who stirs up contagious feelings when the group is together.

At the low end of the emotional energy continuum, the opposite is the case. Low emotional energy is a lack of Durkheimian solidarity. One is not attracted to the group; one is drained or depressed by it; one wants to avoid it. One does not have a good self in the group. And one is not attached to the group's purposes and symbols, but alienated from them.

There are more differentiated variants of emotional energy as well, besides this up/down, high/low in solidarity and enthusiasm. We will see below there are two major dimensions of stratification (power and status) that produce specific qualities of emotional energy. But while we are considering the main, generic level of emotional energy, I will mention one more Durkheimian feature. Emotional energy is not just something that pumps up some individuals and depresses others. It also has a controlling quality from the group side. Emotional energy is what Durkheim . . . called "moral sentiment": it includes feelings of what is right and wrong, moral and immoral. Individuals, who are full of emotional energy, feel like good persons; they feel righteous about what they are doing. Persons with low emotional energy feel bad. Though they do not necessarily interpret this feeling as guilt or evil (that would depend on the religious or other cultural cognitions available for labelling their feelings), at a minimum, they lack the feeling of being morally good persons, which comes from enthusiastic participation in group rituals.

These feelings of moral solidarity can generate specific acts of altruism and love; but there is also a negative side. As Durkheim pointed out, group solidarity makes individuals feel a desire to defend and honor the group. This solidarity feeling is typically focussed on symbols, sacred objects (like a tribal totemic emblem, a Bible or Koran or other holy scripture, a flag, or a wedding ring). One shows respect for the group by participating in rituals venerating these symbolic objects; conversely, failure to respect them is a quick test of nonmembership in the group. It appears that individuals who are already members of the ritual group are under especially strong pressure to continue to respect its sacred symbols. If they do not, the loyal group members feel shock and outrage, that is their righteousness turns automatically into righteous anger. In this way, ritual violations lead to persecution of heretics, scapegoats, and other outcasts.

5   Rituals shape cognitions. The main objects or ideas that were the focus of attention during a successful ritual become loaded with emotional overtones. Those ideas or things become symbols; whatever else the ideas may refer to on the mundane level, there is also a deeper, Durkheimian level on which symbols invoke membership in the group that charged them up with ritual significance.

It is in this way that society gets inside the individual's mind. Our lives consist of a series of interactions, some of which generate more ritual solidarity than others. (This is what I refer to as "interaction ritual chains.") The high-solidarity rituals give individuals a store of cognitions that they carry around with them, and use to think and communicate with. Whenever someone thinks in terms of concepts that were the focus of a successful interaction ritual, they are subjectively reinvoking the feelings of membership in that group. We are, to speak in the idiom of Symbolic Interaction, imagining society in our minds; it would be more accurate, however, to say that we feel the emotions of social solidarity in the various ideas with which we think. This helps explain why persons who derive emotional energy from group interactions continue to have emotional energy even when they are alone. They are pumped up with emotional energy because of a successful interaction; this energy gets attached to ideas, and thinking those ideas allows these individuals to feel a renewed surge of socially-based enthusiasm.

I have couched this on the positive side, in terms of persons with high emotional energy. The same would apply on the negative side as well. Persons with low emotional energy lack the charge of ideas with solidarity; and their ideas may even be charged with antipathy to particular groups. (We shall see how this fits situations of group stratification.) This carries over into their subjective lives; they are depressed even when they are alone, and their thoughts move away from the symbols of groups that make them depressed. Thus, emotionally-charged symbols motivate individuals when they are away from ritual encounters.

From "Historical Events as Transformations of Structures: Inventing Revolution at the Bastille" William H. Sewell, Jr.

William H. Sewell, Jr., "Historical Events as Transformations of Structures: Inventing Revolution at the Bastille," *Theory and Society* 25 (1996), pp. 864–71.

. . . [T]he assault on the Bastille . . . was a theater of heroism, treachery, and bloodshed. The object was an impregnable fortress, whose commandant was thought to have lured the attackers into an outer courtyard in order to gun them down more efficiently. The operation lasted several hours, it afforded many opportunities for signal bravery under fire, and it brought death to nearly one-hundred assailants and serious wounds to a few score more. It is absolutely crucial to recognize the emotional significance of the bloodshed, if we are to understand the unfolding of the event over the following hours and days. The deaths of the assailants made them understandable as martyrs of liberty; the spilling of their blood became a transformative sacrifice, an act of sacred founding violence. . . .

Most social scientists avoid emotion like the plague. They seem to fear that if they take emotion seriously as an object of study, they will be tainted by the irrationality, volatility, subjectivity, and ineffability that we associate with the term – that their own lucidity and scientific objectivity will be brought into question. But if, as I would maintain, high-pitched emotional excitement is a constitutive ingredient of many transformative actions, then we cannot afford to maintain this protective scientific distance. The transformations that occurred as a consequence of the taking of the Bastille are certainly impossible to explain without considering the emotional tone of the event.

　To begin with, the emotional tone of action can be an important sign of structural dislocation and rearticulation. The more or less extended dislocation of structures that characterizes the temporality of the event is profoundly unsettling. It was in part the unresolved dislocations of the spring and summer of 1789 that rendered the Parisians so distraught by the middle of July; the emotion was then raised to a fever pitch when the king's attempted coup against the Assembly threatened to dash all hopes of reform. The widespread incidents of violence in Paris on the 12th and 13th bear witness to the tension and fear that motivated people to acts of both heroism and butchery on the 14th. And the resolution of structural dislocation – whether by restoring the ruptured articulation or by forging new ones – results in powerful emotional release that consolidates the rearticulation. We have already noted the rapturous reception of the delegation of the National Assembly in Paris on July 15, with its clamorous cheering and spontaneous weeping. It was the delegates' experience of this rapture that first induced them to revalue the events of the 14th as a legitimate revolution.

Emotion not only is an important sign of dislocations and rearticulations, but also shapes the very course of events. This is especially true in moments like the afternoon of July 14, when a large number of people interact intensively in a restricted space, experiencing the kind of contagious emotional excitement that Emile Durkheim called "collective effervescence." Collective effervescence lifts people out of their ordinary inhibitions and limitations. As Durkheim puts it, "in the midst of an assembly animated by a common passion, we become susceptible of acts and sentiments of which we are incapable when reduced to our own forces."

The powerful emotions introduced by collective effervescence make events markedly unstable. Joy and rage blend into one another, making possible acts of either generosity or savagery. The descriptions in *Les Révolutions de Paris* of the victorious procession from the Bastille to the city hall capture beautifully this supreme and dangerous exaltation. When the victors came forth from the fortress, escorting their captives,

> they formed a column and exited in the midst of an enormous crowd. Applause, an excess of joy, insults, imprecations hurled at the perfidious prisoners of war, all were mixed together; cries of vengeance and of pleasure leapt forth from every heart. The victors, glorious and covered with honor, carrying the arms and the corpses of the vanquished; the flags of victory; the militia mixed in with the soldiers of the fatherland; the laurels offered to them from all sides; everything offered a terrible and superb spectacle.

This was the prelude to the slaughter of de Launay. When the column arrived at city hall,

> the people, impatient to avenge itself, would permit neither de Launay nor the other officers to mount to the tribunal of the city. They were torn from the hands of their victors, trampled under foot one after the other. De Launay was pierced by a thousand blows, his head was severed, and it was placed on the end of a lance with the blood running down on all sides.

This slaughter did not seem to slake the crowd's thirst; the scene of triumph threatened to degenerate into an orgy of bloodshed. When the rest of the soldiers who had defended the Bastille arrived, "the people called for their execution" as well. But then the mood of the crowd suddenly shifted to generosity. The French Guards, who had been escorting these prisoners, "asked for their grace, and upon this request all voices were united and the pardon was unanimous." The volatility that characterizes events in general can sometimes result, as this example implies, from inherently unpredictable shifts in emotions. And its effects on the future can be extremely important: had the killing of de Launay led to a generalized slaughter of the soldiers who had defended the Bastille, the National Asembly might never have embraced the Parisians' actions as a sublime expression of the people's will and the modern category of revolution might never have come into being. Tracking down the causes and character of structural transformations in political events may require us to be particularly sensitive to the emotional tone of action.

Dislocation of structures, I have suggested, produces in actors a deep sense of insecurity, a real uncertainty about how to get on with life. I think that this uncertainty is a necessary condition for the kind of collective creativity that characterizes so many great historical events. In times of structural dislocation, ordinary routines of social life are open to doubt, the sanctions of existing power relations are uncertain or suspended, and new possibilities are thinkable. . . .

If the extended structural dislocations of 1789 led to widespread experimentation, the rearticulation of structures was accomplished above all at very particular places and times – at the Bastille and the city hall on July 14, in the reception ceremonies for the delegation from the National Assembly and for the king on July 15 and July 17, and in the meeting hall of the National Assembly on July 16, 20, and 23. These were moments when the pressure of rapidly unfolding actions and the massing of bodies in space led to emotionally-charged cultural improvisations that determined the shape of future history. These improvisations were genuinely collective. For example, the notion that the people itself rose up and conquered liberty at the Bastille was not the invention of one particular orator or journalist but a revelation arrived at by a collectivity of actors in the heat of the moment. The itinerary and gestures of the reception ceremonies of July 15 and 17 were made up on the spot. And the speeches that authoritatively established the events of July 14 as a legitimate revolution were not written out the night before, but were improvised by a succession of speakers in the heat of debate – on July 20 in a feverish effort to rebut Lally's blanket censure of political violence, and on July 23 in response to the shocking news of the murders of Bertier and Foullon.

. . . What is ritualistic about all the episodes I cite above is (1) that the actions constituting them are marked off as ritual by the actors and (2) that they align everyone present with the newly posited ultimate source of power: the people-as-nation. . . . Let me be more specific.

Once the Bastille had been captured, the elated victors celebrated their feat by spontaneously forming a triumphal procession. They marched through the streets to the city hall displaying trophies of their victory – captured weapons, freed prisoners, flags, and the defeated soldiers – to the assembled public. The triumphal procession was a preexisting military rite, but one that previously had displayed the armed might of the king's army – an army that was celebrating the defeat of foreign enemies, but that was always also a means of intimidating the king's subjects. In this case, however, an existing ritual form was adapted to a very different situation: the armed men had *defeated* the king's soldiers and in the processions they displayed themselves as members of the people/ nation through whose midst they were marching and whose accolades they accepted. They strategically produced an expedient scheme (the triumphal procession), thereby structuring the environment (the streets mobbed with ordinary citizens) in such a way that it (the assembled people, both marching and looking on) appeared to be the source of the schemes and their values (it was the people whose sovereign power made the triumph and celebration possible). This procession stated in highly dramatic and emotionally powerful terms the identity between the people and the armed force that had taken the Bastille. . . .

To a significant extent, then, the taking of the Bastille was created as a legitimate revolution through the performance of these spontaneous rituals. Most scholarly study of ritual focuses on religious rites of one kind or another. In most religious rituals, the participants are collected into a place marked off as sacred and then participate in a series of activities that induce a certain emotional state – quiet awe, rapt attention, terror, intense pleasure, or frenzied enthusiasm, as the case may be. In many cases, participants enter into what Victor Turner has called liminality – a state of "betwixt and between" in which social constraints and hierarchies momentarily evaporate and the celebrants experience a profound sense of community with one another and with the deity or dieties. It is the creation of this sense of *communitas* that gives rituals their psychological and social power. In episodes like those surrounding the taking of the Bastille, the usual process is reversed: rather than the ritual inducing the emotional excitement and the sense of communion, the emotional excitement and sense of communion – what Durkheim would call the collective effervescence – induce those present to express and concretize their feelings in ritual. The Parisians who participated in these events were massed in confined spaces and their emotions were excited by the crowding and by the memory – very recent in the episodes of the 14th, more distant on the 15th and 17th – of the battle fought and the victory won. They were also aware that they were participating in a momentous event, whose outcome could determine their future as individuals and as a nation. Finally, in the very course of the event, they discovered that they were members of the sovereign people, that their actions constituted a sacred collective will that rightfully determined the fate of the nation. They could manifest this state of liminality and communitas only by spontaneously appropriating known ritual forms to create new and powerful rituals of sovereignty. Through these rituals, the Parisians participated in the invention of the modern revolution.

chapter 5

Individual and Collective Agency

Introduction

Having seen in the preceding three chapters how Durkheim conceptualizes social structure, systems of symbolic classification, and collective emotions, all of which are important determinants of social interaction, we now step back to examine how individual and collective actors can, in turn, effect significant changes in those very frameworks. To some extent, this is a theme that was already foreshadowed in chapter 4, where our focus was upon the ritual processes whereby social actors agentically reproduce and, in certain cases, even transform the broader frameworks of social life within which they are embedded. But in the present chapter, our focus shifts all the more directly to the theme of transformative agency. In a brief extract from *The Elementary Forms of Religious Life* we see how moments of collective effervescence – both large and small, intermittent and more long-lasting – can empower individual as well as collective actors to alter the structural contexts within which they find themselves. And in a longer selection from *The Evolution of Educational Thought*, we see how Durkheim puts these theoretical insights to work by analyzing the historical role that the Jesuits played during one such period of collective effervescence – the Renaissance – in bringing about fundamental transformations in the French educational system. An excerpt by Pierre Bourdieu then introduces the general theme of "classification struggle," followed by a longer selection by Jeffrey Alexander that highlights one specific instance of a classification struggle – the Watergate scandal of the 1970s – and demonstrates the significance within it of (political) ritual processes. Together, these selections go a long way toward laying to rest the conventional image of Durkheimian analysis as essentially static and conservative, and show how certain of Durkheim's ideas can, in fact, help us to better understand the dynamics of social conflict and institutional change.

From *The Elementary Forms of Religious Life*

Emile Durkheim, *The Elementary Forms of Religious Life*, trans. Karen E. Fields (New York: Free Press, 1995), pp. 211–14.

A god is not only an authority to which we are subject but also a force that buttresses our own. The man who has obeyed his god, and who for this reason thinks he has his god with him, approaches the world with confidence and a sense of heightened energy. In the same way, society's workings do not stop at demanding sacrifices, privations, and efforts from us. The force of the collectivity is not wholly external; it does not move us entirely from outside. Indeed, because society can exist only in and by means of individual minds, it must enter into us and become organized within us. That force thus becomes an integral part of our being and, by the same stroke, uplifts it and brings it to maturity.

This stimulating and invigorating effect of society is particularly apparent in certain circumstances. In the midst of an assembly that becomes worked up, we become capable of feelings and conduct of which we are incapable when left to our individual resources. When it is dissolved and we are again on our own, we fall back to our ordinary level and can then take the full measure of how far above ourselves we were. History abounds with examples. Suffice it to think about the night of August 4 [Durkheim is probably alluding to the night of 4 August 1789, when France's new National Assembly ratified the total destruction of the feudal regime.], when an assembly was suddenly carried away in an act of sacrifice and abnegation that each of its members had refused to make the night before and by which all were surprised the morning after. For this reason all parties – be they political, economic, or denominational – see to it that periodic conventions are held, at which their followers can renew their common faith by making a public demonstration of it together. To strengthen emotions that would dissipate if left alone, the one thing needful is to bring all those who share them into more intimate and more dynamic relationship.

In the same way, we can also explain the curious posture that is so characteristic of a man who is speaking to a crowd – if he has achieved communion with it. His language becomes high-flown in a way that would be ridiculous in ordinary circumstances; his gestures take on an overbearing quality; his very thought becomes impatient of limits and slips easily into every kind of extreme. This is because he feels filled to overflowing, as though with a phenomenal oversupply of forces that spill over and tend to spread around him. Sometimes he even feels possessed by a moral force greater than he, of which he is only the interpreter. This is the hallmark of what has often been called the demon of oratorical inspiration. This extraordinary surplus of forces is quite real and comes to him from the very group he is addressing. The feelings he arouses as he speaks return to him enlarged and amplified, reinforcing his own to the same degree. The passionate energies that he arouses reecho in turn within him, and they increase his dynamism. It is then no longer a mere individual who speaks but a group incarnated and personified.

Apart from these passing or intermittent states, there are more lasting ones in which the fortifying action of society makes itself felt with longer-term consequences and often with more striking effect. Under the influence of some great collective shock in certain historical periods, social interactions become much more frequent and active. Individuals seek one another out and come together more. The result is the general effervescence that is characteristic of revolutionary or creative epochs. The result of that heightened activity is a general stimulation of individual energies. People live differently and more intensely than in normal times. The changes are not simply of nuance and degree; man himself becomes something other than what he was. He is stirred by passions so intense that they can be satisfied only by violent and extreme acts: by acts of superhuman heroism or bloody barbarism. This explains the Crusades, for example, as well as so many sublime or savage moments in the French Revolution. We see the most mediocre or harmless bourgeois transformed by the general exaltation into a hero or an executioner. And the mental processes are so clearly the same as those at the root of religion that the individuals themselves conceived the pressure they yielded to in explicitly religious terms. The Crusaders believed they felt God present among them, calling on them to go forth and conquer the Holy Land, and Joan of Arc believed she was obeying celestial voices.

This stimulating action of society is not felt in exceptional circumstances alone. There is virtually no instant of our lives in which a certain rush of energy fails to come to us from outside ourselves. In all kinds of acts that express the understanding, esteem, and affection of his neighbor, there is a lift that the man who does his duty feels, usually without being aware of it. But that lift sustains him; the feeling society has for him uplifts the feeling he has for himself. Because he is in moral harmony with his neighbor, he gains new confidence, courage, and boldness in action – quite like the man of faith who believes he feels the eyes of his god

turned benevolently toward him. Thus is produced what amounts to a
perpetual uplift of our moral being. Since it varies according to a multitude of external conditions – whether our relations with the social
groups that surround us are more or less active and what those groups
are – we cannot help but feel that this moral toning up has an external
cause, though we do not see where that cause is or what it is. So we readily conceive of it in the form of a moral power that, while immanent in
us, also represents something in us that is other than ourselves. This is
man's moral consciousness and his conscience. And it is only with the
aid of religious symbols that most have ever managed to conceive of it
with any clarity at all. . . .

From *The Evolution of Educational Thought*

Emile Durkheim, *The Evolution of Educational Thought: Lectures on the Formation and
Development of Secondary Education in France*, trans. Peter Collins (London: Routledge
and Kegan Paul, 1977), pp. 227–35, 250–1, 258–64, 265–7.

. . . [A]t the time of the Renaissance and as a consequence of changes in
economic and political organisation, all the peoples of Europe came to
feel the need of a new educational system. This resulted in an awaken-
ing of educational thought which was hitherto without precedent. The
most enlightened minds of the age, in order to meet the needs which public opinion experienced as pressing and which they themselves had been
the first to feel, posed the problem of education in all its generality and
undertook to solve it, using all the methods and the whole corpus of knowledge available at the time. Hence arose the great educational doctrines
whose principal features we have tried to delineate and which, all of them,
set themselves the goal of determining those principles according to
which the educational system should be reorganised so that it could enter
into harmony with the demands of the age.

As we find them expounded in the works of Erasmus, Rabelais, Vives
and Ramus, these doctrines are still only systems of ideals, conceptions
which are purely theoretical, schemes and plans for reconstruction. We
must now investigate what happened to them in practice, how these
theories fared when, emerging from the world of the ideal, they sought
to enter that of reality.

If it was the rule that educational doctrines become fully realised in the
self-same form in which they have been conceived by the thinkers who
propounded them, if academic reality did no more than faithfully to reflect

them, the question would only be of secondary interest. But I do not know of a single historical case where the ideal proposed by an educational theorist has passed in its entirety and without essential modifications into practice. . . . This is, in fact, because great educational theorists are most commonly extremists by temperament. They are vividly aware of what is lacking, of recently evolved needs which have not yet been satisfied. As for those needs which have long been receiving satisfaction, precisely because they make no demands, the theorists are only dimly aware of them and consequently they scarcely take them into account at all in constructing their systems. As a result the systems become one-sided and exclusive, needing, in order to become viable, to become more broadly based, to moderate their essentially simplistic tendencies, to open themselves up to concerns quite different from those which in the beginning provided almost their only source of inspiration. Educational ideas shed their initial intransigence when they make contact with reality, when they seek to become actualised. In order to understand what happens to them once they have entered the domain of practice we need to be familiar with them in the form in which they were conceived by the educational revolutionaries; for it was this that fermented the evolutionary process which brought them into being. But as against this, when this evolutionary process does not restrict itself to giving them an outer covering, a material and visible body, but rather transforms them as it actualises them, then it forms part of their internal history and on this account deserves quite special attention.

In the present case the question is all the more important because the educational theory of the Renaissance had posed a problem which it had left unanswered and which was to be resolved by actual practice alone. We have noted the existence of two different educational movements. For some, enamoured above all by knowledge, the principal aim of education was the fashioning of encyclopaedic intellects. Others, by contrast, delighting more in fine speech than in genuine learning, aimed first and foremost to mould the mind so that it would be polished, cultivated, sensible of the charms of fine language, of the refined pleasures to be enjoyed in intercourse with cultivated minds, and capable of taking an honourable part in it. Certainly these two movements never came into complete conflict with one another so that they were mutually exclusive; indeed there is not one from amongst the great geniuses of the Renaissance who did not, to a greater or lesser extent, come under the influence of both of them simultaneously. But at the same time the difference between them was too great for any one mind to be equally responsive to both of them. We have even seen that the educational value of the two viewpoints was very different. Rabelais is capable of appreciating the skill involved in a discourse constructed according to the rules since Eudémon, with whose gracefulness he contrasts the heavy clumsiness of

Gargantua, is a past master of this art; however, there is no doubt that literary preoccupations do not have overwhelming importance for him. Erasmus, for his part, is far from being contemptuous of learning, since he demands that the teacher possess extensive knowledge; but this knowledge for him is only a way of more effectively initiating the pupil into classical literature, of getting him to understand its beauties better and of teaching him to imitate them. Which of these two movements, with their rival claims for dominion over the minds of man, will triumph and leave its stamp on our system of schooling? The seriousness of the problem is apparent. Our national cast of mind had two paths open before it; depending on the one upon which it embarked it would emerge transformed in one of two quite different ways.

Nor is this all. We have seen that these two movements, in spite of the differences which separate them, nevertheless have one feature in common; this is that they are both the product of an aristocratic mentality. In both cases the qualities which it is important for the pupil to acquire are luxuries wholly lacking in utility value. If, as Erasmus claims, we must study classical literature, this is in order to become intellectually elegant, sophisticated in conversation and attractive as a writer. If Rabelais recommends an extensive education in the sciences it is not because, and in as far as, the sciences are useful; it is because in his view knowledge for its own sake is a fine thing. In both cases nobody seems to suspect that the function of education is first and foremost social, integrally bound up with other social functions, and that consequently it must prepare the child to take his place in society, play a useful part in life. To judge from the concept of education common to both movements we might well think that children are destined to a life spent entirely in the company of lords and ladies, just as the inhabitants of Thélème did, conversing learnedly or tenderly, exchanging well-turned observations or noble ideas, but never having to use their powers in the execution of specific tasks. We would not guess that at the same time there were men occupied in fulfilling specific social functions as artisans and merchants, as soldiers and priests, as magistrates and statesmen. But if education is not to prepare the child for any of these particular professions it must nevertheless equip him so that he can profitably take up whichever of them he chooses when the time comes.

Now, *a priori*, it would not seem rash to suppose that when these two educational theories passed from the realm of theory into that of practice they would necessarily divest themselves of this aristocratic character which so flawed them. When one is speculating in the quiet of one's study one can allow one's thoughts to roam in an ideal world where they encounter no resistance, and thus lose sight of the most immediate necessities of existence. But when one seeks to translate these speculations into actualities it is very difficult to avoid being awoken out of this kind of reverie; it is very difficult not to become aware that the serious business of living does not consist exclusively in the noble employment of leisure, that man is not just a work of art to be polished and sculpted. From this it would be reasonable to expect that the educational theory of the Renaissance, when it attempted to penetrate actual academic practice, would have been impelled to correct and transform itself. We might, for example, imagine that instead of demanding from the child useless erudition people would have realised the necessity of making a choice, and of teaching him only those subjects which were best suited either to developing his judgment or to guiding him in the conduct of his life; that instead of introducing him to classical civilisation solely in order to teach him to write and speak elegantly, they would have used it as a means of expanding his experience of men and of things, of acquainting him with a kind of humanity which was different from that which he saw around him and whose beliefs, practices and ways of thinking differed from those to which he was accustomed. I only cite these possible changes by way of example in order to show how the theories of the sixteenth century, without even modifying their essential principles, could nevertheless have acquired a novel aspect in response to an awareness of the necessities of life.

As we shall see, the way in which the problem was in fact resolved is almost the exact opposite of what, by analogy, we might have most reasonably expected. We were saying earlier that generally when an educational doctrine comes to be put into practice it is corrected and attenuated and sheds its original simplistic character. In direct contrast, the educational ideal of the Renaissance, as it became realised in practice, grew more exclusive, more extreme, more one-sided. The aristocratic and aesthetic character for which we have criticised it, far from moderating itself, only became more pronounced. Education became more foreign to the needs of real life. But let us not anticipate events; let us see how they unfolded.

Although the colleges of the University of Paris had been for centuries the refuge of Scholasticism, they opened up relatively quickly to the new thinking. . . .

In order to know what became of the educational theories of the Renaissance when they were translated into practice it would thus seem that we have only to investigate how the University understood them and applied them. But what makes such a procedure impossible, what makes the whole question more complicated, is the great change which took place at this very moment in our academic organisation. Up till that time the University had a complete monopoly and sole responsibility for education, and consequently the future of any educational reforms was dependent upon the University and upon the University alone. However, towards the middle of the sixteenth century, over and against the University corporation there was established a new teaching corporation which was to break the University's monopoly, and was even to achieve with quite remarkable rapidity a kind of hegemony in academic life. This was the corporation of the Jesuits.

The order of the Jesuits was generated by the need felt by the Catholic Church to check the increasingly threatening progress of Protestantism. With extraordinary speed the doctrines of Luther and Calvin had won over England, almost the whole of Germany, Switzerland, the Low Countries, Sweden, and a notable part of France. In spite of all the rigorous measures taken, the Church felt itself impotent and began to fear that its dominion in the world was collapsing completely. It was then that Ignatius Loyola had the idea of raising a wholly new kind of religious militia the better to combat heresy and if possible to crush it. He realised that the days were over when people's souls could be governed from the depths of a cloister. Now that people, carried by their own momentum, were tending to elude the Church it was essential that the Church should move closer to them so as to be able to influence them. Now that particular personalities were beginning to stand out from the homogeneous moral and intellectual mass which had been the rule in preceding centuries, it was essential to be close to individuals, in order to be able to exercise an influence over them which could be accommodated to intellectual and temperamental diversities. In short, the vast monastic masses familiar to the Middle Ages which, stationary at their post, had restricted themselves to repulsing such attacks as occurred, without knowing how to take the offensive themselves, had to be replaced by the establishment of an army of light troops who would be in constant contact with the enemy and consequently well-informed about all his movements. They would at the same time be sufficiently alert and mobile to be able to betake themselves anywhere where there was danger, at the slightest signal, while remaining sufficiently flexible to be able to vary their tactics in accordance with the diversity of people and circumstances. Moreover, they would do all this while always and everywhere pursuing the same goal and co-operating in the same grand design. This army was the Society of Jesus.

What was distinctive about it, in fact, was that it was able to contain within itself two characteristics which the Middle Ages had adjudged irreconcilable and contradictory. On the one hand, the Jesuits belong to a religious order in the same way as the Dominicans or the Franciscans; they have a head, they are all subject to one and the same rule, to a communal discipline; indeed passive obedience and unity of thought and action have never been carried to such an extreme degree in any militia, whether secular or religious. The Jesuit is thus a regular priest. But, on the other hand, he simultaneously possesses all the characteristics of the secular priest; he wears his habit; he fulfils his functions, he preaches, he hears confessions, he catechises; he does not live in the shadow of a monastery, he mingles rather in the life of the world. For him duty consists not in the mortification of the flesh, in fasting, in abstinence, but in action, in the realisation of the goal of the Society. . . .

Not only must the Jesuit mingle with the world, he must also open himself up to the ideas which are dominant within it. In order the better to be able to guide his age he must speak its language, he must assimilate its spirit. Ignatius Loyola sensed that a profound change had taken place in manners and that there was no going back on this; that a taste for well-being, for a less harsh, easier, sunnier existence had been acquired which could not conceivably be stifled or fobbed off; that man had developed a greater degree of pity for his own sufferings and for those of his fellow-men; he was more thrifty about pain, and consequently the old ideal of absolute renunciation was finished. To prevent the faithful from drifting away from religion the Jesuits devoted their ingenuity to divesting religion of its former austerity; they made it pleasant and devised all kinds of accommodating arrangements to make it easy to observe. It is true that in order to remain faithful to the mission which they had assigned themselves, to avoid seeming to encourage the innovators against whom they were struggling by their own example, they had at the same time to stick to the letter of immutable dogma. It is well known how they extricated themselves from this difficulty and were able to reconcile conflicting demands thanks to their casuistry, whose excessive flexibility and over-ingenious refinements have frequently been pointed out. While maintaining in their sacred form the traditional prescriptions of Roman Christianity, they were still able to place these within the scope not only of human weakness in general – there is no religion which has ever managed to escape this necessity – but even of the elegant frivolousness of the leisured classes of the sixteenth century, the leisured classes amongst whom it was so important to triumph against heresy and to preserve in the faith. This is how, while they became essentially men of the past, the defenders of the Catholic tradition, they were able to exhibit towards the ideas, the tastes and even the defects of the time an attitude of indulgence for which they have often been reproached, and not without reason. They thus had a dual identity as conservatives, reactionaries even, on the one hand, and as liberals on the other; a complex policy the nature and origins of which we needed to show here, for we shall encounter it again in the foundations of their educational theory.

They very quickly came to realise that in order to achieve their end it was not enough to preach, to hear confessions, to catechise: the really important instrument in the struggle for mastery of the human soul was the education of the young. Thus they resolved to seize hold of it. One fact in particular made them acutely aware of the urgent need for this. One would have had to be blind to all the evidence not to see that the new methods which were showing a strong tendency to take root in the schools could only have the effect of opening up the road to heresy. The greatest minds of the time, the most illustrious of the Humanists, had been seen openly to become converted to the new religion. . . . Thus it was a fact that Humanism of its very nature constituted a threat to the faith. It is clear that an inordinate taste for paganism was bound to cause people's minds to dwell in a moral environment which had absolutely nothing Christian about it. If this evil was to be attacked at source it would be necessary, instead of abandoning the Humanist movement to its own devices, to gain control of it and to direct it.

In itself this endeavour constituted a step backwards, a retrograde movement which was to put back the organisation of our schools by several centuries. From the beginning of our history we have seen education becoming progressively and consistently more secular. Born in the shadows of the churches and the monasteries, it gradually freed itself from them, and with the universities established itself as a special organ which was distinct from the Church and which, although it retained certain features reminiscent of its earliest origins, nevertheless in part retained a secular character. With the Jesuits we see the centre of academic life once again transported back to where it had been three or four centuries earlier, to the very bosom of the sanctuary. . . . [E]ducation was once again to be in the hands of a religious order.

Precisely because such an undertaking ran counter to the general direction of our academic evolution, it generated formidable resistance. The Jesuits had ranged against them all the great powers of the state, clergy, university and parliament, and yet they triumphed over all the obstacles which were strewn in their path. . . .

Far from seeking to get their pupils to think again the thoughts of antiquity, far from wishing to steep them in the spirit of classical times, one may say that the Jesuits selected for themselves precisely the opposite aim. This was because they could see no other way of extricating themselves from the contradictory situation in which they had quite deliberately placed themselves. Because the fashion was for Humanism, because classical letters were the object of a veritable cult, the Jesuits, always sensitive to the spirit of their age, professed, as we have just seen, a form of Humanism which was even quite uncompromising, since Greek and Latin alone were permitted entry into their colleges. But from another point of view, as we have said, they realised full well that Humanism constituted a threat to faith, that there was a real danger in wishing to fashion Christian souls in the school of paganism. How could these two contradictory needs be reconciled? How could the faith be defended and safeguarded as was required by the self-imposed mission of the Jesuits, while they simultaneously made themselves the apologists and exegetes of pagan literature?

There was only one way of resolving the antinomy: this was, in the very words used by Father Jouvency, to expound the classical authors in such a way "that they became, although pagan and profane, the eulogists of the faith". To make paganism serve the glorification and the propagation of the Christian ethic was a daring undertaking and, it would appear, remarkably difficult; and yet, the Jesuits had enough confidence in their ability to attempt it and to succeed in it. Only in order to do this they had deliberately to denature the ancient world; they had to show the authors of antiquity, the men they were and the men they portray for us, in such a way as to leave in the shadows everything which was genuinely pagan about them, everything which makes them men of a particular city at a particular time, in order to highlight only those respects in which they are simply men, men as they are at all times and in all places. All the legends, all the traditions, all the religious ideas of Rome and Greece were interpreted in this spirit, to give them a meaning which any good Christian could accept.

Thus the Greco-Roman environment in which they made their children live was emptied of everything specifically Greek or Roman. It became a kind of unreal, idealised environment peopled by personalities who had no doubt historically existed but who were presented in such a way that they had, so to speak, nothing historical about them. They were now simply figures betokening certain virtues and vices, and all the great passions of humanity. Achilles is courage; Ulysses is wily prudence; Numa is the archetype of the pious king; Caesar, the man of ambition; Augustus, powerful monarch and lover of learning. Such general and unspecific types could easily be used to exemplify the precepts of Christian morality.

This kind of disinheriting of antiquity was made easier for the Jesuits by the fact that, at least for a long time, all teaching of history was more or less completely absent from their colleges. Even literary history was unknown in them. The works of the writers were expounded without anyone bothering to notice the character of the author, his manner, the way he related to his age, to his environment, to his predecessors. His historical personality mattered so little that it was normal to study not an author, not even a work, but selected passages and extracts. How was it possible to form a picture of a specific man out of such sparse and disjointed fragments, amongst which his individuality was somehow dispersed and dissolved? Each of these pieces could scarcely appear to be anything other than an isolated model of literary style, as a sort of fair copy of exceptional authority.

We can now understand better how it came about that the Jesuits, and perhaps to a lesser extent so many other educators, tended to attribute to the past, and to the distant past, an educational value greater than that which they attributed to the present. This was because the past, at least at a time when the historical sciences had not advanced sufficiently to render it precise and specific almost to the same extent as is the present, the past, because we see it from afar, naturally appears to us in vague, fluid, unstable forms which it is all the more easy to mould according to our will. It constitutes a more malleable and plastic substance which we can even transform and present according to what suits us. It is thus easier to bend it for educational purposes. ... It was in this way that antiquity in the hands of the Jesuits could become an instrument for Christian education; they would not have been able to use the literature of their own age in the same way, imbued as it was with the spirit of rebellion against the Church. In order to attain their goal they had a powerful vested interest in fleeing from the moderns and taking refuge in antiquity.

So far we have only studied the Jesuits' teaching. We must now consider their disciplinary structures. It was perhaps in this area that they showed the most art and originality, and it was their superiority in this respect which best explains their success.

Their entire discipline was founded upon two principles.

The first was that there could be no good education without contact which was at once continuous and personal between the pupil and the educator. This principle served a double end. It ensured that the pupil was never left to his own devices. In order to mould him he had to be subjected to pressure which never let up or flagged; for the spirit of evil is constantly watchful. This is why the Jesuits' pupil was never alone: "A supervisor would follow him everywhere, to church, to class, to the refectory, to his recreation; in the living quarters and sleeping quarters he was always there, examining everything." But his supervision was not intended only to prevent misconduct. It was also to enable the Jesuit to study at his ease "character and habits, so that he might manage to discover the most suitable method of directing each individual child". In other words, this direct and constant intercourse was supposed not only to render the educational process more sustained in its effect but also to make it more personal and better suited to the personality of each pupil. Father Jouvency never stops recommending teachers not to limit themselves to exerting a general and impersonal influence on the anonymous crowd of pupils but to graduate his influence and to vary it according to age, intelligence and situation. If he is conversing with a child in private, "let him examine the child's character so that he can mould what he says in accordance with it and, as they say, 'hook' his interlocutor with the appropriate bait". In order the better to get the pupils to open their minds to him, he will need to get them to open their hearts by making himself loved. Indeed there can be no doubt that in the course of the relationships which were thus cemented between teachers and pupils there frequently formed bonds of friendship which survived school life. Thus Descartes remained very sincerely attached to his former teachers at La Flèche.

One can readily imagine how effective this system of continuous immersion must have been. The child's environment followed him wherever he went; all around him he heard the same ideas and the same sentiments being expressed with the same authority. He could never lose sight of them. He knew of no others. And in addition to the fact that this influence never ceased to make itself felt, it was also all the more powerful because it knew how best to adapt to the diversity of individual personalities, because it was most familiar with the openings through which it could slip in and insinuate itself in the pupil's heart. By comparison with the disciplinary style which had been practised in the Middle Ages it represented a major revolution. The mediaeval teacher addressed himself to large and impersonal audiences, amongst which each individual, that is to say each student, was lost, drowned and consequently abandoned to his own devices. Now education is essentially an individual matter. As long as it was dealing with vast masses it could yield only very crude results. Hence the rowdy discipline of the students of the Middle Ages, in an attempt to counter which the residential colleges were instituted even though they were never fully successful. For the colleges did not have at their disposal a staff of teachers and supervisors who were sufficiently numerous or perhaps sufficiently committed to the task of supervision to be able to exercise the necessary control and influence over each individual.

In order to train pupils in intensive formal work which was, however, pretty lacking in substance, it was not enough to surround them, to envelop them at close quarters with solicitude and vigilance; it was not enough to be constantly concerned to contain and to sustain them: it was also necessary to stimulate them. The goad which the Jesuits employed consisted exclusively in competition. Not only were they the first to organise the competitive system in the colleges, but they also developed it to a point of greater intensity than it has ever subsequently known.

Although today in our classrooms this system still has considerable importance, nevertheless it no longer functions without interruption. It is fair to say that with the Jesuits it was never suspended for a single moment. The entire class was organised to promote this end. The pupils were divided into two camps, the Romans on the one hand and the Carthaginians on the other, who lived, so to speak, on the brink of war, each striving to outstrip the other. Each camp had its own dignitaries. At the head of the camp there was an *imperator* also known as dictator or consul, then came a *praetor*, a tribune and some senators. These honours, which were naturally coveted and contested, were distributed as the outcome of a competition which was held monthly. From another point of view, each camp was divided into groups consisting of ten pupils (*decuries*) each, commanded by a captain (called the *decurion*) who was selected from amongst the worthies we have just mentioned. These groups were not recruited at random. There was a hierarchy amongst them. The first groups were composed of the best pupils, the last groups of the weakest and least industrious of the scholars. Just as the camp as a whole was in competition with the opposite camp, so in each camp each group had its own immediate rival in the other camp at the equivalent level. Finally, individuals themselves were matched, and each soldier in a group had his opposite number in the opposing group. Thus academic work involved a kind of perpetual hand-to-hand combat. Camp challenged camp, group struggled with group, supervised one another, corrected one another, and took one another to task. On some occasions the teacher was not supposed to be afraid of pitting together two pupils of unequal ability. For example a pupil would have his work corrected by a less able pupil, says Father Jouvency, "so that those who have made mistakes may be more ashamed and the more mortified about them". It was even possible for any individual to do battle with a pupil from a higher group and, if victorious, to take his place.

It is interesting to note that these various ennoblements carried with them not only honorific titles but also active functions; and indeed it was these that constituted the prize. The captain enjoyed extensive powers. Seated opposite his group he was responsible for ensuring silence and attentiveness amongst his ten scholars; he noted down absences, made them recite their lessons, and ensured that assignments had been done with care and completed. The consuls exercised the same authority over the captains in their camp as did these over their own group members. Everyone was thus kept constantly in suspense. Never has the idea that the class is a small organised society been realised to systematically. It was a city state where every pupil was a functionary. It was, moreover, thanks to this division of labour between the teacher and the pupils that one teacher was able without too much difficulty to run classes which sometimes numbered as many as two or three hundred pupils.

In addition to such methods of chronically recurring competition there were intermittent competitions too numerous to enumerate.... [A]n infinite wealth of devices maintained the self-esteem of the pupils in a constant state of extreme excitation.

Here again the Jesuits were effecting a revolution compared with what had gone before. We have seen that in the University and the colleges of the Middle Ages the system of competition was completely unknown. In those days there were no rewards to recompense merit and induce effort. Examinations were organised in such a way that for conscientious pupils they were little more than a formality. Then here we have, quite suddenly, a totally different system, which not only establishes itself but which instantaneously develops to the point of super-abundance. It is easier to understand now how the training given by the Jesuits managed to acquire the intensive character which we were recently remarking upon. Their entire system of discipline was organised towards this goal. The state of constant competition in which the pupils lived incited them to strain all the resources of their intelligence and will-power and even rendered this essential. At the same time the careful supervision to which they were subjected diminished the possibility of lapses. They felt themselves guided, sustained, encouraged. Everything was inducing them to exert themselves. As a result within the colleges there was genuinely intensive activity, which was no doubt flawed by being expended on the superficial rather than on the profound, but whose existence was incontestable.

Now that we have noted the transformations which the Jesuits initiated in the realm of school discipline, we must seek for the causes. Where did these two new principles come from? Did they derive exclusively from the particular aim which the Jesuits were pursuing, from the very nature of their institution, from the mission which they had assigned themselves; or were they not, by contrast, rather the effect of more general causes, were they not a response to some change which had occurred in public thought and ethics?

What must immediately rule out the first hypothesis is the fact that if the Jesuits were the first to realise these principles in academic practice, they had nevertheless been already recognised and proclaimed by the educational thinkers of the Renaissance. . . . The Jesuits were thus on these two points, at least in principle, in agreement with their time. . . .

It was the fact that a great change had taken place in the moral constitution of society, which rendered necessary this double change in the system of academic discipline. In the seventeenth century the individual played a much greater part in social life than that which had been accorded to him hitherto. If, in the Middle Ages, teaching was impersonal, if it could be addressed diffusely to the indistinct crowd of pupils without any disadvantage being experienced, this was because at that time the notion of individual personality was still relatively undeveloped. The movements which occur in the Middle Ages are mass movements which carry along large groupings of human beings in the same direction, and in the midst of which individuals become lost. It was Europe in its entirety which rose up at the time of the Crusades; it was the whole of cultivated European society which soon afterwards, under the influence of a veritable collective urge, flooded towards Paris to receive instruction. The didactic style of the time thus accorded with the moral condition of society.

With the Renaissance, by contrast, the individual began to acquire self-consciousness. He was no longer, at least in enlightened circles, merely an undifferentiated fraction of the whole; he was himself already, in a sense, a whole, he was a person with his own physiognomy who had and

who experienced at least the need to fashion for himself his own way of
thinking and feeling. We know that at this period there occurred, as it
were, a sudden blossoming of great personalities. Now, it is quite clear
that in proportion as people's consciousness becomes individualised
education itself must become individualised. From the moment it is
required to exert its influence on distinct and heterogeneous individuals
it cannot continue to develop in blanket fashion, homogeneously and
uniformly. It had to diversify; and this was possible only if the educator,
instead of remaining distant from the pupil, came close to him in order
to get to know him better and to be able to vary his actions according to
the diverse natures of individuals. . . .

. . . Since the moral organisation of the school must reflect that of civil
society, since the methods which are applied to the child cannot differ
in essence from those which, later on, will be applied to the man, it is
clear that the processes of the mediaeval disciplinary system could not
survive; it is clear that discipline had to become more personal and take
greater account of individual feelings, and consequently allow for a degree
of competitiveness.

There was thus nothing intrinsically arbitrary about the two innovations which the Jesuits introduced into the disciplinary system: the principle, at least, was well-grounded in the nature of things, that is to say
the condition of society in the sixteenth century. But if the principle was
right, if it was to be retained, if it deserved to survive, the Jesuits applied
it in a spirit of extremism which is one of the features of their academic
policy and, in simply doing this, they denatured it. It was good to keep
close to the child in order to be able to guide him confidently; the Jesuits
came so close to him that they inhibited all his freedom of movement. In
this way the method worked against the end which it should have been
serving. It was wise to get to know the child well in order to be able to
help in the development of his nascent personality. The Jesuits studied
him rather in order to stifle more effectively his sense of himself; and this
was a potential source of schism. At least, once they had recognised the
value of rivalry and competitiveness, they made such immoderate use of
them that the pupils lived in relationship to one another on a veritable
war footing. How can we fail to consider immoral an academic organisation which appealed only to egotistical sentiments? Was there then no
means of keeping the pupils active other than by tempting them with such
paltry bait?

. . . The University teachers themselves were good Christians and good
Catholics, and regarded it as part of their professional duty to work for
the maintenance and development of religious awareness. But because of
the way they viewed religion, religious education did not strike them as

being a complicated task; they regarded it as the natural and logical crowning achievement of classical education properly understood. . . .

The case was quite different with Jesuits. They were acutely aware of the distance which separates these two civilisations, that they imply different orientations of the will and that it is impossible to rise from the one to the other without making a dramatic break. For them, the study of antiquity could only be a preliminary, a valid preparation for the Christian life. Of course they made use of antiquity; but they used it as a wind-break behind which they could shelter in order to construct a highly sophisticated piece of machinery designed to master the pupil's will and to instil in him the attitude of mind which the interests of the faith seemed to them to demand. This is why their system of discipline was much more personal than their system of teaching. It is because discipline provides the ideal basis for the nurturing of the will. . . .

If we disregard the education of the will and consider only the education of the intelligence, that is teaching in the narrow sense, we can see how the differences between the two competing systems were ultimately of only secondary importance. Both corporations were pursuing roughly the same ideal, the Jesuits with more stringency, vigour and single-mindedness, the University teachers with a greater degree of moderation, a more lively awareness of the complexity of the problem; and also perhaps with less professional ardour. In both cases the important thing was to teach the art of writing by imitation of the ancients. In both cases in order to be able exploit antiquity in this way it had to be uprooted, detached from its historical setting so that the Greeks and the Romans were portrayed as impersonal models belonging to all ages and all nations.

The similarity between these two types of education was finally completed when the University teachers, confronted by the success of their rivals, finally came to adopt their methods. . . .

The *ancien régime* up to the second half of the eighteenth century, when new ideas were coming to light, thus really knew only one intellectual ideal, and it was on the basis of this ideal that French youth was moulded for more than two hundred years. . . .

From *Distinction: A Social Critique of the Judgment of Taste*
Pierre Bourdieu

Pierre Bourdieu, *Distinction: A Social Critique of the Judgment of Taste*, trans. Richard Nice (Cambridge, MA: Harvard University Press, 1984), pp. 479–81.

Principles of division, inextricably logical and sociological, function within and for the purposes of the struggle between social groups; in producing concepts, they produce groups, the very groups which produce the principles and the groups against which they are produced. What is at stake in the struggles about the meaning of the social world is power over the classificatory schemes and systems which are the basis of the representations of the groups and therefore of their mobilization and demobilization: the evocative power of an utterance which puts things in a different light (as happens, for example, when a single word, such as "paternalism", changes the whole experience of a social relationship) or which modifies the schemes of perception, shows something else, other properties, previously unnoticed or relegated to the background (such as common interests hitherto masked by ethnic or national differences); a separative power, a distinction, *diacrisis, discretio,* drawing discrete units out of indivisible continuity, difference out of the undifferentiated.

Only in and through the struggle do the internalized limits become boundaries, barriers that have to be moved. And indeed, the system of classificatory schemes is constituted as an objectified, institutionalized system of classification only when it has ceased to function as a sense of limits so that the guardians of the established order must enunciate, systematize and codify the principles of production of that order, both real and represented, so as to defend them against heresy; in short, they must constitute the doxa as orthodoxy. Official systems of classification, such as the theory of the three orders, do explicitly and systematically what the classificatory schemes did tacitly and practically. Attributes, in the sense of predicates, thereby become *attributions,* powers, capacities, privileges, prerogatives, attributed to the holder of a post, so that war is no longer what the warrior does, but the *officium,* the specific function, the raison d'être, of the *bellator*. Classificatory *discretio*, like law, freezes a certain state of the power relations which it aims to fix forever by enunciating and codifying it. The classificatory system as a principle of logical and political division only exists and functions because it reproduces, in a transfigured form, in the symbolic logic of differential gaps, i.e., of discontinuity, the generally gradual and continuous differences which structure the established order; but it makes its own, that is, specifically symbolic, contribution to the maintenance of that order only because it has the specifically symbolic power to make people see and believe which is given by the imposition of mental structures.

Systems of classification would not be such a decisive object of struggle if they did not contribute to the existence of classes by enhancing the efficacy of the objective mechanisms with the reinforcement supplied by representations structured in accordance with the classification. The imposition of a recognized name is an act of recognition of full social existence which transmutes the thing named. It no longer exists merely de facto, as a tolerated, illegal or illegitimate practice, but becomes a *social* function, i.e., a mandate, a mission (*Beruf*), a task, a role – all words which express the difference between authorized activity, which is assigned to an individual or group by tacit or explicit delegation, and mere usurpation, which creates a "state of affairs" awaiting institutionalization. But the specific effect of "collective representations", which, contrary to what the Durkheimian connotations might suggest, may be the product of the application of the same scheme of perception or a common system of classification while still being subject to antagonistic social uses, is most clearly seen when the word precedes the thing, as with voluntary associations that turn into recognized professions or corporate defence groups (such as the trade union of the "cadres"), which progressively impose the representation of their existence and their unity, both on their own members and on other groups.

A group's presence or absence in the official classification depends on its capacity to get itself recognized, to get itself noticed and admitted, and so to win a place in the social order. It thus escapes from the shadowy existence of the "nameless crafts" of which Emile Benveniste speaks: business in antiquity and the Middle Ages, or illegitimate activities, such as those of the modern healer (formerly called an "empiric"), bone-setter or prostitute. The fate of groups is bound up with the words that designate them: the power to impose recognition depends on the capacity to mobilize around a name, "proletariat", "working class", "cadres" etc., to appropriate a common name and to commune in a proper name, and so to mobilize the union that makes them strong, around the unifying power of a word.

In fact, the order of words never exactly reproduces the order of things. It is the relative independence of the structure of the system of classifying, classified words (within which the distinct value of each particular label is defined) in relation to the structure of the distribution of capital, and more precisely, it is the time-lag (partly resulting from the inertia inherent in classification systems as quasi-legal institutions sanctioning a state of a power relation) between changes in jobs, linked to changes in the productive apparatus, and changes in titles, which creates the space for symbolic strategies aimed at exploiting the discrepancies between the nominal and the real, appropriating words so as to get the things they designate, or appropriating things while waiting to get the words that sanction them; exercising responsibilities without having entitlement to do so, in order to acquire the right to claim the legitimate titles, or, conversely, declining the material advantages associated with devalued titles so as to avoid losing the symbolic advantages bestowed by more prestigious labels or, at least, vaguer and more manipulable ones; donning the most flattering of the available insignia, verging on imposture if need be – like the potters who call themselves "art craftsmen", or technicians who claim to be engineers – or inventing new labels, like physiotherapists (*kinésithérapeutes*) who count on this new title to separate them from mere masseurs and bring them closer to doctors. All these strategies, like all processes of competition, a paperchase aimed at ensuring constant distinctive gaps, tend to produce a steady inflation of titles – restrained by the inertia of the institutionalized taxonomies (collective agreements, salary scales etc.) – to which legal guarantees are attached. The negotiations between antagonistic interest groups, which arise from the establishment of collective agreements and which concern, inseparably, the tasks entailed by a given job, the properties required of its occupants (e.g., diplomas) and the corresponding advantages, both material and symbolic (the name), are an institutionalized, theatrical version of the incessant struggles over the classifications which help to produce the classes, although these classifications are the product of the struggles between the classes and depend on the power relations between them.

From "Culture and Political Crisis: 'Watergate' and Durkheimian Sociology" Jeffrey C. Alexander

Jeffrey C. Alexander, ed., *Durkheimian Sociology* (Cambridge: Cambridge University Press, 1988), pp. 193–209.

In June 1972, employees of the Republican Party made an illegal entry and burglary into the Democratic Party headquarters in the Watergate

Hotel in Washington, DC. . . . With important exceptions, the mass news media decided after a short time to play down the story, not because they were coercively prevented from doing so but because they genuinely felt it to be a relatively unimportant event. Watergate remained, in other words, part of the profane world in Durkheim's sense. . . . Two years later, this same incident, still called "Watergate," had initiated the most serious peacetime political crisis in American history. It had become a riveting moral symbol, one which initiated a long passage through sacred time and space and wrenching conflict between pure and impure sacred forms. It was responsible for the first president voluntarily to resign his office. . . .

If we look at the two-year transformation of the context of Watergate, we see the creation and resolution of a fundamental social crisis, a resolution that involved the deepest ritualization of political life. To achieve this "religious" status, there had to be an extraordinary generalization of opinion *vis-à-vis* a political threat that was initiated by the very center of established power and a successful struggle not just against that power in its social form but against the powerful cultural rationales it mobilized. To understand this process of crisis creation and resolution we must integrate Durkheim's ritual theory with a more muscular theory of social structure and process. Let me lay these factors out generally before I indicate how each became involved in the instance of Watergate.

What must happen for a society to experience fundamental crisis and ritual renewal?

First, there has to be sufficient social consensus so that an event will be considered polluting, or deviant, by more than a mere fragment of the population. Only with sufficient consensus, in other words, can "society" itself be aroused and indignant.

Second, there has to be the perception by significant groups who participate in this consensus that the event is not only deviant but that its pollution threatens the "center" of society.

Third, if this deep crisis is to be resolved, institutional social controls must be brought into play. However, even legitimate attacks on the polluting sources of crisis are often viewed as frightening. For this reason, such controls also mobilize instrumental force and the threat of force to bring polluting forces to heel.

Fourth, social control mechanisms must be accompanied by the mobilization and struggle of elites and publics which are differentiated and relatively autonomous from the structural center of society. Through this process there begins to be the formation of counter-centers.

Finally, fifth, there have to be effective processes of symbolic interpretation, that is, ritual, and purification processes that continue the labeling process and enforce the strength of the symbolic, sacred center of society at the expense of a center which is increasingly seen as merely

structural, profane, and impure. In so doing, such processes demonstrate
conclusively the deviant or "transgressive" qualities that are the sources
of this threat.

In elaborating how each one of these five factors came into play in
the course of Watergate, I will be indicating how, in a complex society,
reintegration and symbolic renewal are far from being automatic processes. Much more than a simple reading of Durkheim's work might
imply, reintegration and renewal rely on the contingent outcomes of specific
historical circumstances.

First, the factor of consensus. . . .

During the summer of 1972 one can trace a very complex symbolic development in the American collective conscience, a consensual development
that laid the basis for everything that followed even while it did not produce consensus at more social levels. It was during this four-month
period that the meaning complex of "Watergate" came to be defined.
In the first weeks which followed the break-in to the Democratic headquarters, "Watergate" existed, in semiotic terms, merely as a sign. The
word simply denoted a single event. In the weeks that followed, this
sign became more complex, referring to a series of interrelated events
touched off by the break-in, including charges of political corruption, presidential denials, legal suits, and arrests. By August of 1972, "Watergate"
had become transformed from a mere sign to a redolent symbol, a
word that rather than denoting actual events connoted multifold moral
meanings.

Watergate had become a symbol of pollution, embodying a sense
of evil and impurity. In structural terms, the things directly associated
with Watergate – those who were immediately associated with the crime,
the apartment complex, the persons implicated later – were placed on the
negative side of a polarized symbolic classification. Those persons or
institutions responsible for ferreting out and arresting these criminal
elements were placed on the other, positive side. This bifurcated model
of pollution and purity was then superimposed onto the traditional
good/evil structure of American civil religion, whose relevant elements
appear in the following form. It is clear, then, that while significant
symbolic structuring had occurred, the "center" of the American social
structure was in no way implicated. . . .

This symbolic development, it should be emphasized, occurred in the
public mind. Few Americans would have disagreed about the moral meanings of "Watergate" as a collective representation. Yet, while the social
basis of this symbol was widely inclusive, the symbol just about
exhausted the meaning complex of Watergate as such. While the term
identified a complex of events and people with moral evil, the collective
consciousness did not connect this symbol to particular significant social
roles or institutional behaviors. Neither the Republican Party, President

Nixon's staff, nor, least of all, President Nixon himself had yet been polluted by the symbol of Watergate. . . .

Yet in the six months following the election the situation began to be reversed. First, consensus began to emerge. The end of an intensely divisive election period allowed a realignment to begin which had been building at least for two years prior to Watergate. The social struggles of the 60s had long been over and many issues had been taken over by centrist groups. Critical universalism had been readopted by these centrist forces without it being linked to the specific ideological themes or goals of the Left. With this emerging consensus, the possibility for common feelings of moral violation emerged and with it began the movement towards generalization *vis-à-vis* political goals and interests. Now, once this first resource of consensus had become available, the other developments I mentioned could be activated.

The second and third factors I mentioned were anxiety about the center and the invocation of institutional social control. Developments in the post-election months provided a much safer and less "political" atmosphere for the operation of social controls. I am thinking here of the activity of the courts, of the Justice Department, of various bureaucratic agencies, and special congressional committees. The very operation of these social control institutions legitimated the media's efforts to extend the Watergate pollution closer to central institutions. It reinforced public doubt about whether Watergate was, in fact, only a limited crime. It also forced more facts to surface. Of course, at this point the ultimate level of generality and seriousness of Watergate remained undetermined. With this new public legitimation, and the beginnings of generalization it implied, fears that Watergate might pose a threat to the center of American society began to spread to significant publics and elites. The question about proximity to the center preoccupied every major group during this early post-election Watergate period. . . . It further rationalized the invocation of coercive social control. Finally, in structural terms, it began to realign the "good" and "bad" sides of the Watergate symbolization. Which side were Nixon and his staff really on?

The fourth factor I mentioned was elite conflict. Throughout this period, the generalization process – pushed by consensus, by the fear for the center, and by the activities of new institutions of social control – was fueled by a desire for revenge against Nixon by alienated institutional elites. These elites had represented "leftism" or simply "sophisticated cosmopolitanism" to Nixon during his first four years in office, and they had been the object of his legal and illegal attempts at suppression or control. They included journalists and newspapers, intellectuals, universities, scientists, lawyers, religionists, foundations, and, last but not least, authorities in various public agencies and the U.S. Congress. Motivated by a desire to get even, to revive their threatened status, and to defend their universalistic values, these elites moved to establish themselves as counter-centers in the years of crisis.

By May of 1973, then, all of these forces for crisis creation and resolution were in motion. Significant changes in public opinion had been mobilized and powerful structural resources were being brought into play. It is only at this point that the fifth crisis factor could emerge. These were the deep processes of ritualism – sacralization, pollution, and purification – though there had certainly already been important symbolic developments as well.

The first fundamental ritual process of the Watergate crisis involved the Senate Select Committee's televised hearings, which began in May and continued through August. This event had significant repercussions on the symbolic patterning of the entire affair. The decision to hold and to televise the Senate Select Committee hearings responded to the tremendous anxiety that had built up within important segments of the population. The symbolic process that ensued functioned to canalize this anxiety in certain distinctive, more generalized, and more consensual directions. The hearings constituted a kind of civic ritual which revivified very general yet nonetheless very crucial currents of critical universalism and rationality in the American political culture. It recreated the sacred, generalized morality upon which more mundane conceptions of office are based, and it did so by invoking the mythical level of national understanding in a way that few other events have in postwar history. . . .

The televised hearings, in the end, constituted a liminal experience . . . one radically separated from the profane issues and mundane grounds of everyday life. A ritual communitas was created for Americans to share, and within this reconstructed community none of the polarizing issues which had generated the Watergate crisis, or the historical justification which had motivated it, could be raised. Instead, the hearings revivified the civic religion upon which democratic conceptions of "office" have depended throughout American history. . . .

If achieving the form of modern ritual is contingent, so is explicating the content, for modern rituals are not nearly so automatically coded as earlier ones. Within the context of the sacred time of the hearings, administration witnesses and senators struggled for moral legitimation, for definitional or ritual superiority and dominance. The end result was in no sense preordained. It depended on successful symbolic work. To describe this symbolic work is to embark on the ethnography, or hermeneutics, of televised ritual. . . .

The hearings ended without laws or specific judgments of evidence, but they had, nevertheless, profound effects. They helped to establish and fully to legitimate a framework that henceforth gave the Watergate crisis its meaning. They accomplished this by continuing and deepening the cultural process which had begun before the election itself. Actual events and characters in the Watergate episode were organized in terms of the higher antitheses between the pure and the impure elements of America's civil religion. Before the hearings "Watergate" already symbolized the structured antitheses of American mythical life, antitheses which were implicitly linked by the American people to the structure of their civil religion. What the hearings accomplished, first, was to make this linkage to civil religion explicit and pronounced. The "good guys" of the Watergate process – their actions and motives – were purified in the resacralization process through their identification with the Constitution, norms of fairness, and citizen solidarity. The perpetrators of Watergate, and the themes which they evoked as justification, were polluted by association with civil symbols of evil: sectarianism, self-interest, particularistic loyalty. As this description implies, moreover, the hearings also restructured the linkages between Watergate elements and the nation's political center. Many of the most powerful men surrounding President Nixon were now implacably associated with Watergate evil, and some of Nixon's most outspoken enemies were linked to Watergate good. As the structural and symbolic centers of the civil religion were becoming so increasingly differentiated, the American public found the presidential party and the elements of civic sacredness more and more difficult to bring together. . . .

The year-long crisis which followed the hearings was punctuated by episodes of moral convulsion and public anger, by renewed ritualization, by the further shifting of symbolic classification to include the structural center, and by the further expansion of the solidary base of this symbolism to include most of the significant segments of American society. . . .

The impeachment hearings conducted by the House Judiciary Committee in June and July of 1974 marked the most solemn and formalized ritual of the entire Watergate episode. It was the closing ceremony, a rite of expulsion in which the body politic rid itself of the last and most menacing source of sacred impurity. By the time of these hearings the symbolization of Watergate was already highly developed; in fact, Watergate had become not only a symbol with significant referents but a powerful metaphor whose self-evident meaning itself served to define unfolding events. The meaning structure associated with "Watergate," moreover, now unequivocally placed a vast part of White House and "center" personnel on the side of civil pollution and evil. The only question which remained was whether President Nixon himself would officially be placed alongside them as well. . . .

. . . [T]his committee, like its Senate counterpart one year before, existed in a liminal, detached place. They, too, operated within sacred time, their deliberations continuous not with the immediate partisan past but with the great constitutive moments of the American republic: the signing of the Bill of Rights, the framing of the Constitution, the crisis of the Union which marked the Civil War.

This aura of liminal transcendence moved many of the most conservative members of the committee, Southerners whose constituents had voted for Nixon by landslide proportions, to act out of conscience rather than political expediency. The Southern bloc, indeed, formed the key to the coalition which voted for three articles of impeachment. These final articles, revealingly, purposefully eschewed a fourth article, earlier proposed by liberal Democrats, which condemned Nixon's secret bombing of Cambodia. Though this earlier article referred to a real violation of law, it was an issue that was interpreted by Americans in specifically political terms, terms about which they widely disagreed. The final three impeachment articles, by contrast, referred only to fully generalized issues. At stake was the code that regulated political authority, the question of whether impersonal obligations of office can and should control personal interest and behavior. It was Nixon's violation of office obligations which made the House vote his impeachment. . . .

part 3

The Institutional Order of Modern Societies

chapter 6

The Modern State

Introduction

Durkheim can be said to have devoted close and systematic attention to three different institutions or institutional complexes within modern society: the modern state, the modern economy, and what many social thinkers today call civil society. The present chapter draws together Durkheim's most important insights into the first of these three institutional realms. It begins with two brief excerpts (from *The Division of Labor*) on the modern state's deep rootedness within the social order – but also its potential autonomy with regard to that social order. One can easily discern here the significance of culture and collective emotions in Durkheim's assertion that the state's "first and foremost function is . . . to defend the common consciousness from all its enemies" (p. 168). One can also recognize the importance of social structure in his arguments regarding the historical linkages between the development of the modern state and the evolution of the division of labor. An excerpt from "Two Laws of Penal Evolution" continues this line of analysis, distinguishing between a strong state (under circumstances of the division of labor) and an absolutist or despotic one (arising from "individual, transitory, and contingent conditions" only (p. 172)). The remaining Durkheim extracts are all from *Professional Ethics and Civic Morals*. Durkheim elaborates there a highly distinctive definition of the state; he argues that "It is only through the State that individualism is possible," and presents the distinguishing characteristics of a "democratic" state (p. 184). Two excerpts by later writers then illustrate the very different directions in which Durkheimian ideas about the state can be developed. One, by Antonio Gramsci, analyzes the modern state in terms of the dynamics of class conflict and links its educative role (also discussed by Durkheim) to the maintenance of the political hegemony of the dominant social class. The other, by Robert Bellah, presents a more liberal democratic image of the modern state, in this case the US state, by linking it to "a set of beliefs, symbols, and rituals with respect to sacred things" – a "civil religion" (p. 190) – in which are celebrated and ongoingly reaffirmed the modern ideals of freedom, equality, and community.

From *The Division of Labor in Society*

Emile Durkheim, *The Division of Labor in Society*, trans. W. D. Halls (New York: Free Press, 1984), pp. 42–3, 167–70.

... [W]herever an authority with power to govern is established its first and foremost function is to ensure respect for beliefs, traditions and collective practices – namely, to defend the common consciousness from all its enemies, from within as well as without. It thus becomes the symbol of that consciousness, in everybody's eyes its living expression. Consequently the energy immanent within the consciousness is communicated to that authority, just as affinities of ideas are transmitted to the words they represent. This is how the authority assumes a character that renders it unrivalled. It is no longer a social function of greater or lesser importance, it is the embodiment of the collectivity. Thus it partakes of the authority that the collectivity exercises over the consciousness of individuals, and from this stems its strength. Yet once this strength has arisen, not breaking free from the source from which it derives and on which it continues to feed, it nevertheless becomes a factor of social life which is autonomous, capable of producing its own spontaneous actions. Precisely because of the hegemony this strength has acquired, these actions are totally independent of any external impulsion. On the other hand, since it is merely derived from the power immanent in the common consciousness, it necessarily possesses the same properties and reacts in similar fashion, even when the common consciousness does not react entirely in unison. ...

... The state that Spencer holds up as an ideal is in reality the state in its primitive form. Indeed, according to the English philosopher, the sole functions peculiar to it are those of justice and war, at least in so far as war is necessary. In lower societies it has in fact no other role. Doubtless these functions are not understood in the same way as they are nowadays, but they are no different because of that. That entirely tyrannical intervention that Spencer points to is only one of the ways in which judicial power is exercised. By repressing attacks on religion, etiquette, or traditions of every kind the state fulfils the same office as do our judges today when they protect the life or property of individuals. On the other hand, the state's attributions become ever more numerous and diverse as one approaches the higher types of society. The organ of justice itself, which in the beginning is very simple, begins increasingly to become differentiated. Different law-courts are instituted as well as distinctive magistratures, and the respective roles of both are determined, as well as the relationships between them. A host of functions that were diffuse become more concentrated. The task of watching over the education of the young, protecting health generally, presiding over the functioning of the public assistance system or managing the transport and communications systems gradually falls within the province of the central body. As a result that body develops. At the same time it extends progressively over the whole area of its territory an ever more densely packed, complex network, with branches that are substituted for existing local bodies or that assimilate them. Statistical services keep it up to date with all that is happening in the innermost parts of the organism. The mechanism of international relations – by this is meant diplomacy – itself assumes still greater proportions. As institutions are formed, which like the great establishments providing financial credit are of general public interest by their size and the multiplicity of functions linked to them, the state exercises over them a moderating influence. Finally, even the military apparatus, which Spencer asserts is disappearing, seems on the contrary to develop, becoming ever more centralised.

This evolution emerges with so much clarity from the lessons of history that it does not seem necessary for us to enter into greater detail in order to demonstrate it. If we compare tribes that lack all central authority with tribes that are centralised, and the latter to the city, the city to feudal societies, feudal societies to those of the present day, we can follow step by step the principal stages in the development whose general progression we have just traced out. Thus it runs counter to all method to regard the present dimensions of the organ of government as a morbid phenomenon attributable to a chance concatenation of circumstances. Everything compels us to look upon it as a normal phenomenon, inherent in the very structure of higher societies, since it advances in a regular, continuous fashion, as societies evolve towards this type.

Moreover, we can show, at least in broad outline, how it is the outcome of the progress of the division of labour itself and of the process of transformation, whose effect is to facilitate the passage of societies of a segmentary type to the organised type.

So long as each segment has a life peculiarly its own, it forms a small society within the larger one and consequently has its own special regulatory organs, just as does the larger one. But their vigour is necessarily proportional to the intensity of this more local activity. Thus they cannot fail to grow weaker when that activity itself grows weaker. We know that this weakening process occurs with the progressive disappearance of the segmentary organisation. The central organ, finding itself faced with less resistance, since the forces that held it in check have lost some of their strength, develops, attracting to itself these functions, similar to those it exercises already, but that can no longer be retained by those entities that held them up to then. The local organs, instead of preserving their individuality and remaining diffuse, therefore come to merge into the central mechanism, which in consequence is enlarged, and this the more society becomes extensive and the fusion complete. This signifies that it is all the more voluminous the more societies belong to a higher species.

This phenomenon occurs with a kind of mechanical necessity and is moreover useful, because it corresponds to the new state of affairs. In so far as society ceases to be formed by a replication of similar segments, the regulatory mechanism must itself cease to be composed of a replication of autonomous segmentary organs. However, we do not mean that normally the state absorbs into itself all the regulatory organs of society of whatever kind, but only those that are of the same nature as its own, that is, those that govern life generally. As for those that control special functions, such as economic functions, they lie outside its zone of attraction. Among these there can certainly be effected a coalescence of the same kind, but not between them and the state − or at least if they are subject to the action of the higher centres they remain distinct from them. With vertebrates the cerebro-spinal system is very developed and it does have influence on the sympathetic nervous system, although it also leaves it great autonomy.

In the second place, so long as society is made up of segments what occurs in one of these has less chance of having any repercussion upon the others, the stronger the segmentary organisation. The alveolar system naturally lends itself to the localisation of social phenomena and their effects. Thus in a colony of polyps one may be sick without the others feeling any ill effect. This is no longer the case when society is made up of a system of organs. As a result of their mutual dependence, what infects one infects the others, and thus any serious change assumes a general interest.

This generalisation is more easily arrived at because of two other circumstances. The more labour is divided up, the less each organ of society consists of distinctive parts. As large-scale is substituted for small-scale industry, the number of separate undertakings grows less. Each undertaking acquires relatively more importance, because it represents a larger fraction of the whole. All that happens in it has therefore social repercussions that are much more extensive. The closing of a small workshop gives rise to only very limited disturbances, which are not felt beyond a small circle. On the contrary, the failure of a large industrial company entails a great public upheaval. Moreover, as the progress of the division of labour determines a greater concentration in the mass of society, between different parts of the same tissue, organ or mechanism there exists a closer contact which renders easier the chances of infection. Motion originating at one point is rapidly passed on to others. We have only to observe, for example, the rapidity with which a strike today becomes general throughout the same trade. A disturbance of a somewhat general character cannot occur without having repercussions upon the higher centres. Since these are painfully affected, they are obliged to intervene, and this intervention occurs all the more frequently the higher the type of society. But consequently they must be organised to do so. They must extend their ramifications in all directions, so as to keep in touch with the different areas of the organism and to maintain in a more immediate state of dependence certain organs whose action could occasionally give rise to exceptionally grave repercussions. In short, since their functions become more numerous and complex, the organ serving as their substratum needs to develop, just as does the body of legal rules determining these functions. . . .

From "Two Laws of Penal Evolution"

Emile Durkheim: On Institutional Analysis, ed. and trans. Mark Traugott (Chicago and London: University of Chicago Press, 1978), pp. 156–7.

. . . [I]t does not follow that the state has become more absolute just because it makes its action felt on a greater number of fronts. It is true that this may occur, but for that to happen, quite different circumstances are necessary than an increase in the complexity of the powers which have devolved upon it. Conversely, having functions of limited scope does not constitute an obstacle to its assuming an absolute character. In effect, if its functions are not very numerous nor often called into action, it is because social life itself, taken as a whole, is poor and languishing; for the more or less considerable development of the central regulatory organ only reflects the development of collective life in general, just as the dimensions of the nervous system in the individual vary according to the importance of organic exchanges. The controlling functions of the society are rudimentary only when the other social functions are of the same nature; and in this way the relationship among all of them remains the same. Consequently, the former retain all their supremacy, and it is enough that they be absorbed by one and the same individual to place

172 *Emile Durkheim*

him on a different plane and to elevate him infinitely above the rest of society. Nothing is more simple than government by a few uncivilized, petty kings; nothing is more absolute.

This observation leads us to another which more directly concerns our subject: the fact *that the more or less absolute character of the government is not an inherent characteristic of any given social type.* If, in effect, it can as easily be found where collective life is extremely simple as where it is extremely complex, it does not belong more exclusively to lower societies than to others. One might believe, it is true, that this concentration of governmental powers always accompanies the concentration of the social mass, either because the former results from the latter, or because the former contributes to the latter's determination. But this is in no way the case. The Roman city, especially after the fall of the monarchy, was until the last century of the Republic free from any absolutism; yet it was precisely under the Republic that the various segments, or partial societies (*gentes*), of which it was formed attained a very high degree of concentration and fusion. Moreover, we observe in the most diverse social types forms of government which deserve to be called absolute – in France in the seventeenth century, as at the end of the Roman state, or as in a multitude of uncivilized monarchies. Conversely, a single people, according to circumstances, can pass from an absolute government to another quite different type; however, a single society can no more change its type in the course of its evolution than an animal can change its species in the course of its individual existence. Seventeenth-century France and nineteenth-century France belong to the same type, yet the supreme regulatory organ has been transformed. It is as inadmissible to say that, from Napoleon I to Louis-Philippe, French society has passed from one social species to another, than it is to submit to an inverse change from Louis-Philippe to Napoleon III. Such transformations contradict the very notion of species.

This special form of political organization – governmental absolutism – does not, therefore, arise from the congenital constitution of the society, but from individual, transitory, and contingent conditions. . . .

From *Professional Ethics and Civic Morals*

Emile Durkheim, *Professional Ethics and Civic Morals*, trans. Cornelia Brookfield (London: Routledge, 1992), pp. 42–51, 55–64, 82–4, 88–9.

. . . [I]t is important to define what we understand by a political society.

An essential element that enters into the notion of any political group is the opposition between governing and governed, between authority and those subject to it. . . . For if this expression has any one meaning, it is, above all, organization, at any rate rudimentary; it is established authority (whether stable or intermittent, weak or strong), to whose action individuals are subject, whatever it be.

But an authority of this type is not found solely in political societies. The family has a head whose powers are sometimes limited by those of a family council. The patriarchal family of the Romans has often been compared to a State in miniature. Although, as we shall soon see, this expression is not justified, we could not quarrel with it if the sole distinguishing feature of the political society were a governmental structure. So we must look for some further characteristic.

This lies possibly in the especially close ties that bind any political society to its soil. There is said to be an enduring relationship between any nation and a given territory. . . . We may add, however, that where cardinal importance attaches to national territory, it is of comparatively recent date. . . .

Leaving territory aside, should we not find a feature of a political society in the numerical importance of the population? It is true we should not ordinarily give this name to social groups comprising a very small number of individuals. Even so, a dividing line of this kind would be extremely fluctuating: for at what precise moment does a concentration of people become of a size to be classified as a political group? . . .

Nevertheless, we touch here on a distinctive feature. To be sure, we cannot say that a political society differs from family groups or from professional groups on the score that it has greater numbers, for the numerical strength of families may in some instances be considerable while the numerical strength of a State may be very small. But it remains true that there is no political society which does not comprise numerous different families or professional groups or both at once. If it were confined to a domestic society or family, it would be identical with it and hence be a domestic society. But the moment it is made up of a certain number of domestic societies, the resulting aggregate is something other than each of its elements. It is something new, which has to be described by a different word. Likewise, the political society cannot be identified with any professional group or with any caste, if caste there be; but is always an aggregate of various professions or various castes, as it is of different families. More often, when we get a society made up of a collection of secondary groups varying in kind, without itself being a secondary group in relation to a far bigger society, then it constitutes a social entity of a specific kind. We should then define the political society as one formed by the coming together of a rather large number of secondary social groups, subject to the same one authority which is not itself subject to any other superior authority duly constituted.

Thus, and it should be noted, political societies are in part distinguished by the existence of secondary groups. . . . They are not only necessary for directing the particular interests, domestic or professional, that
they include and that are their own *raison d'être*; they also form the primary condition for any higher organization. Far from being in opposition
to the social group endowed with sovereign powers and called more
specifically the State, the State presupposes their existence: it exists only
where they exist. No secondary groups, no political authority – at least,
no authority that this term can apply to without being inappropriate.
Later on, we shall see the source of this solidarity that unites the two kinds
of grouping. For the moment, it is enough to record the fact. . . .

It remains true . . . that one and the same society may be political in some
respects, and only constitute a partial and secondary group in others. This
is what occurs in all federal States. Each individual State is autonomous
to a certain degree: this degree is more limited than if there were not a
federation with a regular structure, but the degree, although diminished
by this federation, is not reduced to nil. Each member constitutes a political society, a State in the true meaning of the term, to the extent to which
it is answerable only to itself and is not dependent on the central authority of the federation. On the other hand, to the extent to which it is
subordinate to some organ superior to itself, it is an ordinary secondary
group, a partial one and analagous to a district, a province, a clan or a
caste. It ceases to be a whole and no longer emerges except as a part.
Thus our definition does not establish an absolute line of demarcation
between political societies and others; but that is because there is not
and could not be such a line. On the contrary, the sequence of things is
continuous. The major political societies are formed by the gradual
aggregation of the minor. There are periods of transition when these minor
societies, still keeping something of their original nature, begin to
develop into something different and take on new characteristics, and
when consequently, their status is ambiguous. The main thing is, not to
record a break in continuity where none exists, but to be aware of the
specific features which distinguish political societies and which (according to their degree of "more or less") determine whether these societies
are really more, or less, entitled to this term.

Now that we know the distinguishing marks of a political society, let
us see what the morals are that relate to it. From the very definition just
made, it follows that the essential rules of these morals are those determining the relation of individuals to this sovereign authority, to whose
control they are subject. Since we need a word to indicate the particular
group of officials entrusted with representing this authority, we are
agreed to keep for this purpose the word "State". It is true that very often
we apply the word State not to the instrument of government but to the
political society as a whole, or to the people governed and its government

taken as one, and we ourselves often use the term in this sense. It is in this way that we speak of the European States or that we call France a State. But since it is well to have separate terms for existent things as different as the society and one of its organs, we apply the term "State" more especially to the agents of the sovereign authority, and "political society" to the complex group of which the State is the highest organ. This being granted, the principal duties under civic morals are obviously those the citizen has towards the State and, conversely, those the State owes to the individual. To understand what these duties are, we must first of all determine the nature and function of the State.

It is true it may seem that we have already answered the first question and that the nature of the State has been defined at the same time as the political society. Is not the State the supreme authority to which the political society as a whole is subordinate? But in fact this term authority is pretty vague and needs definition. Where does the group of officials vested with this authority begin and end, and who constitute, properly speaking, the State? The question is all the more called for, since current speech creates much confusion on the subject. Every day, we hear that public services are State services; the Law, the army, the Church – where there is a national Church – are held to form part of the State. But we must not confuse with the State itself the secondary organs in the immediate field of its control, which in relation to it are only executive. At very least, the groups or special groups (for the State is complex) – to which these secondary groups (called more specifically administrative) are subordinate, must be distinguished from the State. The characteristic feature of the special groups is that they alone are entitled to think and to act instead of representing the society. The representations, like the solutions that are worked out in this special *milieu* are inherently and of necessity collective. It is true, there are many representations and many collective decisions beyond those that take shape in this way. In every society there are or have been myths and dogmas, whenever the political society and the Church are one and the same, as well as historical and moral traditions: these make the representations common to all members of the society but are not in the special province of any one particular organ. There exist too at all times social currents wholly unconnected with the State, that draw the collectivity in this or that direction. Frequently it is a case of the State coming under their pressure, rather than itself giving the impulse to them. In this way a whole psychic life is diffused throughout the society. But it is a different one that has a fixed existence in the organ of government. It is here that this other psychic life develops and when in time it begins to have its effect on the rest of the society, it is only in a minor way and by repercussions. When a bill is carried in Parliament, when the government takes a decision within the limits of its competence, both actions, it is true, depend on the general state of social opinion, and on the society. Parliament and the government are in touch with the masses of the nation and the various impressions released by this contact have their effect in deciding them to take this course rather than that. But even if there be this one factor in their decision lying outside themselves, it is none the less true that it is they (Parliament and government) who make this decision and above all it expresses the particular *milieu* where it has its origin. It often happens, too, that there may even be discord between this *milieu* and the nation as a whole, and that decisions taken by the government or parliamentary vote may be valid for the whole community and yet do not square with the state of social opinion. So we may say that there is a collective psychic life, but this life is not diffused throughout the entire social body: although collective, it is localised in a specific organ. And this localisation does not come about simply through concentration on a given point of a life having its origins outside this point. It is in part at this very point that it has its beginning. When the State takes thought and makes a decision, we must not say that it is the society that thinks and decides through the State, but that the State thinks and decides for it. It is not simply an instrument for canalizing and concentrating. It is, in a certain sense, the organizing centre of the secondary groups themselves.

Let us see how the State can be defined. It is a group of officials *sui generis*, within which representations and acts of volition involving the collectivity are worked out, although they are not the product of collectivity. It is not accurate to say that the State embodies the collective consciousness, for that goes beyond the State at every point. In the main, that consciousness is diffused: there is at all times a vast number of social sentiments and social states of mind (*états*) of all kinds, of which the State hears only a faint echo. The State is the centre only of a particular kind of consciousness, of one that is limited but higher, clearer and with a more vivid sense of itself. There is nothing so obscure and so indefinite as these collective representations that are spread throughout all societies – myths, religious or moral legends, and so on. . . . We do not know whence they come nor whither they are tending; we have never had them under examination. The representations that derive from the State are always more conscious of themselves, of their causes and their aims. These have been concerted in a way that is less obscured. The collective agency which plans them realizes better what it is about. There too, it is true, there is often a good deal of obscurity. The State, like the individual, is often mistaken as to the motives underlying its decisions, but whether its decisions be ill motivated or not, the main thing is that they should be motivated to some extent. There is always or at least usually a semblance of deliberation, an understanding of the circumstances as a whole that make the decision necessary, and it is precisely this inner organ of the State that is called upon to conduct these debates. Hence, we have these councils, these regulations, these assemblies, these debates that make it impossible for these kinds of representation to evolve except at a slow pace. To sum up, we can therefore say that the State is a special organ whose responsibility it is to work out certain representations which hold good for the collectivity. These representations are distinguished from the other collective representations by their higher degree of consciousness and reflection.

We may perhaps feel some surprise at finding excluded from this definition all idea of action or execution or achievement of plans outside the State. Is it not generally held that this part of the State (at all events the part more precisely called the government), has the executive power? This view, however, is altogether out of place: the State does not execute anything. The Council of ministers or the sovereign do not themselves take action any more than Parliament: they give the orders for action to be taken. They co-ordinate ideas and sentiments, from these they frame decisions and transmit these decisions to other agencies that carry them out: but that is the limit of their office. In this respect there is no difference between Parliament (or the deliberative assemblies of all kinds surrounding the sovereign or head of State) and the government in the exact meaning of the term, the power known as executive. This power is called executive because it is closest to the executive agencies, but it is not to be identified with them. The whole life of the State, in its true meaning, consists not in exterior action, in making changes, but in deliberation, that is, in representations. It is others, the administrative bodies of all kinds, who are in charge of carrying out the changes. The difference between them and the State is clear: this difference is parallel to that between the muscular system and the central nervous system. Strictly speaking, the State is the very organ of social thought. As things are, this thought is directed towards an aim that is practical, not speculative. The State, as a rule at least, does not think for the sake of thought or to build up doctrinal systems, but to guide collective conduct. None the less, its principal function is to think.

But what is the direction of this thought? or, in other words, what end does the State normally pursue and therefore should it pursue, in the social conditions of the present day? This is the question that still remains. . . .

There is no doubt, in the case of very many societies, what was the true nature of the aims pursued by the State. To keep on expanding its power and to add lustre to its fame – this was the sole or main object of public activity. Individual interests and needs did not come into the reckoning. The ingrained religious character of the political system of societies makes us appreciate this indifference of the State for what concerns the individual. The destiny of a State was closely bound up with the fate of the gods worshipped at its altars. If a State suffered reverses, then the prestige of its gods declined in the same measure – and vice versa. Public religion and civic morals were fused: they were but different aspects of the same reality. To bring glory to the City was the same as enhancing the glory of the gods of the City: it worked both ways. Now, the phenomena in the religious sphere can be recognized because they are wholly unlike those of the human order. They belong to a world apart. The individual *qua* individual is part of the profane world, whilst the gods are the very nucleus of the religious world, and between these two worlds there is a gulf. The gods are, in their substance, different from men: they have other ideas, other needs and an existence with no likeness to that of men. Anyone who holds that the aims of the political system were religious and the religious aims political, might as well say that there was a cleavage between the aims of the State and the ends pursued by individuals on their own. How then came it that the individual could thus occupy himself with the pursuit of aims which were to such a degree foreign to his own private concerns? The answer is this: his private concerns were relatively unimportant to him and his personality and everything that hung on it had but slight moral weight. His personal views, his private beliefs and all his diverse aspirations as an individual seemed insignificant factors. What was prized by all, were the beliefs held in common, the collective aspirations, the popular traditions and the symbols that were an expression of them. That being so, it was gladly and without any demur that the individual yielded to the instrument by which the aims of no immediate concern to himself were secured. Absorbed, as he was, into the mass of society, he meekly gave way to its pressures and subordinated his own lot to the destinies of collective existence without any sense of sacrifice. This is because his particular fate had in his own eyes nothing of the meaning and high significance that we nowadays attribute to it. If we are right in that estimate, it was in the nature of things that it should be so; societies could only exist at that time by virtue of this subservience.

But the further one travels in history, the more one is aware of the process of change. In the early stage, the individual personality is lost in the depths of the social mass and then later, by its own effort, breaks away. From being limited and of small regard, the scope of the individual life expands and becomes the exalted object of moral respect. The individual comes to acquire ever wider rights over his own person and over the possessions to which he has title; he also comes to form ideas about the world that seem to him most fitting and to develop his essential qualities without hindrance. War fetters his activity, diminishes his stature and so becomes the supreme evil. Because it inflicts undeserved suffering on him, he sees in it more and more the supreme form of moral offence. In the light of this, it is utterly inconsistent to require from him the same subordination as before. One cannot make of him a god, a god above all others, and at the same time an instrument in the hands of the gods. One cannot make of him the paramount end and reduce him to the role of means. If he be the moral reality, then it is he who must serve as the pole-star for public as well as private conduct. It should be the part of the State to try to bring his innate qualities to the light. Shall we find some people saying that the cult of the individual is a superstition of which we ought to rid ourselves? That would be to go against all the lessons of history: for as we read on, we find the human person tending to gain in dignity. There is no rule more soundly established. For any attempt to base social institutions on the opposite principle is not feasible and could be convincing only for a moment: we cannot force things to be other than they are. We cannot undo the individual having become what he is – an autonomous centre of activity, an impressive system of personal forces whose energy can no more be destroyed than that of the cosmic forces. It would be just as impossible to transform our physical atmosphere, in the midst of which we breathe and have our being.

Do we not arrive here at a contradiction that cannot be resolved? On the one hand we establish that the State goes on developing more and more: on the other, that the rights of the individual, held to be actively opposed to those of the State, have a parallel development. The government organ takes on an ever greater scale, because its function goes on growing in importance and because its aims, that are in line with its own activity, increase in number; yet we deny that it can pursue aims other than those that concern the individual. Now, these aims are by definition held to belong to individual activity. If, as we suppose, the rights of the individual are inherent, the State does not have to intervene to establish them, that is, they do not depend on the State. But then, if they do not, and are outside its competence, how can the cadre of this competence go on expanding, in face of the fact that it must less and less take in things alien to the individual?

The only way of getting over the difficulty is to dispute the postulate that the rights of the individual are inherent, and to admit that the institution of these rights is in fact precisely the task of the State. Then, certainly, all can be explained. We can understand that the functions of the State may expand, without any diminishing of the individual. We can see too that the individual may develop without causing any decline of the State, since he would be in some respects the product himself of the State, and since the activity of the State would in its nature be liberating to him. Now, what emerges, on the evidence of the facts, is that history gives sound authority for this relation of cause and effect as between the progress of moral individualism and the advance of the State. Except for the abnormal cases we shall discuss later, the stronger the State, the more the individual is respected. . . .

History seems indeed to prove that the State was not created to prevent the individual from being disturbed in the exercise of his natural
rights: no, this was not its role alone – rather, it is the State that creates
and organizes and makes a reality of these rights. And indeed, man is
man only because he lives in society. Take away from man all that has
a social origin and nothing is left but an animal on a par with other
animals. It is society that has raised him to this level above physical
nature: it has achieved this result because association, by grouping the
individual psychic forces, intensifies them. It carried them to a degree of
energy and productive capacity immeasurably greater than any they could
achieve if they remained isolated one from the other. Thus, a psychic
life of a new kind breaks away which is richer by far and more varied
than one played out in the single individual alone. Further, the life thus
freed pervades the individual who shares in it and so transforms him.
Whilst society thus feeds and enriches the individual nature, it tends, on
the other hand, at the same time inevitably to subject that nature to itself
and for the same reason. It is precisely because the group is a moral force
greater to this extent than that of its parts, that it tends of necessity to
subordinate these to itself. The parts are unable *not* to fall under its
domination. Here there is a law of moral mechanics at work, which is
just as inevitable as the laws of physical mechanics. Any group which
exercises authority over its members by coercion strives to model them
after its own pattern, to impose on them its ways of thinking and acting
and to prevent any dissent.

Every society is despotic, at least if nothing from without supervenes
to restrain its despotism. Still, I would not say that there is anything artificial in this despotism: it is natural because it is necessary, and also
because, in certain conditions, societies cannot endure without it. Nor
do I mean that there is anything intolerable about it: on the contrary, the
individual does not feel it any more than we feel the atmosphere that
weighs on our shoulders. From the moment the individual has been
raised in this way by the collectivity, he will naturally desire what it
desires and accept without difficulty the state of subjection to which
he finds himself reduced. If he is to be conscious of this and to resist it,
individualist aspirations must find an outlet, and that they cannot do in
these conditions.

But for it to be otherwise, we may say, would it not be enough for
the society to be on a fairly large scale? There is no doubt that when it is
small – when it surrounds every individual on all sides and at every
moment – it does not allow of his evolving in freedom. If it be always
present and always in action, it leaves no room to his initiative. But it is
no longer in the same case when it has reached wide enough dimensions.
When it is made up of a vast number of individuals, a society can exercise over each a supervision only as close and as vigilant and effective as

when the surveillance is concentrated on a small number. A man is far more free in the midst of a throng than in a small coterie. Hence it follows that individual diversities can then more easily have play, that collective tyranny declines and that individualism establishes itself in fact, and that, with time, the fact becomes a right. Things can, however, only have this course on one condition: that is, that inside this society, there must be no forming of any secondary groups that enjoy enough autonomy to allow of each becoming in a way a small society within the greater. For then, each of these would behave towards its members as if it stood alone and everything would go on as if the full-scale society did not exist. Each group, tightly enclosing the individuals of which it was made up, would hinder their development; the collective mind would impose itself on conditions applying to the individual. A society made up of adjoining clans or of towns or villages independent in greater or lesser degree, or of a number of professional groups, each one auto-nomous in relation to the others, would have the effect of being almost as repressive of any individuality as if it were made up of a single clan or town or association. The formation of secondary groups of this kind is bound to occur, for in a great society there are always particular local or professional interests which tend naturally to bring together those people with whom they are concerned. There we have the very stuff of associations of a special kind, of guilds, of coteries of every variety; and if there is nothing to offset or neutralize their activity, each of them will tend to swallow up its members. . . .

In order to prevent this happening, and to provide a certain range for individual development, it is not enough for a society to be on a big scale; the individual must be able to move with some degree of freedom over a wide field of action. He must not be curbed and monopolised by the secondary groups, and these groups must not be able to get a mastery over their members and mould them at will. There must therefore exist above these local, domestic – in a word, secondary – authorities, some overall authority which makes the law for them all: it must remind each of them that it is but a part and not the whole and that it should not keep for itself what rightly belongs to the whole. The only means of averting this collective particularism and all it involves for the individual, is to have a special agency with the duty of representing the overall collectivity, its rights and its interests, vis-à-vis these individual collectivities.

These rights and these interests merge with those of the individual. Let us see why and how the main function of the State is to liberate the indi-vidual personalities. It is solely because, in holding its constituent soci-eties in check, it prevents them from exerting the repressive influences over the individual that they would otherwise exert. So there is nothing inherently tyrannical about State intervention in the different fields of col-lective life; on the contrary, it has the object and the effect of alleviating tyrannies that do exist. It will be argued, might not the State in turn become despotic? Undoubtedly, provided there were nothing to counter that trend. In that case, as the sole existing collective force, it produces the effects that any collective force not neutralized by any counter-force of the same kind would have on individuals. The State itself then becomes a leveller and repressive. And its repressiveness becomes even harder to endure than that of small groups, because it is more artificial. The State, in our large-scale societies, is so removed from individual interests that it cannot take into account the special or local and other conditions in which they exist. Therefore when it does attempt to regulate them, it succeeds only at the cost of doing violence to them and distorting them. It is, too, not sufficiently in touch with individuals in the mass to be able to mould them inwardly, so that they readily accept its pressure on them. The individual eludes the State to some extent – the State can only be effective in the context of a large-scale society – and individual diversity may not come to light. Hence, all kinds of resistance and distressing conflicts arise. The small groups do not have this drawback. They are close enough to the things that provide their *raison d'être* to be able to adapt their actions exactly and they surround the individuals closely enough to shape them in their own image. The inference to be drawn from this comment, however, is simply that if that collective force, the State, is to be the liberator of the individual, it has itself need of some counter-balance; it must be restrained by other collective forces, that is, by those secondary groups we shall discuss later on. . . . It is not a good thing for the groups to stand alone, nevertheless they have to exist. And it is out of this conflict of social forces that individual liberties are born. Here again we see the significance of these groups. Their usefulness is not merely to regulate and govern the interests they are meant to serve. They have a wider purpose; they form one of the conditions essential to the emancipation of the individual.

It remains a fact that the State is not of its own volition antagonistic to the individual. It is only through the State that individualism is possible, although it cannot be the means of making it a reality, except in certain precise conditions. We might say that in the State we have the prime mover. It is the State that has rescued the child from patriarchal domination and from family tyranny; it is the State that has freed the citizen from feudal groups and later from communal groups; it is the State that has liberated the craftsman and his master from guild tyranny. It may take too violent a course, but the action becomes vitiated only when it is merely destructive. And that is what justifies the increasing scope of its functions. . . .

We must . . . not say that democracy is the political form of a society governing itself, in which the government is spread throughout the *milieu* of the nation. Such a definition is a contradiction in terms. It would be almost as if we said that democracy is a political society without a State. In fact, the State is nothing if it is not an organ distinct from the rest of society. If the State is everywhere, it is nowhere. The State comes into existence by a process of concentration that detaches a certain group of individuals from the collective mass. In that group the social thought is subjected to elaboration of a special kind and reaches a very high degree of clarity. Where there is no such concentration and where the social thought remains entirely diffused, it also remains obscure and the distinctive feature of the political society will be lacking. Nevertheless, communications between this especial organ and the other social organs may be either close or less close, either continuous or intermittent. Certainly in this respect there can only be differences of degree. There is no State with such absolute power that those governing will sever all contact with the mass of its subjects. Still, the differences of degree may be of significance, and they increase in the exterior sense with the existence or non-existence of certain institutions intended to establish the contact, or according to the institutions' being either more or less rudimentary or more or less developed in character. It is these institutions that enable the people to follow the working of government (national assembly – parliament, official journals, education intended to equip the citizen to one day carry out his duties – and so on . . .) and also to communicate the result of their reflections (organ for rights of franchise or electoral machinery) to the organs of government, directly or indirectly. But what we have to decline at all costs is to admit a concept which (by eliminating the State entirely) opens a wide door to criticism. In this sense, democracy is just what we see when societies were first taking shape. If every one is to govern, it means in fact that there is no government. It is collective sentiments, diffused, vague and obscure as they may be, that sway the people. No clear thought of any kind governs the life of peoples. Societies of this description are like individuals whose actions are prompted by routine alone and by preconception. This means they could not be put forward as representing a definite stage in progress: rather, they are a starting point. If we agree to reserve the name democracy for political societies, it must not be applied to tribes without definite form, which so far have no claim to being a State and are not political societies. The difference, then, is quite wide, in spite of apparent likeness. It is true that in both cases – and this gives the likeness – the whole society takes part in public life but they do this in very different ways. The difference lies in the fact that in one case there is a State and in the other there is none.

This primary feature, however, is not enough. There is another, inseparable from it. In societies where it is narrowly localised, the government consciousness has, too, only a limited number of objects within its range. This part of public consciousness that is clear is entirely enclosed within a little group of individuals and it is in itself also only of small compass. There are all sorts of customs, traditions and rules which work automatically without the State itself being aware of it and which therefore are beyond its action. In a society such as the monarchy of the seventeenth century the number of things on which government deliberations have any bearing is very small. The whole question of religion was outside its province and along with religion, every kind of collective prejudice and bias: any absolute power would soon have come to grief if it had attempted to destroy them. Nowadays, on the other hand, we do not admit there is anything in public organization lying beyond the arm of the State. In principle, we lay down that everything may for ever remain open to question, that everything may be examined, and that in so far as decisions have to be taken, we are not tied to the past. The State has really a far greater sphere of influence nowadays than in other times, because the sphere of the clear consciousness has widened. All those obscure sentiments which are diffusive by nature, the many habits acquired, resist any change precisely because they are obscure. What cannot be seen is not easily modified. All these states of mind shift, steal away, cannot be grasped, precisely because they are in the shadows. On the other hand, the more the light penetrates the depths of social life, the more can changes be introduced. This is why those of cultivated mind, who are conscious of themselves, can change more easily and more profoundly than those of uncultivated mind. Then there is another feature of democratic societies. They are more malleable and more flexible, and this advantage they owe to the government consciousness, that in widening has come to hold more and more objects. By the same token, resistance is far more sharply defined in societies that have been unorganized from the start, or pseudo-democracies. They have wholly yielded to the yoke of tradition. Switzerland, and the Scandinavian countries, too, are a good example of this resistance. . . .

To sum up: if we want to get a fairly definite idea of what a democracy is, we must begin by getting away from a number of present concepts that can only muddle our ideas. The number of those governing must be left out of account and, even more important, their official titles. Neither must we believe that a democracy is necessarily a society in which the powers of the State are weak. A State may be democratic and still have a strong organization. The true characteristics are twofold: (1) a greater range of the government consciousness, and (2) closer communications between this consciousness and the mass of individual consciousnesses. The confusions that have occurred can be understood to some extent by the fact that in societies where the government authority is weak and limited, the communications linking it to the rest of the society are of necessity quite close, since it is not distinguishable from the rest. It has no existence outside the mass of the people, it must therefore of necessity be in communication with that mass. In a small primitive tribe, the political leaders are only delegates and always provisional, without any clearly defined functions. They live the life of everyone else, and their decisive discussions remain subject to the check of the whole collectivity. They do not however form a separate and definite organ. And here we find nothing resembling the second feature already mentioned – I mean the pliability deriving from the range of government consciousness, that is, from the field of collective, clear ideas. Societies such as these are the victims of traditional routine. This secondary feature is perhaps even more distinctive than the first. The first criterion, at any rate, can be very useful providing it is used with discernment, and providing we beware of identifying the confused situation arising from the State not yet being detached from the society and separately organized, with the communications that may exist between a clearly defined State and the society it governs.

Seen from this point, a democracy may, then, appear as the political system by which the society can achieve a consciousness of itself in its purest form. The more that deliberation and reflection and a critical spirit play a considerable part in the course of public affairs, the more democratic the nation. It is the less democratic when lack of consciousness, uncharted customs, the obscure sentiments and prejudices that evade investigation, predominate. This means that democracy is not a discovery or a revival in our own century. It is the form that societies are assuming to an increasing degree. . . .

From *Selections from the Prison Notebooks*
Antonio Gramsci

Antonio Gramsci, *Selections from the Prison Notebooks*, trans. Quintin Hoare and Geoffrey Nowell Smith (New York: International Publishers, 1971), pp. 235–63.

... [I]n the case of the most advanced States, ... "civil society" has become a very complex structure and one which is resistant to the catastrophic "incursions" of the immediate economic element (crises, depressions, etc.). The superstructures of civil society are like the trench-systems of modern warfare. In war it would sometimes happen that a fierce artillery attack seemed to have destroyed the enemy's entire defensive system, whereas in fact it had only destroyed the outer perimeter; and at the moment of their advance and attack the the assailants would find themselves confronted by a line of defence which was still effective. The same thing happens in politics, during the great economic crises. A crisis cannot give the attacking forces the ability to organise with lightning speed in time and in space; still less can it endow them with fighting spirit. Similarly, the defenders are not demoralised, nor do they abandon their positions, even among the ruins, nor do they lose faith in their own strength or their own future. ... Hence it is a question of studying "in depth" which elements of civil society correspond to the defensive systems in a war of position. ...

Educative and formative role of the State   Its aim is always that of creating new and higher types of civilisation; of adapting the "civilisation" and the morality of the broadest popular masses to the necessities of the continuous development of the economic apparatus of production; hence of evolving even physically new types of humanity. But how will each single individual succeed in incorporating himself into the collective man, and how will educative pressure be applied to single individuals so as to obtain their consent and their collaboration, turning necessity and coercion into "freedom"? Question of the "Law": this concept will have to be extended to include those activities which are at present classified as "legally neutral", and which belong to the domain of civil society; the latter operates without "sanctions" or compulsory "obligations", but nevertheless exerts a collective pressure and obtains objective results in the form of an evolution of customs, ways of thinking and acting, morality, etc. . . .

. . . [I]t can be said that a State will win a war in so far as it prepares for it minutely and technically in peacetime. The massive structures of the modern democracies, both as State organisations, and as complexes of associations in civil society, constitute for the art of politics as it were the "trenches" and the permanent fortifications of the front in the war of position: they render merely "partial" the element of movement which before used to be "the whole" of war, etc. . . .

. . . If every State tends to create and maintain a certain type of civilisation and of citizen (and hence of collective life and of individual relations), and to eliminate certain customs and attitudes and to disseminate others, then the Law will be its instrument for this purpose (together with the school system, and other institutions and activities). It must be developed so that it is suitable for such a purpose – so that it is maximally effective and productive of positive results.

The conception of law will have to be freed from every residue of transcendentalism and from every absolute; in practice, from every moralistic fanaticism. However, it seems to me that one cannot start from the point of view that the State does not "punish" (if this term is reduced to its human significance), but only struggles against social "dangerousness". In reality, the State must be conceived of as a "educator". . . .

. . . [E]very State is ethical in as much as one of its most important functions is to raise the great mass of the population to a particular cultural and moral level, a level (or type) which corresponds to the needs of the productive forces for development, and hence to the interests of the ruling classes. The school as a positive educative function, and the courts as a repressive and negative educative function, are the most important State activities in this sense: but, in reality, a multitude of other so-called private initiatives and activities tend to the same end – initiatives and activities which form the apparatus of the political and cultural hegemony of the ruling classes. . . . Government with the consent of the governed – but with this consent organised, and not generic and vague as it is expressed in the instant of elections. The State does have and request consent, but is also "educates" this consent, by means of the political and syndical associations; these, however, are private organisms, left to the private initiative of the ruling class. . . .

We are still on the terrain of the identification of State and government – an identification which is precisely a representation of the economic-corporate form, in other words of the confusion between civil society and political society. For it should be remarked that the general notion of State includes elements which need to be referred back to the notion of civil society (in the sense that one might say that State = political society + civil society, in other words hegemony protected by the armour of coercion). In a doctrine of the State which conceives the latter as tendentially capable of withering away and of being subsumed into regulated society, the argument is a fundamental one. It is possible to imagine the coercive element of the State withering away by degrees, as ever-more conspicuous elements of regulated society (or ethical State or civil society) make their appearance. . . .

From "Civil Religion in America"
Robert Bellah

Robert Bellah, *Beyond Belief: Essays on Religion in a Post-Traditional World* (New York: Harper and Row, 1970), pp. 168–76.

While some have argued that Christianity is the national faith, and others that church and synagogue celebrate only the generalized religion of "the American Way of Life," few have realized that there actually exists alongside of and rather clearly differentiated from the churches an elaborate and well-institutionalized civil religion in America. . . .

John F. Kennedy's inaugural address of January 20, 1961, serves as an example and a clue with which to introduce this complex subject. That address began:

> We observe today not a victory of party but a celebration of freedom –
> symbolizing an end as well as a beginning – signifying renewal as well as
> change. For I have sworn before you and Almighty God the same solemn
> oath our forebears prescribed nearly a century and three quarters ago.
>   The world is very different now. For man holds in his mortal hands the
> power to abolish all forms of human poverty and to abolish all forms of
> human life. And yet the same revolutionary beliefs for which our forebears
> fought are still at issue around the globe – the belief that the rights of man
> come not from the generosity of the state but from the hand of God.

And it concluded:

> Finally, whether you are citizens of America or of the world, ask of us
> the same high standards of strength and sacrifice that we shall ask of you.

With a good conscience our only sure reward, with history the final judge
of our deeds, let us go forth to lead the land we love, asking His blessing
and His help, but knowing that here on earth God's work must truly be
our own.

These are the three places in this brief address in which Kennedy mentioned the name of God. . . .

. . . [I]t is worth considering whether the very special placing of the
references to God in Kennedy's address may not reveal something
rather important and serious about religion in American life.

It might be countered that the very way in which Kennedy made his
references reveals the essentially vestigial place of religion today. He did
not refer to any religion in particular. He did not refer to Jesus Christ,
or to Moses, or to the Christian church; certainly he did not refer to the
Catholic church. In fact, his only reference was to the concept of God, a
word that almost all Americans can accept but that means so many different things to so many different people that it is almost an empty sign.
Is this not just another indication that in America religion is considered
vaguely to be a good thing, but that people care so little about it that it
has lost any content whatever? Isn't Dwight Eisenhower reported to
have said "Our government makes no sense unless it is founded in a deeply
felt religious faith – and I don't care what it is," and isn't that a complete
negation of any real religion?

These questions are worth pursuing because they raise the issue of
how civil religion relates to the political society on the one hand and to
private religious organization on the other. President Kennedy was a
Christian, more specifically a Catholic Christian. Thus his general references to God do not mean that he lacked a specific religious commitment.
But why, then, did he not include some remark to the effect that Christ
is the Lord of the world or some indication of respect for the Catholic
church? He did not because these are matters of his own private religious
belief and of his relation to his own particular church; they are not matters relevant in any direct way to the conduct of his public office. Others
with different religious views and commitments to different churches or
denominations are equally qualified participants in the political process.
The principle of separation of church and state guarantees the freedom
of religious belief and association, but at the same time clearly segregates
the religious sphere, which is considered to be essentially private, from
the political one.

Considering the separation of church and state, how is a president
justified in using the word "God" at all? The answer is that the separation of church and state has not denied the political realm a religious
dimension. Although matters of personal religious belief, worship, and
association are considered to be strictly private affairs, there are, at the

same time, certain common elements of religious orientation that the
great majority of Americans share. These have played a crucial role in
the development of American institutions and still provide a religious
dimension for the whole fabric of American life, including the political
sphere. This public religious dimension is expressed in a set of beliefs,
symbols, and rituals that I am calling the American civil religion. The
inauguration of a president is an important ceremonial event in this
religion. It reaffirms, among other things, the religious legitimation of
the highest political authority. . . .

. . . The whole address can be understood as only the most recent statement of a theme that lies very deep in the American tradition, namely
the obligation, both collective and individual, to carry out God's will on
earth. This was the motivating spirit of those who founded America,
and it has been present in every generation since. Just below the surface
throughout Kennedy's inaugural address, it becomes explicit in the
closing statement that God's work must be our own. That this very act-
ivist and noncontemplative conception of the fundamental religious
obligation, which has been historically associated with the Protestant
position, should be enunciated so clearly in the first major statement of
the first Catholic president seems to underline how deeply established it
is in the American outlook. . . .

What we have, then, from the earliest years of the republic is a collection
of beliefs, symbols, and rituals with respect to sacred things and institutionalized in a collectivity. This religion – there seems no other word for
it – while not antithetical to and indeed sharing much in common with
Christianity, was neither sectarian nor in any specific sense Christian. At
a time when the society was overwhelmingly Christian, it seems unlikely
that this lack of Christian reference was meant to spare the feelings of
the tiny non-Christian minority. Rather, the civil religion expressed what
those who set the precedents felt was appropriate under the circumstances.
It reflected their private as well as public views. Nor was the civil religion simply "religion in general." While generality was undoubtedly seen
as a virtue by some . . . the civil religion was specific enough when it
came to the topic of America. Precisely because of this specificity, the
civil religion was saved from empty formalism and [served] as a genuine
vehicle of national religious self-understanding.

But the civil religion was not, in the minds of Franklin, Washington,
Jefferson, or other leaders, with the exception of a few radicals like Tom
Paine, ever felt to be a substitute for Christianity. There was an implicit
but quite clear division of function between the civil religion and
Christianity. Under the doctrine of religious liberty, an exceptionally
wide sphere of personal piety and voluntary social action was left to the
churches. But the churches were neither to control the state nor to be

controlled by it. The national magistrate, whatever his private religious views, operates under the rubrics of the civil religion as long as he is in his official capacity, as we have already seen in the case of Kennedy. This accommodation was undoubtedly the product of a particular historical moment and of a cultural background dominated by Protestantism of several varieties and by the Enlightenment, but it has survived despite subsequent changes in the cultural and religious climate. . . .

chapter 7

The Modern Economy

Introduction

In this chapter, we see Durkheim elaborating a highly original sociology of the modern economy. The chapter begins with an excerpt from *The Division of Labor*, a critique of economic theories that, like the rational actor theories of today, conceptualize "social solidarity [as] nothing more than the spontaneous agreement between individual interests, an agreement of which contracts are the natural expression" (p. 193). In contrast to such theories, Durkheim stresses the importance of the "non-contractual elements" in contract and thereby of society itself, of which contractual relationships are a mere product. The chapter then turns to the topic of socialism. In *Socialism and Saint-Simon*, Durkheim defines socialism, distinguishes its major variants, and, in passages reminiscent of his discussions of anomie in *Suicide* (see chapter 1), reflects upon its inherent moral limitations. Moral reflections continue in *The Division of Labor*, to which the chapter then returns. First we encounter an important statement of Durkheim's moral psychology, a rumination on the sources, meaning, and limitations of individual happiness. Then we turn to more substantive analyses – Durkheim's critiques of the modern economy itself – which we find cast precisely in the same terms as his moral analyses. Extended excerpts on the "anomic" and "forced" variants of the division of labor show Durkheim to be simultaneously a moralist and a profound critic of today's economy, one whose indictments encompass the "pathological" social structure, culture, and collective emotions alike of contemporary industrial capitalism. The usefulness of Durkheim's arguments with respect to economic life is then demonstrated by two brief excerpts by later writers. One, by James Scott, returns to the theme of the non-contractual elements in economic relationships by highlighting the moral principles of "reciprocity" and "right to subsistence" that are "woven into the tissue" of traditional peasant societies. The other, by Amitai Etzioni, shifts attention back to modern industrial capitalism, but similarly underscores the importance of "pre-contractual . . . social bonds" in providing the basic framework for economic institutions and practices.

From *The Division of Labor in Society*

Emile Durkheim, *The Division of Labor in Society*, trans. W. D. Halls (New York: Free Press, 1984), pp. 141, 151–63.

The law we have established . . . in one characteristic, but in one characteristic alone, may have reminded us of the one that dominates the sociology of Spencer. Like him, we have stated that the place of the individual in society, from being originally nothing at all, has grown with civilisation. But this indisputable fact has presented itself in a completely different light than to the English philosopher, so much so that in the end our conclusions are in contradiction to his, more than echoing them. . . .

. . . [I]f higher societies do not rest upon a basic contract which has a bearing on the general principles of political life, they would have – or tend to have – according to Spencer, as their sole basis the vast system of special contracts that link individuals with one another. Individuals would only be dependent upon the group to the extent that they depended upon one another, and they would not depend upon one another save within the limits drawn by private agreements freely arrived at. Thus social solidarity would be nothing more than the spontaneous agreement between individual interests, an agreement of which contracts are the natural expression. The type of social relations would be the economic relationship, freed from all regulation, and as it emerges from the entirely free initiative of the parties concerned. In short, society would be no more than the establishment of relationships between individuals exchanging the products of their labour, and without any social action, properly so termed, intervening to regulate that exchange.

Is this indeed the nature of societies whose unity is brought about by the division of labour? If this were so, one might reasonably doubt their stability. For if mutual interest draws men closer, it is never more than for a few moments. It can only create between them an external bond. In the fact of exchange the various agents involved remain apart from one another and once the operation is over, each one finds himself again "reassuming his self" in its entirety. The different consciousnesses are only superficially in contact: they neither interpenetrate nor do they cleave closely to one another. Indeed, if we look to the heart of the matter we shall see that every harmony of interests conceals a latent conflict, or one that is simply deferred. For where interest alone reigns, as nothing arises to check the egoisms confronting one another, each self finds itself in relation to the other on a war footing, and any truce in this perpetual antagonism cannot be of long duration. Self-interest is, in fact, the least constant thing in the world. Today it is useful for me to unite with you; tomorrow the same reason will make me your enemy. Thus such a cause can give rise only to transitory links and associations of a fleeting kind. We see how necessary it is to examine whether such is effectively the nature of organic solidarity. . . .

It is absolutely true that contractual relationships that originally were rare or completely missing are multiplied as labour in society is divided up. But what Spencer seems to have failed to perceive is that non-contractual relationships are developing at the same time. . . .

. . . On the other hand the social control over the way in which obligations are entered into and dissolved is modified, and is continually increasing. . . .

But it is not only outside the sphere of contractual relationships, but also on the interplay between these relationships themselves that social action is to be felt. For in a contract not everything is contractual. The only undertakings worthy of the name are those that are desired by individuals, whose sole origin is this free act of the will. Conversely, any obligation that has not been agreed by both sides is not in any way contractual. Wherever a contract exists, it is submitted to a regulatory force that is imposed by society and not by individuals: it is a force that becomes ever more weighty and complex. . . .

Undoubtedly when men bind one another by contract it is because, through the division of labour, whether this be simple of complex, they have need of one another. But for them to co-operate harmoniously it is not enough that they should enter into a relationship, nor even be aware of the state of mutual interdependence in which they find themselves. The conditions for their co-operation must also be fixed for the entire duration of their relationship. The duties and rights of each one must be defined, not only in the light of the situation as it presents itself at the moment when the contract is concluded, but in anticipation of circumstances that can arise and can modify it. Otherwise, at every moment there would be renewed conflicts and quarrels. Indeed we must not forget that if the division of labour joins interests solidly together, it does not mix them together: it leaves them distinct, and in competition with one another. Just as within the individual organism each organ is at odds with the others, whilst still acting in concert with them, each contracting party, whilst having need of the other, seeks to obtain at least cost what he needs, that is, to gain the widest possible rights in exchange for the least possible obligations.

Thus it is necessary for the allocation of both rights and obligations to be prescribed in advance, and yet this cannot take place according to some preconceived plan....

... [C]ontractual law exists to determine the legal consequences of those of our acts that we have not settled beforehand. It expresses the normal conditions for attaining equilibrium, as they have evolved gradually from the average case. Epitomising numerous, varied experiences, it foresees what we could not do individually; what we could not regulate is regulated, and this regulation is mandatory upon us, although it is not our handiwork, but that of society and tradition....

Viewed in this light, the law of contract appears very differently. It is no longer a useful supplement to individual agreements, but their basic norm. It imposes itself upon us with the traditional authority of experience, it constitutes the foundation of our contractual relationships. We can only depart from it in part, and by chance....

Finally, beyond this organised, precise pressure exerted by the law, there is another that arises from morals. In the way in which we conclude and carry out contracts, we are forced to conform to rules which, although not sanctioned, either directly or indirectly, by any legal code, are none the less mandatory....

Summing up, therefore, the contract is not sufficient by itself, but is only possible because of the regulation of contracts, which is of social origin....

We need not demonstrate that this intervention, in its various forms, is of an eminently positive kind, since its effect is to determine the manner in which we should co-operate together....

From *Socialism and Saint-Simon*

Emile Durkheim, *Socialism and Saint-Simon*, trans. Charlotte Sattler (Yellow Springs, OH: Antioch Press, 1958), pp. 18–28, 196–200.

... [E]conomic activities have this particularity: they are not in definite and regulated relationships with the organ which is charged with representing and directing the social body in its entirety, namely, what is commonly called the state. This absence of connection can be ascertained both in the way that industrial and commercial life acts on it, as in the manner it acts on the latter. On the one hand, what goes on in factories, in mills, and in private stores, in principle escapes the awareness of the state. It is not directly and specifically informed of what is produced there. The state can indeed, in certain cases, feel its reverberations; but it is not advised in a different way nor in different circumstances than are other branches of society. For that to happen, it is necessary that the economic situation be seriously disturbed and the general state of society noticeably modified. In this case, the state is being injured, and so, vaguely takes notice of it, as do other parts of the organization, but not differently. In other words, there exists no special communication between it and this sphere of collective life. In principle, economic activity is outside of collective consciousness. It functions silently and the conscious centers do not feel it while it is normal. Likewise it is not activated in a specialized and regular way. There is no system of determinate and organized channels by which the influence of the state makes itself felt upon economic organs. In other words, there is no system of functions charged with imposing on it the action coming from the superior centers. It is altogether different in other activities. Everything that occurs in the various administrations, in local deliberating assemblies, in public education, in the army, etc., is susceptible of reaching the "social brain," by paths specially destined to assure these communications, so that the state is kept up to date without the surrounding portions of society being notified. Further, there are other paths of the same kind, by which the state sends back its action to the secondary centers. Between them there are continuing and diversified exchanges. We can say then that these latter functions are organized; for what constitutes the organization of a living body is the institution of a central organ and the connection with this organ of secondary organs. In contrast, we say of present economic functions that they are diffused, the diffusion consisting in the absence of organization.

This granted, it is easy to establish that among economic doctrines, there are some which demand the linking of commercial and industrial activities to the directing and conscious agencies of society, and that these doctrines are opposed to others which, on the contrary, call for a greater diffusion. It seems incontestable that in giving to the first of these doctrines the name socialist, we do not violate the customary meaning of the word. For all the doctrines ordinarily called socialist agree on this claim. . . .

We denote as socialist every doctrine which demands the connection of all economic functions, or of certain among them, which are at the present time diffuse, to the directing and concious centers of society. It is important to note at once that we say connection, not subordination. In fact this bond between the economic life and the state does not imply, according to our belief, that every *action* should come from the latter. On the contrary, it is natural that it receive from it as much as it gives it. One can foresee that the industrial and commercial life, once put in *permanent* contact with it, will affect its functioning, will contribute to determining the manifestations of its activity much more than today, will play in the life of government a much more important role; and this explains how, while complying with the definition we have just obtained, there are socialist systems which tend to anarchy. It is because, for them, this transformation must result in making the state subordinate to economic functions, rather than putting them in its hands. . . .

. . . Socialists do not demand that the economic life be put into the hands of the state, but into contact with it. On the contrary, they declare that it should react on the state at least as much as – if not more than – the latter acts on it. In their thinking, this rapport should have the effect, not of subordinating industrial and commercial interests to "political" interests, but rather of elevating the former to the rank of the latter. For, once this constant communication is assured, these economic interests would effect the functioning of the government organ much more profoundly than today and contribute in much larger measure to determining its course. Very far from relegating economic interests to second place, it would much rather be a question of calling upon them to play, in the whole of social life, a considerably more important role than is permitted today, when precisely because of their distance from the directing centers of society, they can activate the latter only feebly and intermittently. Even according to the most celebrated theoreticians of socialism, the state as we know it would disappear and no longer be the central point of economic life – rather than economic life being absorbed by the state. For this reason, in the definition, we have not used the term "state," but the expression – expanded and somewhat figurative – "the knowing and managing organs of society." . . .

Comparing this definition of the concept with those generally held of socialism, we can now ascertain the differences. Thus, according to the terms of our formula the theories which recommend, as a remedy for the evils suffered by present societies, a greater development of charitable and provident institutions (not only private, but public), would not be called socialist, although very often one does call them this – either to attack or to defend them. But it is not that our definition is in error; it is that by so calling them one gives them an unfitting name. For, however generous they may be, however useful it may be to put them into practice – which is not under discussion – they do not correspond at all to the needs and thoughts socialism has awakened and expresses. . . .

Another important remark our definition gives rise to is that neither class war, nor concern about rendering economic relations more equitable and even more favorable for workers, figures in it. Far from being the whole of socialism, these characteristics do not even represent an essential element of it, nor are they *sui generis*, part of it. We are, it is true, so accustomed to an entirely different conception that at first such a statement is rather surprising and could arouse doubts as to the exactness of our definition. Do not both partisans and adversaries constantly present socialism to us as the philosophy of the working classes? But it is now easy to see that this tendency is far from the only one which inspires it but is actually only a particular, and is a derived form of the more general tendency (in the service of which we have expressed it). In reality, amelioration of the workers' fate is only one goal that socialism desires from the economic organization it demands, just as class war is only one of the means by which this reorganization could result, one aspect of the historic development producing it.

And in fact, what is it, according to socialists that causes the inferiority of the working classes and the injustice whose victims it declares them to be? It is that they are placed in direct dependence, not on society in general, but on a particular class powerful enough to impose its own wishes on them. That is, the "capitalists." The workers do not do business directly with society; it is not the latter which directly remunerates them – it is the capitalist. . . .

These premises posed, it is clear that the only means of at least tempering this subjection and ameliorating this state of affairs, is to moderate the power of capital by another [force] which at first may be of equal or superior strength but which [in addition] can make its action felt in conformity with the general interests of society. For it would be altogether useless to have another individual and private force intervene in the economic mechanism. This would be to replace with another kind – and not to suppress – the slavery from which the proletariat suffers. Therefore, only the state is capable of playing the role of moderator. But for that it is essential that the economic media cease to operate outside of it, without the state being aware of them. On the contrary, by means of a continuing communication the state must know what is happening, and in turn make its own action known. If one wishes to go still further, if one intends not only to attenuate but put a radical stop to this situation, it is necessary to completely suppress the medium of the capitalist who, by wedging himself between worker and society, prevents labor from being properly appreciated and rewarded according to its social value. This last must be directly evaluated and recompensed – if not by the community (which is practically impossible), then at least by the social agency which normally represents it. This is to say that the capitalist class under these conditions must disappear, that the state fulfill these functions at the same time as it is placed in direct relation with the working class, and in consequence, must become the center of economic life. . . .

Thus our definition actually takes into account these special concerns which at first did not seem to enter; only, they are now in their proper place – which is a secondary one. Socialism does not reduce itself to a question of wages, or – as they say – the stomach. It is above all an aspiration for a rearrangement of the social structure, by relocating the industrial set-up in the totality or the social organism, drawing it out of the shadow where it was functioning automatically, summoning it to the light and to the control of the conscience. One can see that this aspiration is not felt uniquely by the lower classes but by the state itself which, as economic activity becomes a more important factor in the general life, is led by force of circumstances, by vital needs of the greatest importance, to increasingly supervise and regulate these economic manifestations. Just as the working masses tend to approach the state, the state also tends to be drawn towards them, for the single reason that it is always further extending its ramifications and its sphere of influence. Socialism is far from being an exclusively workingman's affair! Actually there are two movements under whose influence the doctrine of socialism is formed: one which comes from below and directs itself toward the higher regions of society, and the other which comes from the latter and follows a reverse direction. But since at root each is only an extension of the other, as they mutually imply each other, as they are merely different aspects of the same need of organization, one cannot define socialism by one rather than the other. . . . The result is two different kinds of socialism: a worker's socialism or a state socialism, but the separation is a simple difference of degree. . . .

However, if economic problems are posed by every socialist doctrine, most of the systems do not limit themselves to it. Almost all have more or less extended their claims to other spheres of social activity: to politics, to the family, marriage, morality, to art and literature, etc. There is even one school which has made it a rule to apply the principle of socialism to the whole of collective living. It is what Benoît Malon called "integral socialism." . . . Those schemes of individual reforms then are not neatly joined within a system but are due to the same inspiration and consequently must be given a place in our definition. This is why, after having defined socialist theories as we did in the first place, we add: "Secondly, one also calls socialist those theories which, though not directly related to the economic order, nevertheless have a connection with it." Thus socialism will be defined essentially by its economic concepts, while being able to extend beyond them.

. . . Historically, socialism does not spring from economics, but is derived from a similar source. Born at almost the same time, the two systems should obviously correspond to the same social state they express differently. And . . . not only do they coincide in certain secondary characteristics, not only did we find in both the same tendency to cosmopolitanism, the same sensuous and utilitarian tendency, but further, the fundamental principle on which they rest is identical. Both are industrialist; both proclaim that economic interests are social interests. The difference is that Saint-Simon, and all subsequent socialists, conclude that since economic factors are the substance of common life, they must be organized socially, whereas the economists refuse to subject them to any collective control and believe they can be arranged and harmonized without prior reorganization.

Of these two ways of interpreting this principle, the second is inadmissible for it is self-contradictory. If everything social is economic, the economic domain must include the social, and on the other hand, what is social could not, without contradiction, be regarded and treated as a private thing. Economists cannot escape this objection by maintaining there is nothing basic which is truly collective, that society is only a sum of individuals juxtaposed, and that social interests are the sum of individual interests. But this concept no longer has many defenders, so irreconcilable is it with the facts. If therefore one regards as established the fundamental proposition on which the two doctrines rest, the socialist and Saint-Simonian theses are logically derived. If economic interests do have the supremacy attributed to them, if as a result, it is to these interests that human ends are reduced, the only goal society can set itself is to organize industry in such a way as to secure the maximum production possible, and finally, the only means to attain this goal and to cause individuals to apply themselves, is to apportion the products thus obtained so that everyone, from top to bottom of the ladder, has enough – or better still, as much as possible.

But what is the scientific value of this principle? Saint-Simon established it by demonstrating that the powers which had dominated industry until the present, were going into decline and that this decline was inevitable. From this he concluded that it (industry) did and should tend toward complete enfranchisement, toward absolute liberation, that it was no longer to be subordinated to anything which would surpass it, that henceforth it was to be its own end and draw from itself its own rule. But this conclusion was premature. To assume that the particular state of subjection in which industry had formerly been held could not be in agreement with the new conditions of collective life, does not imply that every other type of dependence would be devoid of reason. It can well be that the transformation now necessary does not consist in suppressing all subordination, but in changing its form – not in making industrial interests a kind of unlimited absolute beyond which there is nothing, but rather in limiting them in a different manner and spirit than formerly. Not only does this hypothesis deserve examination, but in fact it is easy to understand that in any social organization, however skillfully ordered, economic functions cannot co-operate harmoniously nor be maintained in a state of equilibrium unless subjected to moral forces which surpass, contain, and regulate them.

And in fact it is a general law of all living things that needs and appetites are normal only on condition of being controlled. Unlimited need contradicts itself. . . . [A]n appetite that nothing can appease can never be satisfied. Insatiable thirst can only be a source of suffering. Whatever one does, it is never slaked. . . . It is well known that insatiability is a sign of morbidity.

Among animals this limitation comes of itself because the animal's life is essentially instinctive. . . . This is why excesses are rare. When beasts have eaten enough to satisfy their hunger they seek no more. When sexual desire is met, they are in repose.

But it is not the same with man, precisely because instincts play a lesser role in him. . . . [A]s there is nothing within an individual which constrains these appetites, they must surely be contained by some force exterior to him, or else they would become insatiable – that is, morbid. Either, knowing no limits, they become a source of torment for man, exciting him to activity that nothing can satisfy, irritating and plaguing him in a pursuit without possible end, or there must be, outside the individual, some power capable of stopping them, disciplining them, fixing a limit that nature does not.

This is what seems to have escaped Saint-Simon [and the Socialists]. To [them] it appears that the way to realize social peace is to free economic appetites of all restraint on the one hand, and on the other to satisfy them by fulfilling them. But such an undertaking is contradictory. For such appetites cannot be appeased unless they are limited and they cannot be limited except by something other than themselves. They cannot be regarded as the only purpose of society since they must be subordinated to some end which surpasses them, and it is only on this condition that they are capable of being really satisfied. Picture the most productive economic organization possible and a distribution of wealth which assures abundance to even the humblest – perhaps such a transformation, at the very moment it was constituted, would produce an instant of gratification. But this gratification could only be temporary. For desires, though calmed for an instant, will quickly acquire new exigencies. Unless it is admitted that each individual is equally compensated – and such leveling, if it conforms to the communist ideal, is as opposed as possible to the Saint-Simonian doctrine, as to every socialist theory – there will always be some workers who will receive more and others less. So it is inevitable that at the end of a short time the latter find their share meager compared with what goes to the others, and as a result new demands arise, for all levels of the social scale. And besides, even apart from any feeling of envy, excited desires will tend naturally to keep outrunning their goals, for the very reason that there will be nothing before them which stops them. And they will call all the more imperiously for a new satisfaction, since those already secured will have given them more strength and vitality. This is why those at the very top of the hierarchy, who consequently would have nothing above them to stimulate their ambition, could nevertheless not be held at the point they had reached, but would continue to be plagued by the same restlessness that torments them today. What is needed if social order is to reign is that the mass of men be content with their lot. But what is needed for them to be content, is not that they have more or less but that they be convinced they have no right to more. And for this, it is absolutely essential that there be an authority whose superiority they acknowledge and which tells them what is right. For an individual committed only to the pressure of his needs will never admit he has reached the extreme limits of his rightful portion. If he is not conscious of a force above him which he respects, which stops him and tells him with authority that the compensation due him is fulfilled, then inevitably he will expect as due him all that his needs demand. And since in our hypothesis these needs are limitless, their exigency is necessarily without limit. For it to be otherwise, a moral power is required whose superiority he recognizes, and which cries out, "You must go no further." . . .

From *The Division of Labor in Society*

Emile Durkheim, *The Division of Labor in Society*, trans. W. D. Halls (New York: Free Press, 1984), pp. 181–3, 291–308, 310–21.

. . . [I]t is a truth generally recognised today that pleasure does not accompany states of consciousness that are either too intense or are too weak. There is pain when functional activity is insufficient, but excessive activity produces the same effect. . . .

What is more, if states of consciousness of moderate intensity are generally pleasant, they do not all present conditions equally favourable to the production of pleasure. Around the lower limit the changes through which the agreeable activity passes are too small, in absolute value, to arouse feelings of pleasure of great strength. Conversely, when it is close to the point of indifference, that is, near its maximum, the orders of magnitude in which it increases have too weak a relative value. A man possessing a very small capital cannot easily increase it in proportions that are sufficient appreciably to change his condition. This is why the initial economies that he makes bring so little enjoyment. They are too small to better his situation. The insignificant advantages they procure do not compensate for the privations that they have cost. Likewise a man whose fortune is excessive finds no longer any pleasure save in exceptional profits, for he measures their importance against what he already possesses. The state of affairs is completely different in the case of moderate fortunes. Here both the absolute size and the relative size of the variations occur under the best conditions for pleasure to arise from them, for they are easily important enough, and yet they need not be outstanding to be valued at their worth. The standard that serves to measure their value is not so high for a big depreciation in it to occur. The intensity of a pleasant stimulus cannot therefore *usefully* increase save between limits even narrower than we stated at the outset, for it produces its complete effect only in the space that corresponds to the average area of the pleasant activity. Below this and beyond this pleasure still continues, but it is not in proportion to the cause that produces it, whilst in that more temperate zone the slightest variations are savoured and appreciated. Nothing is lost of the force of the stimulus, which is converted wholly into pleasure.

What we have just said about the intensity of each stimulus could be repeated about their number. They cease to be pleasant when they are too many or too few, just as when they exceed or do not reach a certain degree of intensity. Not without reason does human experience see the *aurea mediocritas* as the condition of happiness. . . .

Other considerations lead to the same conclusion.

We cannot state categorically that every pleasurable state is useful, nor that pleasure and utility always vary in the same direction and in the same relationship. Yet an organism that in principle might take pleasure in things that were harmful to it could plainly not sustain itself. Thus we can accept as a very general truth that pleasure is not linked to harmful states, that is, on the whole, happiness coincides with a state of health. Only creatures afflicted with some kind of physiological or psychological abnormality find pleasure in states of sickness. Now health consists in a moderate degree of activity. In fact it implies the harmonious development of all functions and these cannot develop harmoniously unless they moderate one another, that is, contain one another mutually within certain bounds, beyond which sickness begins and pleasure ceases. As for the simultaneous growth of all faculties, this is not possible for any given creature, save to a very restricted extent that is determined by the congenital state of the individual.

In this way we understand what limits human happiness: it is the constitution of man itself, taken at every moment in his history. Given his temperament, the degree of physical and moral development that he has attained, there is a maximum degree of happiness, just as there is a maximum degree of activity, that he cannot exceed. . . .

Up to now we have studied the division of labour only as a normal phenomenon. Yet, like all social facts, and more generally, like all biological ones, it manifests pathological forms that we must analyse. If normally the division of labour produces social solidarity, it can happen, however, that it has entirely different or even opposite results. It is important that we should investigate what makes it deviate in this way from its natural course, for so long as it has not been established that these cases are exceptional, the division of labour might be suspected of logically implying them. Moreover, the study of deviant forms will allow us to determine better the conditions for the existence of the normal state. When we know the circumstances in which the division of labour ceases to engender solidarity, we shall know better what is necessary for it to have its full effect. Here as elsewhere pathology is a precious ancillary to physiology. . . .

A first case of this nature is provided for us by industrial or commercial crises, and by the bankruptcies that are so many partial breaks in organic solidarity. They demonstrate in fact that at certain points of the organism certain social functions are not adjusted to one another. As labour becomes increasingly divided up these phenomena seem to become more frequent, at least in certain cases. . . .

Hostility between labour and capital is another example, a more striking one, of the same phenomenon. As industrial functions specialise more the struggle becomes more fierce, far from solidarity increasing. . . .

What makes these facts serious is that sometimes they have been seen to be a necessary consequence of the division of labour, as soon as it has passed a certain stage in its development. In that case, it has been said, the individual, bent low over his task, will isolate himself in his own special activity. He will no longer be aware of the collaborators who work at his side on the same task, he has even no longer any idea at all of what that common task consists. The division of labour cannot therefore be pushed too far without being a source of disintegration.

Every decomposition of any kind [asserts Auguste Comte] necessarily tending to set off a corresponding dispersion, the basic distribution of human labour cannot avoid creating individual divergences, both intellectual and moral, in proportion, whose combined influence must require to the same extent a permanent discipline, capable of constantly forestalling or containing their discordant upsurge. . . .

Although Auguste Comte recognised that the division of labour is a source of solidarity, he does not appear to have perceived that this solidarity is *sui generis* and is gradually substituted for that which social similarities engender. . . .

Indeed we know that wherever it is to be observed, we meet at the same time a regulatory system sufficiently developed to determine the mutual relationships between functions. For organic solidarity to exist it is not enough for there to be a system of organs necessary to one another that feel their solidarity in a general way. The manner in which they should co-operate, if not on every kind of occasion when they meet, at least in the most common circumstances, must be predetermined. Otherwise, a fresh struggle would be required each time in order to bring them into a state of equilibrium with one another, for the conditions for this equilibrium can only be found by a process of trial and error, in the course of which each party treats the other as an opponent as much as an auxiliary. Such conflicts would therefore break out continually, and in consequence solidarity would be hardly more than virtual, and the mutual obligations would have to be negotiated anew in their entirety for each individual case. It will be objected that contracts exist. But firstly, not every social relationship is capable of assuming this legal form. Moreover, we know that a contract is not sufficient in itself, but supposes a regulatory system that extends and grows more complicated just as does contractual life itself. Moreover, the ties originating in this way are always of short duration. The contract is only a truce, and a fairly precarious one at that; it suspends hostilities only for a while. Doubtless, however precise the regulatory system may be, it will always leave room for much dispute. But it is neither necessary nor even possible for social life to be without struggle. The role of solidarity is not to abolish competition but to moderate it.

Moreover, in the normal state, these rules emerge automatically from the division of labour; they are, so to speak, its prolongation. Certainly if the division of labour only brought together individuals who unite for a brief space of time with a view to the exchange of personal services, it could not give rise to any regulatory process. But what it evokes are functions, that is, definite ways of acting that are repeated identically in given circumstances, since they relate to the general, unchanging conditions of social life. The relationships entertained between these functions cannot therefore fail to arrive at the same level of stability and regularity. . . .

Now, in all the cases we have described above, this regulatory process either does not exist or is not related to the degree of development of the division of labour. Nowadays there are no longer any rules that fix the number of economic undertakings, and in each branch of industry production is not regulated in such a way that it remains exactly at the level of consumption. . . .

The relationships between capital and labour have up to now remained in the same legal state of indeterminacy. The contract for the hiring of services occupies in our legal codes a very small place, particularly when we consider the diversity and complexity of the relationships it is called upon to regulate. Moreover, we need emphasise no further the deficiencies that all peoples feel at the present time and that they are attempting to remedy. . . .

These various examples are therefore varieties of a same species. In all these cases, if the division of labour does not produce solidarity it is because the relationships between the organs are not regulated; it is because they are in a state of *anomie*. . . .

. . . [T]he division of labour does not produce these consequences through some imperative of its own nature, but only in exceptional and abnormal circumstances. For it to be able to develop without having so disastrous an influence on the human consciousness, there is no need to mitigate it by means of its opposite. It is necessary and sufficient for it to be itself, for nothing to come from outside to deform its nature. For normally the operation of each special function demands that the individual should not be too closely shut up in it, but should keep in constant contact with neighbouring functions, becoming aware of their needs and the changes that take place in them, etc. The division of labour supposes that the worker, far from remaining bent over his task, does not lose sight of those co-operating with him, but acts upon them and is acted upon by them. He is not therefore a machine who repeats movements the sense of which he does not perceive, but he knows that they are tending in a certain direction, towards a goal that he can conceive of more or less distinctly. He feels that he is of some use. For this he has no need to take in very vast areas of the social horizon; it is enough for him to perceive enough of it to understand that his actions have a goal beyond themselves. Thenceforth, however specialised, however uniform his activity may be, it is that of an intelligent being, for he knows that his activity has a meaning. The economists would not have left this essential characteristic of the division of labour unclarified and as a result would not have lain it open to this undeserved reproach, if they had not reduced it to being only a way of increasing the efficiency of the social forces, but had seen it above all as a source of solidarity.

However, it is not enough for rules to exist, for occasionally it is these very rules that are the cause of evil. This is what happens in the class war. The institution of classes or castes constitutes one organisation of the division of labour, one that is closely regulated. Yet it is often a source of dissension. Since the lower classes are not, or no longer are, satisfied with the role that has fallen to them by custom or law, they aspire to functions that are prohibited to them and seek to dispossess those who exercise them. Hence civil wars, which arise from the way in which labour is shared out.

No similar phenomenon is to be observed within the organism. Doubtless in moments of crisis its different elements war with one another, feeding at the expense of one another. But a cell or an organ never attempts to usurp any role other than that which is rightfully its own.

The reason for this being the case is that each anatomical element proceeds mechanically towards its goal. Its constitution and place in the organism determine its vocation; its task is a consequence of its nature. It can perform it badly, but it cannot assume that of another, unless the latter abandons it, as happens in . . . rare cases of substitution. . . . The same does not hold good for societies. Here the chance factor is greater. There is a larger gap between the hereditary tendencies of the individual and the social function he will fulfil. Hereditary tendencies do not signify with such direct necessity any set function. The field is open to trial and error and discussion, as well as being open to the free play of a host of causes that may make the individual nature deviate from its normal path, thus creating a pathological state. Since the organisation is more flexible, it is also more delicate and amenable to change. We are certainly not predestined from birth to any particular form of employment, but we nevertheless possess tastes and aptitudes that limit our choice. If no account is taken of them, if they are constantly frustrated in our daily occupation, we suffer, and seek the means of bringing that suffering to an end. There is no solution other than to change the established order and create a new one. For the division of labour to engender solidarity, it is thus not sufficient for everyone to have his task: it must also be agreeable to him.

This condition is not realised in the instance we are examining. Indeed, if the institution of class or caste sometimes gives rise to miserable squabbling instead of producing solidarity, it is because the distribution of social functions on which it rests does not correspond, or rather no longer corresponds, to the distribution of natural abilities. . . . For needs to spread from one class to another, the differences originally separating these classes must have disappeared or grown less. As a result of the changes that have occurred in society, one group must have become capable of carrying out functions that were originally beyond its capacity, at the same time as another group was losing its original superiority. When the plebeians began to dispute with the patricians the honour of performing religious and administrative functions, it was not merely to imitate them, but it was because they [the plebeians] had become more intelligent, more wealthy and more numerous, and their tastes and ambitions had in consequence been modified. Through these transformations the congruence in a whole sector of society was broken between the aptitudes of individuals and the kind of activity allocated to them. Constraint alone, more or less violent, more or less direct, henceforth binds them to these functions. In consequence only an imperfect, troubled form of solidarity can exist.

Such an outcome is therefore not a necessary sequel to the division of labour. It only occurs in very special circumstances, that is, when it is the result of some external constraint. Matters are very different when it is established through some purely internal and spontaneous action, without anything arising to hinder individual initiatives. On this condition, in fact, a harmony between individual natures and social functions cannot fail to occur, at least over the average number of cases. If nothing hampers or favours unduly rivals who are disputing the tasks they perform, inevitably only those most fitted for each type of activity will succeed in obtaining it. The sole cause then determining how labour is divided up is the diversity of abilities. In the nature of things this allocation is made according to aptitude, since there is no reason for it to happen otherwise. Thus a harmony is automatically realised between the constitution of each individual and his condition. It will be argued that this is not always sufficient to satisfy men, for there are some whose desires overreach their abilities. This is true, but these are exceptional cases and may be termed of a morbid kind. Normally a man finds happiness in fulfilling his nature; his needs are proportionate to his means. Thus in the organism each organ claims only that quantity of food consistent with its position.

The forced division of labour is thus a second morbid type that we can distinguish. But we must not mistake the meaning of the term. What causes constraint is not any kind of regulation, since on the contrary the division of labour, as we have just seen, cannot do without this. Even when functions are allocated in accordance with set rules, the distribution is not necessarily the result of constraint. This is what takes place even under a caste regime, so long as it is based upon the nature of society. Indeed the institution of caste is not at all times and places an arbitrary one. When it functions regularly in a society, meeting with no opposition, it is because it at least approximately expresses the immutable way in which professional abilities are distributed throughout society. This is why, although tasks are to a certain extent allocated by law, each organ performs its own spontaneously. Constraint begins only when regulation, no longer corresponding to the true state of affairs and consequently without any moral foundation, is only maintained by force.

Conversely, we may therefore state that the division of labour only produces solidarity if it is spontaneous, and to the degree that it *is* spontaneous. But spontaneity must mean not simply the absence of any deliberate, formal type of violence, but of anything that may hamper, even indirectly, the free unfolding of the social force each individual contains within himself. It not only supposes that individuals are not consigned forcibly to performing certain determined functions, but also that no obstacle whatsoever prevents them from occupying within the ranks of society a position commensurate to their abilities. In short, labour only divides up spontaneously if society is constituted in such a way that social inequalities express precisely natural inequalities. It is a necessary and sufficient condition for these inequalities neither to be emphasised nor played down through some external cause. Perfect spontaneity is therefore only a sequel to, and another form of, this further fact: absolute equality in the external conditions of the struggle. It does not consist of a state of anarchy which would allow men to satisfy freely every inclination they have, good or bad. It rather comprises a finely articulated organisation in which each social value, neither distorted in one direction nor the other by anything outside it, is appreciated at its true worth. It will be objected that even under these conditions, struggle still occurs, because of the fact that there must be victors and vanquished, with the latter accepting their defeat only under constraint. But this constraint does not resemble the other form; it has nothing in common with it save the term. What constitutes real constraint is when even struggle becomes impossible, and one is not even allowed to fight. . . .

Equality in the external conditions of the struggle is not only needed to secure each individual to his function, but also to link these functions with one another.

Indeed, contractual relationships necessarily develop with the division of labour, since the latter is not possible without exchange, of which contract is the legal form. In other words, one of the important varieties of organic solidarity is what might be termed contractual solidarity. It is undoubtedly incorrect to believe that all social relationships can be reduced to a contract, all the more so because a contract assumes the existence of something other than itself. However, there are special ties that originate in the will of individuals. There is a *consensus* of a certain kind that is expressed in contracts and that, in the higher species, represents an important factor in the general *consensus*. Thus it is necessary in higher societies for contractual solidarity to be shielded so far as possible from anything that might disturb it. . . .

But in order to achieve this result, it is not enough for the public authority to ensure that undertakings entered into are kept. It must also, at least in roughly the average number of cases, see that they are spontaneously kept. If contracts were observed only by force or the fear of force, contractual solidarity would be in an extremely parlous state. A wholly external order would ill conceal a state of contestation too general to be contained indefinitely. Yet it may be argued that for this danger not to be feared, it is enough that contracts should be freely agreed. This may be true, but the difficulty is not resolved by this, for what constitutes free consent? . . .

. . . [W]e assert that the contract is not fully agreed to unless the services exchanged are equivalent in social value. In these conditions each person will receive the object that he desires and hand over what he gives in return – what both are worth. This equilibrium of wants that the contract proclaims and embodies therefore happens and is maintained of its own accord, since it is only a consequence and a different form of the very equilibrium of things. It is truly spontaneous. It is occasionally the

case that we desire to receive more for the product that we are sur-
rendering than it is worth. Our ambitions are boundless and are consequently only moderated when they are mutually held in check by one
another. But this constraint, which prevents us from satisfying freely even
our most inordinate wants, cannot be confused with that which removes
from us the means of obtaining a just reward for our labour. . . .

The necessary and sufficient condition for this equivalence to be the
rule governing contracts is that the contracting parties should be placed
externally under equal conditions. As the assessment of matters cannot
be determined *a priori*, but arises from the exchange itself, in order to have
their labour appraised at its precise worth the individuals involved in the
exchange must dispose of no other force than that which they draw from
their social merit. In this way the value of objects corresponds exactly to
the services that they render and the toil that has been expended. For any
other factor capable of causing the value to vary is ruled out by hypothesis. Doubtless their unequal merit will always leave men unequally
placed in society. But these inequalities are only apparently external, for
they merely interpret internal inequalities from the outside. Thus their
only influence over the determination of values is to establish between
them a gradation that runs parallel to the hierarchy of social functions.
It is no longer the same if some receive additional power from some other
source. That power must needs result in displacing the point of equilibrium, and it is clear that such a displacement is independent of the social
value of things. Every form of superiority has repercussions on the way
in which contracts are arrived at. If therefore it does not depend upon
the person of individuals and their services to society, it invalidates the
moral conditions of the exchange. If one class in society is obliged, in order
to live, to secure the acceptance by others of its services, whilst another
class can do without them, because of the resources already at its disposal, resources that, however, are not necessarily the result of some
social superiority, the latter group can lord it over the former. In other
words, there can be no rich and poor by birth without their being unjust
contracts. This was the more true when the social condition was itself
hereditary and the law sanctioned all kinds of inequalities. . . .

It is to the economists that the credit goes for having first pointed out
the spontaneous character of social life, showing that constraint can only
cause it to deviate from its natural course and that normally it arises not
from arrangements imposed from without, but from its free internal
nature. In this respect they have rendered a signal service to the science
of morality, but have erred regarding the nature of that freedom. Since
they see it as a constituent attribute in men and deduce it logically from
the concept of the individual *per se*, such a freedom appears to them to
be absolute even from the state of nature, leaving out of account any kind
of society. According to them, social action has therefore nothing to add

to it; all that it can, and must, do, is to regulate its external functioning in such a way that the liberties vying with one another do not do injury to one another. But if social action does not confine itself strictly within these limits, it encroaches upon their legitimate domain and diminishes it.

Yet, apart from the fact that it is incorrect to say that any form of regulation is the product of constraint, it so happens that liberty itself is the product of regulation. Far from being a type of antagonist to social action, it is the resultant. It is so little a property inherent in the state of nature that it is, on the contrary, a conquest by society over nature. Men are naturally unequal in physical strength; they are placed in external conditions that give unequal advantages. Domestic life itself, with the property inheritance that it implies and the inequalities that flow from this, is, of all forms of social life, the one that most narrowly depends upon natural causes. We have just seen that all these inequalities are the very negation of liberty. In the final analysis what constitutes liberty is the subordination of external to social forces, for it is only on this condition that the latter can develop freely. Yet such a subordination is rather an utter reversal of the natural order. Thus it can only be realised progress-ively, as man raises himself above things so as to regulate them as he wishes, stripping them of their fortuitous, absurd and amoral character, that is, to the extent that he becomes a social being. For he cannot escape from nature save by creating another world in which he dominates it. That world is society.

The task of the most advanced societies may therefore be said to be a mission for justice. That in fact they feel the need to tread this path we have already demonstrated, and this is proved also by everyday experi-ence. Just as the ideal of lower societies was to create or maintain a common life as intense as possible, in which the individual was engulfed, ours is to inject an even greater equity into our social relationships, in order to ensure the free deployment of all those forces that are socially useful. . . .

From *The Moral Economy of the Peasant: Rebellion and Subsistence in Southeast Asia*
James C. Scott

James C. Scott, *The Moral Economy of the Peasant: Rebellion and Subsistence in Southeast Asia* (New Haven: Yale University Press, 1976), pp. 165–77.

The discussion of the norm of fairness brings us directly up against the fact that our approach to exploitation has thus far been too one-sidedly materialistic. An analysis that begins, as this one has, with the givens of the peasant household budget, and deduces peasant needs and interests from them, runs the risk of what one writer has aptly called "methodological individualism." That is, it risks treating the peasant purely as a kind of marketplace individualist who amorally ransacks his environment so as to reach his personal goal – that is, the stabilization of his subsistence arrangements. The individual and society are set apart from this perspective and society is simply the milieu in which he must act.

To be sure, the goal of assuring subsistence exists as an irreducible given in the lives of most peasants. But to stop there is to miss the critical social context of peasant action. It is to miss the central fact that the peasant is born into a society and culture that provide him with a fund of moral values, a set of concrete social relationships, a pattern of expectations about the behavior of others, and a sense of how those in his culture have proceeded to similar goals in the past. The same might be said for any goal of man in society. . . .

Woven into the tissue of peasant behavior, then, whether in normal local routines or in the violence of an uprising, is the structure of a shared moral universe, a common notion of what is just. It is this moral heritage that, in peasant revolts, selects certain targets rather than others, certain forms rather than others, and that makes possible a collective (though rarely coordinated) action born of moral outrage. . . .

. . . How can we grasp the peasant's sense of social justice? We can begin, I believe, with two moral principles that seem firmly embedded in both the social patterns and injunctions of peasant life: the *norm of reciprocity* and the *right to subsistence.* . . . Reciprocity serves as a central moral formula for interpersonal conduct. The right to subsistence, in effect, defines the minimal needs that must be met for members of the community within the context of reciprocity. Both principles correspond to vital human needs within the peasant economy; both are embodied in many concrete social patterns that owe their strength and longevity to the force of moral approval or disapproval that villagers can bring to bear.

The moral principle of reciprocity permeates peasant life, and perhaps social life in general. It is based on the simple idea that one should help those who help him or (its minimalist formulation) at least not injure them. More specifically, it means that a gift or service received creates, for the recipient, a reciprocal obligation to return a gift or service of at least comparable value at some future date. Durkheim claimed that this notion of equal exchange was a general moral principle to be found in all cultures. Many anthropologists, including Malinowski and Mauss, have found that reciprocity served as the basis for the structure of friendship and alliance in traditional societies. . . .

For our purposes, it is critical to understand that the obligation of reciprocity is a moral principle par excellence and that it applies as strongly to relationships between unequals as between equals. In peasant societies not yet permeated by class cleavage, these relationships commonly take the form of patron-client bonds. . . . As a general rule the patron is expected to protect his client and provide for his material needs whereas the client reciprocates with his labor and his loyalty. The moral tone of the relationship is often reinforced by ceremonies of ritual kinship or other symbolic ties. . . .

If the growth in permanent disparities in power opens the way to what we might call patronage, it also opens the way to exploitation. For it is such differences that allow the stronger party to take advantage of the needs of weaker parties and thus violate the norm of equivalent reciprocity. . . .

Thus, the crucial question in rural class relations is whether the relationship of dependence is seen by clients as primarily collaborative and legitimate or as primarily exploitative. . . .

If the legitimacy of elites, in the eyes of peasants, were simply a direct linear function of the balance of exchange, our task would be deceptively simple. The discontinuous character of human needs, however, makes such an easy formula inconceivable. . . .

There is strong evidence that, along with reciprocity, the right to subsistence is an active moral principle in the little tradition of the village. It is certainly inherent in the preference for social arrangements that minimize the danger of going under. . . . More important, it is reflected in the social pressures on the relatively well-to-do within the village to be open-handed toward their less fortunate neighbors. . . .

The operating assumption of the "right to subsistence" is that all members of a community have a presumptive right to a living so far as local resources will allow. This subsistence claim is morally based on the common notion of a hierarchy of human needs, with the means for physical survival naturally taking priority over all other claims to village wealth. In a purely logical sense, it is difficult to imagine how any disparities in wealth and resources can be legitimated unless the right to subsistence is given priority. This right is surely the minimal claim that an individual makes in his society and it is perhaps for this reason that it has such moral force. . . .

From *The Moral Dimension: Toward a New Economics*
Amitai Etzioni

Amitai Etzioni, *The Moral Dimension: Toward a New Economics* (New York: Free Press, 1988), pp. 208–11.

The perfect competition model assumes that the relations among the actors are impersonal, as the actors proceed independently of one another in an anonymous market. "The fortunes of any one firm are independent of what happens to any other firm: one farmer is not benefited [sic] if his neighbor's crop is destroyed." . . . One might add: or, if his neighbor's crop thrives. And each actor is out to maximize what he or she can gain. This orientation is not problematic in the neoclassical paradigm of perfect competition because it is assumed that self-interest will sustain the system. It is problematic, however, in other paradigms, which acknowledge conflict, recognize the significance of positive, mutually supporting *social* bonds, and in which actors treat each other as persons, as ends, and care for one another, as contributing to the continuity of *economic* relations.

A well-known illustration of the conflict limiting role of social bonds is found in a political arena, that of the U.S. Senate. Senators are reported to be keenly aware that they are members of one "club"; that although they are in conflict on some issues, they soon will have to work together concerning others. Hence, they endeavor to limit the scope of their conflicts; for instance, personal attacks are considered highly improper.

Similarly, among traders in the market there are social bonds that help to sustain the relationships of trust (by and large, people trust those they know much more than they do strangers), and to limit conflicts. This observation has been referred to as the pre-contractual base of contracts. This is a point sociologists have made at least since Durkheim. His work . . . shows that contracts, while on the face of it being voluntary calculated deals among uncommitted individuals, in effect draw on prior shared bonds which are not subject to negotiation, and of which the parties are often unaware. Without such bonds, contracts are nearly impossible to formulate and their enforcement costs would be often so high, that they would be impractical. . . .

Although social bonds and normative factors are frequently mutually supportive, they are independent factors and are not to be viewed as one variable. Social bonds tend to unite people through positive mutual feelings, often enhanced by compatibility of background (social bonds tend to be stronger among people of similar ethnic class and educational background than among those of highly divergent ones), by compatible or complementary personalities, and by shared social activities (from golf to bowling). Such bonds are not inherently normative; they bind as readily a group of thieves as they bind police officers sharing a beat. . . . That is, they constitute a distinct category.

Social bonds exist on both micro – one to one, or small group – and macro, society-wide, levels. Micro-bonds help transactions between brokers and their clients, sales representatives and their customers, suppliers and manufacturers, and numerous others. Socio-economic analysis need not deny that *in part* the incentives for investment is such bonds, as distinct from trying to garner maximum benefit from every transaction, are due to "enlightened" (long-term) self-interest. However, it maintains that (1) social bonds, that precede and accompany economic relations, say among members of a work crew, generate economic benefits; and (2) that they bind people to some extent even when the social bonds exact some economic costs in the short *and* in the longer run (as for example if, in order to stay in the good graces of a group, one must regularly contribute to a given charity). . . .

On the societal level, social bonds exist among regions, races, classes, and generations. In the United States macro-social bonds were quite weak between the South and the North, but strengthened after the Civil War during the Reconstruction Era. And, while during the nineteenth century and well into the twentieth, American workers were treated as socially unfit, gradually their social acceptance grew. This greater acceptance is often cited as one reason that American labor is much less radical, and more accepting of the political and the competitive economic system, than its European counterparts. Strikes and violence are reported to be less common in the United States.

The next step in developing this part of socio-economic theory is to take these observations (often made, but also often overlooked) and to render them more specific. To specify them, measurements of various attributes of the social bonds have to be tied (or correlated) to the scope (and other attributes) of competition. *A curvilinear relationship is hypothesized to exist between social bonds and competition.* All things being equal, when the bonds are absent or very weak, the capsule that contains competition is expected to be insufficient, with competition showing signs of threatening to break down the containing capsule, leading toward all-out conflict. In labor relations, long and destructive strikes, shut-outs, wild-cat strikes, acts of sabotage and violence, and use of strike breakers are indications of such a tendency. In contrast, when various ranks of the employees consider themselves as one social community, a one We (as they are said to do at Delta Airlines), labor relations are expected to be much more harmonious. (This is not to suggest that labor conflicts are caused only by weak social bonds, but that weakness of bonds is a contributing factor, or indicates the weakness of other factors that might contain conflict.)

At the opposite extreme, where social bonds are very powerful, encompassing, and tight, economic competition is likely to be restrained, if not suppressed. For example, members of a close knit family find it difficult to charge one another for services rendered, and to engage in economic transactions and competition. This is one reason market economies tend to be limited, if not absent, in small, highly communal, tribal societies.

Accordingly, *competition thrives not in impersonal, calculative systems* of independent actors unbound by social relations, as implied by the neo-classical paradigm, *nor in the socially tight world of communal societies, but in the middle range,* where social bonds are strong enough to sustain mutual trust and low transaction costs but not so strong as to suppress exchange orientations. Aside from being of middle strength (more than between total strangers, but less than between kin and close friends), social bonds support competition when they distinguish relatively clearly between behaviors that are socially offensive (e.g., cheating), and those that are acceptable or at least tolerable (e.g., trading). This is the point at which social bonds and normative factors are intertwined. . . .

chapter 8

Civil Society (1): Occupational Groups and Family

Introduction

Despite the depth and originality of his analyses of the modern state and modern economy, Durkheim is perhaps most significant as a theorist of what is today termed "civil society": that sphere of social life outside the state and the economy that is organized around the principle of solidarity and that encompasses such organizations, voluntary associations, and mediating bodies as occupational groups, the family, and educational institutions. This present chapter, together with the one that follows, presents a strong case for Durkheim as the most penetrating and insightful sociologist of modern civil society. It begins with two selections on occupational groups, one from *Suicide*, the other from *The Division of Labor* (specifically, its Preface to the Second Edition), which together formulate practical remedies or solutions to the maladies in industrial capitalism that Durkheim had specified in his earlier analyses of the modern economy. (Accordingly, the present chapter is profitably read in tandem with chapter 7.) Durkheim's solution to these economic problems is the development of "corporative organizations" or "professional groups" that mediate between the individual and larger economic institutions and that provide an encompassing moral community for that individual, while also being firmly grounded in the specific conditions of his or her economic existence. The subsequent two selections (in particular, excerpts from "The Conjugal Family") reveal the close parallels between these envisioned occupational groups and the "domestic morality" of the family – indeed, their common origins – and the very similar ways in which Durkheim conceptualizes them and understands their moral functions. A short selection by two later authors, Peter Berger and Richard John Neuhaus, speaks of "mediating structures" and argues for their supreme importance for a new public policy that would seek "empowerment" and democracy.

From *Suicide*

Emile Durkheim, *Suicide: A Study in Sociology*, trans. John A. Spaulding and George Simpson (New York: Free Press, 1951), pp. 386–91.

... The maladjustment from which we suffer does not exist because the objective causes of suffering have increased in number or intensity; it bears witness not to greater economic poverty, but to an alarming poverty of morality. . . .

... Society was originally organized on the family basis; it was formed by the union of a number of smaller societies, clans, all of whose members were or considered themselves kin. This organization seems not to have remained long in a pure state. The family quite soon ceases to be a political division and becomes the center of private life. Territorial grouping then succeeds the old family grouping. Individuals occupying the same area gradually, but independently of consanguinity, contract common ideas and customs which are not to the same extent those of their neighbors who live farther away. Thus, little aggregations come to exist with no other material foundation than neighborhood and its resultant relations, each one, however, with its own distinct physiognomy; we have the village, or better, the city-state and its dependent territory. Of course, they do not usually shut themselves off in savage isolation. They become confederated, combine under various forms and thus develop more complex societies which they enter however without sacrificing their personalities. They remain the elemental segments of which the whole society is merely an enlarged reproduction. But bit by bit, as these confederations become tighter, the territorial surroundings blend with one another and lose their former moral individuality. From one city or district to another, the differences decrease. The great change brought about by the French Revolution was precisely to carry this levelling to a point hitherto unknown. Not that it improvised this change; the latter had long since been prepared by the progressive centralization to which the ancient regime had advanced. But the legal suppression of the former provinces and the creation of new, purely artificial and nominal divisions definitely made it permanent. Since then the development of means of communication, by mixing the populations, has almost eliminated the last traces of the old dispensation. And since what remained of occupational organization was violently destroyed at the same time, all secondary organs of social life were done away with.

Only one collective form survived the tempest: the State. By the nature of things this therefore tended to absorb all forms of activity which had a social character, and was henceforth confronted by nothing but an unstable flux of individuals. But then, by this very fact, it was compelled to assume functions for which it was unfitted and which it has not been able to discharge satisfactorily.... While the State becomes inflated and hypertrophied in order to obtain a firm enough grip upon individuals, but without succeeding, the latter, without mutual relationships, tumble over one another like so many liquid molecules, encountering no central energy to retain, fix and organize them.

To remedy this evil, the restitution to local groups of something of their old autonomy is periodically suggested. This is called decentralization. But the only really useful decentralization is one which would simultaneously produce a greater concentration of social energies. Without loosening the bonds uniting each part of society with the State, moral powers must be created with an influence, which the State cannot have, over the multitude of individuals....

The only decentralization which would make possible the multiplication of the centers of communal life without weakening national unity is what might be called *occupational decentralization*. For, as each of these centers would be only the focus of a special, limited activity, they would be inseparable from one another and the individual could thus form attachments there without becoming less solidary with the whole. Social life can be divided, while retaining its unity, only if each of these divisions represents a function. This has been understood by the ever growing number of authors and statesmen, who wish to make the occupational group the base of our political organization, that is, divide the electoral college, not by sections of territory but by corporations. But first the corporation must be organized. It must be more than an assemblage of individuals who meet on election day without any common bond. It can fulfill its destined role only if, in place of being a creature of convention, it becomes a definite institution, a collective personality, with its customs and traditions, its rights and duties, its unity. The great difficulty is not to decree that the representatives shall be selected by occupation and what each occupation's share shall be, but to make each corporation become a moral individuality. Otherwise, only another external and artificial subdivision will be added to the existing ones which we wish to supplant....

From Preface to the Second Edition of
The Division of Labor in Society

Emile Durkheim, Preface to the Second Edition of *The Division of Labor in Society*, trans. W. D. Halls (New York: Free Press, 1984), pp. xxxv–lvii.

. . . If anomie is an evil it is above all because society suffers through it, since it cannot exist without cohesion and regulation. Thus moral or legal rules essentially express social needs which society alone can identify. They rest upon a climate of opinion, and all opinion is a collective matter, the result of being worked out collectively. To be shot of anomie a group must thus exist or be formed within which can be drawn up the system of rules that is now lacking.

Political society as a whole, or the state, clearly cannot discharge this function. Economic life, because it is very special and is daily becoming increasingly specialised, lies outside their authority and sphere of action. Activity within a profession can only be effectively regulated through a group close enough to that profession to be thoroughly cognisant of how it functions, capable of perceiving all its needs and following every fluctuation in them. The sole group that meets these conditions is that constituted by all those working in the same industry, assembled together and organised in a single body. This is what is termed a corporation, or professional group.

Yet in the economic field the professional group no more exists than does a professional ethic. Since the last century when, *not without reason*, the ancient corporations were dissolved, hardly more than fragmentary and incomplete attempts have been made to reconstitute them on a different basis. Doubtless, individuals who are busy in the same trade are in contact with one another by the very fact that their activities are similar. Competition with one another engenders mutual relationships. But these are in no way regular; depending upon chance meetings, they are very often entirely of an individual nature. One industrialist finds himself in contact with another, but he body of industrialists in some particular speciality do not meet to act in concert. Exceptionally, we do see all members of the same profession come together at a conference to deal with some problem of common interest. But such conferences last only a short while: they do not survive the particular circumstances that gave rise to them. Consequently the collective life for which they provided an opportunity dies more or less entirely with them.

The sole groups that have a certain permanence are what today are called unions, either of employers or workers. There is no doubt that this represents the beginnings of any organisation by occupation, although still in a rudimentary and amorphous form. In the first place, this is because a union is a private association, lacking legal authority and consequently any regulatory power. The number of such unions is theoretically unlimited, even within a particular branch of industry. As each one is independent of the others, unless they federate or unite there is nothing about them that expresses the unity of the profession as a whole. Finally, not only are unions of employers and unions of employees distinct from each other, *which is both legitimate and necessary*, but there are no regular contacts between them. They lack a common organisation to draw them together without causing them to lose their individuality, one within which they might work out a common set of rules and which, fixing their relationship to each other, would bear down with equal authority upon both. Consequently it is always the law of the strongest that decides any disputes, and a state of out and out warfare prevails. Except for actions of theirs that are dependent upon ordinary morality, in their relation to each other employers and workers are in the same situation as two autonomous states, but unequal in strength. They can, as peoples do through their governments, draw up contracts with each other. But these contracts merely express the respective state of the economic forces present, just as the treaties concluded by two belligerents do no more than express the state of their respective military forces. They confirm a state of fact; they cannot make of it a state of law.

For a professional morality and code of law to become established within the various professions in the economy, instead of the corporation remaining a conglomerate body lacking unity, it must become, or rather become once more, a well-defined, organised group – in short, a public institution. . . .

. . . Within a political society, as soon as a certain number of individuals find they hold in common ideas, interests, sentiments and occupations which the rest of the population does not share in, it is inevitable that, under the influence of these similarities, they should be attracted to one another. They will seek one another out, enter into relationships and associate together. Thus a restricted group is gradually formed within society as a whole, with its own special features. Once such a group is formed, a moral life evolves within it which naturally bears the distinguishing mark of the special conditions in which it has developed. It is impossible for men to live together and be in regular contact with one another without their acquiring some feeling for the group which they constitute through having united together, without their becoming attached to it, concerning themselves with its interests and taking it into account in their behaviour. And this attachment to something that transcends the individual, this subordination of the particular to the general interest, is the very well-spring of all moral activity. Let this sentiment only crystallise and grow more determinate, let it be translated into well-defined formulas by being applied to the most common circumstances of life, and we see gradually being constituted a corpus of moral rules.

This outcome is not only effected of its own accord; by the very nature of things it also possesses utility, and this sentiment of its utility contributes to its strength. Moreover, society is not alone in having an interest in these special groups being constituted and regulating their own activities, which otherwise would degenerate into anarchy. For his part the individual finds in them a source of satisfaction, for anarchy is personally harmful to him. . . . This is why, when individuals discover they have interests in common and come together, it is not only to defend those interests, but also so as to associate with one another and not feel isolated in the midst of their adversaries, so as to enjoy the pleasure of communicating with one another, to feel at one with several others, which in the end means to lead the same moral life together.

Domestic morality did not arise any differently. Because of the prestige that the family retains in our eyes, if it appears to us to have been and continue to be a school of altruism and abnegation, the highest seat of morality, it is through the very special characteristics it is privileged to possess, ones that could not be found at any level elsewhere. . . . Quite simply, it is a group of individuals who have drawn close to one another within the body politic through a very specially close community of ideas, feelings and interests. Blood kinship was able to make such a concentration of individuals easier, for it naturally tends to have the effect of bringing different consciousnesses together. Yet many other factors have also intervened: physical proximity, solidarity of interest, the need to unite to fight a common danger, or simply to unite, have been causes of a different kind which have made people come together.

Such causes are not peculiar to the family but are to be found, although in different forms, within the corporation. Thus if the former group has played so important a role in the moral history of humanity, why should not also the latter be capable of so doing? Undoubtedly one difference will always exist between them, inasmuch as family members share in common their entire existence, whereas the members of a corporation share only their professional concerns. The family is a kind of complete society whose influence extends to economic activity as well as to that of religion, politics, and science, etc. Everything of any importance that we do, even outside the home, has repercussions upon it and sparks off an appropriate reaction. In one sense the corporation's sphere of influence is more limited. Yet we must not forget the ever more important place that our profession assumes in our lives as work becomes increasingly segmented. The field of each individual's activity tends to be restricted by the limits prescribed by the functions especially entrusted to each individual. Moreover, if the influence of the family extends to everything, this can only be very generally so. Thus the detail escapes it. Finally, and above all, the family, by losing its former unity and indivisibility, has lost at the same time much of its effectiveness. Since nowadays the family is dispersed with each generation, man spends a not inconsiderable part of his existence far removed from any domestic influence. The corporation does not experience any such interruptions: it is as continuous as life itself. Thus the inferior position it may evince as compared with the family is in certain respects not uncompensated.

If we have thought it necessary to compare the family and the corporation in this way, it is not merely to establish between them an instructive parallel, but it is because the two institutions are not wholly unconnected. This is particularly illustrated in the history of the Roman corporations. We saw in fact that they were modelled on domestic society, of which at first they were merely a new and enlarged form. A professional grouping would not to this extent recall to mind the family grouping unless there was something akin about them. Indeed in one sense the corporation was heir to the family. So long as the economy remains exclusively agricultural, it possesses in the family and in the village (which itself is only a kind of large family) its direct organ, and it needs no other. As exchange is not at all, or only slightly developed, the peasant's life does not draw him beyond the family circle. Since economic activity has no repercussions outside the home, the family suffices to regulate it, thus itself serving as the professional grouping. But this is no longer so when trades develop, for to live off a trade one must have customers, and go outside the home to find them. One has also to go outside it in order to come into contact with one's competitors, to vie with them, and to reach an understanding with them. Moreover, directly or indirectly trades imply towns, and towns have always been created and in the main peopled by migrants, that is, individuals who have left their birthplace. Thus in this way a new form of activity was constituted, one that went beyond the primitive family organisation. For the activity not to remain in a state without any organisation, a new framework had to be created, one particular to it. In other words, a secondary group of a new kind had to be constituted. Thus the corporation was born. Exercising a function that had first been domestic, but that could no longer remain so, it replaced the family. Yet these origins do not justify our attributing to it that kind of constitutionally amoral state with which we gratuitously credit it. Just as the family had been the environment within which domestic morality and law had been worked out, so the corporation was the natural environment within which professional morality and law had to be elaborated.

... A society made up of an extremely large mass of unorganised individuals, which an overgrown state attempts to limit and restrain, constitutes a veritable sociological monstrosity. For collective activity is always too complex to be capable of finding expression in the one single organ of the state. Moreover, the state is too remote from individuals, its connections with them too superficial and irregular, to be able to penetrate the depths of their consciousness and socialise them from within. This is why, when the state constitutes the sole environment in which men can fit themselves for the business of living in common, they inevitably "contract out", detaching themselves from one another, and thus society disintegrates to a corresponding extent. A nation cannot be maintained unless, between the state and individuals, a whole range of secondary groups are interposed. These must be close enough to the individual to attract him strongly to their activities and, in so doing, to absorb him into the mainstream of social life. We have just demonstrated how professional groupings are fitted to perform this role, and how indeed everything marks them out for it. Hence we can comprehend how important it is, particularly in the economic sphere, that they should emerge from that inchoate and disorganised state in which they have lain for a century, since professions of this kind today absorb the greater part of the energies of society.

We shall perhaps now be in a better position to explain the conclusions we reached at the end of our book, *Suicide*. We proposed in it already a strong corporative organisation as a means of curing the malaise whose existence is demonstrated by the increase in suicide, linked as well to many other symptoms. Certain critics have considered that the remedy we propounded did not match up to the extent of the evil. But this is because they have misunderstood the true nature of the corporation, the place where it rightfully belongs in our collective life as a whole, and the serious anomaly arising from its abolition. They have regarded it only as a utilitarian body whose entire effect would be to improve the way in which we organise our economic interests, whereas in reality it should constitute the essential element in our social structure. The absence of any corporative institution therefore creates, in the organisation of a people such as ours, a vacuum the significance of which it is difficult to overestimate. We therefore lack a whole system of organs necessary to the normal functioning of social life. Such a structural defect is plainly not some local affliction limited to one segment of society: it is a sickness *totius substantiae*, one that affects the entire organism. Consequently any venture whose purpose is to effect a cure cannot fail to have the most far-reaching consequences. The general health of the body social is at stake.

Yet this is not to say that the corporation is a kind of cure-all which can serve any purpose. The crisis from which we are suffering does not stem from one single, unique cause. For it to be dispelled, it is not enough to establish some kind of regulatory system wherever necessary: the system should also be fair, as is fitting. But, as we shall state later on, "So long as there are rich and poor from birth, there can exist no just contract," nor any just distribution of social status. Yet if corporative reform does not remove the need for other reforms, it is the *sine qua non* of their effectiveness. Let us suppose that the overriding consideration of ideal justice has been finally realised, that men begin their lives in a state of perfect economic equality, that is, that wealth has completely ceased to be hereditary. The problems with which we are now grappling would not thereby have been resolved. In fact, the economic mechanism will always continue to exist, as will the various actors who co-operate in its workings. Thus their rights and duties will have to be determined, and indeed for every type of industry. For each profession a set of rules will have to be drawn up, fixing the amount of labour required, the just reward for the various people engaged in it, and their duties towards the community and towards one another, etc. Thus, just as at the present time, we shall be faced with a clean sweep. Merely because wealth will not be handed down according to the same principles as at the present time, the state of anarchy will not have disappeared. That state does not only depend upon the fact that things are located here rather than there, or in the hands of this person rather than in another's, but will depend upon the fact that the activity for which these matters are the occasion, or the instrument, remains unregulated. Nor will it become regulated as if by magic as soon as it becomes useful to do so, unless the forces needed to institute that regulatory system have been mobilised and organised beforehand.

Something else must be added: new difficulties would then arise which would remain insoluble without a corporative organisation. Up to now it has been the family which, either by the institution of property held in common or by that of inheritance, had maintained the continuity of economic life. Either it possessed and exploited wealth on an indivisible basis or, as soon as this ancient family form of communism was upset, it was the family which received the wealth bequeathed – the family represented by the closest relatives, upon the death of the owner. In the first case no change was even wrought through death, and the relationship of things to persons remained as they were, with no modification even through the accession of new generations. In the second case the change was effected automatically and there was no perceptible time when the wealth remained idle, with no one available to utilise it. But if domestic society is no longer to play this role, another social organ must indeed replace it in order to exercise this most necessary function. For there is only one means by which to prevent the functioning of affairs from being interrupted from time to time. This is if a group – such as the family – which is an enduring entity, either owns or exploits possessions itself, or receives them as deaths occur, in order to hand them on, where appropriate, to someone else to whom they are entrusted for development. But we have stated, and repeat, that the state is ill-suited for these economic tasks, which are too specialised for it. Hence there remains only the professional grouping which can usefully perform them. It does indeed meet the two necessary conditions: it is too closely bound up with economic life not to be conscious of the economy's every need, and at the same time is at least as equally enduring as the family. But in order to fulfil that office, it must first exist, and indeed have achieved sufficient consistency and maturity to be equal to the new and complex role that may befall it.

Thus, although the problem of the corporation is not the only one which imposes itself upon public attention, there is certainly none more pressing, for other problems can only be tackled when this one has been resolved. No notable innovation of a legal kind can be introduced unless we begin by creating the body needed for the creation of the new law. This is why it is otiose to waste time in working out in too precise detail what that law should be. In the present state of scientific knowledge we cannot foresee what it should be, except in ever approximate and uncertain terms. How much more important it is to set to work immediately on constituting the moral forces which alone can give that law substance and shape!

From "Introduction to the Sociology of the Family"

Emile Durkheim: On Institutional Analysis, ed. and trans. Mark Traugott (Chicago and London: University of Chicago Press, 1978), p. 211.

. . . The modern family contains within itself, in abbreviated form, the entire historical development of the family.

From "The Conjugal Family"

Emile Durkheim: On Institutional Analysis, ed. and trans. Mark Traugott (Chicago and London: University of Chicago Press, 1978), pp. 233–8.

The great change which [has] occurred [is] the progressive disruption of familial communism. In the beginning, it extended to all kinship relations; all the relatives lived in common, possessed in common. But as soon as a first dissociation occurred in the heart of originally amorphous masses, as soon as the secondary zones appeared, communism withdrew and concentrated itself exclusively in the primary or central zone. When the agnatic family emerged from the clan, communism ceased to be the basis of the agnatic family. Finally, little by little, it was confined to the primary circle of relatedness. In the patriarchal family, the father of the family was liberated from it, since he freely and personally controlled the family property. In the paternal family, it was more marked, because the familial types belonged to a lower species. However, the members of the family could have title to personal wealth even though they could not dispose of or administer it personally. Finally, in the conjugal family, only vestiges of this right remained: this development was, therefore, linked to the same causes as the preceding one. The same causes which had the effect of progressively restricting the family circle also allowed the personalities of the family members to come forth more and more. The more the social milieu extended, the less, we are saying, the development of private divergences was contained. But, among these divergences, there were some which were specific to the individual, to each member of the family, and these continually became more numerous and more important as the field of social relations became more vast. Therefore, wherever they encountered weak resistance, it was inevitable that they reproduce themselves outside, that they be accentuated, consolidated, and, as they were the property of the individual personality, they necessarily tended to develop. Each individual increasingly assumed his own character, his personal manner of thinking and feeling. In these circumstances, communism became more and more impossible because it, on the contrary, presupposed the identity and fusion of all consciousnesses within a single common consciousness which embraced them. We can be certain that this disappearance of communism which characterizes our domestic law not only is not a transient, chance event but, on the contrary, that it will become ever more pronounced – unless, by some unforeseen and nearly incomprehensible miracle, the fundamental conditions which have dominated social evolution since its beginning do not remain the same.

Does domestic solidarity emerge weakened or reinforced by these changes? It is very difficult to respond to this question. In one sense, it is stronger, since the bonds of relatedness are today indissoluble; but in another, the obligations to which it gives rise are less numerous and less important. What is certain is that it is transformed. It depends on two factors: persons and things. We retain solidarity with our family because we feel solidarity with the persons who compose it; but we also retain solidarity with it because we cannot do without certain things and because, under a system of familial communism, it is the family which possesses them. The result of the breakdown of communism is that things cease, to an ever greater extent, to act as a cement for domestic society. Domestic solidarity becomes entirely a matter of persons. We are attached to our family only because we are attached to the person of our father, our mother, our wife, or our children. It was quite different formerly, when the links which derived from things took precedence over those which derived from persons, when the whole familial organization had as its primary object to keep the domestic property within the family, and when all personal considerations appeared secondary to these considerations.

That is how the family has tended to develop. But if this is an accurate description, if things possessed in common cease to be a factor in domestic life, then the right of inheritance no longer has any reason to exist. It is nothing but familial communism being continued under a system of private property. If, therefore, communism goes away, disappears from all the zones of the family, how can the right of inheritance maintain itself? In fact, it regresses in the most regular manner. At first it belongs in an imprescriptible manner to all relatives, even the most distant collaterals. But soon the right of testament appears and paralyzes it as far as the secondary zones are concerned. The right of collaterals to inherit from the deceased only comes into play if the deceased has not created any obstacle, and the power which the individual exercises in this regard becomes more extensive every day. Finally, the right to leave a will penetrates even the central zone, enters into the group formed by the parents and children. The father can disinherit his children either totally or partially. There is no doubt that this regression is destined to continue. I mean that not only will the right of testament become absolute, but that a day will come when a man will no longer be permitted, even through a will, to leave his fortune to his descendants; that, since the French Revolution, he is not permitted to leave them his offices and honors. For conveying one's estate in a will is but the final and most diminished form of hereditary transmission. As of the present, there are valuable commodities of the greatest importance which can no longer be transmitted by any hereditary means; [these are, to be precise,] offices and honors. At present, there is a whole category of workers who can no longer transmit to their children the fruits of their labor, namely, those whose work brings only honor and respect rather than wealth. It is certain that this rule will tend to be generalized more and more and that hereditary transmission will tend to become more and more distinct.

From still another point of view, the change becomes more and more necessary. As long as riches are transmitted hereditarily, there are some who are rich and some who are poor by birth. The moral conditions of our social life are such that societies can be maintained only if the external inequalities with which individuals are faced are leveled to an ever greater degree. This does not mean that men must become more equal among themselves – on the contrary, their internal inequality continually increases – but that there should be no social inequalities other than those which derive from the personal worth of each individual, and this inequality must not be exaggerated or reduced through some external cause. But hereditary wealth is one of these causes. It gives to some advantages which do not derive from their own merit but which confer upon them this superiority over others. This injustice, which seems more and more intolerable to us, becomes increasingly incompatible with the conditions of existence of our societies. Everything converges, therefore, in proving that the right of inheritance, even in the form of a will, is destined progressively to disappear.

But, as necessary as this transformation may be, it will hardly be easy. Without doubt, the rule of hereditary transmission of property has its cause in the ancient familial communism, and the latter is in the process of disappearing. But, in the course of this development, we have become so used to this rule and it has been so closely linked to our entire organization that, were it to be abolished without being replaced, the vital source of social life would run dry. In effect, we are so well conditioned, so accustomed to it, that the prospect of hereditarily transmitting the fruits of our labor has become the preeminent force behind our activity. If we pursued purely personal ends, we would be far less encouraged to work, for our work makes sense only because it serves something other than ourselves. The individual is not an end sufficient unto himself. When he looks for his purpose within himself, he falls into a state of moral misery which leads him to suicide. What binds us to our work is the fact that it is our means of enriching the domestic patrimony, of increasing the well-being of our children. If this prospect were withdrawn, this extremely powerful and moral stimulant would be taken away as well. The problem is not, therefore, as simple as it first appeared. If it is to be possible for the ideal which we have just outlined to be realized, this driving force, which we risk losing, must be replaced, little by little, by another. We must be stimulated to work by something other than personal or domestic interest. On the other hand, social interest is too distant from us, too vaguely glimpsed, too impersonal for it to serve as an effective motive force. We must, therefore, be integrated into some group outside the family, one more limited than political society and closer to us. It is to this group that the very rights which the family is no longer capable of exercising will be transferred.

What can this group be? Will matrimonial society do? We have, indeed, seen it grow in the most regular fashion; it has been consolidated and become more and more coherent. The importance it assumes in the conjugal family marks the apogee of this development. Not only has marriage become almost completely indissoluble in this type of family, not only has monogamy become just about complete, but it presents two new characteristics which demonstrate the force it has assumed with time.

In the first place, it has completely ceased to be a personal contract and become a public act. A [magistrate] presides over the contracting of the marriage. Not only does the ceremony have this public character, but if the constituent formalities are not accurately fulfilled, the marriage is not valid. And we know that no legal act assumes solemn forms unless it assumes great importance.

If, from another point of view, we pass from the external conditions of marriage to the organization of matrimonial relationships, they present us with a peculiarity without parallel in the history of the family. This is the appearance of the system of community property between spouses, whether this community is all-encompassing or limited to acquisitions. Indeed, community is the rule of matrimonial society. It can be qualified, but it exists with full legitimacy if there are no contrary conventions. Thus, while communism was retreating from domestic society, it appeared in matrimonial society. Is not the latter destined to replace the former in the function we have been discussing, and isn't conjugal love the force capable of producing the same effects as love of the family?

Not at all. For conjugal society, taken by itself, is too ephemeral for that. It does not provide us with sufficiently vast perspectives. In order that we be bound to our work, we must feel that it will survive us, that some portion of it will remain after us, that even when we are no longer around, it will serve persons whom we love. We quite naturally have this feeling when we are working for our family, since it continues to exist after us. But conjugal society, on the contrary, dissolves with death in every generation. The spouses do not survive one another very long. As a result, they cannot be for one another an object sufficient to tear them from the search for fleeting sensations. That is why marriage alone does not have an influence on suicide comparable to that of the family.

There seems to be only one group close enough to the individual for him to adhere tightly to it, yet durable enough for him to aspire to its perspective. That is the occupational group. In my view, only it can succeed the family in the economic and moral functions, which the family is becoming more and more incapable of fulfilling. To extricate ourselves from the state of crisis which we are passing through, the suppression of the rule of hereditary transmission is not enough. Men must gradually be bound to professional life and must establish strong groups of this kind. Professional duty must assume the same role in men's hearts which domestic duty has hitherto played. This is the moral level already attained by the entire elite which we have discussed, and this proves that this transformation is not impracticable. (Moreover, this change will not be accomplished in an absolute manner, and there will long remain a great many vestiges of the old laws. Parents will always be encouraged to work by the desire to feed and raise their families, but this driving force would not, by itself, be sufficient to) [disperse and eliminate the family. On the contrary, the occupational group is, in its essence, a perpetual entity.] . . .

From *To Empower People: From State to Civil Society*
Peter L. Berger and Richard John Neuhaus

Peter L. Berger and Richard John Neuhaus, *To Empower People: From State to Civil Society* (Washington, DC: American Enterprise Institute for Public Policy Research, 1977), pp. 1–21.

... [W]e suggest that the modern welfare state is here to stay, indeed that it ought to expand the benefits it provides – but that *alternative mechanisms are possible to provide welfare-state services....*

Of course there are no panaceas. The alternatives proposed here, we believe, can solve *some* problems. Taken seriously, they could become the basis of far-reaching innovations in public policy, perhaps of a new paradigm for at least sectors of the modern welfare state.

The basic concept is that of what we are calling mediating structures. The concept in various forms has been around for a long time. What is new is the systematic effort to translate it into specific public policies. For purposes of this study, mediating structures are defined as *those institutions standing between the individual in his private life and the large institutions of public life.*

Modernization brings about an historically unprecedented dichotomy between public and private life. The most important large institution in the ordering of modern society is the modern state itself. In addition, there are the large economic conglomerates of capitalist enterprise, big labor, and the growing bureaucracies that administer wide sectors of the society, such as in education and the organized professions. All these institutions we call the *megastructures.*

Then there is that modern phenomenon called private life. It is a curious kind of preserve left over by the large institutions and in which individuals carry on a bewildering variety of activities with only fragile institutional support.

For the individual in modern society, life is an ongoing migration between these two spheres, public and private. The megastructures are typically alienating, that is, they are not helpful in providing meaning and identity for individual existence. Meaning, fulfillment, and personal identity are to be realized in the private sphere. While the two spheres interact in many ways, in private life the individual is left very much to his own devices, and thus is uncertain and anxious. Where modern society is "hard," as in the megastructures, it is personally unsatisfactory; where it is "soft," as in private life, it cannot be relied upon. Compare, for example, the social realities of employment with those of marriage.

The dichotomy poses a double crisis. It is a crisis for the individual who must carry on a balancing act between the demands of the two spheres. It is a political crisis because the megastructures (notably the state) come to be devoid of personal meaning and are therefore viewed as unreal or even malignant. Not everyone experiences this crisis in the same way. Many who handle it more successfully than most have access to institutions that *mediate* between the two spheres. Such institutions have a private face, giving private life a measure of stability, and they have a public face, transferring meaning and value to the megastructures. Thus, mediating structures alleviate each facet of the double crisis of modern society. Their strategic position derives from their reducing both the anomic precariousness of individual existence in isolation from society and the threat of alienation to the public order.

Our focus is on four such mediating structures – neighborhood, family, church, and voluntary association. This is by no means an exhaustive list, but these institutions were selected for two reasons: first, they figure prominently in the lives of most Americans and, second, they are most relevant to the problems of the welfare state with which we are concerned. The proposal is that, if these institutions could be more imaginatively recognized in public policy, individuals would be more "at home" in society, and the political order would be more "meaningful."

Without institutionally reliable processes of mediation, the political order becomes detached from the values and realities of individual life. Deprived of its moral foundation, the political order is "delegitimated." When that happens, the political order must be secured by coercion rather than by consent. And when that happens, democracy disappears. . . .

In his classic study of suicide, Emile Durkheim describes the "tempest" of modernization sweeping away the "little aggregations" in which people formerly found community, leaving only the state on the one hand and a mass of individuals, "like so many liquid molecules," on the other. . . .

Liberalism's blindness to mediating structures can be traced to its Enlightenment roots. Enlightenment thought is abstract, universalistic, addicted to what Burke called "geometry" in social policy. The concrete particularities of mediating structures find an inhospitable soil in the liberal garden. There the great concern is for the individual ("the rights of man") and for a just public order, but anything "in between" is viewed as irrelevant, or even an obstacle, to the rational ordering of society. What lies in between is dismissed, to the extent it can be, as superstition, bigotry, or (more recently) cultural lag. . . .

The left, understood as some version of the socialist vision, has been less blind to the problem of mediation. Indeed the term alienation derives from Marxism. The weakness of the left, however, is its exclusive or nearly exclusive focus on the capitalist economy as the source of this evil, when in fact the alienations of the socialist states, insofar as there are socialist states, are much more severe than those of the capitalist states. . . .

On the right of the political broad center, we also find little that is helpful. To be sure, classical European conservatism had high regard for mediating structures, but, from the eighteenth century on, this tradition has been marred by a romantic urge to revoke modernity – a prospect that is, we think, neither likely nor desirable. . . .

As is now being widely recognized, we need new approaches free of the ideological baggage of the past. The mediating structures paradigm cuts across current ideological and political divides. . . .

The argument of this essay – and the focus of the research project it is designed to introduce – can be subsumed under three propositions. The first proposition is analytical: *Mediating structures are essential for a vital democratic society.* The other two are broad programmatic recommendations: *Public policy should protect and foster mediating structures,* and *Wherever possible, public policy should utilize mediating structures for the realization of social purposes.* The research project will determine, it is hoped, whether these propositions stand up under rigorous examination and, if so, how they can be translated into specific recommendations.

The analytical proposition assumes that mediating structures are the value-generating and value-maintaining agencies in society. Without them, values become another function of the megastructures, notably of the state, and this is a hallmark of totalitarianism. In the totalitarian case, the individual becomes the object rather than the subject of the value-propagating processes of society.

The two programmatic propositions are, respectively, minimalist and maximalist. Minimally, public policy should cease and desist from damaging mediating structures. Much of the damage has been unintentional in the past. We should be more cautious than we have been. As we have learned to ask about the effects of government action upon racial minorities or upon the environment, so we should learn to ask about the effects of public policies on mediating structures.

The maximalist proposition ("utilize mediating structures") is much the riskier. We emphasize, "wherever possible." The mediating structures paradigm is not applicable to all areas of policy. Also, there is the real danger that such structures might be "co-opted" by the government in a too eager embrace that would destroy the very distinctiveness of their function. The prospect of government control of the family, for example, is clearly the exact opposite of our intention. The goal in utilizing mediating structures is to expand government services without producing government oppressiveness. Indeed it might be argued that the achievement of that goal is one of the acid tests of democracy. . . .

The theme is *empowerment*. One of the most debilitating results of modernization is a feeling of powerlessness in the face of institutions controlled by those whom we do not know and whose values we often do not share. . . . The mediating structures under discussion here are the principal expressions of the real values and the real needs of people in our society. They are, for the most part, the people-sized institutions. Public policy should recognize, respect, and, where possible, empower these institutions. . . .

. . . [M]odernization has already had a major impact on the family. It has largely stripped the family of earlier functions in the areas of education and economics, for example. But in other ways, modernization has made the family more important than ever before. It is the major institution within the private sphere, and thus for many people the most valuable thing in their lives. Here they make their moral commitments, invest their emotions, plan for the future, and perhaps even hope for immortality.

There is a paradox here. On the one hand, the megastructures of government, business, mass communications, and the rest have left room for the family to be the autonomous realm of individual aspiration and fulfillment. This room is by now well secured in the legal definitions of the family. At the same time, the megastructures persistently infringe upon the family. We cannot and should not eliminate these infringements entirely. After all, families exist in a common society. We can, however, take positive measures to protect and foster the family institution, so that it is not defenseless before the forces of modernity.

This means public recognition of the family *as an institution*. It is not enough to be concerned for individuals more or less incidentally related to the family as institution. Public recognition of the family as an institution is imperative because every society has an inescapable interest in how children are raised, how values are transmitted to the next generation. Totalitarian regimes have tried – unsuccessfully to date – to supplant the family in this function. Democratic societies dare not try if they wish to remain democratic. Indeed they must resist every step, however well intended, to displace or weaken the family institution.

Public concern for the family is not antagonistic to concern for individual rights. On the contrary, individuals need strong families if they are to grow up and remain rooted in a strong sense of identity and values. Weak families produce uprooted individuals, unsure of their direction and therefore searching for some authority. They are ideal recruits for authoritarian movements inimical to democratic society.

Commitment to the family institution can be combined, although not without difficulty, with an emphatically libertarian view that protects the private lives of adults against public interference of any kind. Public interest in the family is centered on children, not adults; it touches adults insofar as they are in charge of children. The public interest is institutional in character. That is, the state is to view children as members of a family. . . .

We have no intention of glorifying the bourgeois family. Foster parents, lesbians and gays, liberated families, or whatever – all can do the job *as long as* they provide children the loving and the permanent structure that traditional families have typically provided. Indeed, virtually any structure is better for children than what experts or the state can provide.

Most modern societies have in large part disfranchised the family in the key area of education. The family becomes, at best, an auxiliary agency to the state, which at age five or six coercively (compulsory school laws) and monopolistically (for the most part) takes over the child's education. Of course there are private schools, but here class becomes a powerful factor. Disfranchisement falls most heavily on lower-income parents who have little say in what happens to their children in school. This discrimination violates a fundamental human right, perhaps the most fundamental human right – the right to make a world for one's children. . . .

chapter 9

Civil Society (2): Education

Introduction

Durkheim's analyses of modern civil society continue in this chapter, which is concerned specifically with his educational sociology. A first selection, from "Education: Its Nature and Its Role," sets forth Durkheim's definition of the educational process, his assessment of its social functions and moral significance, and his conception of the "duties and . . . rights" of the modern state with respect to it. A second selection, from *Moral Education*, further develops the theme of schooling as a moral enterprise, suggesting that education would serve as "intermediary between the affective morality of the family and the more rigorous morality of civic [including occupational] life" (p. 243). Here, in its twofold concern with the teaching of discipline as well as of group attachment, we see a recapitulation of arguments first encountered in *Suicide* (chapter 1), arguments regarding the functional significance of both moral regulation and moral integration. Here, too, we encounter the famous Durkheimian analogy between the lay teacher and the priest, both "instrument[s] of a great moral reality which surpasses" them (p. 244). A third selection, from *The Evolution of Educational Thought*, argues for a more historical perspective upon the educational process and thereby complements the largely functionalist perspective of the earlier excerpts. It underscores the social and historical relativity of the organization of schooling and of "the educational ideals which this organisation was designed to achieve" (pp. 246–7). "The history of educational thought," it concludes, "and the study of social *mores* are indeed closely linked" (p. 248). The next selection, by Talcott Parsons, amply bears out this insight, reaffirming the importance of schooling as a socializing agency, alongside the family and other sectors of civil society, but within this overall function singling out the inculcation of "achievement-motivation" as its primary contribution, at least within the context of US society. The final selection, by bell hooks, takes a different approach altogether; it stresses the "counter-hegemonic" possibilities of the classroom community and recalls the "antiracist . . . mission" in which hooks's own teachers in all-black schools had been involved during the years before desegregation.

From "Education: Its Nature and its Role"

Emile Durkheim, *Education and Sociology*, trans. Sherwood D. Fox (New York: Free Press, 1956), pp. 71–81.

. . . Education is the influence exercised by adult generations on those that are not yet ready for social life. Its object is to arouse and to develop in the child a certain number of physical, intellectual and moral states which are demanded of him by both the political society as a whole and the special milieu for which he is specifically destined.

It follows from the definition that precedes, that education consists of a methodical socialization of the young generation. In each of us, it may be said, there exist two beings which, while inseparable except by abstraction, remain distinct. One is made up of all the mental states that apply only to ourselves and to the events of our personal lives: this is what might be called the individual being. The other is a system of ideas, sentiments and practices which express in us, not our personality, but the group or different groups of which we are part; these are religious beliefs, moral beliefs and practices, national or professional traditions, collective opinions of every kind. Their totality forms the social being. To constitute this being in each of us is the end of education.

It is here, moreover, that are best shown the importance of its role and the fruitfulness of its influence. Indeed, not only is this social being not given, fully formed, in the primitive constitution of man; but it has not resulted from it through a spontaneous development. Spontaneously, man was not inclined to submit to a political authority, to respect a moral discipline, to dedicate himself, to be self-sacrificing. There was nothing in our congenital nature that predisposed us necessarily to become servants of divinities, symbolic emblems of society, to render them worship, to deprive ourselves in order to do them honor. It is society itself which, to the degree that it is firmly established, has drawn from within itself those great moral forces in the face of which man has felt his inferiority. Now, if one leaves aside the vague and indefinite tendencies which can be attributed to heredity, the child, on entering life, brings to it only his nature as an individual. Society finds itself, with each new generation, faced with a *tabula rasa*, very nearly, on which it must build anew. To the egoistic and asocial being that has just been born it must, as rapidly as possible, add another, capable of leading a moral and social life. Such is the work of education, and you can readily see its great importance. It is not limited to developing the individual organism in the direction indicated by its nature, to elicit the hidden potentialities that need only be manifested. It creates in man a new being.

This creative quality is, moreover, a special prerogative of human education. Anything else is what animals receive, if one can apply this name to the progressive training to which they are subjected by their parents. It can, indeed, foster the development of certain instincts that lie dormant in the animal, but such training does not initiate it into a new life. It facilitates the play of natural functions, but it creates nothing. Taught by its mother, the young animal learns more quickly how to fly or build its nest; but it learns almost nothing that it could not have been able to discover through its own individual experience. This is because animals either do not live under social conditions or form rather simple societies, which function through instinctive mechanisms that each individual carries within himself, fully formed, from birth. Education, then, can add nothing essential to nature, since the latter is adequate for everything, for the life of the group as well as that of the individual. By contrast, among men the aptitudes of every kind that social life presupposes are much too complex to be able to be contained, somehow, in our tissues, and to take the form of organic predispositions. It follows that they cannot be transmitted from one generation to another by way of heredity. It is through education that the transmission is effected.

However, it will be said, if one can indeed conceive that the distinctively moral qualities, because they impose privations on the individual, because they inhibit his natural impulses, can be developed in us only under an outside influence, are there not others which every man wishes to acquire and seeks spontaneously? Such are the divers qualities of the intelligence which allow him better to adapt his behavior to the nature of things. Such, too, are the physical qualities, and everything that contributes to the vigor and health of the organism. For the former, at least, it seems that education, in developing them, may only assist the development of nature itself, may only lead the individual to a state of relative perfection toward which he tends by himself, although he may be able to achieve it more rapidly thanks to the co-operation of society.

But what demonstrates, despite appearances, that here as elsewhere education answers social necessities above all, is that there are societies in which these qualities have not been cultivated at all, and that in every case they have been understood very differently in different societies. The advantages of a solid intellectual culture have been far from recognized by all peoples. . . .

It is not otherwise with physical qualities. Where the state of the social milieu inclines public sentiment toward asceticism, physical education will be relegated to a secondary place. . . . Thus, even the qualities which appear at first glance so spontaneously desirable, the individual seeks only when society invites him to, and he seeks them in the fashion that it prescribes for him.

We are now in a position to answer a question raised by all that precedes. Whereas we showed society fashioning individuals according to its needs, it could seem, from this fact, that the individuals were submitting to an insupportable tyranny. But in reality they are themselves interested in this submission; for the new being that collective influence, through education, thus builds up in each of us, represents what is best in us. Man is man, in fact, only because he lives in society. It is difficult, in the course of an article, to demonstrate rigorously a proposition so general and so important, and one which sums up the works of contemporary sociology. But first, one can say that it is less and less disputed. And more, it is not impossible to call to mind, summarily, the most essential facts that justify it.

First, if there is today an historically established fact, it is that morality stands in close relationship to the nature of societies, since, as we have shown along the way, it changes when societies change. This is because it results from life in common. It is society, indeed, that draws us out of ourselves, that obliges us to reckon with other interests than our own, it is society that has taught us to control our passions, our instincts, to prescribe law for them, to restrain ourselves, to deprive ourselves, to sacrifice ourselves, to subordinate our personal ends to higher ends. As for the whole system of representation which maintains in us the idea and the sentiment of rule, of discipline, internal as well as external – it is society that has established it in our consciences. It is thus that we have acquired this power to control ourselves, this control over our inclinations which is one of the distinctive traits of the human being and which is the more developed to the extent that we are more fully human.

We do not owe society less from the intellectual point of view. It is science that elaborates the cardinal notions that govern our thought: notions of cause, of laws, of space, of number, notions of bodies, of life, of conscience, of society, and so on. All these fundamental ideas are perpetually evolving, because they are the recapitulation, the resultant of all scientific work, far from being its point of departure as Pestalozzi believed. We do not conceive of man, nature, cause, even space, as they were conceived in the Middle Ages; this is because our knowledge and our scientific methods are no longer the same. Now, science is a collective work, since it presupposes a vast co-operation of all scientists, not only of the same time, but of all the successive epochs of history. Before the sciences were established, religion filled the same office; for every mythology consists of a conception, already well elaborated, of man and of the universe. Science, moreover, was the heir of religion. Now, a religion is a social institution.

In learning a language, we learn a whole system of ideas, distinguished and classified, and we inherit from all the work from which have come these classifications that sum up centuries of experiences. There is more: without language, we would not have, so to speak, general ideas; for it is the word which, in fixing them, gives to concepts a consistency sufficient for them to be able to be handled conveniently by the mind. It is language, then, that has allowed us to raise ourselves above pure sensation; and it is not necessary to demonstrate that language is, in the first degree, a social thing.

One sees, through these few examples, to what man would be reduced if there were withdrawn from him all that he has derived from society: he would fall to the level of an animal. If he has been able to surpass the stage at which animals have stopped, it is primarily because he is not reduced to the fruit only of his personal efforts, but co-operates regularly with his fellow-creatures; and this makes the activity of each more productive. It is chiefly as a result of this that the products of the work of one generation are not lost for that which follows. Of what an animal has been able to learn in the course of his individual existence, almost nothing can survive him. By contrast, the results of human experience are preserved almost entirely and in detail, thanks to books, sculptures, tools, instruments of every kind that are transmitted from generation to generation, oral tradition, etc. The soil of nature is thus covered with a rich deposit that continues to grow constantly. Instead of dissipating each time that a generation dies out and is replaced by another, human wisdom accumulates without limit, and it is this unlimited accumulation that raises man above the beast and above himself. But, just as in the case of the co-operation which was discussed first, this accumulation is possible only in and through society. For in order that the legacy of each generation may be able to be preserved and added to others, it is necessary that there be a moral personality which lasts beyond the generations that pass, which binds them to one another: it is society. Thus the antagonism that has too often been admitted between society and individual corresponds to nothing in the facts. Indeed, far from these two terms being in opposition and being able to develop only each at the expense of the other, they imply each other. The individual, in willing society, wills himself. The influence that it exerts on him, notably through education, does not at all have as its object and its effect to repress him, to diminish him, to denature him, but, on the contrary, to make him grow and to make of him a truly human being. No doubt, he can grow thus only by making an effort. But this is precisely because this power to put forth voluntary effort is one of the most essential characteristics of man.

This definition of education provides for a ready solution of the controversial question of the duties and the rights of the State with respect to education.

The rights of the family are opposed to them. The child, it is said, belongs first to his parents; it is, then, their responsibility to direct, as they understand it, his intellectual and moral development. Education is then conceived as an essentially private and domestic affair. When one takes this point of view, one tends naturally to reduce to a minimum the intervention of the State in the matter. The State should, it is said, be limited to serving as an auxiliary to, and as a substitute for, families. When they are unable to discharge their duties, it is natural that the State should take charge. It is natural, too, that it make their task as easy as possible, by placing at their disposal schools to which they can, if they wish, send their children. But it must be kept strictly within these limits, and forbidden any positive action designed to impress a given orientation on the mind of the youth.

But its role need hardly remain so negative. If, as we have tried to establish, education has a collective function above all, if its object is to adapt the child to the social milieu in which he is destined to live, it is impossible that society should be uninterested in such a procedure. How could society not have a part in it, since it is the reference point by which education must direct its action? It is, then, up to the State to remind the teacher constantly of the ideas, the sentiments that must be impressed upon the child to adjust him to the milieu in which he must live. If it were not always there to guarantee that pedagogical influence be exercised in a social way, the latter would necessarily be put to the service of private beliefs, and the whole nation would be divided and would break down into an incoherent multitude of little fragments in conflict with one another. One could not contradict more completely the fundamental end of all education. Choice is necessary: if one attaches some value to the existence of society – and we have just seen what it means to us – education must assure, among the citizens, a sufficient community of ideas and of sentiments, without which any society is impossible; and in order that it may be able to produce this result, it is also necessary that education not be completely abandoned to the arbitrariness of private individuals.

Since education is an essentially social function, the State cannot be indifferent to it. On the contrary, everything that pertains to education must in some degree be submitted to its influence. This is not to say, therefore, that it must necessarily monopolize instruction. . . . One can believe that scholastic progress is easier and quicker where a certain margin is left for individual initiative; for the individual makes innovations more readily than the State. But from the fact that the State, in the public interest, must allow other schools to be opened than those for which it has a more direct responsibility, it does not follow that it must remain aloof from what is going on in them. On the contrary, the education given in them must remain under its control. It is not even admissible that the function of the educator can be fulfilled by anyone who does not offer special guarantees of which the State alone can be the judge. No doubt, the limits within which its intervention should be kept may be rather difficult to determine once and for all, but the principle of intervention could not be disputed. There is no school which can claim the right to give, with full freedom, an antisocial education.

It is nevertheless necessary to recognize that the state of division in which we now find ourselves, in our country, makes this duty of the State particularly delicate and at the same time more important. It is not, indeed, up to the State to create this community of ideas and sentiments without which there is no society; it must be established by itself, and the State can only consecrate it, maintain it, make individuals more aware of it. Now, it is unfortunately indisputable that among us, this moral unity is not at all points what it should be. We are divided by divergent and even sometimes contradictory conceptions. There is in these divergences a fact which it is impossible to deny, and which must be reckoned with. It is not a question of recognizing the right of the majority to impose its ideas on the children of the minority. The school should not be the thing of one party, and the teacher is remiss in his duties when he uses the authority at his disposal to influence his pupils in accordance with his own preconceived opinions, however justified they may appear to him. But in spite of all the differences of opinion, there are at present, at the basis of our civilization, a certain number of principles which, implicitly or explicitly, are common to all, that few indeed, in any case, dare to deny overtly and openly: respect for reason, for science, for ideas and sentiments which are at the base of democratic morality. The role of the State is to outline these essential principles, to have them taught in its schools, to see to it that nowhere are children left ignorant of them, that everywhere they should be spoken of with the respect which is due them. There is in this connection an influence to exert which will perhaps be all the more efficacious when it will be less aggressive and less violent, and will know better how to be contained within wise limits.

From *Moral Education*

Emile Durkheim, *Moral Education: A Study in the Theory and Application of the Sociology of Education*, trans. Everett K. Wilson and Herman Schnurer (New York: Free Press, 1973), pp. 148–9, 154–5, 228–9.

. . . Each social group, each type of society, has and could not fail to have its own morality, which expresses its own make-up.

Now, the class is a small society. It is therefore both natural and necessary that it have its own morality corresponding to its size, the character of its elements, and its function. Discipline is this morality. The obligations we shall presently enumerate are the student's duties, just as the civic or professional obligations imposed by state or corporation are the duties of the adult. On the other hand, the schoolroom society is much closer to the society of adults than it is to that of the family. For aside from the fact that it is larger, the individuals – teachers and students – who make it up are not brought together by personal feelings or preferences but for altogether general and abstract reasons, that is to say, because of the social function to be performed by the teacher, and the immature mental condition of the students. For all these reasons, the rule of the classroom cannot bend or give with the same flexibility as that of the family in all kinds and combinations of circumstances. It cannot accommodate itself to given temperaments. There is already something colder and more impersonal about the obligations imposed by the school: they are now concerned with reason and less with feelings; they require more effort and greater application. And although . . . we must guard against over-doing it, it is nevertheless indispensable in order that school discipline be everything that it should be and fulfill its function completely. For only on this condition will it be able to serve as intermediary between the affective morality of the family and the more rigorous morality of civil life. It is by respecting the school rules that the child learns to respect rules in general, that he develops the habit of self-control and restraint simply because he should control and restrain himself. It is a first initiation into the austerity of duty. Serious life has now begun.

This, then, is the true function of discipline. It is not a simple procedure aimed at making the child work, stimulating his desire for instruction, or husbanding the energies of the teacher. It is essentially an instrument – difficult to duplicate – of moral education. The teacher to whom it is entrusted cannot guard it too conscientiously. . . .

Now, what is the source of the teacher's authority? Does it derive from a physical power with which he is armed, from his right of punishment and reward? The fear of punishment is something altogether different from respect for authority. It has a moral character and moral value only if the penalty is regarded as just by those subjected to it, which implies that the authority which punishes is itself recognized as legitimate. However, this is what is in question. It is not from the outside, from the fear he inspires, that the teacher should gain his authority; it is from himself. This cannot come to him except from his innermost being. He must believe, not perhaps in himself or in the superior quality of his intelligence or will, but in his task and the greatness of that task. It is the priest's lofty conception of his mission that gives him the authority that so readily colors his language and bearing. For he speaks in the name of a God, who he feels in himself and to whom he feels himself much closer than the laymen in the crowds he addresses. So, the lay teacher can and should have something of this same feeling. He also is an instrument of a great moral reality which surpasses him and with which he communicates more directly than does the child, since it is through his intermediation that the child communicates with it. Just as the priest is the interpreter of God, he is the interpreter of the great moral ideas of his time and country. Whatever is linked with these ideas, whatever the significance and authority attributed to them, necessarily spreads to him and everything coming from him since he expresses these things and embodies them in the eyes of children. . . .

Above all we must give the child the clearest possible idea of the social groups to which he belongs. It is here that the role of the educator is most important. . . . Now, in order to attach the child to these groups, which is the final goal of moral education, it is not enough to give him an image of them. Beyond this, the image must be repeated with such persistence that it becomes, through the sole fact of repetition, an integrating element in himself, such that he can no longer do without it. Once again, we can only become attached to things through the impressions or images we have of them. To say that the idea we acquire of these social groups is a part of our consciousness is really to say that it cannot disappear without creating a painful void. Not only must we repeat this representation, but in repeating it, give the idea enough color, form, and life to stimulate action. It must warm the heart and set the will in motion. The point here is not to enrich the mind with some theoretical notion, a speculative conception; but to give it a principle of action, which we must make as effective as necessary and possible. In other words, the representation must have something emotional; it must have the characteristic of a sentiment more than of a conception. Since, in the long run, one only learns to do by doing, we must multiply the opportunities in which the sentiments thus communicated to the child can manifest themselves in actions. To learn the love of collective life we must live it, not only in our minds and imaginations, but in reality. It is not enough to form in a child the potential for attaching himself to the group. We must stimulate this power by effective exercise; for only thus can it take shape and become strengthened. . . .

From *The Evolution of Educational Thought*

Emile Durkheim, *The Evolution of Educational Thought: Lectures on the Formation and Development of Secondary Education in France*, trans. Peter Collins (London: Routledge and Kegan Paul, 1977), pp. 8–13, 18.

... [I]t is no use trying to conceal the fact that secondary education finds itself intellectually disorientated between a past which is dying and a future which is still undecided, and as a consequence lacks the vigour and vitality which it once possessed. To say this is not to imply that anyone is to blame but rather to take note of something which is a product of the nature of things. The old faith in the perennial virtue of the classics has been definitively shaken. Even those who by inclination look most naturally towards the past have a strong sense that something has changed, that needs have arisen which will have to be satisfied. As against this, however, no new faith has yet appeared to replace the one which is disappearing. The task of educational theory is precisely to help in the development of this new faith and, consequently, of a new life. For an educational faith is the very soul which animates a teaching body.

Thus the necessity for study of educational theory turns out to be far more pressing in the case of the secondary school teacher than in that of the primary. It's not a question of simply instructing our future teachers in how to apply a number of sound recipes. They must be confronted with the problems of secondary school culture in its entirety. This is precisely what the course of study we are going to begin this year seeks to achieve.

I know that both those who over-generalise and those who are meticulously scholarly (for in this instance diametrically opposed types of mind find themselves in agreement) will claim that nothing of practical utility can be learned from history. What on earth, they ask, can the colleges of the Middle Ages tell us about secondary schools today? In what way can the scholasticism of the trivium and the quadrivium help us to discover what, here and now, we ought to be teaching to our children and how we ought to be teaching it? It is sometimes even additionally suggested that these retrospective studies can only have disadvantageous consequences; since it is the future for which we have to prepare, it is the future to which we should be looking and on which we should be concentrating our attention; excessive contemplation of the past can only hold us back. I believe, by contrast, that it is only by carefully studying the past that we can come to anticipate the future and to understand the present; consequently a history of education provides the soundest basis for the study of educational theory.

Indeed is it not already highly instructive to survey the various sorts
of education which have followed one another in the course of our history. Of course – as is too often the case – the successive variations are
attributed to the feebleness of the human intellect which has failed to grasp
the one-and-for-all-time ideal system, if they are regarded simply as a series
of mistakes painfully and imperfectly correcting themselves one after the
other, then this whole history can only be of marginal interest. At most
it could put us on our guard against repeating old mistakes; but then
again, since the realm of errors knows no bounds, error itself can appear
in an infinite variety of forms; a knowledge of the mistakes made in
the past will enable us neither to foresee nor to avert those which may
be made in the future. We shall see, however, that there was nothing
arbitrary about any of these theories and these systems, which have
undergone the test of experience and been incarnated in reality. If one
of them has not survived, this was not because it was merely the product of human aberration but rather that it was the result of specific and
mutually interacting social forces. If it has changed, this is because society
itself has changed. . . .

. . . [I]sn't it obvious that in order to play his part in that organism which
is the school, the teacher needs to know what the organism is, what are
the component parts out of which it is constituted and how they are interrelated so as to form a unity? . . . If we are to know what they are really
like and how consequently we shall behave towards them, it is not
enough to be apprised of the letter of the laws which stipulate the relevant form they are to take and lay down (in theory) how they are to be
organised. What we need to know is, as it were, the inner life of the institutions, how they are motivated and what goals they seek to achieve. For
they have acquired a momentum of their own, which drives them in
some particular direction and it is this which we need to know about more
than anything else. Now just as we need more than one point in order
to specify any particular line (especially a relatively tortuous one), so the
geometrical point which is constituted by the present moment is by itself
quite useless if what we wish to do is to plot the trajectory of a particular institution. What tends to make it move in one direction rather than
another are forces which are internal to it, which give it life, but which
do not reveal themselves clearly on the surface. In order to understand
them we need to see them at work in the course of history, for only in
history do they manifest themselves through the accumulation of their
effects. This is why no educational subject can be truly understood
except by placing it in the context of the institutional development, the
evolutionary process of which it forms a part but of which it is only the
contemporary and provisional culmination.

But it is not only the organisation of education which history helps us
to understand; it also illuminates the educational ideals which this

organisation was designed to achieve, the aims which determine and justify its existence.

Here again, it looks on the surface as if so much historical investigation was really unnecessary for solving the problem. Isn't the object of education to turn our pupils into men of their times, and in order to know what we need to produce a man of his own times is it really necessary to investigate the past? ... What we need to understand is not the man of the moment, man as we experience him at a particular point in time, influenced as we are by momentary needs and passions, but rather man in his totality throughout time.

To do this we need to cease studying man at a particular moment and instead try to consider him against the background of the whole process of his development. Instead of confining ourselves to our own particular age, we must on the contrary escape from it in order to escape from ourselves, from our narrow-minded points of view, which are both partial and partisan. And that is precisely why a study of the history of education is so important and worthwhile. Instead of starting out by what the contemporary ideal ought to be we must transport ourselves to the other end of the historical time-scale; we must strive to understand the educational ideology most remote in time from our own, the one which was the first to be elaborated in European culture. We will study it, describe it and, as far as we are able, explain it. Then, step by step, we will follow the series of changes which it has undergone, parallel to changes in society itself, until finally we arrive at the contemporary situation. That is where we must end, not where we must begin; and when, by travelling along this road, we arrive at the present-day situation it will appear in a light quite different from that in which we would have seen it, had we abandoned ourselves at once and unreservedly to our contemporary passions and prejudices. In this way we shall avoid the risk of succumbing to the prestigious influence exercised by transitory passions and predilections, because these will be counter-balanced by the newly acquired sensitivity to differences in needs and necessities – all equally legitimate – with which the study of history will have furnished us. Thus the problem, instead of being arbitrarily over-simplified, will become susceptible of a dispassionate examination, in all its complexity and in a form which is no less relevant for the student of the social ethos of our own age than it is for the historian. ...

... What we are going to try and chart is the development of all the most essential features of the French educational ideal, by scrutinising the doctrines in which it has from time to time sought to articulate itself self-consciously as well as the academic institutions whose function it was to realise it. Moreover, since the most important intellectual forces of the nation were, from the fourteenth or fifteenth century onwards, formed in our secondary schools, we shall, as we progress, be driven to what almost amounts to writing a history of the French intellectual. It is additionally true that this disproportionate role played by secondary education in the totality of that social life which is peculiar to our nation and which is not to be found anywhere else to the same extent, will, as we can be sure in advance, derive from some personally distinctive characteristic, some idiosyncrasy in our national temperament which we shall come to uncover simply because we shall be seeking the causes of this peculiarity in the history of our educational thought. The history of educational thought and the study of social *mores* are indeed closely linked. . . .

From "The School Class as a Social System: Some of its Functions in American Society" Talcott Parsons

Talcott Parsons, *Social Structure and Personality* (London: Free Press, 1964), pp. 130–41.

Our main interest . . . , is in a dual problem: first of how the school class functions to internalize in its pupils both the commitments and capacities for successful performance of their future adult roles, and second of how it functions to allocate these human resources within the role-structure of the adult society. The primary ways in which these two problems are interrelated will provide our main points of reference.

First, from the functional point of view the school class can be treated as an agency of socialization. That is to say, it is an agency through which individual personalities are trained to be motivationally and technically adequate to the performance of adult roles. It is not the sole such agency; the family, informal "peer groups," churches, and sundry voluntary organizations all play a part, as does actual on-the-job training. But, in the period extending from entry into first grade until entry into the labor force or marriage, the school class may be regarded as the focal socializing agency.

The socialization function may be summed up as the development in individuals of the commitments and capacities which are essential prerequisites of their future role-performance. Commitments may be broken down in turn into two components: commitment to the implementation of the broad *values* of society, and commitment to the performance of a specific type of role within the *structure* of society. Thus a person in a relatively humble occupation may be a "solid citizen" in the sense of commitment to honest work in that occupation, without an intensive and sophisticated concern with the implementation of society's higher-level values. Or conversely, someone else might object to the anchorage of the feminine role in marriage and the family on the grounds that such anchorage keeps society's total talent resources from being distributed equitably to business, government, and so on. Capacities can also be broken down into two components, the first being competence or the skill to perform the tasks involved in the individual's roles, and the second being "role-responsibility" or the capacity to live up to other people's expectations of the interpersonal behavior appropriate to these roles. Thus a mechanic as well as a doctor needs to have not only the basic "skills of his trade," but also the ability to behave responsibly toward those people with whom he is brought into contact in his work.

While on the one hand, the school class may be regarded as a primary agency by which these different components of commitments and capacities are generated, on the other hand, it is, from the point of view of the society, an agency of "manpower" allocation. It is well known that in American society there is a very high, and probably increasing, correlation between one's status level in the society and one's level of educational attainment. Both social status and educational level are obviously related to the occupational status which is attained. Now, as a result of the general process of both educational and occupational upgrading, completion of high school is increasingly coming to be the norm for minimum satisfactory educational attainment, and the most significant line for future occupational status has come to be drawn between members of an age-cohort who do and do not go to college.

We are interested, then, in what it is about the school class in our society that determines the distinction between the contingents of the age-cohort which do and do not go to college. Because of a tradition of localism and a rather pragmatic pluralism, there is apparently considerable variety among school systems of various cities and states. Although the situation in metropolitan Boston probably represents a more highly structured pattern than in many other parts of the country, it is probably not so extreme as to be misleading in its main features. There, though of course actual entry into college does not come until after graduation from high school, the main dividing line is between those who are and are not enrolled in the college preparatory course in high school; there is only a small amount of shifting either way after about the ninth grade when the decision is normally made. Furthermore, the evidence seems to be that by far the most important criterion of selection is the record of school performance in elementary school. These records are evaluated by teachers and principals, and there are few cases of entering the college preparatory course against their advice. It is therefore not stretching the evidence too far to say broadly that the primary selective process occurs through differential school performance in elementary school, and that the "seal" is put on it in junior high school.

The evidence also is that the selective process is genuinely assortative. As in virtually all comparable processes, ascriptive as well as achieved factors influence the outcome. In this case, the ascriptive factor is the socio-economic status of the child's family, and the factor underlying his opportunity for achievement is his individual ability. . . .

The essential points here seem to be that there is a relatively uniform criterion of selection operating to differentiate between the college and the non-college contingents, and that for a very important part of the cohort the operation of this criterion is not a "put-up job" – it is not simply a way of affirming a previously determined ascriptive status. To be sure, the high-status, high-ability boy is very likely indeed to go to college, and the low-status, low-ability boy is very unlikely to go. But the "cross-pressured" group for whom these two factors do not coincide is of considerable importance.

Considerations like these lead me to conclude that the main process of differentiation (which from another point of view is selection) that occurs during elementary school takes place on a single main axis of *achievement*. Broadly, moreover, the differentiation leads up through high school to a bifurcation into college-goers and non-college-goers.

To assess the significance of this pattern, let us look at its place in the socialization of the individual. Entering the system of formal education is the child's first major step out of primary involvement in his family of orientation. Within the family certain foundations of his motivational system have been laid down. But the only characteristic fundamental to later roles which has clearly been "determined" and psychologically stamped in by that time is sex role. The post-oedipal child enters the system of formal education clearly categorized as boy or girl, but beyond that his *role* is not yet differentiated. The process of selection, by which persons will select and be selected for categories of roles, is yet to take place.

On grounds which cannot be gone into here, it may be said that the most important single predispositional factor with which the child enters the school is his level of *independence*. By this is meant his level of self-sufficiency relative to guidance by adults, his capacity to take responsibility and to make his own decisions in coping with new and varying situations. This, like his sex role, he has as a function of his experience in the family.

The family is a collectivity within which the basic status-structure is ascribed in terms of biological position, that is, by generation, sex, and age. There are inevitably differences of performance relative to these, and they are rewarded and punished in ways that contribute to differential character formation. But these differences are not given the sanction of institutionalized social status. The school is the first socializing agency in the child's experience which institutionalizes a differentiation of status on nonbiological bases. Moreover, this is not an ascribed but an achieved status; it is the status "earned" by differential performance of the tasks set by the teacher, who is acting as an agent of the community's school system. . . .

Seen in this perspective, the socialization function of the school class assumes a particular significance. The socialization functions of the family by this time are relatively residual, though their importance should not be underestimated. But the school remains adult-controlled and, moreover, induces basically the same kind of identification as was induced by the family in the child's pre-oedipal stage. This is to say that the learning of achievement-motivation is, psychologically speaking, a process of identification with the teacher, of doing well in school in order to please the teacher (often backed by the parents) in the same sense in which a pre-oedipal child learns new skills in order to please his mother.

In this connection I maintain that what is internalized through the process of identification is a reciprocal pattern of role-relationships. Unless there is a drastic failure of internalization altogether, not just one, but both sides of the interaction will be internalized. There will, however, be an emphasis on one or the other, so that some children will more nearly identify with the socializing agent, and others will more nearly identify with the opposite role. Thus, in the pre-oedipal stage, the "independent" child has identified more with the parent, and the "dependent" one with the child-role vis-à-vis the parent.

In school the teacher is institutionally defined as superior to any pupil in knowledge of curriculum subject-matter and in responsibility as a good citizen of the school. In so far as the school class tends to be bifurcated (and of course the dichotomization is far from absolute), it will broadly be on the basis, on the one hand, of identification with the teacher, or acceptance of her role as a model; and, on the other hand, of identification with the pupil peer group. This bifurcation of the class on the basis of identification with teacher or with peer group so strikingly corresponds with the bifurcation into college-goers and non-college-goers that it would be hard to avoid the hypothesis that this structural dichotomization in the school system is the primary source of the selective dichotomization. Of course in detail the relationship is blurred, but certainly not more so than in a great many other fields of comparable analytical complexity. . . .

From *Teaching to Transgress: Education as the Practice of Freedom*
bell hooks

bell hooks, *Teaching to Transgress: Education as the Practice of Freedom* (New York and London: Routledge, 1994), pp. 2–8.

... For black folks teaching – educating – was fundamentally political because it was rooted in antiracist struggle. Indeed, my all-black grade schools became the location where I experienced learning as revolution.

Almost all our teachers at Booker T. Washington were black women. They were committed to nurturing intellect so that we could become scholars, thinkers, and cultural workers – black folks who used our "minds." We learned early that our devotion to learning, to a life of the mind, was a counter-hegemonic act, a fundamental way to resist every strategy of white racist colonization. Though they did not define or articulate these practices in theoretical terms, my teachers were enacting a revolutionary pedagogy of resistance that was profoundly anticolonial. Within these segregated schools, black children who were deemed exceptional, gifted, were given special care. Teachers worked with and for us to ensure that we would fulfill our intellectual destiny and by so doing uplift the race. My teachers were on a mission.

To fulfill that mission, my teachers made sure they "knew" us. They knew our parents, our economic status, where we worshipped, what our homes were like, and how we were treated in the family. I went to school at a historical moment where I was being taught by the same teachers who had taught my mother, her sisters, and brothers. My effort and ability to learn was always contextualized within the framework of generational family experience. Certain behaviors, gestures, habits of being were traced back.

Attending school then was sheer joy. I loved being a student. I loved learning. School was the place of ecstasy – pleasure and danger. To be changed by ideas was pure pleasure. But to learn ideas that ran counter to values and beliefs learned at home was to place oneself at risk, to enter the danger zone. Home was the place where I was forced to conform to someone else's image of who and what I should be. School was the place where I could forget that self and, through ideas, reinvent myself.

School changed utterly with racial integration. Gone was the messianic zeal to transform our minds and beings that had characterized teachers and their pedagogical practices in our all-black schools. Knowledge was suddenly about information only. It had no relation to how one lived, behaved. It was no longer connected to antiracist struggle. Bussed to white schools, we soon learned that obedience, and not a zealous will to learn, was what was expected of us. Too much eagerness to learn could easily be seen as a threat to white authority.

When we entered racist, desegregated, white schools we left a world where teachers believed that to educate black children rightly would require a political commitment. Now, we were mainly taught by white teachers whose lessons reinforced racist stereotypes. For black children, education was no longer about the practice of freedom. Realizing this, I lost my love of school. The classroom was no longer a place of pleasure or ecstasy.

School was still a political place, since we were always having to counter white racist assumptions that we were genetically inferior, never as capable as white peers, even unable to learn. Yet, the politics were no longer counter-hegemonic. We were always and only responding and reacting to white folks.

That shift from beloved, all-black schools to white schools where black students were always seen as interlopers, as not really belonging, taught me the difference between education as the practice of freedom and education that merely strives to reinforce domination. The rare white teacher who dared to resist, who would not allow racist biases to determine how we were taught, sustained the belief that learning at its most powerful could indeed liberate. A few black teachers had joined us in the desegregation process. And, although it was more difficult, they continued to nurture black students even as their efforts were constrained by the suspicion they were favoring their own race. . . .

. . . As a classroom community, our capacity to generate excitement is deeply affected by our interest in one another, in hearing one another's voices, in recognizing one another's presence. Since the vast majority of students learn through conservative, traditional educational practices and concern themselves only with the presence of the professor, any radical pedagogy must insist that everyone's presence is acknowledged. That insistence cannot be simply stated. It has to be demonstrated through pedagogical practices. To begin, the professor must genuinely *value* everyone's presence. There must be an ongoing recognition that everyone influences the classroom dynamic, that everyone contributes. These contributions are resources. Used constructively they enhance the capacity of any class to create an open learning community. Often before this process can begin there has to be some deconstruction of the traditional notion that only the professor is responsible for classroom dynamics. That responsibility is relative to status. Indeed, the professor will always be more responsible because the larger institutional structures will always ensure that accountability for what happens in the classroom rests with the teacher. It is rare that any professor, no matter how eloquent a lecturer, can generate through his or her actions enough excitement to create an exciting classroom. Excitement is generated through collective effort.

Seeing the classroom always as a communal place enhances the likelihood of collective effort in creating and sustaining a learning community. . . .

part 4

Morality and Modernity

chapter 10

Individuality and Autonomy

Introduction

This concluding chapter draws together ideas that are already adumbrated in most of the chapters that have come before. Its theme is Durkheim as the great sociologist of individuality and of moral autonomy. We see in a first selection from *The Division of Labor* how Durkheim explains the rise of the individual personality in terms of "the disappearance of the segmentary type of society" and of "the progress of specialisation" (p. 261). In an excerpt from *Suicide*, in fact, we see how "the cult of man," "the exaltation of human personality," has itself become one of the hallmarks of modern society (p. 266). In the next two selections, from *Moral Education* and "The Determination of Moral Facts," we follow Durkheim's careful linkage of this ideal of individual personality to that of moral self-determination and his argument that we only realize this ideal, we only "liberate ourselves" as autonomous moral actors, "through understanding" and through "reasoned evaluations" (aided, of course, by the new "science of morality" that Durkheim himself is concerned with developing). An excerpt from "The Dualism of Human Nature" then suggests that this moral dimension of our nature "come[s] to us from society . . . and connect[s] us with something that surpasses us" (p. 273). This theme is further developed in a lengthy selection from "Individualism and the Intellectuals," in which Durkheim answers critics of modern individualism by emphasizing that the individual personality possesses a "sacred" status in the modern "religion of humanity" and that individualism, far from being anarchical, is "the only system of beliefs which can ensure . . . moral unity" in modern society (p. 276). In the first of two modern selections, Erving Goffman then illustrates how this cult of the individual is observed and reenacted in everyday life, and how the self is regarded as "in part a ceremonial thing, a sacred object which must be treated with proper ritual care" (p. 280). In the second, Viviana Zelizer traces the rise of this new religion (at least in the US) to the late nineteenth and early twentieth centuries, when childhood was sentimentalized and a new "sacred child" was produced – a "priceless child" – who "occuped a special and separate world, regulated by affection and education, not work or profit" (p. 281).

From *The Division of Labor in Society*

Emile Durkheim, *The Division of Labor in Society*, trans. W. D. Halls (New York: Free Press, 1984), pp. 83–5, 117–18, 334–7.

. . . [W]e shall identify two kinds of positive solidarity, distinguished by the following characteristics:

1   The first kind links the individual directly to society without any intermediary. With the second kind he depends upon society because he depends upon the parts that go to constitute it.
2   In the two cases, society is not viewed from the same perspective. In the first, the term is used to denote a more or less organised society composed of beliefs and sentiments common to all the members of the group: this is the collective type. On the contrary, in the second case the society to which we are solidly joined is a system of different and special functions united by definite relationships. Moreover, these two societies are really one. They are two facets of one and the same reality, but which none the less need to be distinguished from each other.
3   From this second difference there arises another which will serve to allow us to characterise and delineate the features of these two kinds of solidarity.

The first kind can only be strong to the extent that the ideas and tendencies common to all members of the society exceed in number and intensity those that appertain personally to each one of those members. The greater this excess, the more active this kind of society is. Now what constitutes our personality is that which each one of us possesses that is peculiar and characteristic, what distinguishes it from others. This solidarity can therefore only increase in inverse relationship to the personality. As we have said, there is in the consciousness of each one of us two consciousnesses: one that we share in common with our group in its entirety, which is consequently not ourselves, but society living and acting within us; the other that, on the contrary, represents us alone in what is personal and distinctive about us, what makes us an individual. The solidarity that derives from similarities is at its *maximum* when the collective consciousness completely envelops our total consciousness, coinciding with it at every point. At that moment our individuality is zero. That individuality cannot arise until the community fills us less completely. Here there are two opposing forces, the one centripetal, the other centrifugal, which cannot increase at the same time. We cannot ourselves develop simultaneously in two so opposing directions. If we have a strong inclination to think and act for ourselves we cannot be strongly inclined to think and act like other people. If the ideal is to create for ourselves a special, personal image, this cannot mean to be like everyone else. Moreover, at the very moment when this solidarity exerts its effect, our personality, it may be said by definition, disappears, for we are no longer ourselves, but a collective being.

The social molecules that can only cohere in this one manner cannot therefore move as a unit save in so far as they lack any movement of their own, as do the molecules of inorganic bodies. This is why we suggest that this kind of solidarity should be called mechanical. The word does not mean that the solidarity is produced by mechanical and artificial means. We only use this term for it by analogy with the cohesion that links together the elements of raw materials, in contrast to that which encompasses the unity of living organisms. What finally justifies the use of this term is the fact that the bond that thus unites the individual with society is completely analogous to that which links the thing to the person. The individual consciousness, considered from this viewpoint, is simply a dependency of the collective type, and follows all its motions, just as the object possessed follows those which its owner imposes upon it. In societies where this solidarity is highly developed the individual, as we shall see later, does not belong to himself; he is literally a thing at the disposal of society. Thus, in these same social types, personal rights are still not yet distinguished from "real" rights.

The situation is entirely different in the case of solidarity that brings about the division of labour. Whereas the other solidarity implies that individuals resemble one another, the latter assumes that they are different from one another. The former type is only possible in so far as the individual personality is absorbed into the collective personality; the latter is only possible if each one of us has a sphere of action that is peculiarly our own, and consequently a personality. Thus the collective consciousness leaves uncovered a part of the individual consciousness, so that there may be established in it those special functions that it cannot regulate. The more extensive this free area is, the stronger the cohesion that arises from this solidarity. Indeed, on the one hand each one of us depends more intimately upon society the more labour is divided up, and on the other, the activity of each one of us is correspondingly more specialised, the more personal it is. Doubtless, however circumscribed that activity may be, it is never completely original. Even in the exercise of our profession we conform to usages and practices that are common to us all within our corporation. Yet even in this case, the burden that we bear is in a different way less heavy than when the whole of society bears down upon us, and this leaves much more room for the free play of our initiative. Here, then, the individuality of the whole grows at the same time as that of the parts. Society becomes more effective in moving in concert, at the same time as each of its elements has more movements that are peculiarly its own. This solidarity resembles that observed in the higher animals. In fact each organ has its own special characteristics and autonomy, yet the greater the unity of the organism, the more marked the individualisation of the parts. Using this analogy, we propose to call "organic" the solidarity that is due to the division of labour. . . .

. . . [O]n the whole the common consciousness comprises ever fewer strong and well-defined sentiments. This is therefore the case because the average intensity and degree of determinateness of the collective states of feeling . . . diminish, . . . [and] the sole collective sentiments that have gained in intensity are those that relate, not to social matters, but to the individual. For this to be so the individual personality must have become a much more important factor in the life of society. For it to have been able to acquire such importance it is not enough for the personal consciousness of each individual to have increased in absolute terms; it must have increased more than the common consciousness. The personal consciousness must have thrown off the yoke of the common consciousness, and consequently the latter must have lost its power to dominate and that determining action that it exerted from the beginning. If indeed the relationship between these two elements had remained unchanged, if both had developed in extent and vitality in the same proportion, the collective sentiments that relate to the individual would likewise have remained unchanged. Above all, they would not have been the sole sentiments to have grown. This is because they depend solely on the social value of the individual factor, which in turn is determined not by any absolute development of that factor, but by the relative size of the share that falls to him within the totality of social phenomena.

. . . [D]oes not the division of labour, by rendering each one of us an incomplete being, not entail some curtailment of the individual personality? This criticism has often been made.

Firstly, let us note that it is difficult to see why it might be more in accord with the logic of human nature to develop more superficially rather than in depth. Why should a more extensive activity, one that is more dispersed, be superior to one more concentrated and circumscribed? Why should more dignity attach to being complete and mediocre than in leading a more specialised kind of life but one more intense, particularly if we can recapture in this way what we have lost, through our association with others who possess what we lack and who make us complete beings? We start from the principle that man must realise his nature as man – as Aristotle said, accomplish his οἰχέί ον ἔργον. But at different moments in history this nature does not remain constant; it is modified with societies. Among lower peoples, the act that connotes a man is to resemble his fellows, to realise within himself all the characteristics of the collective type which, even more than today, was then confused with the human type. In more advanced societies man's nature is mainly to be a part of society; consequently the act that connotes a man is for him to play his part as one organ of society.

There is something more: far from the progress of specialisation whittling away the individual personality, this develops with the division of labour.

Indeed to be a person means to be an autonomous source of action. Thus man only attains this state to the degree that there is something within him that is his and his alone, that makes him an individual, whereby he is more than the mere embodiment of the generic type of his race and group. It will in any case be objected that he is endowed with free will, and that this is sufficient upon which to base his personality. But whatever this freedom may consist of – and it is the subject of much argument – it is not this impersonal, invariable, metaphysical attribute that can serve as the sole basis for the empirical, variable and concrete personality of individuals. That personality cannot be formed by the entirely abstract capacity to choose between two opposites. This faculty must be exercised in relation to ends and motives that are peculiar to the person acting. In other words the stuff of which his consciousness is made up must have a personal character. Now we have seen . . . that is an outcome that occurs progressively as the division of labour itself progresses. The disappearance of the segmentary type of society, at the same time as it necessitates greater specialisation, frees the individual consciousness in part from the organic environment that supports it, as it does from the social environment that envelops it. This dual emancipation renders the individual more independent in his own behaviour. The division of labour itself contributes to this liberating effect. Individual natures become more complex through specialising; by this very fact they are partly shielded against the effects of the collectivity and the influences of heredity, which can scarcely enforce themselves except in simple, general matters.

Thus, as a consequence of a veritable illusion, one could occasionally believe that the personality was more whole, so long as it had not been breached by the division of labour. Doubtless, viewing from the outside the variety of occupations that the individual embarks upon, it may seem that the personality then develops more freely and completely. But in reality the activity he displays is not his own. It is society, it is the race, which act in and through him; he is only the intermediary through which they are realised. His liberty is only apparent, his personality is borrowed. Since the life of societies is in certain respects less regular, we imagine that original talents can more easily come to light, that it is easier for each individual to follow his own tastes, that greater room is left for the free play of fantasy. Yet this is to forget that personal sentiments are then very rare. If the motives governing conduct do not occur with the same regularity as they do today, they do not cease to be collective, and consequently impersonal. The same is true for the actions they inspire. We have moreover shown above how the activity becomes richer and more intense the more specialised it becomes.

Thus the advance of the individual personality and that of the division of labour depend on one and the same cause. Thus also it is impossible to will the one without willing the other. Nowadays no one questions the obligatory nature of the rule that ordains that we should exist as a person, and this increasingly so.

One final consideration will show to what extent the division of labour is linked to our whole moral life.

It has long been a dream cherished by men to succeed at last in achieving as a reality the ideal of human brotherhood. Peoples raise their voices to wish for a state of affairs where war would no longer govern international relations, where relationships between societies would be regulated peacefully as are already those between individuals, and where all men would co-operate in the common task and live the same life. Although these aspirations are partly neutralised by others that relate to the particular society of which we form part, they remain very strong and are continually gathering strength. However, they cannot be satisfied unless all men form part of one and the same society, subject to the same laws. For, just as private conflicts can only be contained by the regulatory action of a society that embraces all individuals, so inter-social conflicts can only be contained by the regulatory action of a society that embraces all societies. The only power that can serve to moderate individual egoism is that of the group; the only one that can serve to moderate the egoism of groups is that of another group that embraces them all.

Really, once the problem has been posed in these terms, we must acknowledge that this ideal is not on the verge of being realised in its entirety. Between the different types of society coexisting on earth there are too many intellectual and moral divergences to be able to live in a spirit of brotherhood in the same society. Yet what is possible is that societies of the same species should come together, and it is indeed in this direction that our society appears to be going. We have seen already that there is tending to form, above European peoples, in a spontaneous fashion, a European society that has even now some feeling of its own identity and the beginnings of an organisation. If the formation of one single human society is for ever ruled out – and this has, however, not yet been demonstrated – at least the formation of larger societies will draw us continually closer to that goal. Moreover, these facts do not at all contradict the definition we have given of morality. If we cling to humanity and ought to continue to do so, it is because it is a society in the process of realising itself in this way, one to which we are solidly bound.

Yet we know that more extensive societies cannot be formed without the development of the division of labour. Without a greater specialisation of functions not only could they not sustain their equilibrium, but the increase in the number of elements in competition would also automatically suffice to bring about that state. Even more would this be the case, for an increase in volume does not generally occur without an increase in population density. Thus we may formulate the following proposition: the ideal of human brotherhood cannot be realised unless the division of labour progresses. We must choose: either we must abandon our dream, if we refuse to limit our individual activity any further; or we can pursue the consummation of our dream, but only on the condition just stated.

From *Suicide*

Emile Durkheim, *Suicide: A Study in Sociology*, trans. John A. Spaulding and George Simpson (New York: Free Press, 1951), pp. 332–7.

... Regardless of differences in detail in repressive measures of different peoples, legislation on [suicide] clearly passed through two chief phases. In the first, the individual is forbidden to destroy himself on his own authority; but the State may permit him to do so. The act is immoral only when it is wholly private and without collaboration through the organs of collective life. Under specific circumstances, society yields slightly and absolves what it condemns on principle. In the second period, condemnation is absolute and universal. The power to dispose of a human life, except when death is the punishment for a crime, is withheld not merely from the person concerned but from society itself. It is henceforth a right denied to collective as well as to private disposition. Suicide is thought immoral in and for itself, whoever they may be who participate in it. Thus, with the progress of history the prohibition, instead of being relaxed, only becomes more strict. If the public conscience seems less assured in its opinion of this matter today, therefore, this uncertainty may rise from fortuitous and passing causes; for it is wholly unlikely that moral evolution should so far reverse itself after having developed in a single direction for centuries.

The ideas that set it in this direction are in fact still alive. It has occasionally been said that if suicide is and should be forbidden, it is because a man evades his obligations towards society by killing himself. But if we were moved only by this thought we, like the Greeks, should leave society free to abrogate a prohibition issued only for its own benefit. If we refuse it this authority, it is because we see in the suicide more than an unscrupulous debtor to society. A creditor may always remit a debt by which he benefits. Besides, if this were the only reason for disapproving [of] suicide, the reprobation should be more formal the more strictly the individual is subject to the State; so that it would be at its height in lower societies. On the contrary, its rigor increases with the growth of individual as contrasted with State rights. If it has become so formal and severe in Christian societies, this is not because of the idea of the State held by these people but because of their new conception of the human personality. It has become sacred, even most sacred in their eyes, something which no one is to offend. Of course, even under the city-state regime the individual's existence was no longer as self-effacing as among primitive tribes. Then it was accorded a social value, but one supposed to belong wholly to the State. The city-state could therefore dispose of him freely without the individual having the same right over himself. But today he has acquired a kind of dignity which places him above himself as well as above society. So long as his conduct has not caused him to forfeit the title of man, he seems to us to share in some degree in that quality *sui generis* ascribed by every religion to its gods which renders them inviolable by everything mortal. He has become tinged with religious value; man has become a god for men. Therefore, any attempt against his life suggests sacrilege. Suicide is such an attempt. No matter who strikes the blow, it causes scandal by violation of the sacrosanct quality within us which we must respect in ourselves as well as in others.

Hence, suicide is rebuked for derogating from this cult of human personality on which all our morality rests. Proof of this explanation is the difference between our view and that of the nations of antiquity. Once suicide was thought only a simple civil wrong committed against the State; religion had little or no interest in the matter. Now it has become an act essentially involving religion. The judges condemning it have been church councils, and lay power in punishing it has only followed and imitated ecclesiastical authority. Because we have an immortal soul in us, a spark of divinity, we must now be sacred to ourselves. We belong completely to no temporal being because we are kin to God.

But if this is why suicide has been classed among illicit actions, should we not henceforth consider the condemnation to be without basis? It seems that scientific criticism cannot concede the least value to these mystical conceptions, nor admit that man contains anything whatever that is superhuman. Reasoning thus, Ferri in his *Omicidio-suicidio* thought himself justified in regarding all prohibitions of suicide as survivals from the past, doomed to disappear. Considering it absurd from the rationalist point of view that the individual could have an extra-personal aim, he deduces that we are always free to renounce the advantages of community existence by renouncing life itself. The right to live seems to him logically to imply the right to die.

But this method of argument draws its conclusion too abruptly from form to content, from the verbal expression through which we translate our feeling to the feeling itself. It is true that, both intrinsically and abstractly, the religious symbols by means of which we explain the respect inspired in us by human personality are not adequate to reality, and this is easily proveable; but from all this it does not follow that this respect is itself unreasonable. On the contrary, its preponderant role in our law and in our morality must warn us against such an interpretation. Instead of taking a literal interpretation of this conception, let us examine it in itself, let us discover its make-up, and we shall see that in spite of the crudeness of the popular formula the conception nevertheless has objective value.

Indeed, the sort of transcendency we ascribe to human personality is not a quality peculiar to it. It is found elsewhere. It is nothing but the imprint of all really intense collective sentiments upon matters related to them. Just because these feelings derive from the collectivity, the aims to which they direct our actions can only be collective. Society has needs beyond our own. The acts inspired in us by its needs therefore do not depend on our individual inclinations; their aim is not our personal interest, but rather involves sacrifices and privations. When I fast, when I accept mortification to be pleasing in God's sight, when I undertake some inconvenience out of respect for a tradition the meaning and import of which are usually unknown to me; when I pay my taxes, when I give any labor or life to the State, I renounce something of myself; and by the resistance offered by our egoism to these renunciations, we readily see that they are forced from us by a power to which we have submitted. Even when we defer gladly to its commands we feel that our conduct is guided by a sentiment of reverence for something greater than ourselves. However willingly we obey the voice dictating this abnegation, we feel sure that its tone is imperative beyond that of instinct. That is why we cannot indisputably consider it our own, though it speaks within our consciences. We ascribe it to other sources, as we do our sensations; we project it outside of ourselves, referring it to an existence we think of as exterior and superior to ourselves, since it commands us and we obey. Of course, whatever seems to us to come from the same origin shares the same quality. Thus we have been forced to imagine a world beyond this one and to people it with realities of a different order.

Such is the source of all the ideas of transcendency which form the bases of religions and morals; for moral obligation is explicable only in this way. To be sure, the definite form in which we usually clothe these ideas is without scientific value. Whether we ascribe them to a personal being of a special nature or to some abstract force which we vaguely hypostasize under the title of moral ideal, they are solely metaphorical conceptions, giving no adequate explanation of the facts. But the process which they symbolize is none the less real. It remains true that in every case we are urged to act by an authority exceeding ourselves, namely society, and that the aims to which it attaches us thus enjoy real moral supremacy. If so, all the objections applicable to the common conceptions by which men have tried to represent this sensed supremacy to themselves cannot lessen its reality. Such criticism is superficial, not reaching to the basis of things. If it is demonstrable that exaltation of human personality is one of the aims pursued, and which should be pursued, by modern societies, all moral regulation deriving from this principle is justified by that fact itself, whatever the manner of its usual justification. Though the reasons satisfying the crowd are open to criticism, they need only be transposed into another idiom to be given their full import.

Now, not only is this aim really one of the aims of modern societies, but it is a law of history that peoples increasingly detach themselves from every other objective. Originally society is everything, the individual nothing. Consequently, the strongest social feelings are those connecting the individual with the collectivity; society is its own aim. Man is considered only an instrument in its hands; he seems to draw all his rights from it and has no counter-prerogative, because nothing higher than it exists. But gradually things change. As societies become greater in volume and density, they increase in complexity, work is divided, individual differences multiply, and the moment approaches when the only remaining bond among the members of a single human group will be that they are all men. Under such conditions the body of collective sentiments inevitably attaches itself with all its strength to its single remaining object, communicating to this object an incomparable value by so doing. Since human personality is the only thing that appeals unanimously to all hearts, since its enhancement is the only aim that can be collectively pursued, it inevitably acquires exceptional value in the eyes of all. It thus rises far above all human aims, assuming a religious nature.

This cult of man is something, accordingly, very different from the egoistic individualism above referred to, which leads to suicide. Far from detaching individuals from society and from every aim beyond themselves, it unites them in one thought, makes them servants of one work. For man, as thus suggested to collective affection and respect, is not the sensual, experiential individual that each one of us represents, but man in general, ideal humanity as conceived by each people at each moment of its history. None of us wholly incarnates this ideal, though none is wholly a stranger to it. So we have, not to concentrate each separate person upon himself and his own interests, but to subordinate him to the general interests of humankind. Such an aim draws him beyond himself; impersonal and disinterested, it is above all individual personalities; like every ideal, it can be conceived of only as superior to and dominating reality. This ideal even dominates societies, being the aim on which all social activity depends. This is why it is no longer the right of these societies to dispose of this ideal freely. While we recognize that they too have their reason for existence, they have subjected themselves to the jurisdiction of this ideal and no longer have the right to ignore it; still less, to authorize men themselves to do so. Our dignity as moral beings is therefore no longer the property of the city-state; but it has not for that reason become our property, and we have not acquired the right to do what we wish with it. How could we have such a right if society, the existence greater than ourselves, does not have it?

Under these conditions suicide must be classed among immoral acts; for in its main principle it denies this religion of humanity. A man who kills himself, the saying goes, does wrong only to himself and there is no occasion for the intervention of society; for so goes the ancient maxim *Volenti non fit injuria*. This is an error. Society is injured because the sentiment is offended on which its most respected moral maxims today rest, a sentiment almost the only bond between its members, and which would be weakened if this offense could be committed with impunity. How could this sentiment maintain the least authority if the moral conscience did not protest its violation? From the moment that the human person is and must be considered something sacred, over which neither the individual nor the group has free disposal, any attack upon it must be forbidden. No matter that the guilty person and the victim are one and the same; the social evil springing from the act is not affected merely by the author being the one who suffers. If violent destruction of a human life revolts us as a sacrilege, in itself and generally, we cannot tolerate it under any circumstances. A collective sentiment which yielded so far would soon lose all force.

From *Moral Education*

Emile Durkheim, *Moral Education: A Study in the Theory and Application of the Sociology of Education*, trans. Everett K. Wilson and Herman Schnurer (New York: Free Press, 1973), pp. 106–8, 111–16.

Heretofore we have, in effect, viewed morality as a system of rules, external to the individual, which impose themselves on him from outside; not, certainly, by any physical force, but by virtue of the ascendancy that they enjoy. From this point of view, it is certainly true that the individual will seems to be controlled by a law not of its own making. It is not we, in effect, who create morality. Doubtless, since we constitute part of the society that elaborates it, in a sense each of us collaborates in the development giving rise to morality. But the part played by each generation in the evolution of morality is quite restricted. The morality of our time is fixed in its essentials from the moment of our birth; the changes it undergoes during the course of an individual's life – those in which we can share – are infinitely limited. Great moral transformations always presuppose a long period of time. Furthermore, each of us is only one among innumerable units who collaborate in such a change. Our personal contribution is therefore never more than a minute factor in the complex result in which it disappears anonymously. Thus, one cannot fail to recognize that if the moral rule is a collective product, we receive much more than we contribute. Our posture is much more passive than active. We are influenced to a greater extent than we influence.

Now, this passivity is in opposition to an actual tendency of the moral consciousness – one that becomes continually stronger. Indeed, one of the fundamental axioms of our morality – perhaps even *the* fundamental axiom – is that the human being is the sacred thing par excellence. He merits the respect that the faithful of all religions reserve for their Gods. We ourselves express this when we make the idea of humanity the end and the *raison d'être* of the nation.

As a result of this principle, any kind of restriction placed upon our consciences seems immoral since it does violence to our personal autonomy. Today, everyone acknowledges, at least in theory, that never in any case should a predetermined mode of thought be arbitrarily imposed on us, even in the name of moral authority. It is not only a rule of logic but of morality that our reason should accept as true only that which it itself has spontaneously recognized as such. . . .

. . . On the one hand, moral rules seem, from all the evidence, external to the will. They are not of our fashioning, consequently, in conforming to them, we defer to a law not of our own making. We undergo a constraint that, however moral, is nonetheless real. On the other hand, it is certain that conscience protests such dependency. We do not regard an act as completely moral except when we perform it freely without coercion of any sort. We are not free if the law by which we regulate our behavior is imposed on us, if we have not freely desired it. The tendency of the moral conscience to link the morality of an act with the autonomy of the actor is a fact one cannot deny and which must be accounted for. . . .

. . . Since we are and always will be sensate as well as rational human beings, there will always be conflict between these two parts of ourselves, and heteronomy will always be the rule in fact if not by right. What the moral conscience demands is an effective autonomy, it is true; not only for some unspecified ideal being, but for such beings as we ourselves are. Indeed, the fact that our requirements on this score are continually increasing certainly suggests that it is not a matter of a simple logical possibility, always equally true in the sense of an altogether abstract truth, but of something that grows, is progressively becoming, that evolves through history.

To understand the nature of progressive autonomy, let us look first at the way it materializes in our relations with the physical universe. It is not only in the realm of moral ideas that we seek and gain a greater independence. We are increasingly liberated from direct dependence on things, and we are quite aware of this process. But we cannot regard man's reason as the legislator of the physical universe. It has not received its laws from us. If we have in some respects liberated ourselves, it is not the result of our own efforts. It is to science that we owe this relative liberation. To simplify the argument let us suppose that we have complete knowledge of things and that each of us has this knowledge. Thus, the world, properly speaking, is no longer outside us; it has become a part of ourselves, since we have within us a system of symbolic representations that adequately express it. Everything in the physical world is represented in our consciousnesses by an idea; and, since these ideas are scientific – that is to say, distinct and clearly defined – we can manipulate them, combine them readily, as we do, for example, with the propositions of geometry. Consequently, in order to know at a given moment in time what the physical world is like and how we should adapt to it, we no longer need go beyond ourselves to understand physical phenomena. It is enough to look within ourselves and to analyze our ideas about the objects we deal with, just as the mathematician can determine the relationships between magnitudes through a simple mental calculation and without having to observe the actual relationships of such magnitudes as they obtain outside of him.

Thus, to understand the world and to order our conduct as it should be in relationship to it, we only have to take careful thought, to be fully

aware of that which is in ourselves. This constitutes a first degree of autonomy. Moreover, because we then understand the laws of everything, we
also understand the reasons for everything. We can then understand the
reason for the universal order. In other words, to resurrect an old expression, if it is not we who made the plan of nature, we rediscover it through
science, we re-think it, and we understand why it is as it is. Hence, to the
extent that we see that it is everything it ought to be – that it is as the
nature of things implies – we can conform, not simply because we are
physically restrained and unable to do otherwise without danger, but
because we deem it good and have no better alternative. What prompts
the faithful to see that the world is good in principle because it is the work
of a good being, we can establish a posteriori to the extent that science
permits us to establish rationally what faith postulates a priori. Such
conformity does not amount to passive resignation but to enlightened
allegiance. Conforming to the order of things because one is sure that it
is everything it ought to be is not submitting to a constraint. It is freely
desiring this order, assenting through an understanding of the cause.
Wishing freely is not desiring the absurd. On the contrary, it implies wishing what is rational – that is to say, it implies the desire to act in agreement
with the nature of things. True, it happens that things sometimes depart
from their own nature under the influence of abnormal or accidental
circumstances. But then science warns us, while at the same time providing means for balancing and rectifying things, since it gives us knowledge of the normal and natural state of things and the sources of these
abnormal deviations.

Of course, what we have just been discussing is altogether hypothetical. Knowledge of nature is not and never will be complete. But
what I have just dealt with as a *fait accompli* is an ideal limit that
we approach asymptotically. To the extent that science builds itself,
we, in our relationship with the physical universe, tend increasingly to
rely only on ourselves. We liberate ourselves through understanding;
there is no other means of liberation. Science is the wellspring of our
autonomy.

In the moral order there is room for the same autonomy; and there is
place for no other. Since morality expresses the nature of society and since
this nature is no more directly apprehended by us than the nature of the
physical world, individual reason can no more be the lawmaker for the
moral world than that of the physical world. The layman's confused notions
of society express the reality of society no more adequately than our aud-
itory and visual sensations express sound or color, the objective nature
of physical phenomena to which they correspond. However, it is possible
through science to get hold of this order, which the individual, *qua* individual, has not created and for which he has not deliberately wished. We
can investigate the nature of these moral rules, which the child receives

from without, through education, and which impose themselves on him by virtue of their authority. We can investigate the reasons for their being, their immediate and more remote conditions. In a world, we can create a scientific study of the moral order. . . .

From "The Determination of Moral Facts"

Emile Durkheim, *Sociology and Philosophy*, trans. D. F. Pocock (New York: Free Press, 1974), pp. 59–62.

. . . If morality is the product of the collective, it necessarily imposes itself upon the individual, who is in no position to question it whatever form it may take, and must accept it passively. We are thus condemned to follow opinion without ever having the right to rebel against its dictates.

But here, as elsewhere, the science of reality puts us in a position to modify the real and to direct it. The science of moral opinion furnishes us with the means of judging it and the need of rectifying it. . . .

. . . The science of morals allows us to take up a position between these two divergent moralities, the one now existing and the one in the process of becoming. It teaches us, for example, that the first is related to an order which has disappeared or is disappearing, and that the new ideas on the contrary are related to recent changes in the conditions of collective existence and are made necessary by these changes. Our science may help us to render these ideas more precise and to direct them, etc.

We are not then obliged to bend our heads under the force of moral opinion. We can even in certain cases feel ourselves justified in rebelling against it. It may, in fact, happen that, for one of the reasons just indicated, we shall feel it our duty to combat moral ideas that we know to be out of date and nothing more than survivals. The best way of doing this may appear to be the denial of these ideas, not only theoretically but also in action. No doubt here I am touching on points of conscience that are always delicate, and I do not intend to resolve the problem in a word. I wish merely to indicate that the method I have laid down permits the posing of these problems.

But in any case we cannot aspire to a morality other than that which is related to the state of our society. We have here an objective standard with which to compare our evaluations. The reason which is the judge on these matters is not the individual reason, subject as it is to all sorts of private aspirations and personal preferences, but the reason supported by the methodical observation of a given reality, the social reality. It is from society and not from the individual that morality derives. No doubt we shall often be bound to take sides on these questions without waiting for our science to be sufficiently advanced to guide us; the necessity for action often forces us to precede science. In such cases we do what we can; we replace methodical science, in the circumstances impossible, by a more summary and premature science which looks in moments of doubt to the inspirations of sensibility. I am not trying to suggest that this new-born science is already in a condition to act as the sovereign guide of conduct. All I want to show here is that this science, far from preventing us from evaluating reality, gives us the means by which we can arrive at *reasoned* evaluations. . . .

From "The Dualism of Human Nature"

Emile Durkheim: On Morality and Society, trans. Charles Blend, ed. Robert N. Bellah (Chicago and London: University of Chicago Press, 1973), pp. 151–62.

Our intelligence, like our activity, presents two very different forms: on the one hand, are sensations and sensory tendencies; on the other, conceptual thought and moral activity. Each of these two parts of ourselves represents a separate pole of our being, and these two poles are not only distinct from one another but are opposed to one another. Our sensory appetites are necessarily egoistic: they have our individuality and it alone as their object. When we satisfy our hunger, our thirst, and so on, without bringing any other tendency into play, it is ourselves, and ourselves alone, that we satisfy. [Conceptual thought] and moral activity are, on the contrary, distinguished by the fact that the rules of conduct to which they conform can be universalized. Therefore, by definition, they pursue impersonal ends. Morality begins with disinterest, with attachment to something other than ourselves. . . .

These two aspects of our psychic life are, therefore, opposed to each other as are the personal and the impersonal. There is in us a being that represents everything in relation to itself and from its own point of view; in everything that it does, this being has no other object but itself. There is another being in us, however, which knows things *sub specie aeternitatis*, as if it were participating in some thought other than its own, and which, in its acts, tends to accomplish ends that surpass its own. The old formula *homo duplex* is therefore verified by the facts. Far from being simple, our inner life has something that is like a double center of gravity. On the one hand is our individuality – and, more particularly, our body in which it is based; on the other is everything in us that expresses something other than ourselves.

Not only are these two groups of states of consciousness different in their origins and their properties, but there is a true antagonism between them. They mutually contradict and deny each other. We cannot pursue moral ends without causing a split within ourselves, without offending the instincts and the penchants that are the most deeply rooted in our bodies. There is no moral act that does not imply a sacrifice, for, as Kant has shown, the law of duty cannot be obeyed without humiliating our individual, or, as he calls it, our "empirical" sensitivity. We can accept this sacrifice without resistance and even with enthusiasm, but even when it is accomplished in a surge of joy, the sacrifice is no less real. The pain that the ascetic seeks is pain nonetheless, and this antinomy is so deep and so radical that it can never be completely resolved. How can we belong entirely to ourselves, and entirely to others at one and the same time? The ego cannot be something completely other than itself, for, if it were, it would vanish – this is what happens in ecstasy. In order to think, we must be, we must have an individuality. On the other hand, however, the ego cannot be entirely and exclusively itself, for, if it were, it would be emptied of all content. If we must be in order to think, then we must have something to think about. To what would consciousness be reduced if it expressed nothing but the body and its states? We cannot live without representing to ourselves the world around us and the objects of every sort which fill it. And because we represent it to ourselves, it enters into us and becomes part of us. Consequently, we value the world and are attached to it just as we are to ourselves. Something else in us besides ourselves stimulates us to act. It is an error to believe that it is easy to live as egoists. Absolute egoism, like absolute altruism, is an ideal limit which can never be attained in reality. Both are states that we can approach indefinitely without ever realizing them completely. . . .

It is not without reason, therefore, that man feels himself to be double: he actually is double. There are in him two classes of states of consciousness that differ from each other in origin and nature, and in the ends toward which they aim. One class merely expresses our organisms and the objects to which they are most directly related. Strictly individual, the states of consciousness of this class connect us only with ourselves, and we can no more detach them from us than we can detach ourselves from our bodies. The states of consciousness of the other class, on the contrary, come to us from society; they transfer society into us and connect us with something that surpasses us. Being collective, they are impersonal; they turn us toward ends that we hold in common with other men; it is through them and them alone that we can communicate with others. It is, therefore, quite true that we are made up of two parts, and are like two beings, which, although they are closely associated, are composed of very different elements and orient us in opposite directions.

In brief, this duality corresponds to the double existence that we lead concurrently: the one purely individual and rooted in our organisms, the other social and nothing but an extension of society. The origin of the antagonism that we have described is evident from the very nature of the elements involved in it. The conflicts of which we have given examples are between the sensations and the sensory appetites, on the one hand, and the intellectual and moral life, on the other; and it is evident that passions and egoistic tendencies derive from our individual constitutions, while our rational activity – whether theoretical or practical – is dependent on social causes. We have often had occasion to prove that the rules of morality are norms that have been elaborated by society; the obligatory character with which they are marked is nothing but the authority of society, communicating itself to everything that comes from it. . . .

From "Individualism and the Intellectuals"

Emile Durkheim: On Morality and Society, trans. Charles Blend, ed. Robert N. Bellah (Chicago and London: University of Chicago Press, 1973), pp. 45–54.

. . . [W]e have come a long way from that apotheosis of well-being and private interest, from that egoistic cult of the self for which utilitarian individualism has been rightly criticized. Quite the contrary, according to . . . moralists [such as Kant and Rousseau], duty consists in disregarding all that concerns us personally, all that derives from our empirical individuality, in order to seek out only that which our humanity requires and which we share with all our fellowmen. This ideal so far surpasses the level of utilitarian goals that it seems to those minds who aspire to it to be completely stamped with religiosity. This human person (*personne humaine*), the definition of which is like the touchstone which distinguishes good from evil, is considered sacred in the ritual sense of the word. It partakes of the transcendent majesty that churches of all time lend to their gods; it is conceived of as being invested with that mysterious property which creates a void about sacred things, which removes them from vulgar contacts and withdraws them from common circulation. And the respect which is given it comes precisely from this source. Whoever makes an attempt on a man's life, on a man's liberty, on a man's honor, inspires in us a feeling of horror analogous in every way to that which the believer experiences when he sees his idol profaned. Such an ethic is

therefore not simply a hygenic discipline or a prudent economy of existence; it is a religion in which man is at once the worshiper and the god.

But this religion is individualistic, since it takes man as its object and
since man is an individual by definition. What is more, there is no system whose individualism is more intransigent. Nowhere are the rights
of the individual affirmed with greater energy, since the individual is
placed in the ranks of sacrosanct objects; nowhere is the individual more
jealously protected from encroachments from the outside, whatever their
source. The doctrine of utility can easily accept all sorts of comprom-
ises without belying its fundamental axiom; it can admit of individual
liberties being suspended whenever the interest of the greater number
requires that sacrifice. But no compromise is possible with a principle which
is thus placed outside and above all temporal interests. There is no political reason which can excuse an attack upon the individual when the rights
of the individual are above those of the state. If then, individualism is,
in and of itself, the catalyst of moral dissolution, we should see it here
manifest its antisocial essence. Now we understand the gravity of the question. For this eighteenth-century liberalism which is at bottom the whole
object of the dispute is not simply a drawing-room theory, a philosophical construct; it has become a fact, it has penetrated our institutions and
our mores, it has blended with our whole life, and if, truly, we had to
give it up, we would have to recast our whole moral organization at the
same stroke.

Now it is already a remarkable fact that all those theoreticians of individualism are no less sensitive to the rights of the collectivity than to those
of the individual. . . .

And, in fact, once we have stopped confusing individualism with its
opposite – that is, with utilitarianism – [this] supposed contradiction disappear[s] like magic. This religion of humanity has everything it needs
to speak to its faithful in a no less imperative tone than the religions it
replaces. Far from limiting itself to flattering our instincts, it fixes before
us an ideal which infinitely surpasses nature. For ours is not naturally
a wise and pure reason which, purged of all personal motives, would
legislate in the abstract its own conduct. Doubtless, if the dignity of the
individual came from his personal characteristics, from the peculiarities
which distinguish him from others, we might fear that it would shut him
off in a sort of moral egoism which would make any solidarity impossible. But in reality he receives dignity from a higher source, one which
he shares with all men. If he has a right to this religious respect, it is because
he partakes of humanity. It is humanity which is worthy of respect and
sacred. Now it is not all in him. It is diffused among all his fellowmen
and consequently he cannot adopt it as the aim of his conduct without
being obliged to come out of himself and relate to others. The cult, of which
he is at once both object and agent, does not address itself to the particular

being which he is and which bears his name, but to the human person (*la personne humaine*) wherever it is to be found, and in whatever form it is embodied. Impersonal and anonymous, such an aim, then, soars far above all individual minds (*consciences particulières*) and can thus serve them as a rallying point. The fact that it is not alien to us (by the simple fact that it is human) does not prevent it from dominating us. Now, the only thing necessary for a society to be coherent is that its members have their eyes fixed on the same goal, concur in the same faith. But it is in no way necessary that the object of this common faith be unrelated to individual natures. After all, individualism thus extended is the glorification not of the self but of the individual in general. It springs not from egoism but from sympathy for all that is human, a broader pity for all sufferings, for all human miseries, a more ardent need to combat them and mitigate them, a greater thirst for justice. Is there not herein what is needed to place all men of good will in communion? . . .

But I am anxious to come to the great objection. This cult of man has as its primary dogma the autonomy of reason and as its primary rite the doctrine of free inquiry. But, we are told, if all opinions are free, by what miracle will they be in harmony? If they are formed without mutual awareness and without having to take one another into account, how can they not be incoherent? Intellectual and moral anarchy would thus be the inevitable result of liberalism. . . . Yes, it is quite true that individualism implies a certain intellectualism; for freedom of thought is the first of the freedoms. But where has it been seen to have as a consequence this absurd infatuation with oneself which shuts everyone up in his own feelings and creates a vacuum between intellects? What it requires is the right for each individual to know the things he legitimately can know. But it in no way consecrates some sort of right to incompetence. On a question on which I can form no knowledgeable opinion, it costs my intellectual independence nothing to follow more competent opinions. The collaboration of learned men is possible only thanks to this mutual deference; every science constantly borrows from its neighboring disciplines propositions that it accepts without further verification. However, my reason requires reasons before it bows before someone else's. Respect for authority is in no way incompatible with rationalism as long as the authority is rationally grounded. . . .

Not only is individualism not anarchical, but it henceforth is the only system of beliefs which can ensure the moral unity of the country.

We often hear it said today that religion alone can produce this harmony. This proposition, which modern prophets believe they must develop in mystic tones, is essentially a simple truism about which everyone can agree. For we know today that a religion does not necessarily imply symbols and rites, properly speaking, or temples and priests. This whole exterior apparatus is only the superficial part. Essentially, it is nothing other than a body of collective beliefs and practices endowed with a certain authority. As soon as a goal is pursued by an entire people, it acquires, in consequence of this unanimous adherence, a sort of moral supremacy which raises it far above private aims and thus gives it a religious character. From another viewpoint, it is apparent that a society cannot be coherent if there does not exist among its members a certain intellectual and moral community. However, after recalling once again this sociological truism, we have not gotten very far. For if it is true that religion is, in a sense, indispensable, it is no less certain that religions change – that the religion of yesterday could not be the religion of tomorrow. What is important therefore is to say what the religion of today should be.

Now everything converges in the belief that this religion of humanity, of which the individualistic ethic is the rational expression, is the only one possible. Hereafter, to what can the collective sensitivity cling? To the extent that societies become more voluminous and expand over vaster territories, traditions and practices, in order to accommodate themselves to the diversity of situations and to the mobility of circumstances, are obliged to maintain themselves in a state of plasticity and inconstancy which no longer offers enough resistance to individual variations. These variations, being less well restrained, are produced more freely and multiply; that is to say, everyone tends to go off in his own direction. At the same time, as a result of a more developed division of labor, each mind finds itself oriented to a different point on the horizon, reflecting a different aspect of the world, and consequently the contents of consciousness (*conscience*) differ from one person to another. Thus, we make our way, little by little, toward a state, nearly achieved as of now, where the members of a single social group will have nothing in common among themselves except their humanity, except the constitutive attributes of the human person (*personne humaine*) in general. This idea of the human person, given different nuances according to the diversity of national temperaments, is therefore the only idea which would be retained, unalterable and impersonal, above the changing torrent of individual opinions. And the feelings it awakens would be the only ones which could be found in almost every heart. The communion of spirits can no longer be based on definite rites and prejudices, since rites and prejudices are overcome by the course of events. Consequently, nothing remains which men can love and honor in common if not man himself. That is how man has become a god for man and why he can no longer create other gods without lying to himself. And since each of us incarnates something of humanity, each individual consciousness contains something divine and thus finds itself marked with a character which renders it sacred and inviolable to others. Therein lies all individualism; and that is what makes it a necessary doctrine. For in order to halt its advance it would be necessary to prevent men from differentiating themselves more and more from each other, to equalize their personalities, to lead them back to the old conformism of former times, to contain, as a result, the tendency for societies to become always more extended and more centralized, and to place an obstacle in the way of the unceasing progress of the division of labor. Such an enterprise, whether desirable or not, infinitely exceeds all human capability.

Moreover, what are we offered in place of this despised individualism? The merits of Christian morality are praised and we are discreetly invited to embrace them. But are we to ignore the fact that the originality of Christianity consisted precisely in a remarkable development of the individualistic spirit? Whereas the religion of the ancient city-state was quite entirely made of external practices, from which the spiritual was absent, Christianity demonstrated in its inner faith, in the personal conviction of the individual, the essential condition of piety. . . . And looking at it from another point of view, if this restrained individualism which is Christianity was necessary eighteen centuries ago, there is a good chance that a more fully developed individualism is indispensable today. For things have changed. It is therefore a singular error to present the individualistic ethic as the antagonist of Christian morality. Quite the contrary – the former derived from the latter. By attaching ourselves to the first, we do not deny our past; we only continue it.

We are now in a better position to understand why certain minds believe they must oppose an opinionated resistance against everything that seems to threaten the individualistic creed. If every enterprise directed against the rights of an individual revolts them, it is not only out of sympathy for the victim; nor is it from fear of having to suffer similar injustices. Rather, it is because such attempts cannot remain unpunished without compromising the national existence. Indeed, it is impossible for them to occur freely without weakening the feelings they transgress against. And since these feelings are the only ones we hold in common, they cannot be weakened without disturbing the cohesion of society. A religion which tolerates sacrilege abdicates all dominion over men's minds (*consciences*). The religion of the individual therefore cannot let itself be scoffed at without resistance, under penalty of undermining its authority. And since it is the only tie which binds us all to each other, such a weakness cannot exist without a beginning of social dissolution. Thus the individualist who defends the rights of the individual defends at the same time the vital interests of society, for he prevents the criminal inpoverishment of that last reserve of collective ideas and feelings which is the very soul of the nation. He renders to his country the same service the aged Roman once rendered to his city in defending the traditional rites against foolhardy innovators. And if there is a country among all others where the cause of individualism is truly national, it is our own;

for there is no other which has created such rigorous solidarity between its fate and the fate of these ideas. We have given them their most recent formulation, and it is from us that other peoples have received them. And this is why even now we are considered their most authoritative representatives. Therefore we cannot disavow them today without disavowing ourselves, without diminishing ourselves in the eyes of the world, without committing a veritable moral suicide. . . .

From "The Nature of Deference and Demeanor"
Erving Goffman

Erving Goffman, *Interaction Ritual: Essays on Face-to-Face Behavior* (New York: Pantheon, 1967), pp. 90–1.

The rules of conduct which bind the actor and the recipient together are the bindings of society. But many of the acts which are guided by these rules occur infrequently or take a long time for their consummation. Opportunities to affirm the moral order and the society could therefore be rare. It is here that ceremonial rules play their social function, for many of the acts which are guided by these rules last but a brief moment, involve no substantive outlay, and can be performed in every social interaction. Whatever the activity and however profanely instrumental, it can afford many opportunities for minor ceremonies as long as other persons are present. Through these observances, guided by ceremonial obligations and expectations, a constant flow of indulgences is spread through society, with others who are present constantly reminding the individual that he must keep himself together as a well demeaned person and affirm the sacred quality of these others. The gestures which we sometimes call empty are perhaps in fact the fullest things of all.

It is therefore important to see that the self is in part a ceremonial thing, a sacred object which must be treated with proper ritual care and in turn must be presented in a proper light to others. As a means through which this self is established, the individual acts with proper demeanor while in contact with others and is treated by others with deference. It is just as important to see that if the individual is to play this kind of sacred game, then the field must be suited to it. The environment must ensure that the individual will not pay too high a price for acting with good demeanor and that deference will be accorded him. Deference and demeanor practices must be institutionalized so that the individual will be able to project a viable, sacred self and stay in the game on a proper ritual basis.

An environment, then, in terms of the ceremonial component of activity, is a place where it is easy or difficult to play the ritual game of having a self. . . .

From *Pricing the Priceless Child:*
The Changing Social Value of Children
Viviana Zelizer

Viviana Zelizer, *Pricing the Priceless Child: The Changing Social Value of Children* (Princeton: Princeton University Press, 1994), pp. 209–11.

Between the 1870s and the 1930s, the value of American children was transformed. The twentieth-century economically useless but emotionally priceless child displaced the nineteenth-century useful child. To be sure, the most dramatic changes took place among the working class; by the turn of the century middle-class children were already experienced "loafers." But the sentimentalization of childhood intensified regardless of social class. The new sacred child occupied a special and separate world, regulated by affection and education, not work or profit.

 . . . the expulsion of working-class children from the market was a controversial process, vehemently supported by reformers but resisted with equal conviction by working-class and middle-class advocates of a productive childhood. It was partly a matter of conflicting economic interest but mostly an ideological dispute between two opposing views of childhood. The sacred child prevailed. Children were to be kept off the market, useless but loving, and off the streets, protected and supervised. The economic role of the child, however, did not disappear but was profoundly transformed, both in families [and] in adoptive homes. Child work and child money became defined primarily in educational not instrumental terms. A child was now entitled to an allowance; after all, how else could he or she learn to become a proper consumer? Children's token participation in household work was justified as moral training, seldom as a real labor contribution.

As the sentimental uniqueness of children was stressed, pragmatic pecuniary assessments of their value were considered not only impractical but morally offensive. Pricing the priceless child, therefore, became a complex task, creating confusion in legal thought and practice, controversy in the insurance business, and uncertainty in the "exchange" of adoptive children. New sentimental criteria were established to determine the monetary worth of child life. Courts began awarding damages for loss of a child's companionship; insurance was legally justified as coverage against the loss of affection; child sellers now sold a baby's cuteness and beauty. Ironically, both the "surrender" cash value of children at death and their "exchange" price increased even as children's economic value disappeared.

A profound paradox was created. The twentieth-century family was defined as a sentimental institution, "the antithesis of a market economy's concept of human relations," as Carl Degler aptly puts it. Yet, even the family seemed to capitulate to the dominant cash nexus, as the value of its most precious member, the sacred child, was now routinely converted into its monetary equivalent. Had the child lost its economic value only to become another commercial commodity? My findings strongly suggest that the sentimental value of children served as a bulwark against the market. The historical development of the three institutions examined shows that the insurance business, compensation for the wrongful death of children, and the sale of children were profoundly shaped by children's noneconomic value. Priceless values were being priced, but the pricing process itself was transformed by its association to value. In child death awards, insurance policies for children, and adoptive payments for a child, money is to a certain extent deprived of its economic worth. Instead, such monetary payments acquire powerful symbolic meanings. An insurance policy, for instance, never sold as a sensible investment but as a token of respect for the dying child in the nineteenth century, and later as a token of love for the living child. Damage cases for the economically useless child were surrounded by emotional ambiguities and settled in unusual ways. Similarly, payments for sacred adoptive children have seldom been conducted as ordinary business deals.

Durkheim's Methodological Manifesto

Introduction

This appendix consists entirely of extracts from *The Rules of Sociological Method* and is perhaps most profitably read in conjunction with the selections from *Suicide* (chapter 1). Durkheim begins here with a definition and explication of the concept of "social facts" and with the stipulation that such objects must be "studied from the outside, as external things, because it is in this guise that they present themselves to us" (p. 286). He proceeds to note the existence of two entirely different orders of social facts – the normal and the pathological – and to provide rigorous criteria for distinguishing between the two, criteria that, in Durkheim's view, will allow sociology to speak scientifically about social maladies and "to throw light on practical matters while remaining true to its own method" (p. 287). ("Between science and art," he proclaims, "there is no longer a gulf" (p. 287).) A famous passage follows in which Durkheim gives the example of crime as itself "among the phenomena of normal sociology." But he quickly observes that social facts, including crime, "can only be labelled normal or abnormal in relation to a given social species," and he then turns to a discussion of how these different species or types might be constituted and classified, declaring social morphology to be the key to such a grouping. But morphological analysis is itself "only one step towards the truly explanatory part of the science" (p. 291). Accordingly, Durkheim devotes considerable attention to two other major steps in sociological analysis: namely, functionalist and causal inquiry. The former entails seeking "[t]he determining cause of a social fact . . . among antecedent social facts and not among the states of the individual consciousness," while the latter entails seeking "[t]he function of a social fact . . . in the relationship that it bears to some social end" (p. 293). The two methods, Durkheim adds, must be carefully dissociated from one another and pursued separately. And for "demonstrating that one phenomenon is the cause of another," the only suitable method is that of "indirect experimentation, or the comparative method" (p. 293).

From *The Rules of Sociological Method*

Emile Durkheim, *The Rules of Sociological Method and Selected Texts on Sociology and its Method*, trans. W. D. Halls, ed. Steven Lukes (New York: Free Press, 1982), pp. 50–9, 60–70, 85–102, 108–15, 119–34, 147–50.

Before beginning the search for the method appropriate to the study of social facts it is important to know what are the facts termed "social". . . .

When I perform my duties as a brother, a husband or a citizen and carry out the commitments I have entered into, I fulfil obligations which are defined in law and custom and which are external to myself and my actions. Even when they conform to my own sentiments and when I feel their reality within me, that reality does not cease to be objective, for it is not I who have prescribed these duties; I have received them through education. Moreover, how often does it happen that we are ignorant of the details of the obligations that we must assume, and that, to know them, we must consult the legal code and its authorised interpreters! Similarly the believer has discovered from birth, ready fashioned, the beliefs and practices of his religious life; if they existed before he did, it follows that they exist outside him. The system of signs that I employ to express my thoughts, the monetary system I use to pay my debts, the credit instruments I utilise in my commercial relationships, the practices I follow in my profession, etc., all function independently of the use I make of them. Considering in turn each member of society, the foregoing remarks can be repeated for each single one of them. Thus there are ways of acting, thinking and feeling which possess the remarkable property of existing outside the consciousness of the individual.

Not only are these types of behaviour and thinking external to the individual, but they are endued with a compelling and coercive power by virtue of which, whether he wishes it or not, they impose themselves upon him. Undoubtedly when I conform to them of my own free will, this coercion is not felt or felt hardly at all, since it is unnecessary. None the less it is intrinsically a characteristic of these facts; the proof of this is that it asserts itself as soon as I try to resist. If I attempt to violate the rules of law they react against me so as to forestall my action, if there is still time.

Alternatively, they annul it or make my action conform to the norm if it is already accomplished but capable of being reversed; or they cause me to pay the penalty for it if it is irreparable. If purely moral rules are at stake, the public conscience restricts any act which infringes them by the surveillance it exercises over the conduct of citizens and by the special punishments it has at its disposal. In other cases the constraint is less violent; nevertheless, it does not cease to exist. If I do not conform to ordinary conventions, if in my mode of dress I pay no heed to what is customary in my country and in my social class, the laughter I provoke, the social distance at which I am kept, produce, although in a more mitigated form, the same results as any real penalty. In other cases, although it may be indirect, constraint is no less effective. I am not forced to speak French with my compatriots, nor to use the legal currency, but it is impossible for me to do otherwise. If I tried to escape the necessity, my attempt would fail miserably. As an industrialist nothing prevents me from working with the processes and methods of the previous century, but if I do I will most certainly ruin myself. Even when in fact I can struggle free from these rules and successfully break them, it is never without being forced to fight against them. Even if in the end they are overcome, they make their constraining power sufficiently felt in the resistance that they afford. There is no innovator, even a fortunate one, whose ventures do not encounter opposition of this kind.

Here, then, is a category of facts which present very special characteristics: they consist of manners of acting, thinking and feeling external to the individual, which are invested with a coercive power by virtue of which they exercise control over him. Consequently, since they consist of representations and actions, they cannot be confused with organic phenomena, nor with psychical phenomena, which have no existence save in and through the individual consciousness. Thus they constitute a new species and to them must be exclusively assigned the term *social*. . . .

Yet since the examples just cited (legal and moral rules, religious dogmas, financial systems, etc.) consist wholly of beliefs and practices already well established, in view of what has been said it might be maintained that no social fact can exist except where there is a well defined social organisation. But there are other facts which do not present themselves in this already crystallised form but which also possess the same objectivity and ascendancy over the individual. These are what are called social "currents". Thus in a public gathering the great waves of enthusiasm, indignation and pity that are produced have their seat in no one individual consciousness. They come to each one of us from outside and can sweep us along in spite of ourselves. If perhaps I abandon myself to them I may not be conscious of the pressure that they are exerting upon me, but that pressure makes its presence felt immediately I attempt to struggle against them. If an individual tries to pit himself against one of

these collective manifestations, the sentiments that he is rejecting will be turned against him. . . .
. . . Our definition will therefore subsume all that has to be defined if it states:

A social fact is any way of acting, whether fixed or not, capable of exerting over the individual an external constraint;

or:

which is general over the whole of a given society whilst having an existence of its own, independent of its individual manifestations.

The first and most basic rule is *to consider social facts as things.* . . .
Social phenomena must therefore be considered in themselves, detached from the conscious beings who form their own mental representations of them. They must be studied from the outside, as external things, because it is in this guise that they present themselves to us. . . .

Observation conducted according to the preceding rules mixes up two orders of facts, very dissimilar in certain respects: those that are entirely appropriate and those that should be different from what they are – normal phenomena and pathological phenomena. We have even seen that it is necessary to include both in the definition with which all research should begin. Yet if, in certain aspects, they are of the same nature, they nevertheless constitute two different varieties between which it is important to distinguish. Does science have the means available to make this distinction?

The question is of the utmost importance, for on its solution depends one's conception of the role that science, and above all the science of man, has to play. According to a theory whose exponents are recruited from the most varied schools of thought, science cannot instruct us in any way about what we ought to desire. It takes cognisance, they say, only of facts which all have the same value and the same utility; it observes, explains, but does not judge them; for it, there are none that are reprehensible. For science, good and evil do not exist. Whereas it can certainly tell us how causes produce their effects, it cannot tell us what ends should be pursued. To know not what is, but what is desirable, we must resort to the suggestions of the unconscious – sentiment, instinct, vital urge, etc., – by whatever name we call it. Science . . . can well light up the world, but leaves a darkness in the human heart. The heart must create its own illumination. Thus science is stripped, or nearly, of all practical effectiveness and consequently of any real justification for its existence. For what good is it to strive after a knowledge of reality if the knowledge we acquire cannot serve us in our lives? . . .

The solution to the problem just posed will nevertheless allow us to lay claim to the rights of reason without falling back into ideology. For societies, as for individuals, health is good and desirable; sickness, on the other hand, is bad and must be avoided. If therefore we find an objective criterion, inherent in the facts themselves, to allow us to distinguish scientifically health from sickness in the various orders of social phenomena, science will be in a position to throw light on practical matters while remaining true to its own method. . . . Under these conditions we are no longer justified in stating that thought is useless for action. Between science and art there is no longer a gulf. . . .

Every sociological phenomenon, just as every biological phenomenon, although staying essentially unchanged, can assume a different form for each particular case. Among these forms exist two kinds. The first are common to the whole species. They are to be found, if not in all, at least in most individuals. If they are not replicated exactly in all the cases where they are observed, but vary from one person to another, their variations are confined within very narrow limits. On the other hand, other forms exist which are exceptional. These are encountered only in a minority of cases, but even when they occur, most frequently they do not last the whole lifetime of an individual. They are exceptions in time as they are in space. We are therefore faced with two distinct types of phenomena which must be designated by different terms. Those facts which appear in the most common forms we shall call normal, and the rest morbid or pathological. . . .

It can be seen that a fact can be termed pathological only in relation to a given species. The conditions of health and sickness cannot be defined *in abstracto* or absolutely. . . .

Since the reference point for judging the state of health or sickness varies according to the species, it can vary also within the same species, if that happens to change. . . . Health for the old person is not the same as it is for the adult, just as the adult's is different from the child's. The same is likewise true of societies. Thus a social fact can only be termed normal in a given species in relation to a particular phase, likewise determinate, of its development. Consequently, to know whether the term is merited for a social fact, it is not enough to observe the form in which it occurs in the majority of societies which belong to a species: we must also be careful to observe the societies at the corresponding phase of their evolution. . . .

Since the generality which outwardly characterises normal phenomena, once directly established by observation, is itself an explicable phenomenon, it demands explanation. Doubtless we can have the prior conviction that it is not without a cause, but it is better to know exactly what that cause is. The normality of the phenomenon will be less open to question if it is demonstrated that the external sign whereby it was revealed to us is not merely apparent but grounded in the nature of things. . . .

Circumstances even exist where this verification is indispensable, because the first method, if it were applied in isolation, might lead to error. This is what occurs in transition periods when the whole species is in the process of evolving, without yet being stabilised in a new and definitive form. In that situation the only normal type extant at the time and grounded in the facts is one that relates to the past but no longer corresponds to the new conditions of existence. A fact can therefore persist through a whole species but no longer correspond to the requirements of the situation. It therefore has only the appearance of normality, and the generality it displays is deceptive; persisting only through the force of blind habit, it is no longer the sign that the phenomenon observed is closely linked to the general conditions of collective existence. . . . The sociologist may therefore be at a loss to know whether a phenomenon is normal, since he lacks any reference point.

He can get out of this difficulty by proceeding along the lines we have just laid down. Having established by observation that the fact is general, he will trace back the conditions which determined this general character in the past and then investigate whether these conditions still pertain in the present or, on the contrary, have changed. In the first case he will be justified in treating the phenomenon as normal; in the other eventuality he will deny it that characteristic. . . .

. . . We can then formulate the three following rules:

1   A social fact is normal for a given social type, viewed at a given phase of its development, when it occurs in the average society of that species, considered at the corresponding phase of its evolution.
2   The results of the preceding method can be verified by demonstrating that the general character of the phenomenon is related to the general conditions of collective life in the social type under consideration.
3   This verification is necessary when this fact relates to a social species which has not yet gone through its complete evolution.

Let us in fact apply the rules previously laid down. Crime is not only observed in most societies of a particular species, but in all societies of all types. There is not one in which criminality does not exist, although it changes in form and the actions which are termed criminal are not everywhere the same. Yet everywhere and always there have been men who have conducted themselves in such a way as to bring down punishment upon their heads. If at least, as societies pass from lower to higher types, the crime rate (the relationship between the annual crime figures and population figures) tended to fall, we might believe that, although still remaining a normal phenomenon, crime tended to lose that character of normality. Yet there is no single ground for believing such a regression to be real. Many facts would rather seem to point to the existence of a movement in the opposite direction. From the beginning of the century statistics provide us with a means of following the progression of criminality. It has everywhere increased, and in France the increase is of the order of 300 per cent. Thus there is no phenomenon which represents more incontrovertibly all the symptoms of normality, since it appears to be closely bound up with the conditions of all collective life. To make crime a social illness would be to concede that sickness is not something accidental, but on the contrary derives in certain cases from the fundamental constitution of the living creature. This would be to erase any distinction between the physiological and the pathological. It can certainly happen that crime itself has normal forms; this is what happens, for instance, when it reaches an excessively high level. There is no doubt that this excessiveness is pathological in nature. What is normal is simply that criminality exists, provided that for each social type it does not reach or go beyond a certain level which it is perhaps not impossible to fix in conformity with the previous rules.

We are faced with a conclusion which is apparently somewhat paradoxical. Let us make no mistake: to classify crime among the phenomena of normal sociology is not merely to declare that it is an inevitable though regrettable phenomenon arising from the incorrigible wickedness of men; it is to assert that it is a factor in public health, an integrative element in any healthy society. At first sight this result is so surprising that it disconcerted even ourselves for a long time. However, once that first impression of surprise has been overcome it is not difficult to discover reasons to explain this normality and at the same time to confirm it.

In the first place, crime is normal because it is completely impossible for any society entirely free of it to exist.

Crime, as we have shown elsewhere, consists of an action which offends certain collective feelings which are especially strong and clear-cut. In any society, for actions regarded as criminal to cease, the feelings that they offend would need to be found in each individual consciousness without exception and in the degree of strength requisite to counteract the opposing feelings. Even supposing that this condition could effectively be fulfilled, crime would not thereby disappear; it would merely change in form, for the very cause which made the well-springs of criminality to dry up would immediately open up new ones. . . .

. . . Imagine a community of saints in an exemplary and perfect monastery. In it crime as such will be unknown, but faults that appear venial to the ordinary person will arouse the same scandal as does normal crime in ordinary consciences. . . .

... [S]ince there cannot be a society in which individuals do not diverge to some extent from the collective type, it is also inevitable that among these deviations some assume a criminal character. What confers upon them this character is not the intrinsic importance of the acts but the importance which the common consciousness ascribes to them. Thus if the latter is stronger and possesses sufficient authority to make these divergences very weak in absolute terms, it will also be more sensitive and exacting. By reacting against the slightest deviations with an energy which it elsewhere employs against those what are more weighty, it endues them with the same gravity and will brand them as criminal.

Thus crime is necessary. It is linked to the basic conditions of social life, but on this very account is useful, for the conditions to which it is bound are themselves indispensable to the normal evolution of morality and law. . . .

From this viewpoint the fundamental facts of criminology appear to us in an entirely new light. Contrary to current ideas, the criminal no longer appears as an utterly unsociable creature, a sort of parasitic element, a foreign, unassimilable body introduced into the bosom of society. He plays a normal role in social life. For its part, crime must no longer be conceived of as an evil which cannot be circumscribed closely enough. Far from there being cause for congratulation when it drops too noticeably below the normal level, this apparent progress assuredly coincides with and is linked to some social disturbance. . . .

Since a social fact can only be labelled normal or abnormal in relation to a given social species, what has been stated up to now implies that a branch of sociology must be devoted to the constitution and classification of these species. . . .

But how should we set about constituting these species? . . .

. . . [I]t is not difficult to surmise in what area to look for the characteristic properties of social types. We know that societies are made up of a number of parts added on to each other. Since the nature of any composite necessarily depends upon the nature and number of the elements that go to make it up and the way in which these are combined, these characteristics are plainly those which we must take as our basis. It will be seen later that it is on them that the general facts of social life depend. Moreover, as they are of a morphological order, one might term that part of sociology whose task it is to constitute and classify social types *social morphology.*

The principle of this classification can be defined even more precisely. It is known in fact that the constituent parts of every society are themselves societies of a simpler kind. A people is produced by the combination of two or more peoples that have preceded it. If therefore we knew the simplest society that ever existed, in order to make our classification we should only have to follow the way in which these simple societies joined together and how these new composites also combined. . . .

We shall begin by classifying societies according to the degree of organisation they manifest, taking as a base the perfectly simple society or the single-segment society. Within these classes different varieties will be distinguished, according to whether a complete coalescence of the initial segments takes place.

The constitution of species is above all a means of grouping the facts so as to facilitate their interpretation, but social morphology is only one step towards the truly explanatory part of the science. What is the method appropriate for explanation?

Most sociologists believe they have accounted for phenomena once they have demonstrated the purpose they serve and the role they play. They reason as if phenomena existed solely for this role and had no determining cause save a clear or vague sense of the services they are called upon to render. This is why it is thought that all that is needful has been said to make them intelligible when it has been established that these services are real and that the social need they satisfy has been demonstrated. . . .

But this method confuses two very different questions. To demonstrate the utility of a fact does not explain its origins, nor how it is what it is. The uses which it serves presume the specific properties characteristic of it, but do not create it. Our need for things cannot cause them to be of a particular nature; consequently, that need cannot produce them out of nothing, conferring in this way existence upon them. They spring from causes of another kind. . . .

What clearly demonstrates the duality of these two avenues of research is that a fact can exist without serving any purpose, either because it has never been used to further any vital goal or because, having once been of use, it has lost all utility but continues to exist merely through force of custom. There are even more instances of such survivals in society than in the human organism. There are even cases where a practice or a social institution changes its functions without for this reason changing its nature. The rule of *is pater est quem justae nuptiae declarant* has remained substantially the same in our legal code as it was in ancient Roman law. But while its purpose was to safeguard the property rights of the father over children born of his legitimate wife, it is much more the rights of the children that it protects today. The swearing of an oath began by being a kind of judicial ordeal before it became simply a solemn and impressive form of attestation. The religious dogmas of Christianity have not changed for centuries, but the role they play in our modern societies is no longer the same as in the Middle Ages. Thus words serve to express new ideas without their contexture changing. Moreover, it is a proposition true in sociology as in biology, that the organ is independent of its function, i.e. while staying the same it can serve different ends. Thus the causes which give rise to its existence are independent of the ends it serves. . . .

Therefore when one undertakes to explain a social phenomenon the efficient cause which produces it and the function it fulfils must be investigated separately. We use the word "function" in preference to "end" or "goal" precisely because social phenomena generally do not exist for the usefulness of the results they produce. We must determine whether there is a correspondence between the fact being considered and the general needs of the social organism, and in what this correspondence consists, without seeking to know whether it was intentional or not. All such questions of intention are, moreover, too subjective to be dealt with scientifically.

Not only must these two kinds of problems be dissociated from each other, but it is generally appropriate to deal with the first kind before the second. This order of precedence corresponds to that of the facts. It is natural to seek the cause of a phenomenon before attempting to determine its effects. This method is all the more logical because the first question, once resolved, will often help to answer the second. Indeed, the solid link which joins cause to effect is of a reciprocal character which has not been sufficiently recognised. Undoubtedly the effect cannot exist without its cause, but the latter, in turn, requires its effect. It is from the cause that the effect derives its energy, but on occasion it also restores energy to the cause and consequently cannot disappear without the cause being affected. . . .

If we must proceed only at a second stage to the determination of the function, it is none the less necessary for the complete explanation of the phenomenon. Indeed, if the utility of a fact is not what causes its existence, it must generally be useful to continue to survive. If it lacks utility, that very reason suffices to make it harmful, since in that case it requires effort but brings in no return. Thus if the general run of social phenomena had this parasitic character, the economy of the organism would be in deficit, and social life would be impossible. Consequently, to provide a satisfactory explanation of social life we need to show how the phenomena which are its substance come together to place society in harmony with itself and with the outside world. Undoubtedly the present formula which defines life as a correspondence between the internal and the external environments is only approximate. Yet in general it remains true; thus to explain a fact which is vital, it is not enough to show the cause on which it depends. We must also – at least in most cases – discover the part that it plays in the establishment of that general harmony.

Having distinguished between these two questions, we must determine the method whereby they must be resolved. . . .

   Hence we arrive at the following rule: *The determining cause of a social fact must be sought among antecedent social facts and not among the states of the individual consciousness.* Moreover, we can easily conceive that all that has been stated above applies to the determination of the function as well as the cause of a social fact. Its function can only be social, which means that it consists in the production of socially useful effects. Undoubtedly it can and indeed does happen that it has repercussions which also serve the individual. But this happy result is not the immediate rationale for its existence. Thus we can complement the preceding proposition by stating: *The function of a social fact must always be sought in the relationship that it bears to some social end.* . . .

We have only one way of demonstrating that one phenomenon is the cause of another. This is to compare the cases where they are both simultaneously present or absent, so as to discover whether the variations they display in these different combinations of circumstances provide evidence that one depends upon the other. When the phenomena can be artificially produced at will by the observer, the method is that of experimentation proper. When, on the other hand, the production of facts is something beyond our power to command, and we can only bring them together as they have been spontaneously produced, the method used is one of indirect experimentation, or the comparative method.

   We have seen that sociological explanation consists exclusively in establishing relationships of causality, that a phenomenon must be joined to its cause, or, on the contrary, a cause to its useful effects. Moreover, since social phenomena clearly rule out any control by the experimenter, the comparative method is the sole one suitable for sociology. . . .

   . . . If therefore we wish to use the comparative method scientifically, i.e., in conformity with the principle of causality as it arises in science itself, we shall have to take as the basis of the comparisons established the following proposition: *To the same effect there always corresponds the same cause.* Thus . . . if suicide depends on more than one cause it is because in reality there are several kinds of suicide. It is the same for crime. For punishment, on the other hand, if we have believed it also explicable by different causes, this is because we have not perceived the common element to be found in all its antecedents, by virtue of which they produce their common effect.

Index

economy (*cont'd*)
  importance of regulation, 20, 42–4,
    200–2, 204–6, 210–11, 224–5
  role of occupational groups, 20, 220,
    224–6
education, 2, 22, 236–54
  definition, 237
  disenfranchisement of the family, 235
  duties and rights of the state, 241–2
  impact of morphological structures
    on change, 9–10
  and maintenance of political
    hegemony, 186–7
  mediating function, 22
  moral and social functions, 237–41,
    243–4
  as the practice of freedom, 252–4
  Renaissance doctrines, 142–5
  shift from depth to breadth, 79–82
  "State Durkheimianism", 7
  value of studying history, 245–8
  see also French educational system;
    schools
"Education: Its Nature and Role", 236,
    237–42
educational capital, 51
egoism, 2, 38–9, 40, 46, 273
  distinguished from the religion of
    humanity, 6, 267, 274–6
egoistic suicide, 6, 39–40, 44, 46
Eisenhower, Dwight, 189
Elementary Forms of Religious Life, The,
    7–8, 9, 11, 12, 14, 15, 16, 19, 83,
    84–91, 107, 109–22, 139, 140–2
elite conflict
  in social crisis and renewal, 159
  in "Watergate", 161–2
Emirbayer, Mustafa, 8, 10, 15, 23
"emotional energy" (EE), 132
emotions, *see* collective emotions
empowerment, 234
Engels, Friedrich, 130
England, 99, 146
Enlightenment, 191, 232–3
Epinal, France, 3–4
equality
  importance for contractual
    solidarity, 209–10

  and the injustice of hereditary
    wealth, 224, 228
  and the need for economic
    regulation, 224–5
  and spontaneous division of labour,
    208–9
Erasmus, Desiderius, 144
Erikson, Kai, 83, 103–5
Etzioni, Amitai, 192, 214–16
Eurocentrism, 23–4
European society, formation, 263
Evolution of Educational Thought, The,
    9, 13, 22, 139, 142–55, 236, 245–8

face-work, 128–9
family, 2, 21–2
  clan organization, 218
  compared with clan, 65–6
  compared with occupational
    groups, 217, 222–3
  compared with political society, 173
  conjugal, 21–2, 226–30
  defined as sentimental institution,
    282
  domestic morality, 222
  educational rights, 235, 241
  former importance as mediating
    institution, 18
  historical development, 21, 226–7
  and maintenance of economic
    continuity, 225
  need for recognition as an
    institution, 234–5
  as safeguard against suicide, 37–8
  socialization functions, compared
    with school, 251
fatalistic suicide, 44
federal states, 174
forced division of labour, 6, 19, 192,
    206–9
Foucault, Michel, 83, 105–6
France
  Durkheim's background, 3–4
  effect of revolutions on suicide, 38
  examples of creative effervescence, 16
  increase in crime, 289
  medieval sacred powers, 98, 99
  transformation of the state, 172

evolution, 168–71
externality of economy, 170, 195–6, 220
federalism, 174
function in promoting individualism, 17–18, 178–82
indifference to the individual, 177–8
maintenance of political hegemony, 186–8
permission for suicide, 263
and public/private dichotomy, 231–2
religious dimension in America, 167, 188–91
as sole collective organ, 219, 223–4, 232
"Stratification, Emotional Energy, and the Transient Emotions" (Collins), 129–33
structural functionalism, 15
structure and agency, 8–9
substantive rules, 126–7
suicide, 32–49
   altruistic, 40–1, 46
   anomic, 6, 44, 46–7
   changing legislation, 263–4
   classification by causes, 35
   and domestic society, 37–8
   egoistic, 6, 39–40, 44, 46
   fatalistic, 44
   immorality, in denial of religion of humanity, 264–7
   limited effects of marriage, 230
   and modern social pathology, 31, 48–9
   as part of normal sociology, 31, 45–8
   and political society, 38
   and the principle of causality, 293
   reduced by development of occupational groups, 224
   religious, 89
   and religious society, 35–7
   as result of purely personal ends, 229
   role of individual factors, 45
   as social fact, 31, 33–4

Suicide, 5, 6, 13, 31, 32–49, 217, 218–19, 224, 236, 257, 263–7, 293
supernatural, religion and, 85–6
symbolic boundaries
   around deviancy, 103–5
   changes in schools, 81–2
   created by prisons, 105–6
symbolic classification
   purity and pollution, 12, 101–2
   sacred and profane, 7, 12, 83, 87–9
   and the savage mind, 99–101
   social origins, 83, 91–4
   transformation of "Watergate", 160–1, 163
symbolic formations
   binary logic, 12
   social situatedness, 11
symbols, *see* sacred objects

Ta-ta-thi, 92
taste, 31, 51–4
   criteria of pertinence, 50–1
   and distance from necessity, 51–3
   and sense of distinction, 53–4
teachers
   changing roles, 79, 80–1
   compared with priests, 22, 236, 243–4
   constant contact with pupils in Jesuit schools, 150–1
Teaching to Transgress: Education as the Practice of Freedom (hooks), 252–4
territorial division, 69–70, 218
Third Republic, 4, 6, 7, 18, 20
Thompson, E. P., 11
Tilly, Charles, 13, 20
To Empower People: From State to Civil Society (Berger and Neuhaus), 231–5
Tocqueville, Alexis de, 12, 20
totalitarianism, 233, 234
totemism, 90–1, 107, 112–16
   as aspect of classification, 99–101
towns and cities, 10, 70, 73, 223
Traugott, Mark, 11, 13
Turner, Victor, 107, 125–6
"Two Laws of Penal Evolution", 167, 171–2

Made in the USA
Lexington, KY
15 January 2015